CW01188239

B-2 BAZENVILLE

INVASION AIRFIELDS
THEN AND NOW

*I was able to announce on the morning of June 9 that for the first time since 1940
Allied air forces were operating from France. Within three weeks of D-Day,
31 Allied squadrons were operating from the beach-head bases.*

GENERAL DWIGHT D. EISENHOWER,
Supreme Commander, Allied Expeditionary Force
Report to the Combined Chiefs of Staff, July 13, 1945.

342-AF-52433AC

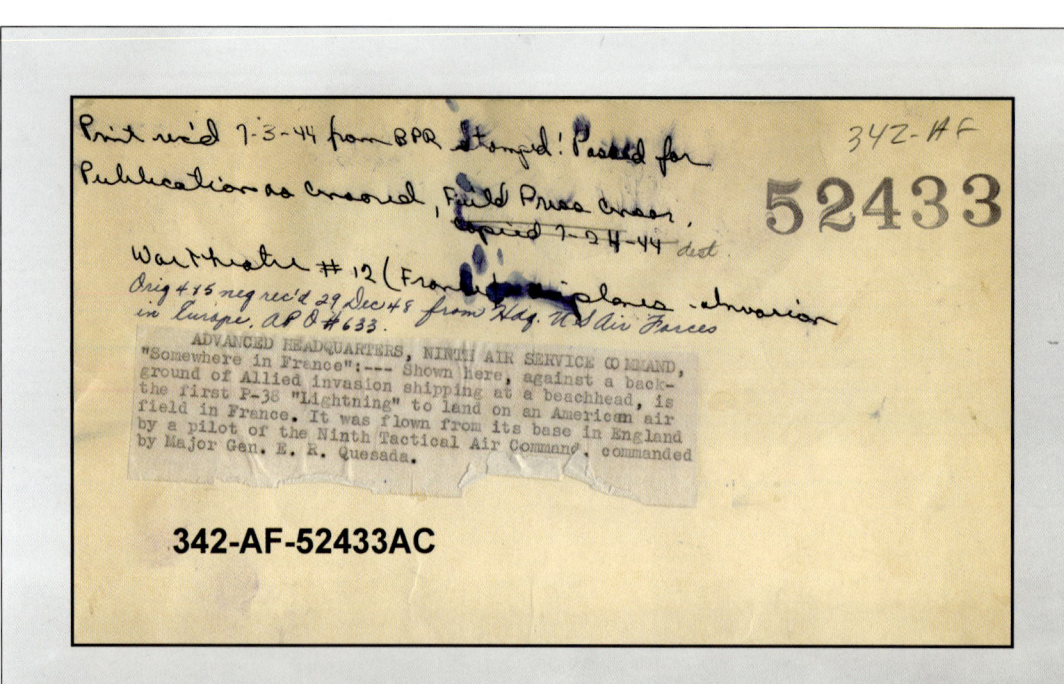

ADVANCED HEADQUARTERS, NINTH AIR SERVICE COMMAND, "Somewhere in France":--- Shown here, against a background of Allied invasion shipping at a beachhead, is the first P-38 "Lightning" to land on an American air field in France. It was flown from its base in England by a pilot of the Ninth Tactical Air Command, commanded by Major Gen. E. R. Quesada.

INVASION AIRFIELDS
THEN AND NOW

Edited by Winston Ramsey

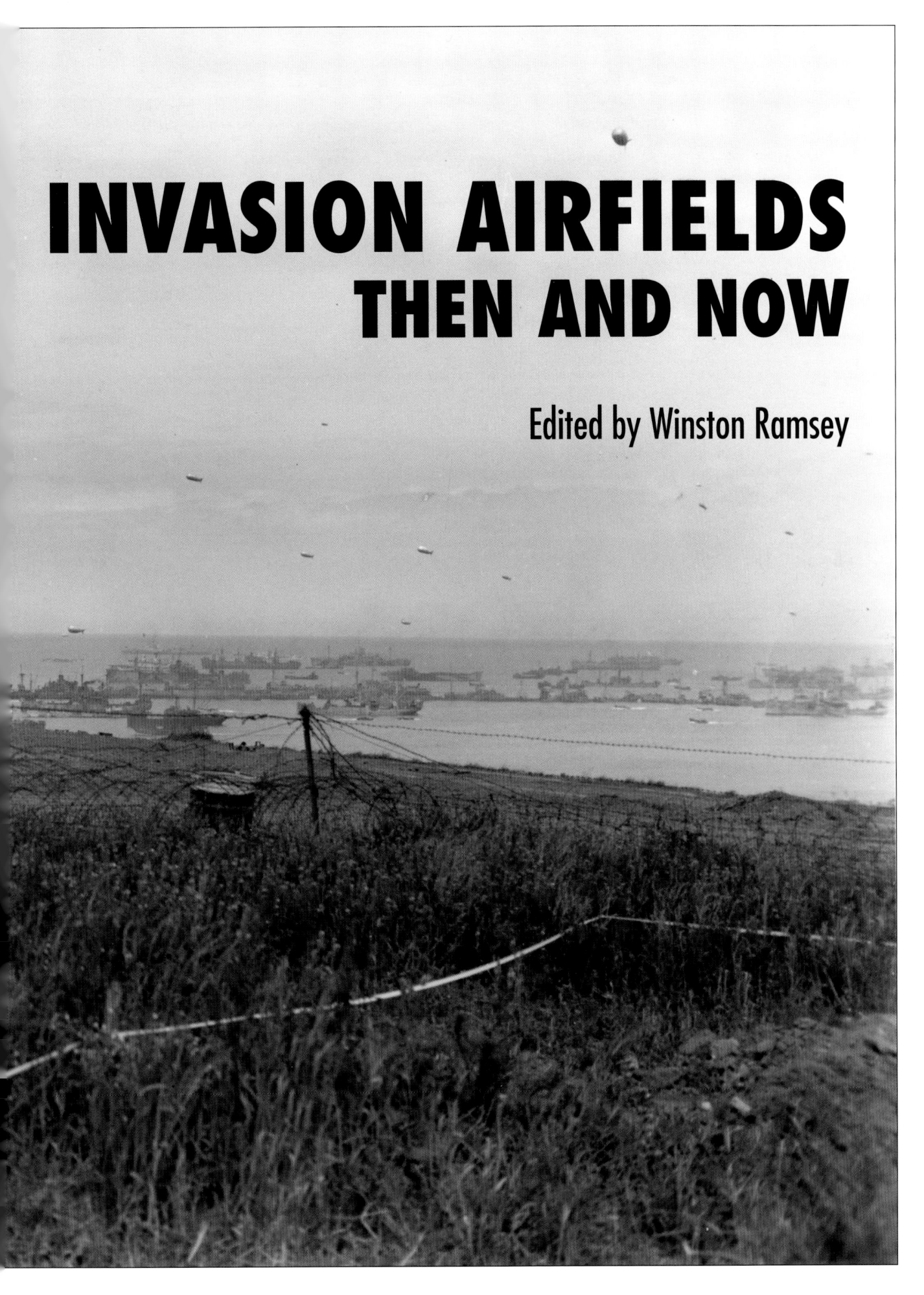

Credits

ISBN: 978-1-870067-91-1

© *After the Battle* 2017

Edited and designed by
Winston Ramsey, Editor-in-Chief

PUBLISHERS
Battle of Britain International Ltd
The Mews, Hobbs Cross House,
Hobbs Cross, Old Harlow,
Essex CM17 0NN

Telephone: 01279 41 8833.
Fax: 01279 41 9386
E-mail: hq@afterthebattle.com
Website: www.afterthebattle.com

PRINTERS
Printed by Ozgraf S. A., Olsztyn, Poland.

PHOTOGRAPHS
All photographs are from the *After the Battle* archive unless stated otherwise. **Steve Casely:** 62 top. **Tom Doziel:** 88 top left, right and bottom. **Stéphane Duchemin:** 39 bottom. **Adrian Farwell:** 94 bottom. **John Flaherty:** 96 centre right. **Chris Goss:** 136 top, 150 top, 188 top, 208 top. **Imperial War Museum:** 73 top (CL570). **National Archives:** 98-99. **Jean Paul Pallud:** 181 bottom right. **G. Ruppelt:** 160 top. **Society for the Study of the ETO:** 18 both, 19 both, 20 top, 89 top right. **Ed Storey:** 6 top, 10 top, 24-25, 40 both, 42 top right, 59 top and centre, 60 top, 78 top, 82 centre, 83 both, 84 both, 85 top left, 86 bottom, 87 bottom, 89 top left, 92 all, 93 top and bottom left, 99 top, 100 both, 130 top, 138 top, 144 top left and right and centre, 145 top, 155 all. **Denis Sweeting:** 80 top. **Chris Thomas:** 5 top, 35 top left, right and centre, 42 bottom left, 43 centre right and bottom, 60 bottom, 69 bottom left and right, 70 bottom, 71 bottom, 72 centre, 78 bottom, 88 centre, 91 bottom, 104 top, 187 centre, 204 top, 210 top left and right. **US National Archives:** 39 top left and right, 46 top, 54 top and bottom, 115 bottom 118 bottom, 127 both, 132 top. **Ken Wakefield:** 175 top.

From the Author

Many years ago, the late Roger Freeman gave me a loose-leaf folder of wartime plans covering airstrips built in Normandy to support Operation 'Overlord'. They provided me with the essential background to be able to tell the story of how the American Ninth Air Force and the British Second Tactical Air Force were able to quickly support the invasion using airstrips in France, without the necessity of flying across the Channel from the UK. Although Roger is no longer with us, having died in 2005, it is a story he would have loved to have done so I would like to dedicate this book to his memory.

Although the airfields have previously appeared in various publications, they are always listed in the order of their prefixes, i.e. American beginning with A-1 followed by the British prefixed by 'B'. However, I felt it was very important to tell the story chronologically as it happened, so the airfields appear here in the order that each received its first aircraft, i.e. became operational. In this way, the book tells the story of the landings and subsequent break-out, and forms a useful follow-on to our earlier two volumes: *D-Day Then and Now*.

Comparison 'then and now' photographs are central to all our publications but in this case they would be meaningless as one would just be showing a repetition of ploughed fields. So instead I decided it would be far more relevant to show the area that each airfield occupied from above so that we can see the way the landscape has changed over the past 70 years.

Absolutely essential reading which enabled me to piece together the movements of the squadrons that operated from the airstrips were the following: Wing Commander C. G. Jefford's masterly volume *RAF Squadrons A Comprehensive Record of the Movement and Equipment of all RAF Squadrons and their Antecedents since 1912* published by Airlife; *Combat Squadrons of the Air Force World War II*, edited by Maurer Maurer for the USAF Historical Division Air University, and *Air Force Combat Units of World War II*, also edited by Maurer for the Department of the Air Force.

Christopher Shores and Chris Thomas are the joint authors of the incredibly detailed volumes covering the day-to-day operations carried out by the *2nd Tactical Air Force* published by Ian Allen, and I am indebted to them for their generous help and advice, including the supply of photographs.

Seb Cox and his staff at the RAF's Air Historical Branch also came to the rescue in supplying certain plans missing from Roger's set and clarifying other details, and Jean Paul Pallud helped enormously in pinpointing the location of memorials that have since been erected on the airfields. The RAF Museum were able to fill in gaps concerning the fate of particular aircraft, and Ed Storey in Canada, who tracked down some wonderful photos of the period.

Chris Ransted's help in searching out War Diaries of the Royal Engineers was invaluable and others who helped in various ways were Hugh Alexander at the National Archives, Peter Cornwell, Stéphane Duchemin, Jim Parker, Gordon Riley, Chris Goss, Cato Guhnfeldt, Dr Klaus Schmider at the Royal Military Academy, and Kathy Struss of The Dwight D. Eisenhower Presidential Library.

Finally, my thanks and appreciation to Karel Margry, Editor of *After the Battle*, who visited Normandy to photograph the memorials; to Rob Green, my long-suffering computer whizz-kid who works alongside me, and to my wife Gail who spent hours checking our GoogleEarth comparisons which are reproduced under licence.

WINSTON RAMSEY, 2017

Contents

The airfields are listed in order of the date they were declared operational, i.e. the date on which the first aircraft landed. During the first 90 days following D-Day, 74 airfields and airstrips were in use or being constructed.

JUNE

7th	ELS-1	Pouppeville	26
	B-1	Asnelles-sur-Mer	28
	A-21C	St Laurent-sur-Mer	30
15th	B-3	Ste Croix-sur-Mer	32
16th	A-3	Cardonville	36
	B-2	Bazenville	40
17th	A-1	St Pierre-du-Mont	44
	A-2	Cricqueville	48
	A-6	Beuzeville	54
18th	B-4	Bény-sur-Mer	58
	A-4	Deux-Jumeaux	62
20th	B-6	Coulombs	66
24th	B-5	Camilly	70
	A-10	Carentan	74
25th	B-7	Martragny	78
	B-11	Longues-sur-Mer	82
27th	B-10	Plumetot	86
	B-9	Lantheuil	90
	A-7	Azeville	94
29th	B-8	Sommervieu	98
	A-8	Picauville	102

JULY

3rd	A-14	Cretteville	106
	A-15	Maupertus	110
5th	A-9	Le Molay	114
6th	A-5	Chippelle	118
7th	A-12	Lignerolles	120
	A-16	Brucheville	122
8th	B-15	Ryes	124
13th	A-22C	Colleville	126
16th	B-12	Ellon	128
17th	A-24C	Biniville	132
19th	A-13	Tour-en-Bessin	134
25th	B-17	Carpiquet	136
29th	A-23C	Querqueville	140

AUGUST

6th	A-11	St Lambert	143
7th	B-14	Amblie	144
	A-25C	Bolleville	146
8th	B-18	Cristot	148
10th	A-27	Rennes	150
11th	A-31	Gaël	152
13th	B-19	Lingèvres	154
	A-30C	Courtils	156
14th	A-28	Pontorson	157
	B-21	Ste Honorine-de-Ducy	158
15th	A-19	La Vieille	160
16th	A-17	Méautis	164
18th	A-33N	Vannes	166
20th	B-16	Villons-les-Buissons	168
	A-29	St James	172
23rd	A-40D	Chartres	174
24th	A-41	Dreux	176
26th	A-20	Lessay	178
28th	B-24	St André-de-l'Eure	180
	B-26	Illiers-l'Évêque	184
	A-36	St Léonard	185
	B-30	Créton	187
	A-39	Châteaudun	188
	A-48	Brétigny	191
29th	B-28	Évreux	192
	A-35	Le Mans	194
	A42D	Villacoublay	196
	A-46	Toussus-le-Noble	198
30th	A-26	Gorges	200
31st	A-18	St Jean-de-Daye	202

SEPTEMBER

1st	B-27	Boisney	203
	B-33	Campneuseville	204
	B-34	Avrilly	205
2nd	B-29	Valailles	207
	B-40/A-61	Beauvais/Tillé	208
	A-43	St Marceau	212
3rd	B-23	La Rue Huguenot	213
	B-48	Amiens/Glisy	214
	A-34	Gorron	216
4th	A-44	Peray	217
		Index	220

No. 198 Squadron pictured in July at airstrip B-10 at Plumetot. Tempest MN1526 is nearest the camera.

Editorial Note

Prior to in invasion of Normandy, more than 450 aerodromes, airfields, sites for advanced landing grounds, refuelling and re-armament strips and major airports across France, Belgium, Holland and Germany had been earmarked by planners for use by the Allied air forces.

Just days before he met his death in the French Alps while travelling to his next assignment, Air Chief Marshal Sir Trafford Leigh-Mallory, who had been the Air Commander of the Allied Expeditionary Force for Operation 'Overlord', submitted his report to the Supreme Allied Commander, General Dwight D. Eisenhower.

'It was appreciated that the effort of the fighters and fighter-bombers over the beach-head would inevitably be seriously reduced after three or four days if they had to operate at such distances from their bases in the UK. In the early planning therefore, a high priority had been arranged for naval lift of the stores and equipment which would be needed to operate the fighters and fighter-bomber squadrons planned to be flown into bases on the Continent as soon as possible after D-Day. This was made possible only by the work of the airfield construction engineers, of the maintenance personnel, and of the supply organisation.

'In the early stages, the terrain in the British sector was generally more favourable than that in the American. However, the airfield engineers achieved very fine results in both sectors and, as well as constructing the airfields, they often had to lay down their tools to deal with stray snipers in the area around the strip.'

The initial programme for the construction of the airstrips to accommodate the forces allocated for transfer to the Continent was as follows: Three Emergency Landing Strips (ELS) — two American and one British — by the evening of D-Day. Four Refuelling and Re-arming Strips (R&RS), two American and two British, by the evening of D+3. Ten Advanced Landing Grounds (ALGs), five American and five British which were to include four of the R&RSs, by D+8. Eighteen airfields (eight American and ten British) by D+14; 27 airfields (12 American and 15 British) by D+24, and 43 (18 American and 25 British) by D+40. The position at the end of the pre-planned period was to be a total of 93 airfields — 48 American and 45 British — by D+90.

In this volume we cover all those airstrips and airfields that were operational within that period i.e. up to September 4, 1944. Dates of completion for the invasion airfields are fluid as on many occasions squadrons moved in while engineers were still working on them. Also some were initially opened as crash or short fighter strips while work continued to extend the runway. Our criterion has been to list the airfields by the date of the arrival of the first squadron.

The plan shows the forecast by the D-Day planners for the Phase Lines to be achieved during the three months following the landings. They proved very conservative as by September American and French forces had reached Paris and the British and Canadians were entering Belgium.

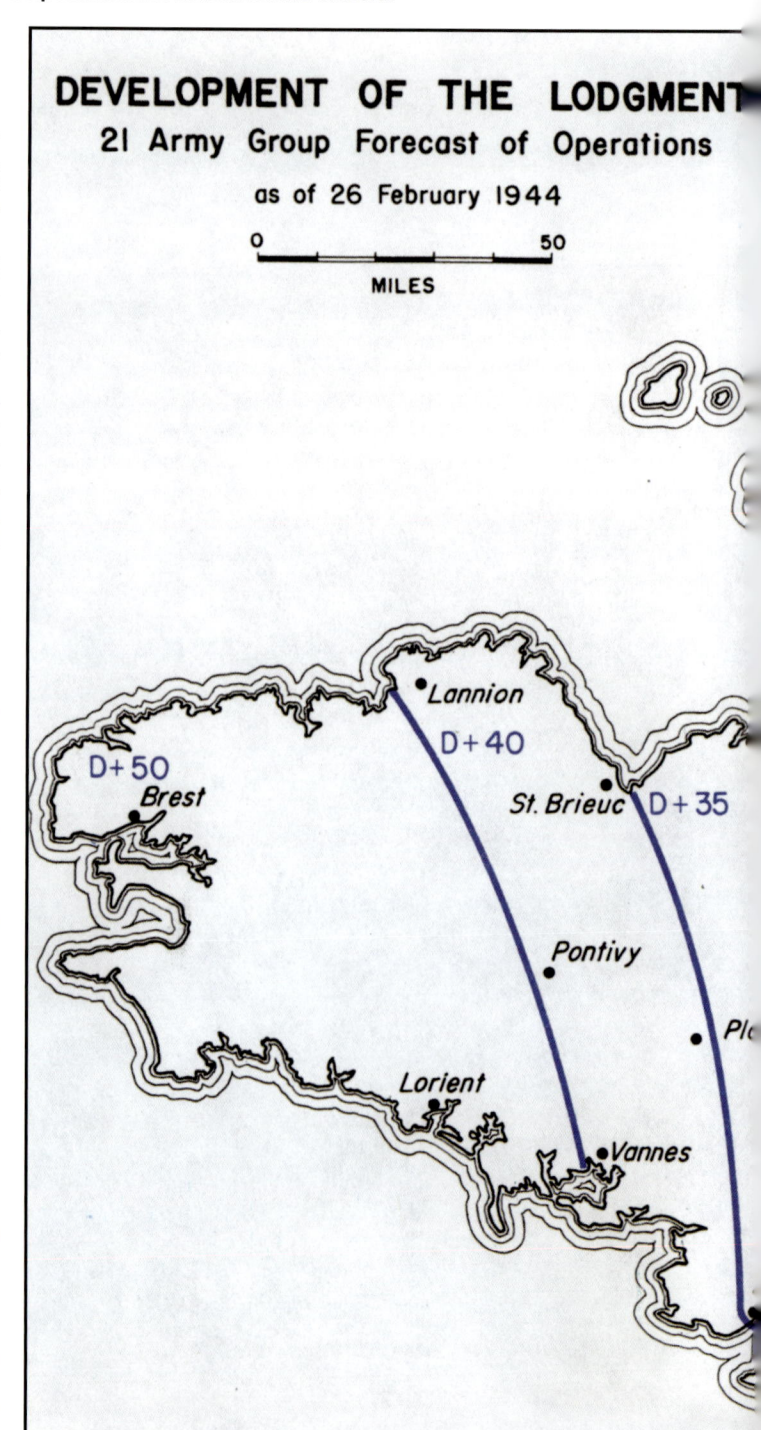

DEVELOPMENT OF THE LODGMENT
21 Army Group Forecast of Operations
as of 26 February 1944

0 — 50 MILES

D+50 Brest
Lannion D+40
St. Brieuc D+35
Pontivy
Lorient
Vannes

P-47s of the 368th Fighter Group at A-3 Cardonville which became operational on June 16.

Introduction

Air supremacy was vital for a successful outcome to defeat of Germany and two special air forces were established in Britain to support the ground forces. Air Chief Marshal Trafford Leigh-Mallory was designated Allied Air Commander-in-Chief as the overall commander of the RAF's Second Tactical Air Force and USAAF's Ninth Air Force. The commander of the American tactical air force had already been decided back in July 1943 when Lieutenant General Lewis H. Brereton was in the Middle East. There, he had worked closely with Air Marshal Arthur Coningham who was appointed to command the RAF's Second Tactical Air Force in January 1944.

Although each air force had separate headquarters in Berkshire (Brereton's at Sunninghill Park near Ascot and Coningham's at Ramslade House, Bracknall), a new combined HQ was established at Hillingdon House, Uxbridge, the former headquarters of the RAF's No. 11 Group. Pierre Closterman, who was serving with No. 602 Squadron, spent two weeks at Uxbridge in May 1944.

'I never saw so many stars and so much braid, and the most insignificant little man you met was at least an Air Commodore. Air Marshals were thick on the ground — it was an absolute Tower of Babel.'

On January 16, 1944, General Dwight D. Eisenhower was appointed as the Supreme Commander of the Allied Expeditionary Force (SHAEF) with Air Chief Marshal Sir Arthur Tedder as his deputy. Sir Trafford Leigh-Mallory (right) had been confirmed as the Allied Air Commander-in-Chief the previous November. Standing behind in this photograph taken on January 27 at Bentley Priory, Stanmore, the HQ of RAF Fighter Command, is Tedder's deputy, Major General William O. Butler.

February 13, 1944 — the Allied air chiefs are pictured in conference. L-R: Air Marshal Roderic M. Hill, Air Officer Commanding Air Defence of Great Britain; Major General William O. Butler, Deputy Commander-in-Chief, Allied Expeditionary Air Force: Air Chief Marshal Sir Trafford Leigh-Mallory; Air Vice-Marshal Philip Wigglesworth, Senior Air Staff Officer, Allied Expeditionary Air Force; Brigadier General Aubrey C. Strickland, Deputy Senior Air Staff Officer; (seated in the foreground) Lieutenant General Lewis H. Brereton, Commanding General US Ninth Air Force, and (extreme right) Air Marshal Sir Arthur Coningham, the Air Officer Commanding the RAF's Second Tactical Air Force. The documents on the table were blanked out at the request of the censor.

Air Chief Marshal Leigh-Mallory set out the requirements that had to be addressed by the D-Day planners:

'In combined operations it is obviously advantageous that fighters, fighter-bombers and reconnaissance aircraft of the Tactical Air Forces should be able to work from bases in the operational theatre as early as possible, and therefore airfield accommodation is of paramount importance.

'The extent to which airfield requirements could be met in this operation depended, in the main, on the ability of the field engineers to locate and develop suitable sites. It also depended upon having a sufficiently high priority within the available shipping space for the movement of equipment and material.

'In the initial stages, the terrain in the British sector was generally more favourable than that in the American. However, the position in the British sector deteriorated because the good area to the east and south-east around Caen was not secured as rapidly as had been planned. Neither did the situation in the American sector greatly improve until the advance had progressed to Le Mans and beyond.

'The minimum programme for airfields to accommodate the forces allocated was as follows:

Emergency Landing Strip (ELS)

'This was a strip having sufficient length of level surface to enable pilots in distress to make a landing. These strips were to have a minimum length of 600 yards and, while not fit for the operation of aircraft, were of inestimable value when operations are conducted a long way from bases, especially when a long sea crossing on the way home is involved.

Refuelling and Re-arming Strip (R&RS)

'This strip had to possess a sufficient length of level compact surface for landing and taking off, adequate marshalling areas for the rapid turn-round of aircraft, and adequate tracking to ensure operation under all normal summer and autumn conditions. These strips were to have a minimum length of 1,200 yards with marshalling areas of 100 by 50 yards at each end.

Advanced Landing Ground (ALG)

'An ALG was a landing ground possessing the same facilities as an R&RS, and was to be brought up to ALG standard by the addition of dispersal facilities and capable of use to capacity by adoption of the "Roulement" system. This was a means of using landing ground facilities to the maximum capacity by flying in squadrons to replace others as they complete their scale of effort appropriate to the period.

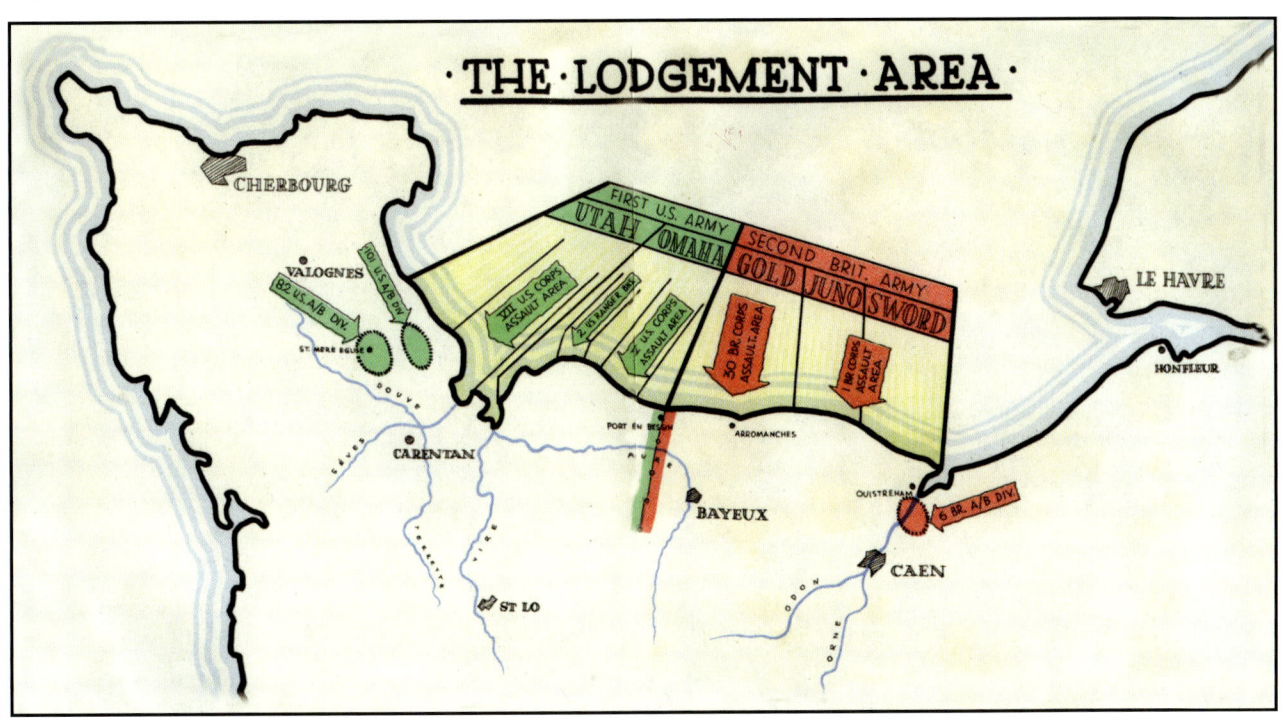

'Pictured in front of a map of the area from which they helped to drive Rommel, the Anglo-American tactical air force chiefs relax after their first conference on British soil leading up to the invasion of France. Air Marshal Coningham, Air Officer Commanding the Second Tactical Force, has with him Lieutenant General Brereton, of the US Ninth (Tactical) Air Force which has now been assigned its Second Front duties.' The 1944 caption writer also explained that 'Sir Arthur inaugurated the First Tactical Air Force in the desert — the force that put into operation Air Chief Marshal Tedder's complete army-air plan — and Lieutenant General Brereton is the man who planned the Liberator assault on the Ploesti oil refineries.'

Each tactical air force had its own facilities for constructing airstrips in Normandy. The Royal Engineers had five Airfield Construction Groups, the RAF four Airfield Construction Wings, and the Americans 16 Engineer (Aviation) Battalions. The latter had the advantage of much more heavy earth-moving plant being available, as admitted by Leigh-Mallory in his report, although it was the British developments of Square Mesh Track (SMT), and Prefabricated Bituminous Surfaces (PBS) that were used to line the majority of the airfields.

Airfield

'These had the same facilities as an ALG but with improved dispersal facilities and on which squadrons were established and not operated on the "Roulement" system, as on an ALG. The minimum lengths for both ALGs and Airfields are 1,200 yards for fighters, with dispersal facilities for 54 aircraft, and 1,650 yards for fighter-bombers with the same dispersal facilities.

All-Weather Airfield.

'This category had the same requirements as for an Airfield but possessing hard-surfaced runways and fit for operation throughout all seasons and all conditions of weather for the appropriate type of aircraft. Within the limits of operational requirements, it was planned that all enemy airfields with hard-surfaced runways would be re-instated, as and when they were captured if, in the opinion of the airfield engineers, reinstatement could be effected without excessive labour and/or material.

'The requirements were for two American and one British ELS to be completed on D-Day, and two American and two British R&RSs by the evening of D+3 and not later than D+4. Ten ALGs, five American and five British, were to be useable by D+8, this total including four of the R&RSs. We required 18 airfields (eight American and ten British) to be operational by D+14; 27 (12 American and 15 British) by D+24; 43 airfields (18 American and 25 British) by D+40, and 93 airfields (48 American and 45 British) by D+90.

'The following construction units were available for allocation as required in the beach-head: 16 American Engineer (Aviation) Battalions, plus two Airborne Aviation Engineering Battalions, and five Airfield Construction Groups (ACG) of the Royal Engineers. There were also four RAF Airfield Construction Wings (ACW), each comprising 58 officers and 2,368 other ranks, but these were not to be used in forward areas but in the lines of communication and base areas on improving and extending existing aerodromes

'Because we failed in the initial phases to gain the ground anticipated in the optimum plan in the vicinity of Caen, the development of all of the pre-selected sites could not be started. This naturally caused some delay and made necessary a re-allotment of sites in the British beach-head area. As a very high proportion of potential sites selected from air photographs proved to be suitable for rapid construction, the intensive preparation of the beach-head area permitted the leeway to be made up. Later, when the Allied advance became rapid, the problem of finding space to prepare airfields was eased. It became more a problem of getting the airfields constructed rapidly in the now adequate space available.

'The system adopted for constructing airfields near the front line was to prepare dirt strips 15-20 miles to the rear of the ground forces. These strips were then visited by transport aircraft, which brought in stores and tools. As a general rule, fighter strips were 50-70 miles behind the front line and bomber strips 100-120 miles behind. As the ground forces moved forward, so the dirt strips previously prepared were constructed as airfields and became bases for fighters and later for bombers.'

It goes without saying that aircraft need fuel to operate . . . and lots of it. Port-en-Bessin was chosen as the petroleum port. After its capture on D+1, the port was found to be in better condition than had been expected, and instead of it only being capable of shallow-draft craft, it proved to be adequate to take tankers up to 14 feet draft in the outer harbour. The quays were also relatively undamaged. Both British and US tankers used the port, the British pipeline being on the east of the harbour and the American on the west. The first ship-to-shore petrol line was in operation on July 1. The prefabricated ports — Mulberry 'A' on Omaha Beach and Mulberry 'B' at Arromanches — were discharging in the order of 2,000 tons of supplies per day by D+12, including fuel in jerrycans, but then the American port was totally lost in the storm on June 19 and Mulberry 'B' severely damaged. Nevertheless, within four days overall discharge had risen to 40,000 tons per day. Meanwhile, considerable construction work was carried out at Port-en-Bessin and by July 25 36,000 tons of bulk spirit had been brought ashore.

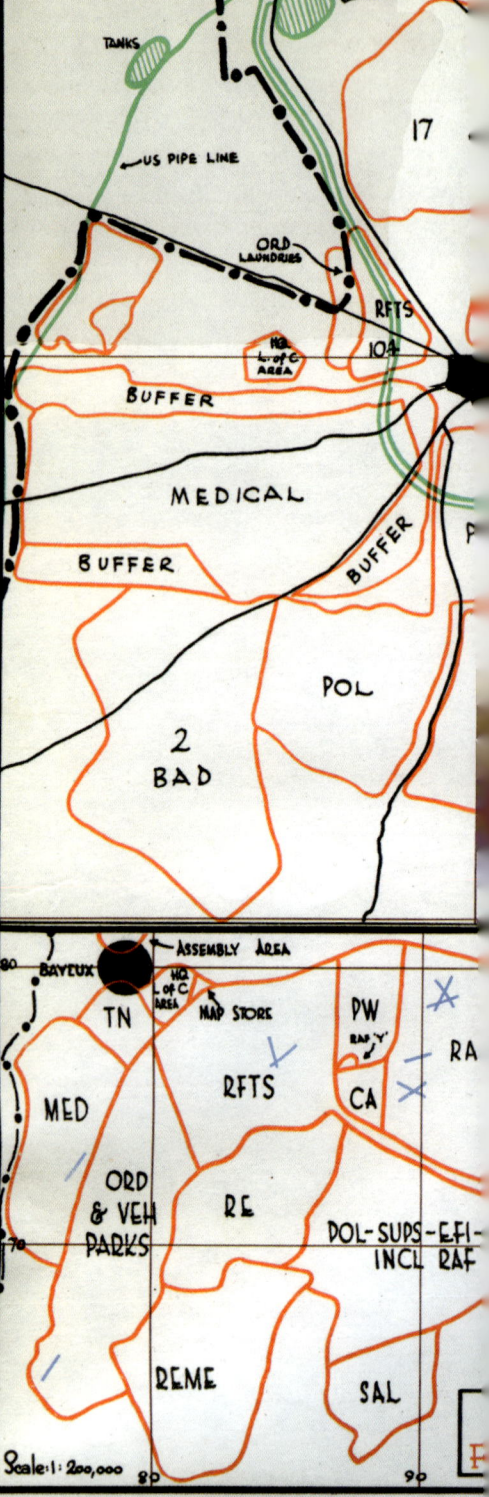

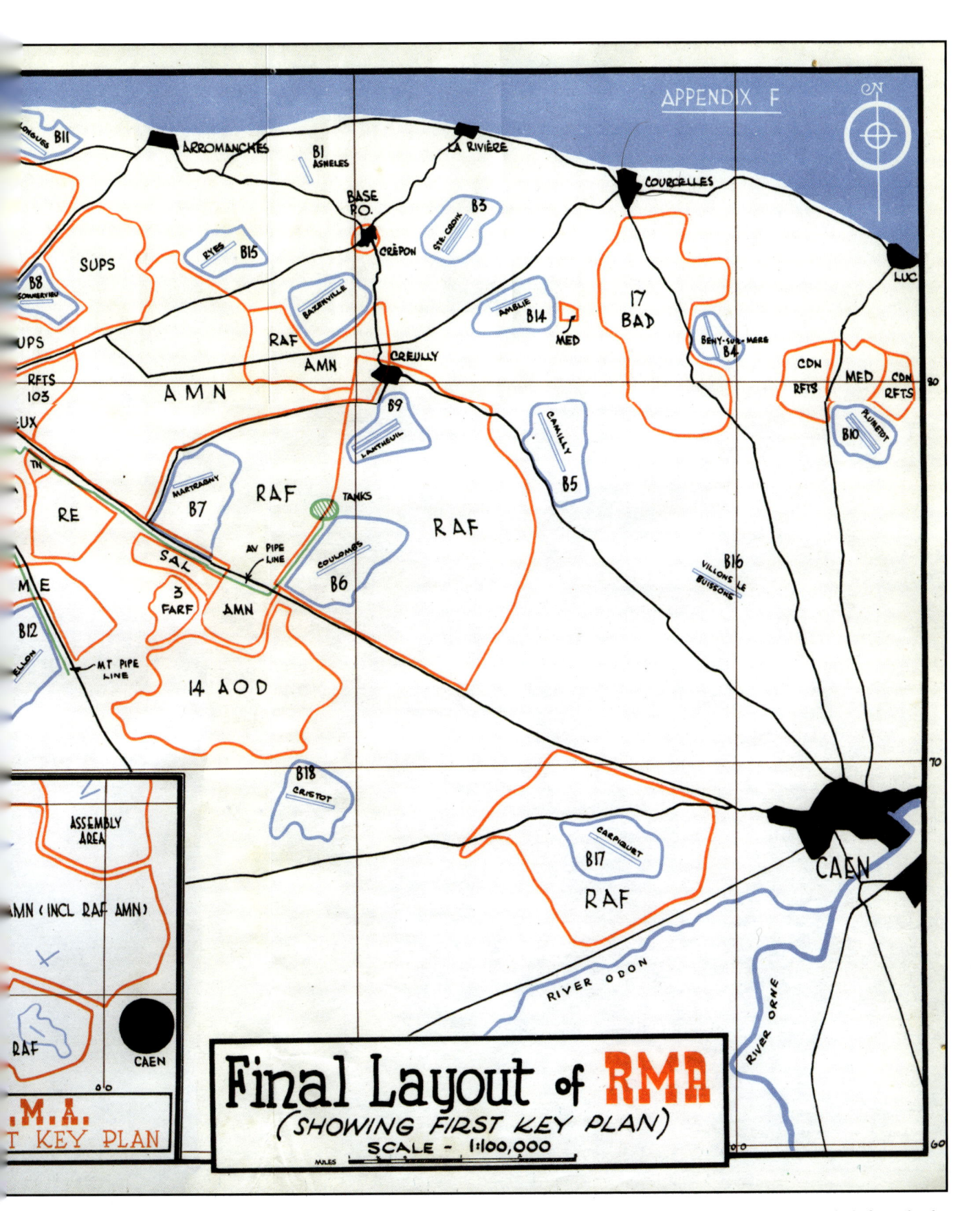

By then, two ship-to-shore pipelines had been completed; six tanker berths were in operation with pipe connections, and tankage had been erected for 9,800 tons of MT fuel and 2,000 tons of aviation spirit. Three six-inch pipelines (in green on the map) had been laid to Blary, south-east of Bayeux, where an additional 1,040 tons of storage had been erected and another pipeline to Isigny in the American sector was nearly finished. In addition, a six-inch aviation fuel line had been laid to B-6 at Coulombs. This plan gives an idea of the pre-invasion planning necessary to allocate areas for the army and air force in the Rear Maintenance Area (RMA) in the British lodgement area. (AMN — Ammunition; AOD — Advanced Ordnance Depot; APO — Army Post Office; BAD — Base Ammunition Depot; CA — Civil Affairs; EFI — Expeditionary Forces Institute, NAAFI; FARF — Field Ammunition Repair Factory; MED — Medical; ORD — Ordnance; POL — Petrol Oil and Lubricants; PW — Prisoners of War; REME — Royal Electrical and Mechanical Engineers; RFTS — Reinforcements; SAL — Salvage; SUPS — Supplies.

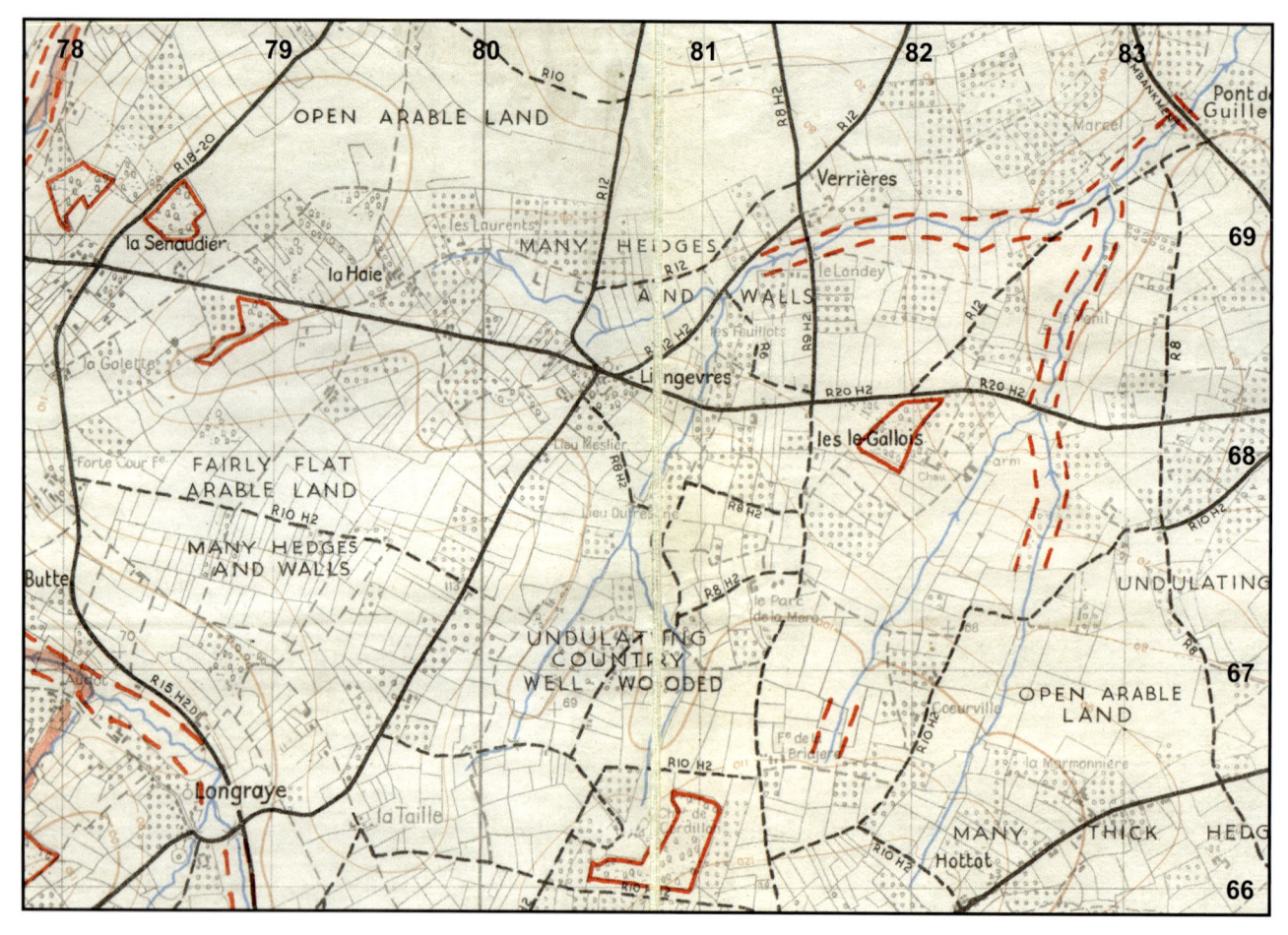

The whole of the lodgement area had been surveyed through aerial photographs and detailed maps produced showing the contours and nature of the terrain to select the best locations for airfields. This section of GSGS Sheet 4347 covers the location where B-19 was built at the grid reference T-805695 just north of Lingèvres (see page 154).

Major General Cecil R. Moore, the US Chief Engineer for the European Theater of Operations, explained that 'the whole program was a huge task and many special problems were involved in it. The provision of fields for the Ninth Air Force was so closely linked with the tactical operations of that force that it was considered desirable to provide a special engineer force with an undivided interest in the one mission of providing airfields and other air force installations. Therefore, to facilitate the execution of this great engineering task, a new organization was established: the IX Engineer Command.

'Beginning in December 1943, engineer aviation troop units in the United Kingdom, where they had been engaged in building airfields, were released on a phased schedule from their construction assignments to this new command in order that necessary pre-invasion training might be initiated.

'As of D-Day, the command was organised into four regiments of four Engineer Aviation Battalions each. The headquarters was able to control the efforts of its units directly through these regiments only during the Normandy operations, where distances were limited. With the St Lô breakthrough and the rapid movement following, flexibility became paramount and to achieve this two Engineer Aviation Brigade headquarters were organised.

'As the number of fields constructed increased, maintenance also increased and became an ever-pyramiding problem. In addition, this organisation conducted necessary salvage of pierced steel plank, hangars, etc. In September, the 6th Army Group pushing up from southern France joined up with the 12th Army Group. At this time it became necessary to bring the 923rd Engineer Aviation Regiment with three battalions from the United Kingdom to the Continent.

'Joint American-British airfields standards were established in November 1943. At this time, 3,600ft runways 120ft wide were agreed upon as were standard methods of marking and identification. It later became necessary to increase the length of American fields to 5,000ft due to the employment of heavier P-47 Thunderbolt fighter aircraft. The lighter P-51s and P-38s originally intended for the operation were being employed as long-range bomber escorts and were not available for fighter use. In addition shortly after D-Day, with the German air force crushed, the necessity for fighters diminished and the P-47s were utilised as fighter-bombers carrying 500lb and 1,000lb bombs. This made the longer runway a "must".

'All site selection in this pre-invasion planning was based on data secured from the Intelligence Division, Office of the Chief Engineer. Aerial photos, multiplex site maps, soil studies plus other technical intelligence were combined to permit the selection of the most suitable sites for rapid development. In planning this airfield construction program based on established phase lines, it was necessary to provide for the development of airfield "clutches" — usually four or five fields to a clutch — to facilitate air force control of its operations.

'Another consideration was the "leapfrogging" of tactical units to ensure continuous close air co-operation for the associated army. In all this planning, the maximum utilisation of existing airfields, particularly hard surfaced ones, was visualised.

'For the operation two light-weight temporary airfield surfacing materials were developed, basically by the British. These were Square Mesh Track (SMT) and Prefabricated Bituminous Surfacing (PBS). While it was originally intended that either one or the other of these materials would be used depending on the situation, in actual practice it proved that a combination of the two was more durable. SMT was also used in conjunction with Pierced Steel Plank (PSP) in non-critical areas of PSP fields when logistics prevented the use of PSP throughout. Cement and asphalt were also required in large amounts to effect the rehabilitation of captured hard-surfaced airfields. Because of the great amounts of lift necessary to move engineer aviation units with their heavy

In July, the US First Army had begun to show signs of being bogged down in the Cherbourg peninsula so General Omar N. Bradley set in motion plans for Operation 'Cobra' in which 2,500 aircraft would obliterate German defences along the St Lô—Périers road. Eisenhower flew to France early on July 25 to watch the bombing. Four Spitfires from No. 127 Squadron escorted him from Tangmere to A-9. Here, Ike thanks the leader of his escort, Flying Officer Arnold Asboe from New South Wales, Australia (he died in 1968). Right up into August, General Eisenhower was still commuting from the UK but Tedder was pressing the Supreme Commander to establish a tactical headquarters on the Continent to permit closer liaison with the forces on the battlefield. On August 7, his Advanced Command Post code-named 'Shellburst' was opened 12 miles south-west of Bayeux. Nearby, A-9 was a convenient airfield at Le Molay. Note the Square Mesh Tracking and also Eisenhower's battledress — a special version of the US 1944 field jacket which had been specially altered for him by the SHAEF tailor, Sergeant Michael Popp.

S E C R E T

DESCRIPTION OF AIRFIELD　　　　　　　　　　　　　　　　　　FIRST EDITION

FRANCE　　　　　　　　　　　　A 67　　　　　　　　　　　　AIRFIELD

NAME: VITRY　　　　　　　CO-ORDINATES: LAT. 48°44'52"N. Long. 04°38'36"E

MAG VAR: 07°10' W (1944)　ANNUAL CHANGE: 10' E.

MAP REF: France 1:50,000　GRID REF: vT 729211　　　HEIGHT (ASL)

LOCAL POSITION
AND LANDMARKS:

OBSTRUCTIONS: None

POSITION OF WIND
 INDICATOR:　　　Both ends of strip

DIMENSIONS: Flying Strip 5000'　　　　　　　　　　QDM:

SURFACE:

RUNWAY:　　S.M.T.

TAXY TRACK AND
MARSHALLING AREA:　25' wide. untracked.

SERVICEABILITY: _____ ON _____ (DATE)

FACILITIES:
 (a) Night landing: Complete portable airfield lighting
 (b) Telephone:
 (c) Radio: VHF Homing, 24 hour darky watch
 (d) Method of refuelling: Fuel servicing truck
 (e) Fuel and oil bulk storage: 35,000 U.S. Gal. Avaition. M.T. in cans.
 (f) Meteorological Staff: Yes
 (g) Rearming: Adaquate for type in occupancy
 (h) Hangars:
 (i) Billeting:
 (j) Water: Adaquate

DISPERSAL: area dispersal for 100 A/C.

ACCESS: Road:
　　　　 Rail: Vitry - 4 Miles.

OCCUPIED BY:

REMARKS:

S E C R E T

Schedules were prepared by IX Engineer Command and 21st Army Group covering each American and British airstrip, with operating conditions and a schematic plan drawn up to a common design. This is an example although, as Vitry-le-François only became operational after D+90, it falls outside the remit of this book. Work to prepare the A-67 airstrip was carried out by the 850th Engineer Aviation Battalion between September 9 and 15 whereupon the three squadrons (365th, 366th and 367th) of the 358th Fighter Group flew in from A-28 at Pontorson.

equipment, and to move forward the large tonnages of airfield surfacing materials required, it was necessary to develop all plans in great detail and with the maximum co-ordination.

'The availability of various types of surfacing materials had direct effects on the rate of construction progress; the number of fields which could be built in a given area, and the standards used. In general during the Normandy period, PBS and SMT were used with PSP being utilised solely for medium bomber fields. Following the breakthrough and all during the rapid movement across France, logistics limited surfacing on new sites to PBS.

'During this period many existing hard-surfaced airfields were uncovered and rehabilitated thus alleviating the supply problem a great deal. As winter came on and the static period of operation began it was necessary and possible to utilise PSP as the primary construction material. Over 800 ground reconnaissances were made for site selection in addition to some 300 aerial reconnaissance flights. The latter were developed until the closing days of the war by special P-38 aircraft.

'On D+40, about a week prior to the break-out from the beach area, the IX Engineer Command had 18 American fields in operation. At this time the initial build-up of personnel was complete and there were some 16,000 engineer aviation troops on the Continent. From D+30 until D+50 progress was held up due to the lack of good sites in the limited areas in our control and by the decision to phase forward the four medium bomber group fields which were immediately taken under construction. From D+50 to D+80 when Paris was liberated, 14 additional fields were placed in operation and the tactical aircraft build-up actually exceeded that originally planned.

'By D+90 some 50,000 tons of surfacing materials had been used. The rapid advance of our forces to the German border produced an ever-increasing shortage of surfacing materials. Rehabilitation of fields was carried out to the maximum, and in the first 100 days — that is by September 15 — 67 fields had been completed, 18 were under construction and 10 of these were operational.

'During the period of rapid movement, supply and evacuation airfields became increasingly important in order that the drive of armoured spearheads might be sustained. By D+90, 30,000 tons of supplies had been flown to France from the United Kingdom and landed on these special fields some of which were later fully developed to tactical use. In addition, during this same period, some 40,000 of our wounded were evacuated by air from these fields.

'Late in September rains began and continued well into November when the freezing weather set in. During this rainy period mud became the major problem. During the static period of operations extending through to February 1945, forward fighter clutches of US airfields were developed in the Nancy area, the Metz area, and to the north in Belgium. In the rear, airfields in the Paris and Reims areas were developed for medium bombers, troop carrier and administrative purposes.

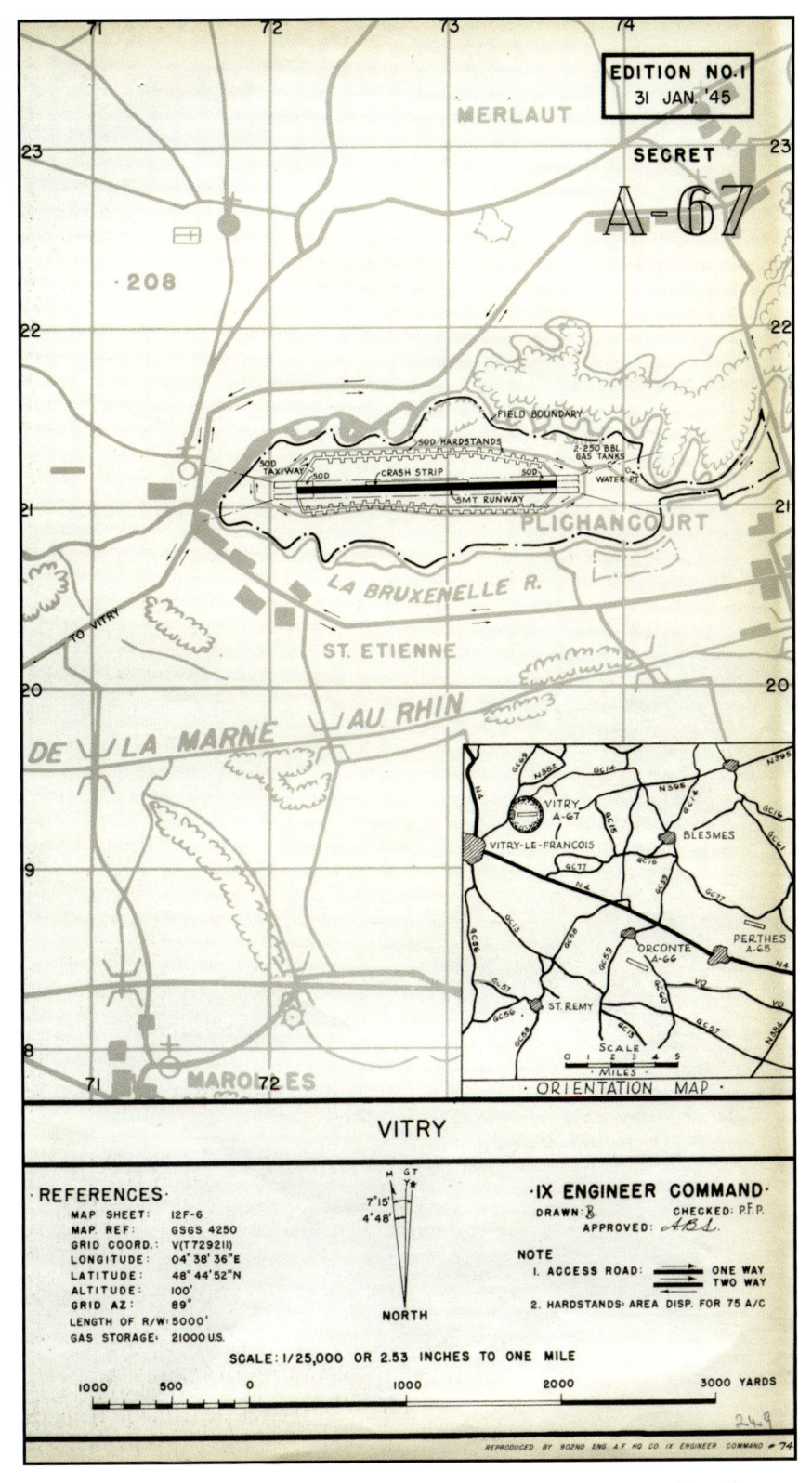

'By the middle of March the large Dutch hard-surfaced airfield at Venlo had been made operational in six days, and the first American-built airfield in Germany was in operation at Aachen.

'Experience during the rapid movement across France had developed an appreciation of the value of supply and evacuation (S&E) airfields. Provision of such fields was planned for the drive into and across Germany. Detachments of Aviation Engineers operated with spearhead task forces. From March 21 to May 9 (49 days), a total of 84 such fields were placed in operation. Using these airfields, C-47s landed 60,000 tons of supplies, about two-thirds of which was gasoline, and evacuated some 108,000 repatriates and 80,000 wounded.

'By VE-Day 120 airfields had been constructed or rehabilitated in Germany and over 100 of these were east of the Rhine. A total of 241 had been constructed or rehabilitated since D-Day.'

After preparing the ground by grubbing out trees and filling ditches, the surface was graded and rolled, ready for the tracking to be laid. Although this particular landing strip is not identified in the censored 1944 caption, as the photo was taken on June 17, and it is being completed by laying rolls of Square Mesh Tracking, our guess is that it probably shows work proceeding on A-2 at Cricqueville (page 48) or A-6 at Beuzeville (page 54).

Metal track surfacing played a crucial role in the success story as Major Reginald Grigson of the Royal Engineers explains:

'Possibly the first occasion on which metal tracking was used as an aid to vehicular movement occurred in the Middle East during the 1914-18 war when it was discovered that ordinary wire-netting (sometimes referred to as "chicken wire") laid on the surface of the desert sand facilitated the passage of vehicles.

'Two types of metal track were provided for the use of airfield engineers of the 21st Army Group and the American Armies in the invasion of North-West Europe: Square Mesh Track — a lightweight wire mesh developed and produced in the United Kingdom in 1943 and 1944 — and Pierced Steel Plank which had been developed in the USA and was ready for production at the time that America entered the war.

'When it is realised that a single average-size airfield may require 250,000 square yards of track, it will be appreciated that only those tracks which require simple manufacturing processes and which utilise raw materials readily available in large quantities in wartime can be considered satisfactory. Also the units which make up the track — whether they be in roll, panel or planks — should be of such dimensions and weights as will permit their transport by ship, rail, or cargo aircraft.

'The types of aircraft which may safely be operated from tracked runways depend upon soil conditions as well as upon the nature of the track. The use of light tracks is confined as far as possible to fighters, fighter-bombers, and light cargo aircraft having wheelloads not exceeding 15,000lbs. The heavy tracks may, under favourable conditions, take wheel loads up to 37,000lbs.

SQUARE MESH TRACK

'This track is a development of the welded mesh used as reinforcement in concrete roads and other structures. It consists of a 3in square mesh of No. 5 s.w.g. cold-drawn steel wire (ultimate tensile strength 34 to 42 tons per square inch), the wires being resistance-welded together at their intersections. It is made in panels measuring approximately 12ft by 6ft or, more commonly, in rolls 7ft 3in wide, each containing a 77ft 3in length of track. It is easy to fabricate, and at one time production in the United Kingdom was at the rate of over 1,000,000 square yards per month. In this type of track weld-strength is of very great importance as the stresses induced by aircraft touching down and braking are very large. Hence, a minimum shear strength of 1,400lbs was specified for the welds.

These RAF engineers are laying SMT at B-19 located near Lingèvres.

'Panels or rolls are connected together transversely and longitudinally in the field by overlapping one or two meshes and clipping them together with mild-steel strap-type clips.

'Square Mesh Track runways were tested with aircraft by British and American army engineers independently in the spring of 1944. It was found that there was a pronounced tendency for a billow or wave to form in front of the wheels of aircraft, particularly where little or no "key" existed between the soil underlying the track and the track itself. In some cases, the magnitude of the wave reached alarming proportions, causing clips to fly out and damage aircraft undercarriages. The waving tendency was eventually prevented by tensioning the track longitudinally and picketing it down.

As untensioned SMT was prone to billowing, the mesh had to be secured down.

The problem was solved by either crimping (left) **and fixing strap-type clips** (above).

No. 5357 Airfield Construction Wing laying SMT at B-19 at Lingèvres where a 5,000ft runway was prepared for No. 125 Wing.

PIERCED STEEL PLANK

'American engineers had, from the outset, concentrated on producing tracks embodying a far more generous quantity of steel in their design than had been considered practicable in the United Kingdom. Pierced Steel Plank was developed in the United States prior to their entry into the war.

'The track consists of panels or planks 1ft 3ins wide by 10ft long, pressed from No. 10 US gauge mild-steel plate. Longitudinal ribs are formed in the sheet to increase stiffness, and to reduce weight three parallel lines of $2^{5}/_{8}$ in diameter holes, spaced at 4-inch centres, are punched out of the sheets on each side of the longitudinal ribs. To obtain additional stiffness the edges of the holes are bent down.

'Side connexions between planks are made by interlocking projecting lugs or "bayonets" along the side of one plank with slots punched out of the side of the adjoining plank. Lugs and slots are provided on both edges of the planks. Spring-steel clips are driven into the slots behind the lug projections to prevent the latter from slipping out. There is no connexion between the ends of planks.

'The planks are laid in rows parallel to the transverse centre-line of the runway and planks in successive rows are staggered by half a panel-length. Each row of planks is laid with the lugs pointing in the opposite direction to those of the adjacent row as this enables individual planks to be removed for repair. Half-length planks are made for filling in the spaces left at the edges of the runway by the staggering of the 10ft planks.

'The principal advantage of this type of track over others is its simplicity of manufacture which has enabled it to be produced by the sheet-metal plants in the USA speedily and in vast quantities.

Pierced Steel Planking was laid parallel to the transverse centre-line of the runway and successive rows were staggered by half a panel-length. On well-drained soil, a relatively long life could be obtained even when the types of aircraft using the track were heavy.

Furthermore, it requires less shipping space per ton than any other type.

'However it does have limitations in use. It tends to retain moisture under it, and, when subjected to repeated applications of load in wet weather, the planks pump up water and mud from the soil on which they are laid through the pierced holes on to the surface. The presence of this mud is very undesirable; it progressively interferes with the passage of traffic until a stage is reached when the track becomes unusable. To reduce this tendency and also to reduce dust in hot weather, the track is frequently laid on a bed of straw. Also when Pierced Steel Plank is laid on ground of bearing capacity inadequate for the traffic loads which it has to carry, a tendency for the panels to curl at the edges develops. Owing to the lack of end connexions between panels, the edges of planks are exposed, thus forming a dangerous hazard to aircraft.

Men from three Engineer Aviation Battalions (the 830th, 833rd and 878th) worked on A-55 at Melun, surfacing it with Pierced Steel Planking in September 1944 as it was to be allocated to the 416th Bomb Group with A-20 Havocs from Wethersfield in Essex. Then, in February 1945, the 436th Troop Carrier Group flew in with C-47 Skytrains.

To cater for heavy transport aircraft, PSP was the preferred surface althought the first of its type was not opened until July 3.

And here an RAF Construction unit are pictured preparing the hundredth airfield for the Second Tactical Air Force since D-Day.

PREFABRICATED BITUMINOUS SURFACING

'PBS differs fundamentally from the metal-track types of airfield surfacing in that its prime function is to maintain or stabilise the bearing capacity of the ground and not to decrease the bearing pressure induced by wheel-loads.

'The War Office first gave serious consideration to the construction of temporary landing grounds utilising waterproof carpets early in 1943, and PBS was used by both British and American army engineers to provide a rapidly laid surface for temporary airfield runways. Its primary function was to waterproof the ground surface, thus preventing or delaying deterioration of the bearing capacity of the underlying soil from the action of rain or other forms of moisture precipitation. Secondary functions were to protect the ground surface from abrasion by traffic, and, in dry weather, to provide a reasonably dust-free surface from which aircraft may operate.

'The first trial took place in June 1943 when a runway 16,000 square yards in area, consisting of heavy clay in a dry condition, was surfaced with rot-proofed hessian cloth impregnated on the site with hot bitumen or soft pitch. Although no damage or marking of the surfacing resulted from aircraft landing and slewing during dry weather, large soft areas developed under the carpet soon after rain, rendering the runway unserviceable.

'From that trial it was apparent that a satisfactory waterproof material having a coating of adequate and consistent thickness could not be manufactured in the field. The temperature of the bitumen required critical control, which was extremely difficult to achieve; also damp hessian could not be successfully impregnated. The latter limitation was as serious as the former, as the storage of large quantities of hessian under dry conditions could not normally be achieved in the field.

'A second trial runway was laid in August 1943 with hessian that had been impregnated and coated with bitumen in a roofing-felt plant. Owing to bad laying, sections of this runway softened after rain, but results were sufficiently promising to justify further trials with prefabricated — as distinct from site-fabricated — material. These further trials were reasonably successful and, after full-scale and laboratory investigations, commercial manufacture was commenced in the United Kingdom in February 1944. Shortly afterwards, manufacture of similar material commenced in the United States so by June 1944, ample stocks of prefabricated bituminous surfacing were available for the British and American armies in their invasion task.

'PBS consisted of jute hessian cloth 40 inches wide impregnated with a relatively soft bitumen and subsequently coated equally on each side with a mixture of oxidised bitumen of a harder grade and a fine mineral filler. After being lightly dusted with a mineral flour, the material is cut into 80-yard lengths and rolled up onto timber or steel formers.

'PBS was normally laid on a smooth surface, graded by mechanical equipment as grass was seldom sufficiently level to permit direct surfacing. Grading was carried out with great care in order to avoid the formation of local depressions which would collect rain-water after surfacing. Stones or other loose

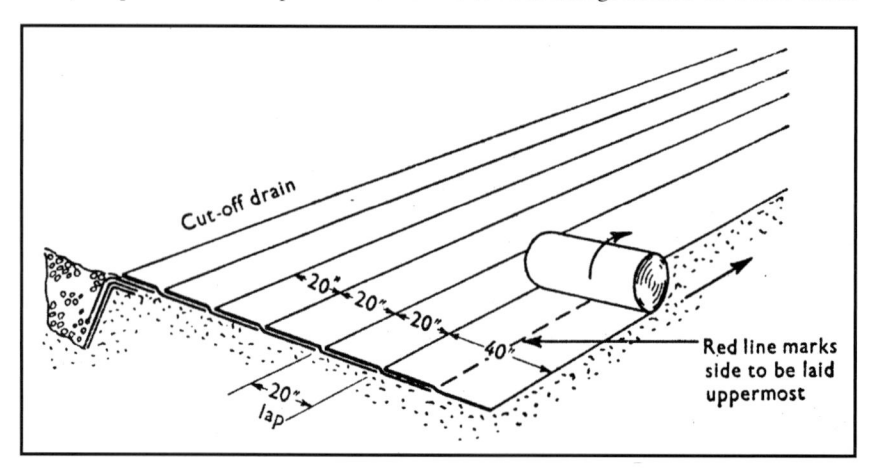

PBS was usually laid by machine, with six laying machines and nine lorries being used to construct one runway. PBS provided an impermeable surface comprising layers of hessian cloth which had been impregnated with bitumen. Each strip was bonded with a 20-inch overlap. Although there was no bond between the ground and the PBS, there was no tendency for the surface to move under the action of aircraft providing there was good adhesion between the individual strips.

objects on the surface of the ground had to be either removed or rolled well into the ground. Dusty surfaces were watered and rolled just prior to the commencement of laying.

'PBS was unrolled and laid on the runway longitudinally; the strips, 80 yards in length, overlapping each other by 20 inches (half their width), thus providing a double thickness of material. To facilitate accurate overlapping and alignment, PBS was unrolled so that the side marked with a centre line was uppermost. Adjacent strips were stuck to each other by applying to their underside a liquid in which bitumen was soluble. This liquid could be petrol, white spirit, diesel oil, or a mixture of these, the action of which was to soften the bituminous coating, thus making it tacky.

'Although manual laying was possible, PBS was usually put down by a machine specially evolved for this purpose. It consisted of a two-wheeled, pneumatic-tired chassis on which were mounted an upper and a lower tank each containing solvent liquid. A canvas-covered wooden roller, half-submerged, rotated in the solvent in the upper tank, the level of the fluid being maintained by a chain-driven pump. Six small rollers for guiding and tensioning the material through the machine and a brush for removing free dusting powder were provided. An articulating road-roller was attached to the rear of the machine which, in operation, is towed by a lorry on which is mounted a rack supporting a roll of PBS.

'The best method of surfacing a runway with laying machines is dependent upon local and operational conditions. Usually six machines and nine lorries were provided to construct one runway. The machines operated in two groups of three, each group starting at opposite ends and opposite sides of the runway and working in a clockwise direction. The machines in a group were placed in echelon and spaced about 100 yards apart longitudinally.

A sighting rod was fitted to the front of the lorry to aid the driver in keeping a straight line.

'Great care had to be exercised in laying the outer strips along each side of the runway accurately to line, since they controlled the alignment of all subsequent strips. The lorry driver was assisted in maintaining alignment by means of a sighting rod fitted to the front of the vehicle. The towing lorries are loaded with a sufficient number of rolls to enable a strip to be laid the entire length of the runway in one operation.

'For successful results to be obtained, PBS had to be laid on ground of bearing strength adequate for the contemplated loading. This normally restricted the season in which it could be used in north-west Europe to the months of May to October.

'Most satisfactory results were obtained when PBS was laid on cohesive ground which had an appreciable clay-content and which was in a hard condition. Results when laid on soft ground, whether the softness be due to excess of plasticity or to lack of cohesion, were unsatisfactory.

'If it is laid on plastic soil, such as wet clays, more harm than good may result, since, although deterioration in bearing capacity through rain may be prevented, at the same time the surfacing prevents any improvement occurring from drying out.

'To protect the end areas of runways from damage which might occur through turning and slewing of aircraft, surfacing with Square Mesh Track was sometimes carried out.

'Provided that all materials are available on the site beforehand, it is possible to surface a runway 3,600ft long by 120ft wide, using six laying-machines and a labour strength of 150 men in approximately 14 working hours.'

Nevertheless, PBS had its drawbacks. *Left:* **This damage was caused by a Dakota landing with an all-up weight of 30,000lbs.** *Right:* **Damage from a locked wheel turn.**

US NINTH AIR FORCE

IX FIGHTER COMMAND

422nd Night Fighter Squadron
P-61 Black Widow

425th Night Fighter Squadron
P-61 Black Widow

IX TACTICAL AIR COMMAND

67th Tactical Reconnaissance Group
12th TRS, 15th TRS, 107th TRS, 109th TRS, 153rd LS.
30th PRS, 9th WRS(P)
F-6 Mustang, F-5 Lightning

70th FIGHTER WING

48th Fighter Group
492nd FS, 493rd FS, 494th FS
P-47 Thunderbolt

367th Fighter Group
392nd FS, 393rd FS, 394th FS
P-38 Lightning

371st Fighter Group
404th FS, 405th FS, 406th FS
P-47 Thunderbolt

474th Fighter Group
428th FS, 429th FS, 430th FS
P-38 Lightning

71st FIGHTER WING

366th Fighter Group
389th FS, 390th FS, 391st FS
P-47 Thunderbolt

368th Fighter Group
395th FS, 396th FS, 397th FS
P-47 Thunderbolt

370th Fighter Group
401st FS, 402nd FS, 485th FS
P-38 Lightning

84th FIGHTER WING

50th Fighter Group
10th FS, 81st FS, 313th FS
P-47 Thunderbolt

365th Fighter Group
386th FS, 387th FS, 388th FS
P-47 Thunderbolt

404th Fighter Group
506th FS, 507th FS, 508th FS
P-47 Thunderbolt

405th Fighter Group
509th FS, 510th FS, 511th FS
P-47 Thunderbolt

XIX TACTICAL AIR COMMAND

10th Photo Reconnaissance Group
30th PRS, 31st PRS, 33rd PRS, 34th PRS, 155th NPS, 12th TRS, 15th TRS
F-5 Lightning, F-6 Mustang, A-20 Havoc

100th FIGHTER WING

354th Fighter Group
353rd FS, 355th FS, 356th FS
P-51 Mustang

358th Fighter Group
365th FS, 366th FS, 367th FS
P-47 Thunderbolt

362nd Fighter Group
377th FS, 378th FS, 379th FS
P-47 Thunderbolt

363rd Fighter Group
380th FS, 381st FS, 382nd FS
P-51 Mustang

303rd FIGHTER WING

36th Fighter Group
22nd FS, 23rd FS, 53rd FS
P-47 Thunderbolt

373rd Fighter Group
410th FS, 411th FS, 412th FS
P-47 Thunderbolt

406th Fighter Group
512th FS, 513th FS, 514th FS
P-47 Thunderbolt

IX BOMBER COMMAND

97th COMBAT BOMB WING

409th Bomb Group
640th BS, 641st BS, 642nd BS, 643rd BS
A-20 Havoc

410th Bomb Group
644th BS, 645th BS, 646th BS, 647th BS
A-20 Havoc

416th Bomb Group
668th BS, 669th BS, 670th BS, 671st BS
A-20 Havoc

98th COMBAT BOMB WING

323rd Bomb Group
453rd BS, 454th BS, 455th BS, 456th BS
B-26 Marauder

387th Bomb Group
556th BS, 557th BS, 558th BS, 559th BS
B-26 Marauder

394th Bomb Group
584th BS, 585th BS, 586th BS, 587th BS
B-26 Marauder

397th Bomb Group
596th BS, 597th BS, 598th BS, 599th BS
B-26 Marauder

99th COMBAT BOMB WING

1st Pathfinder Squadron (P)
B-26 Marauder

322nd Bomb Group
449th BS, 450th BS, 451st BS, 452nd BS
B-26 Marauder

344th Bomb Group
494th BS, 495th BS, 496th BS, 497th BS
B-26 Marauder

386th Bomb Group
552nd BS, 553rd BS, 554th BS, 555th BS
B-26 Marauder, A-26 Invader

391st Bomb Group
572nd BS, 573rd BS, 574th BS, 575th BS
B-26 Marauder

IX TROOP CARRIER COMMAND

IX TCC Pathfinder Group (P)
1st PFS(P), 2nd PFS(P), 3rd PFS(P), 4th PFS(P)
C-47 Skytrain

50th TROOP CARRIER WING

439th Troop Carrier Group
91st TCS, 92nd TCS, 93rd TCS, 94th TCS
C-47 Skytrain

440th Troop Carrier Group
95th TCS, 96th TCS, 97th TCS, 98th TCS
C-47 Skytrain

441st Troop Carrier Group
99th TCS, 100th TCS, 301st TCS, 302nd TCS
C-47 Skytrain

442nd Troop Carrier Group
303rd TCS, 304th TCS, 305th TCS, 306th TCS
C-47 Skytrain

52nd TROOP CARRIER WING

61st Troop Carrier Group
14th TCS, 15th TCS, 53rd TCS, 59th TCS
C-47 Skytrain

313th Troop Carrier Group
29th TCS, 47th TCS, 48th TCS, 49th TCS
C-46 Commando, C-47 Skytrain

314th Troop Carrier Group
32nd TCS, 50th TCS, 61st TCS, 62nd TCS
C-47 Skytrain

315th Troop Carrier Group
34th TCS, 43rd TCS, 309th TCS, 310th TCS
C-47 Skytrain

316th Troop Carrier Group
36th TCS, 37th TCS, 44th TCS, 45th TCS
C-47 Skytrain

349th Troop Carrier Group
23rd TCS, 312th TCS, 313th TCS, 314th TCS
C-46 Commando

53rd TROOP CARRIER WING

434th Troop Carrier Group
71st TCS, 72nd TCS, 73rd TCS, 74th TCS
C-47 Skytrain

435th Troop Carrier Group
75th TCS, 76th TCS, 77th TCS, 78th TCS
C-47 Skytrain

436th Troop Carrier Group
79th TCS, 80th TCS, 81st TCS, 82nd TCS
C-47 Skytrain

437th Troop Carrier Group
83rd TCS, 84th TCS, 85th TCS, 86th TCS
C-47 Skytrain

438th Troop Carrier Group
87th TCS, 88th TCS, 89th TCS, 90th TCS
C-47 Skytrain

RAF SECOND TACTICAL AIR FORCE

HEADQUARTERS

No. 34(PR) Wing
No. 16 Squadron — Spitfire XI
No. 140 Squadron — Mosquito XVI
No. 69 Squadron — Wellington XIII
No. 1401 (Met) Flight — Spitfire IX

No. 2 GROUP

No. 137 Wing
Nos. 88, 342 (French) Squadrons — Boston IIIA
No. 226 Squadron — Mitchell II

No. 138 Wing
Nos. 107, 305 (Polish), 613 Squadrons — Mosquito VI

No. 139 Wing
Nos. 98, 180, 320 (Dutch) Squadrons — Mitchell II

No. 140 Wing
Nos. 21, 464 (RAAF), 487 (RNZAF) Squadrons — Mosquito VI

No. 83 GROUP

No. 39 (Recce) Wing
Nos. 168, 430 (RCAF) Squadrons — Mustang I
No. 400 (RCAF) 414 (RCAF), Squadron — Spitfire XI

No. 121 Wing
Nos. 174, 175, 245 Squadrons — Typhoon 1B

No. 122 Wing
Nos. 19, 65, 122 Squadrons — Mustang III

No. 124 Wing
Nos. 181, 182, 247 Squadrons — Typhoon 1B

No. 125 Wing
Nos. 132, 453 (RAAF), 602 Squadrons — Spitfire IX

No. 126 Wing
Nos. 401 (RCAF), 411 (RCAF), 412 (RCAF) Squadrons — Spitfire IX

No. 127 Wing
Nos. 403 (RCAF), 416 (RCAF), 421 (RCAF) Squadrons — Spitfire IX

No. 129 Wing
No. 184 Squadron — Typhoon 1B

No. 143 Wing
Nos. 438 (RCAF), 439 (RCAF), 440 (RCAF) Squadrons — Typhoon 1B

No. 144 Wing
Nos. 441 (RCAF), 442 (RCAF), 443 (RCAF) Squadrons — Spitfire IX

AOP Units
Nos. 653, 658, 659, 662 Squadrons — Auster IV

No. 84 GROUP

No. 35 (Recce) Wing
Nos. 2, 268 Squadrons — Mustang 1A
No. 4 Squadron — Spitfire XI

No. 123 Wing
Nos. 198, 609 Squadrons — Typhoon 1B

No. 131 Wing
Nos. 302 (Polish), 308 (Polish), 317 (Polish) Squadrons — Spitfire IX

No. 132 Wing
Nos. 66, 331 (Norwegian), 332 (Norwegian) Squadrons — Spitfire IX

No. 133 Wing
Nos. 129, 306 (Polish), 315 (Polish) Squadrons — Mustang III

No. 134 Wing
Nos. 310 (Czech), 312 (Czech), 313 (Czech) Squadrons — Spitfire IX

No. 135 Wing
Nos. 222, 349 (Belgian), 485 (RNZAF) Squadrons — Spitfire IX

No. 136 Wing
Nos. 164, 183 Squadrons — Typhoon 1B

No. 145 Wing
Nos. 329 (French), 340 (French), 341 (French) Squadrons — Spitfire IX

No. 146 Wing
Nos. 193, 197, 257, 266 Squadrons — Typhoon 1B

AOP Units
Nos. 652, 660, 661 Squadrons — Auster IV

No. 85 GROUP

No. 141 Wing
Nos. 264, 410 (RCAF) Squadrons — Mosquito XIII
No. 322 (Dutch) Squadron — Spitfire XIV

No. 142 Wing
No. 124 Squadron — Spitfire VII

No. 147 Wing
Nos. 488 (RNZAF), 604 Squadrons — Mosquito XIII

No. 148 Wing
Nos. 29, 409 (RCAF) Squadrons — Mosquito XIII
No. 91 Squadron — Spitfire XIV

No. 150 Wing
Nos. 3, 486 (RNZAF) Squadrons — Tempest V
No. 56 Squadron — Spitfire IX

Air Spotting Pool
Nos. 26, 63 Squadrons — Spitfire V
No. 1320 Flight — Typhoon 1B
Nos. 808 (FAA), 885 (FAA), 886 (FAA), 897 (FAA) Squadrons — Seafire/Spitfire V
VCS-7 (US Navy) — Spitfire V

On July 23, Winston Churchill made a tour of RAF airstrips in a captured German aircraft piloted by Air Vice-Marshal Harry Broadhurst.

THE INVASION AIRFIELDS

Although uncaptioned, this photograph shows him addressing Canadian aircrews at either B-2 at Bazenville or B-4 at Bény-sur-Mer.

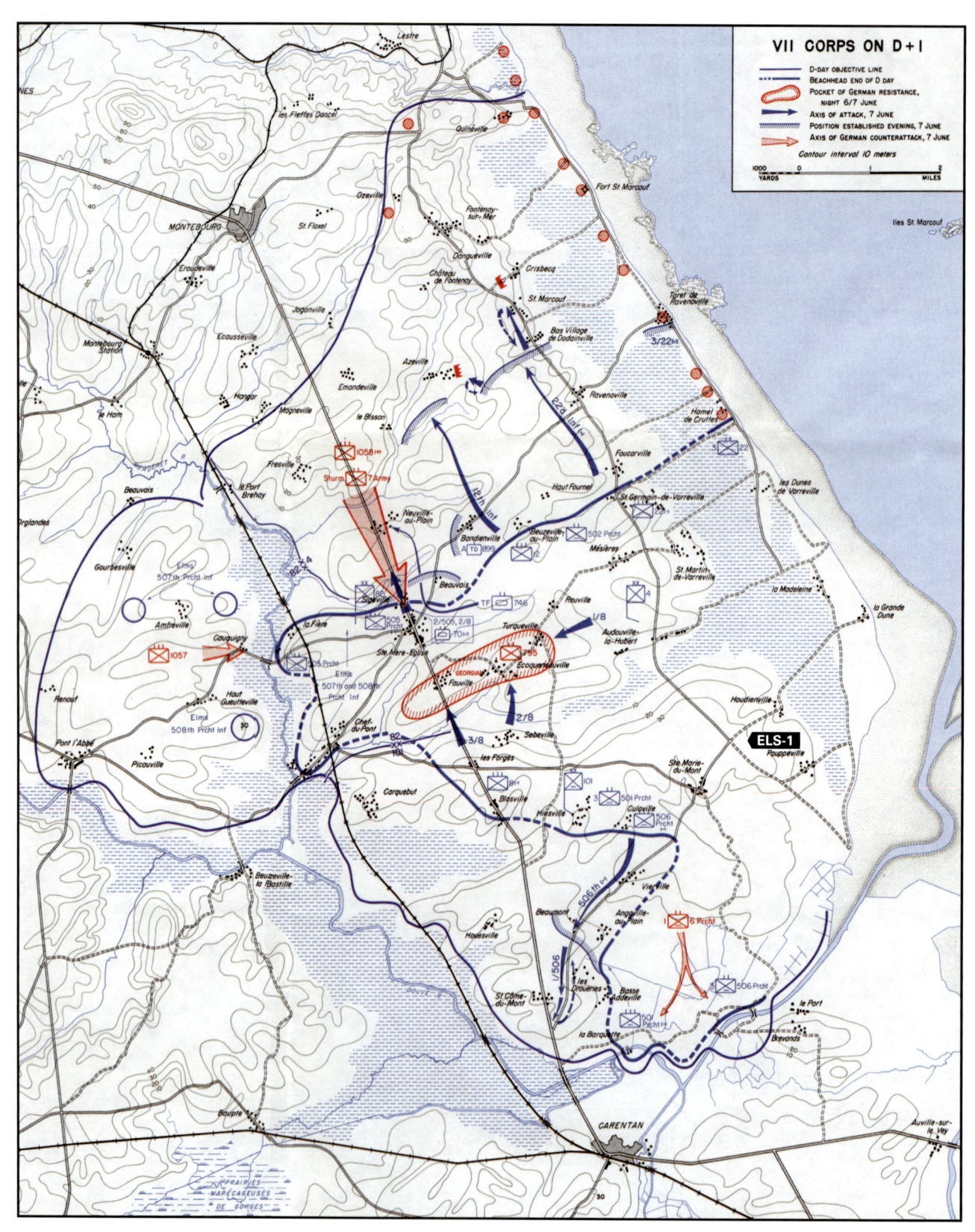

By the evening of D-Day it had been planned to have two Emergency Landing Strips (ELS) operational in the US area and one in the British sector. The operation to secure the Cotentin peninsula was a vital part of the 'Overlord' planning as the early capture of the port of Cherbourg was required to bring in supplies. Utah Beach was to be assaulted both from the sea by the 4th Infantry Division and from the air by two airborne divisions, the 82nd and 101st. However, the drops of the latter were widely scattered and through a series of mishaps by the beach control vessels, part of the seaborne forces came ashore a mile to the south of its designated beach, but, in the event, it proved to be a blessing in disguise as it brought the troops ashore further from the German coastal batteries at St Marcouf and Azeville. Apart from sporadic shelling, the 1,200 men of the 1st and 2nd Battalions of the 8th Infantry came ashore unopposed. The airborne plan was for the 502nd Parachute Infantry of the 101st to destroy the coastal battery at St Martin-de-Varreville and then join up with the 82nd Airborne landing further to the west. A small force of some 40 men from another regiment, the 501st, had already assembled to try to clear Pouppeville at the inland end of Exit 1. They were held up all morning by resistance in the village, but troops of the 2nd Battalion of the 8th Infantry (Lieutenant Colonel Carlton O. MacNeely) advancing from Utah made contact with the airborne force about noon.

ELS-1 POUPPEVILLE

On the evening of D-Day, Captain Lawrence McBee of the 27th Photo Recon Squadron (7th Photo Group) took a strip of photos along the invasion beaches. This print shows the location of the Emergency Landing Strip although no activity can be seen.

OPERATIONAL JUNE 7

Latitude: 49°23'N
Longitude: 01°12'W
Grid reference: T-433933
Altitude: 45ft

It was the task of the 101st Airborne Division to seize the western edge of the inundated Utah Area between St Martin-de-Varreville and Pouppeville. Although the drop did not go to plan, nevertheless the 3rd Battalion of the 501st Parachute Infantry Regiment secured Pouppeville within a few hours of landing, meeting up there with the 2nd Battalion, 8th Infantry of the 4th Division — the first contact between seaborne and airborne forces.

A 2,000ft earth strip on a rough NE-SW alignment was marked out under fire by the 819th Engineer Aviation Battalion of IX Engineer Command to serve for emergency crash-landings although there is no record of it being used.

Seventy years later, the strip is again under the camera lens.

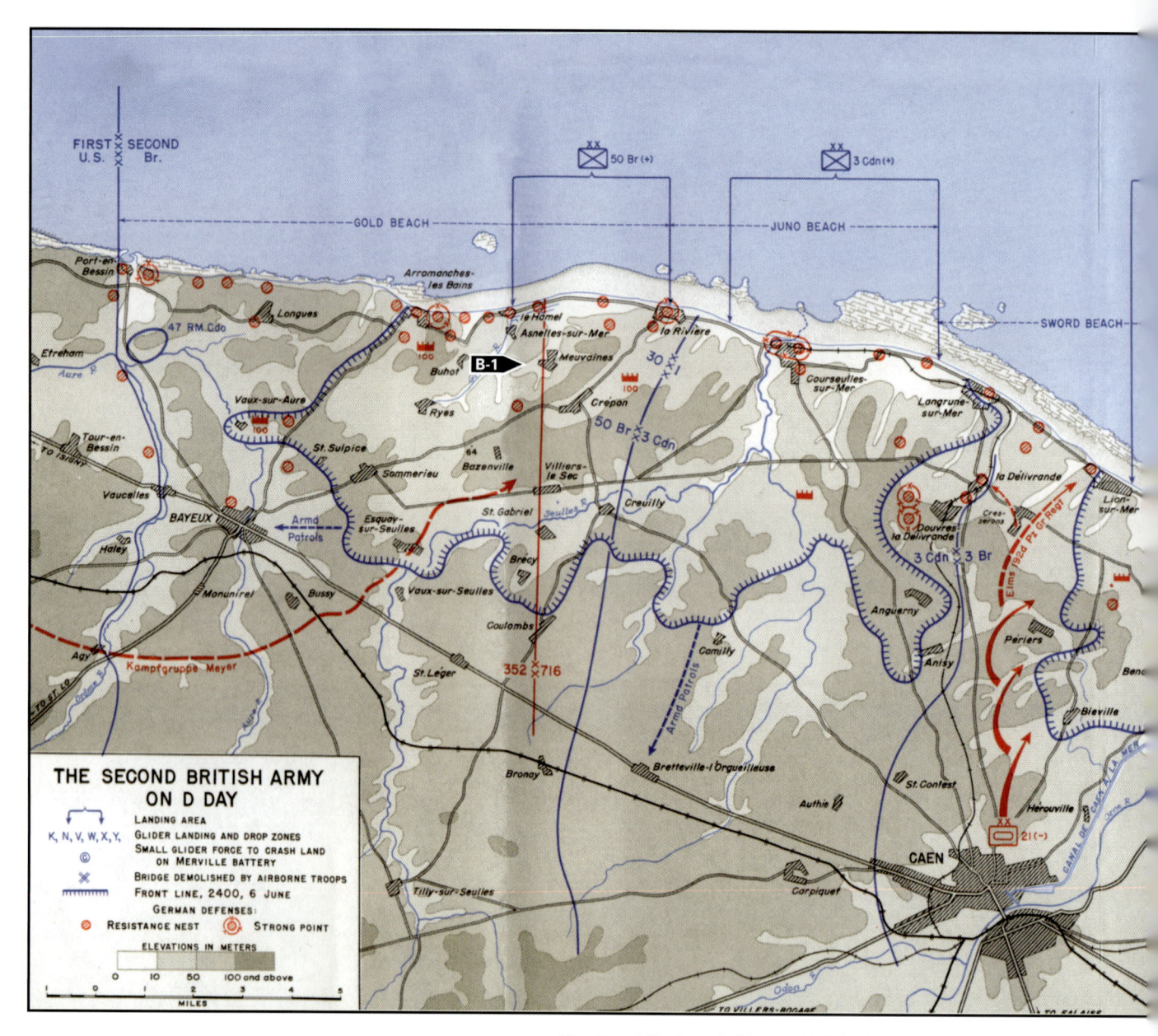

B-1 ASNELLES-SUR-MER

The Royal Engineer's No. 16 Airfield Construction Group were detailed to lay down the Emergency Landing Strip B-1 just inland from Asnelles-sur-Mer on Gold Beach.

OPERATIONAL JUNE 7

Latitude: 49°20'N
Longitude: 00°34'W
Grid reference: T-885853
Altitude: 60ft

This location had been planned for an Emergency Landing Strip (ELS) to be in place on D-Day to be used solely by aircraft in distress. It lay within Gold Area, half a mile inland from Jig Beach. Of the five airfield construction groups of the Corps of Royal Engineers phased into Normandy between D-Day and D+3, responsibility for this particular ELS was that of 'A' Detachment of No. 16 Airfield Construction Group. They prepared a strip 1,800ft long of roughly graded earth, 120ft wide, which was only suitable for crash landings. It was in operation on D+1 but its use as an ELS was discontinued on July 10 and it was used thereafter only as a site for parking crashed aircraft.

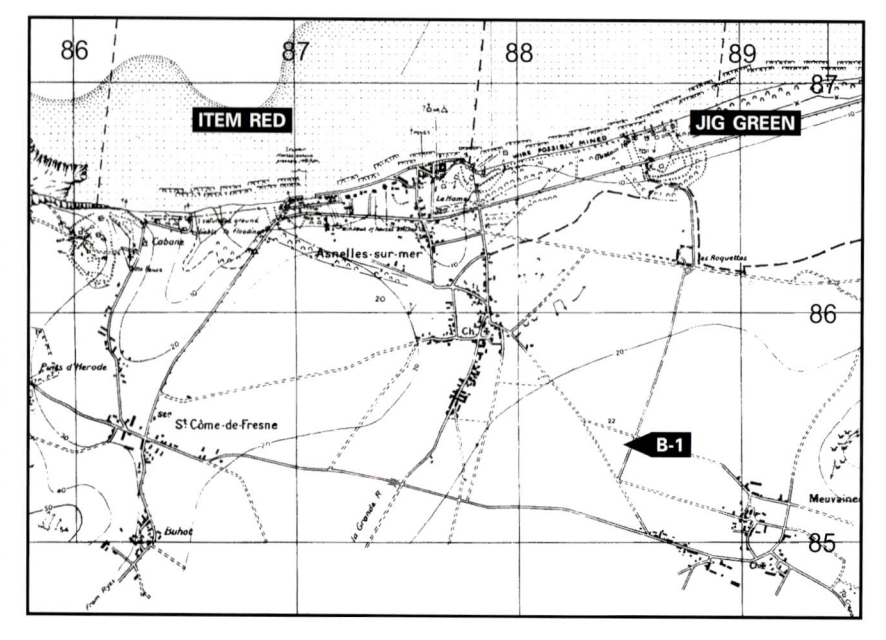

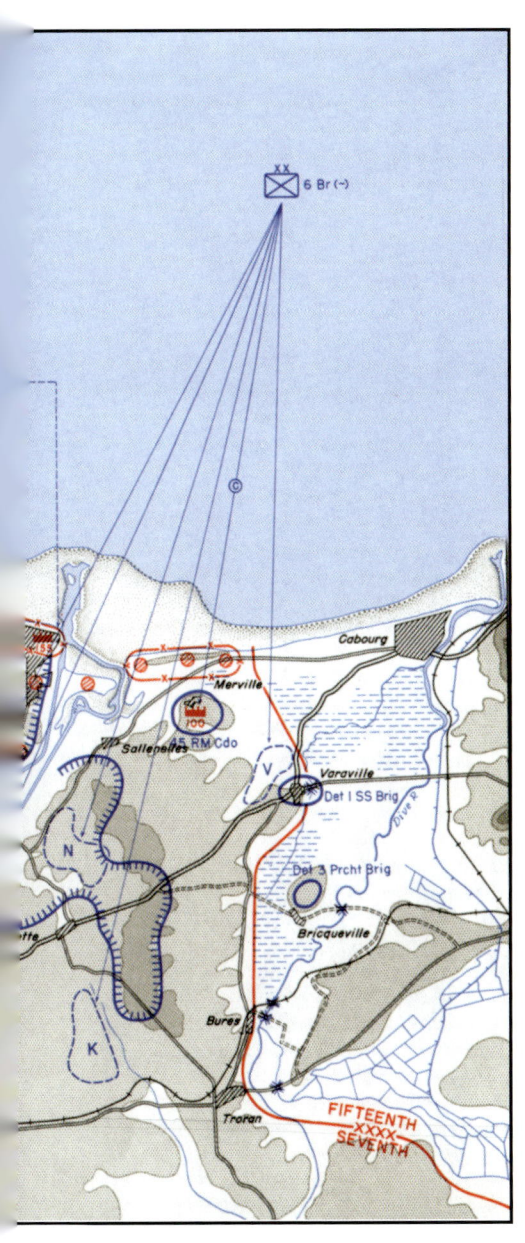

The landing got off to a bad start as the sea was too rough to launch the duplex-drive 'swimming' tanks (DDs) of the Nottinghamshire Yeomanry and they were landed instead directly onto the beach after the armoured fighting vehicles (AVREs) of the Royal Engineers had come ashore from the tank landing craft (LCTs). However, the LCTs beached some 400 yards further to the east than intended. Major Harold Elphinstone, commanding the 82nd Assault Squadron, was killed in the turret of his AVRE and within minutes of the arrival of the 1st Hampshires (3rd Division), their CO, Lieutenant-Colonel David Nelson-Smith, had also become a casualty, together with the forward observation officer and the battery commander from the field artillery. The casemate which accounted for the destruction of at least six tanks was finally put out of action by firing an explosive Petard round through the rear entrance. The position was only finally cleared at 1530 permitting the advance inland. No. 689 Road Construction Company and No. 231 Company of the Pioneer Corps which were to construct the airstrip got ashore at 1800 hours.

29

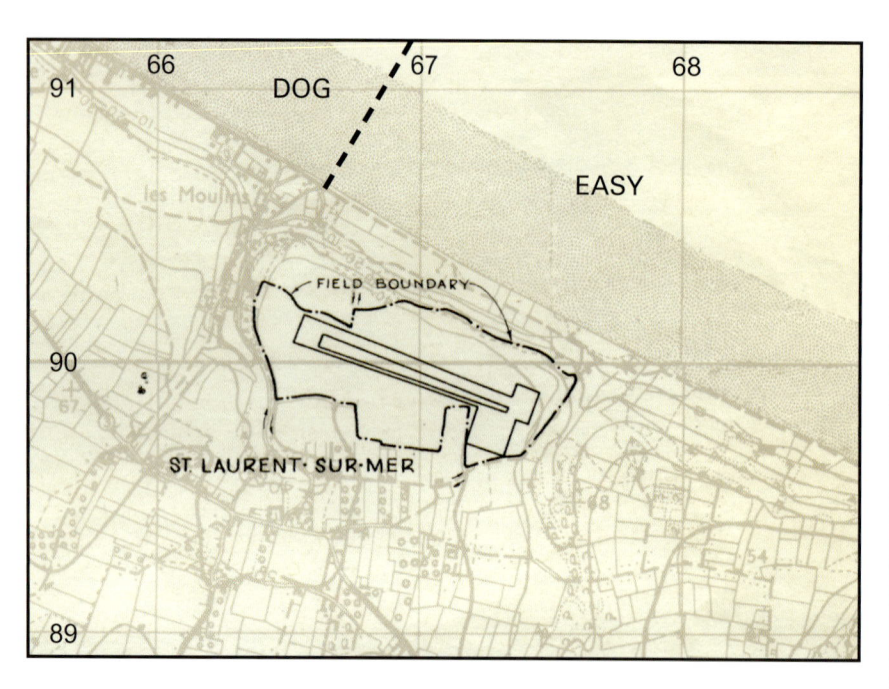

A-21C ST LAURENT-SUR-MER

OPERATIONAL JUNE 7

Latitude: 49°21'N
Longitude: 00°52'W
Grid reference: T-670900
Altitude: 142ft

At Omaha, the 116th Infantry Regiment of the 29th Division came ashore on Easy Green and Easy Red Beaches and, together with the 5th Ranger Battalion, attacks were launched on both sides of the D-3 exit at Les Moulins. On the eastern side, the 3rd Battalion mounted a series of simultaneous independent advances up the bluffs, successfully gaining the top. Encountering no resistance on the crest, they moved off towards St Laurent leaving the way clear for the engineers to step in.

When the 834th Engineer Aviation Battalion was prevented from working

The third ELS was to be located in the American sector at St Pierre-du-Mont but due to the difficulty experienced with the landing at Omaha, the site was not captured as quickly as anticipated. The 834th Engineers were therefore diverted to work on an earth strip on the bluffs at St Laurent-sur-Mer. A report by the IX Engineer Command to 21st Army Group dated June 14, refers to the St Laurent strip as A-1 but as that code had already been allocated to the airstrip at St Pierre, at some later stage St Laurent was renumbered A-21C. ('A' of course stood for American, 'B' for British with the suffix 'C' standing for a courier airstrip.)

In post-war years local communities or squadron associations have placed memorials on many of the temporary strips, most of which have been returned to agriculture. The one at A-21C was erected in 1994, dedicated to the 834th 'Air' Engineer Battalion 'in the memory of those who gave their life for Liberty'.

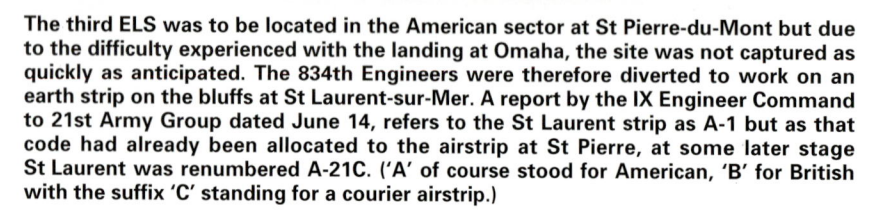

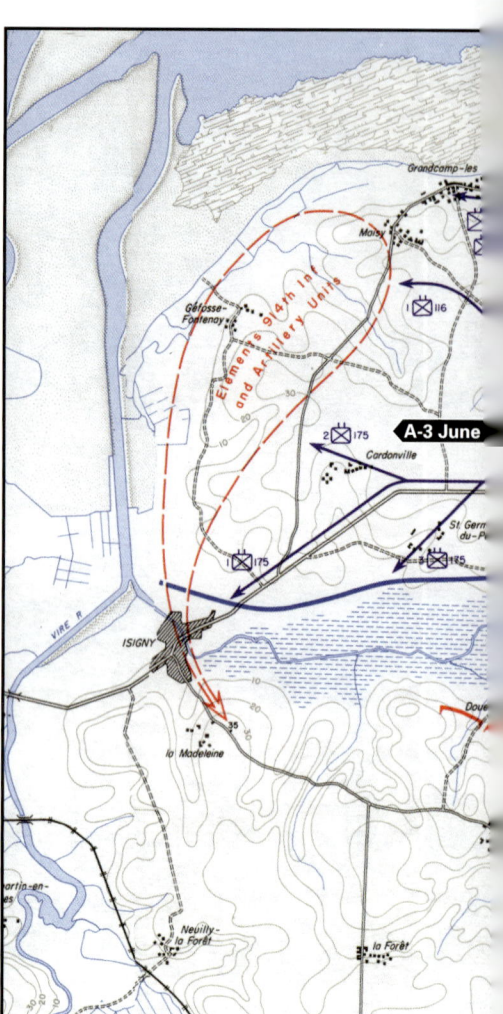

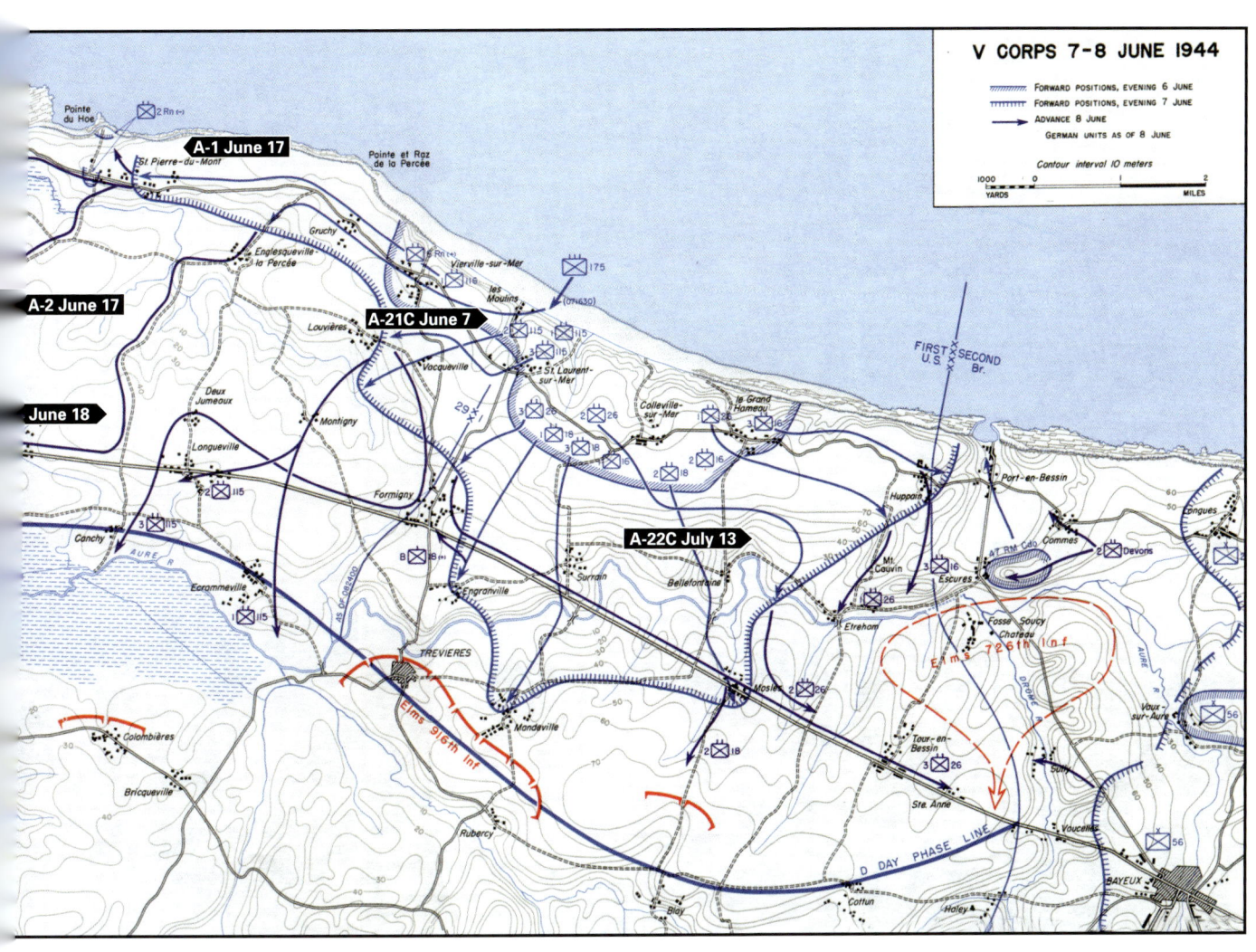

on their designated airfield at St Pierre-du-Mont as the area was still held by German forces, instead the battalion quickly reconnoitred the terrain that had just been cleared on the high ground at Les Moulins. They decided that the fields were suitable and after labouring for 16 hours they had cleared a 3,400ft strip that would be suitable for crash-landings.

In the event, A-21C, although untracked, was used from D+1 for C-47s evacuating wounded. Remaining in use right up to July 16, it handled the major portion of air transport between the Continent and the United Kingdom.

With no number allocated, and St Pierre already designated as A-1, St Laurent became A-21C, the suffix denoting it as a 'courier' airfield.

On the 50th anniversary of D-Day in 1994, a memorial was dedicated at the site of the airfield by the commune of St Laurent-sur-Mer.

Although the data sheet lists A-21C as 'a crash strip only', nevertheless by June 9 it was being used by twin-engined P-38 Lightnings and C-47s flying in from Britain transporting commanders to the battlefield (see also pages 2-3 and 46).

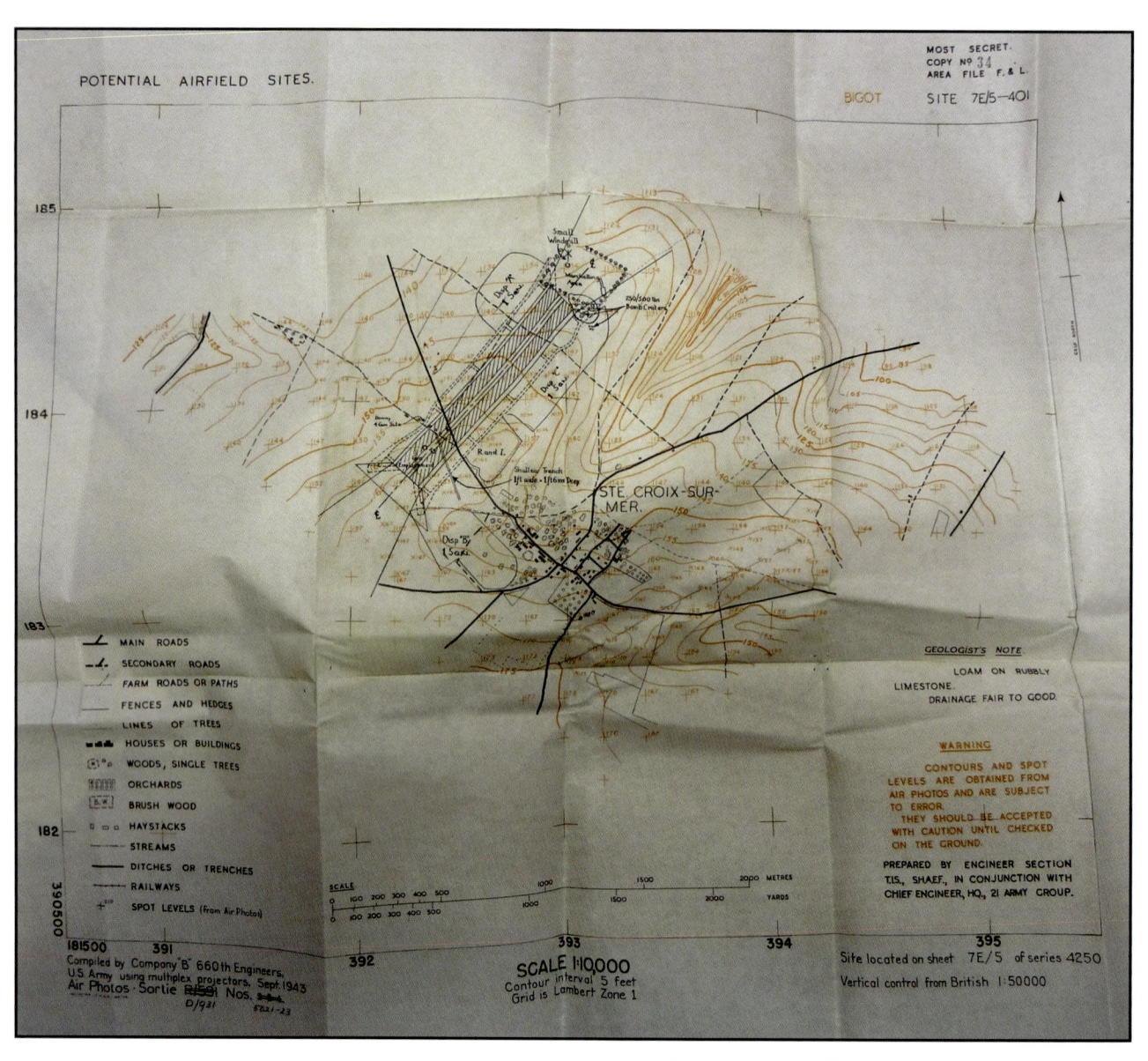

B-3 STE CROIX-SUR-MER

OPERATIONAL JUNE 15

Latitude: 49°19'N
Longitude: 00°31'W
Grid reference: T-928840
Altitude: 161ft

Situated one mile inland from Mike Sector of Juno Area, Sainte Croix was captured on D-Day by 'A' Company of the Royal Winnipeg Rifles, assisted by the 6th Canadian Armoured Regiment. No. 24 Airfield Construction Group were delayed in landing and further held up while enemy defence posts and snipers were cleared from the site.

Work began on D+1 and a 3,600ft by 120ft R&RS was in use by the RAF on D+4. A parallel strip was then started and was completed on D+7 having a runway of graded earth tracked with SMT. Work finally finished on June 15 and when the Spitfires of No. 144 Wing (Nos. 441, 442 and 443 Squadrons) touched down on June 15 they became the first RAF squadrons to operate from French soil since 1940.

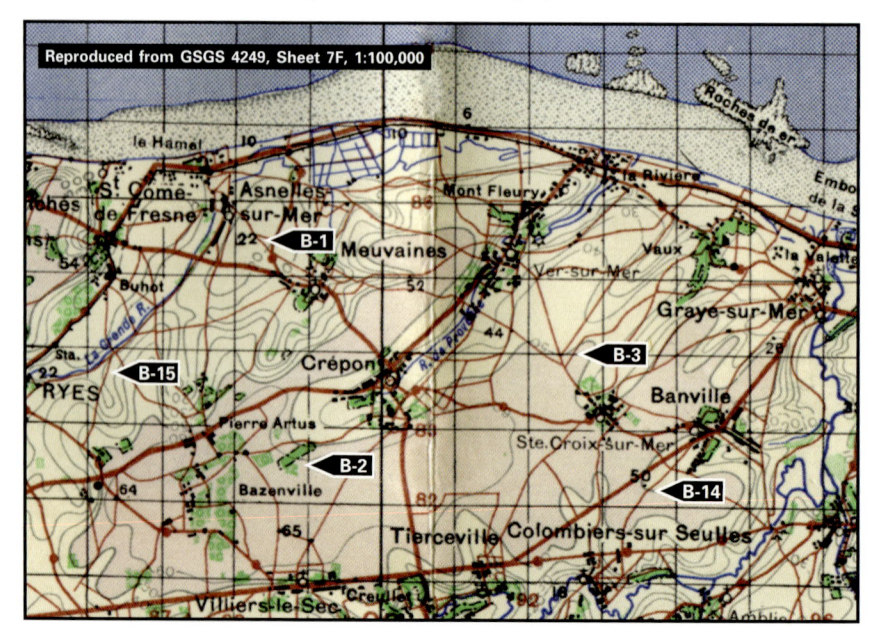

Plans had been prepared by SHAEF engineers for all the invasion airfields, this one by Company B of the US 660th Engineers dating from September 1943 showing a potential site at Ste Croix-sur-Mer.

Apart from Asnelles (B-1), close by were B-2 Bazenville; B-14 at Amblie and B-15 at Ryes.

Whereas the first three airstrips had simple runways of graded earth, a tracked airfield was desperately needed. The Americans were still confined to a restricted area in the west, and the tactical situation in the British sector held up work on B-2 at Bazenville (see page 40) which No. 16 ACG were due to complete as an R&RS by midday on D+4 and as a tracked ALG by last light on D+5. Instead a recce of the site for B-3 at Ste Croix was carried out by No. 24 ACG on the evening of D-Day and two 'dozers had arrived to begin work by 1800 the next day, followed by other plant. Local horse and tractor-drawn cutters were used to harvest the standing crops while two hedges were grubbed out and seven ditches filled in. Once the crops had been cut, lorries, trailers and M-14s were used to roll and compact the 3,600ft R&RS runway that was ready on D+4. Work then started on tracking a parallel strip and this completed Ste Croix as an ALG on D+7. Another tracked ALG (B-5) was scheduled to be completed at Camilly by D+6 but the site was still in enemy hands on D+3. The material did not reach the site until D+9 and the SMT was still being laid on June 15 so Camilly did not become operational until the 24th (see page 70). The proposed site for B-16 at Villons-les-Buissons was also still in enemy hands and the RAF could not begin using it until August 20 (see page 168).

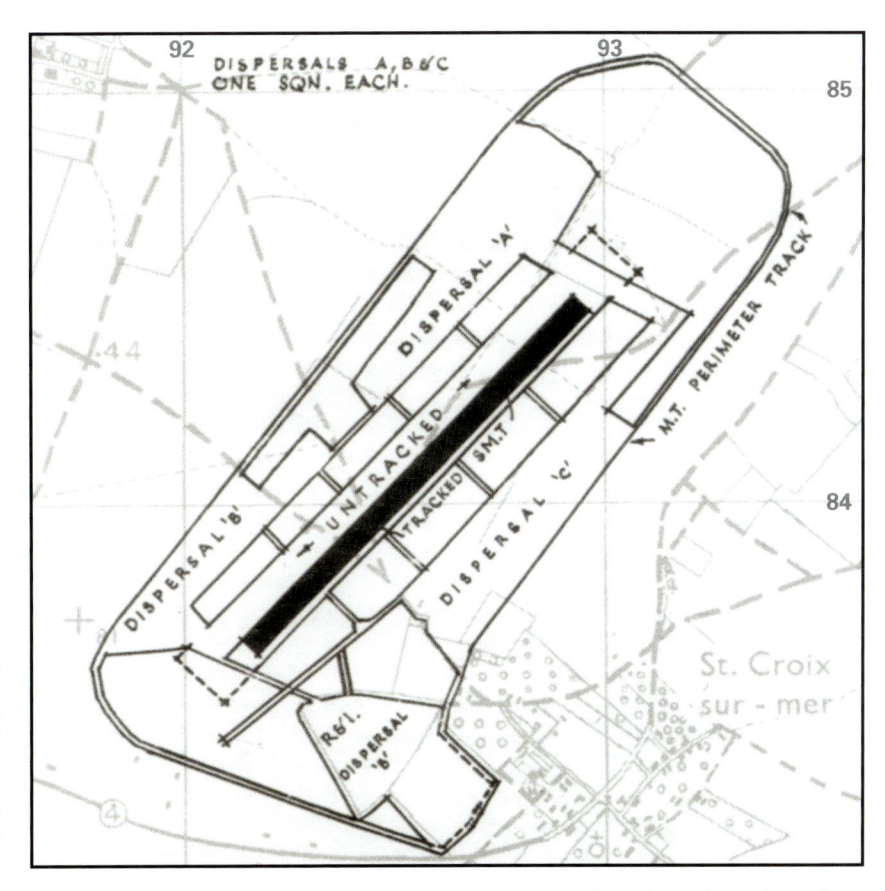

Each departed on July 15: No. 441 to B-11, No. 442 to B-4 and No. 443 to B-2. Then, from June 20-24, Ste Croix briefly hosted the Typhoons of No. 175, but it was not until July 15-20 when No. 146 Wing arrived with its four squadrons (Nos. 193, 197, 257 and 266) that B-3 really became a Typhoon base. No. 266 stayed for five days, but the others remained into August and September. Also No. 263 spent a month there with Typhoons from August 6 to September 6.

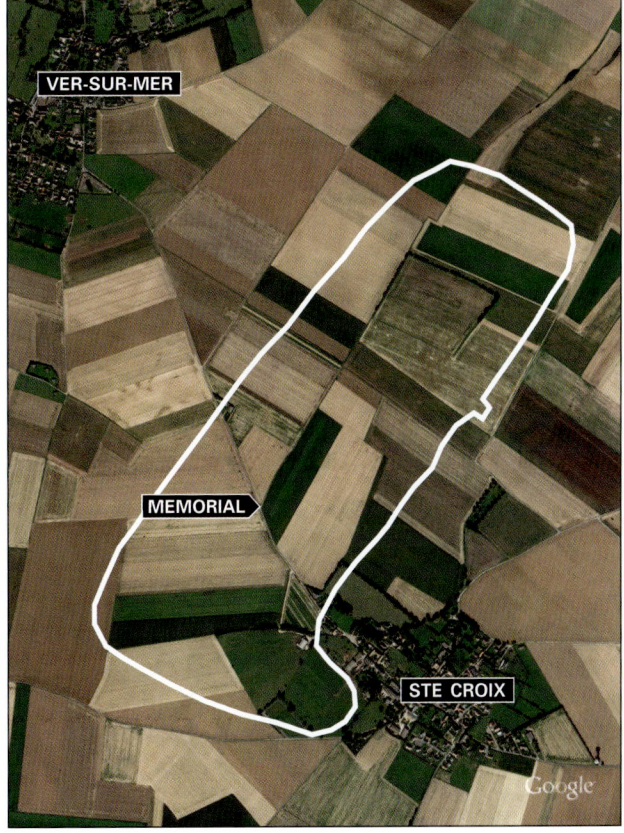

Left: **At the same time, work was proceeding laying down the SMT on the second runway as the layout had been designed to accommodate two parallel strips. In all, it took 4,000 man hours and 200 machine hours to complete.** *Right:* **Little to show today of the first tracked airstrip constructed in Normandy.**

The Royal Engineer recce party, which had been phased to arrive on D+2, was late sailing from the UK so it did not disembark until 1800 hours on D+4, 60 hours late. Also it had been planned to off-load 700 tons of Square Mesh Tracking by D+5 but, due to adverse weather which greatly delayed the transfer of stores from ship to shore, there was a bottleneck in obtaining suitable craft to trans-ship the bulky airfield stores to the beach.

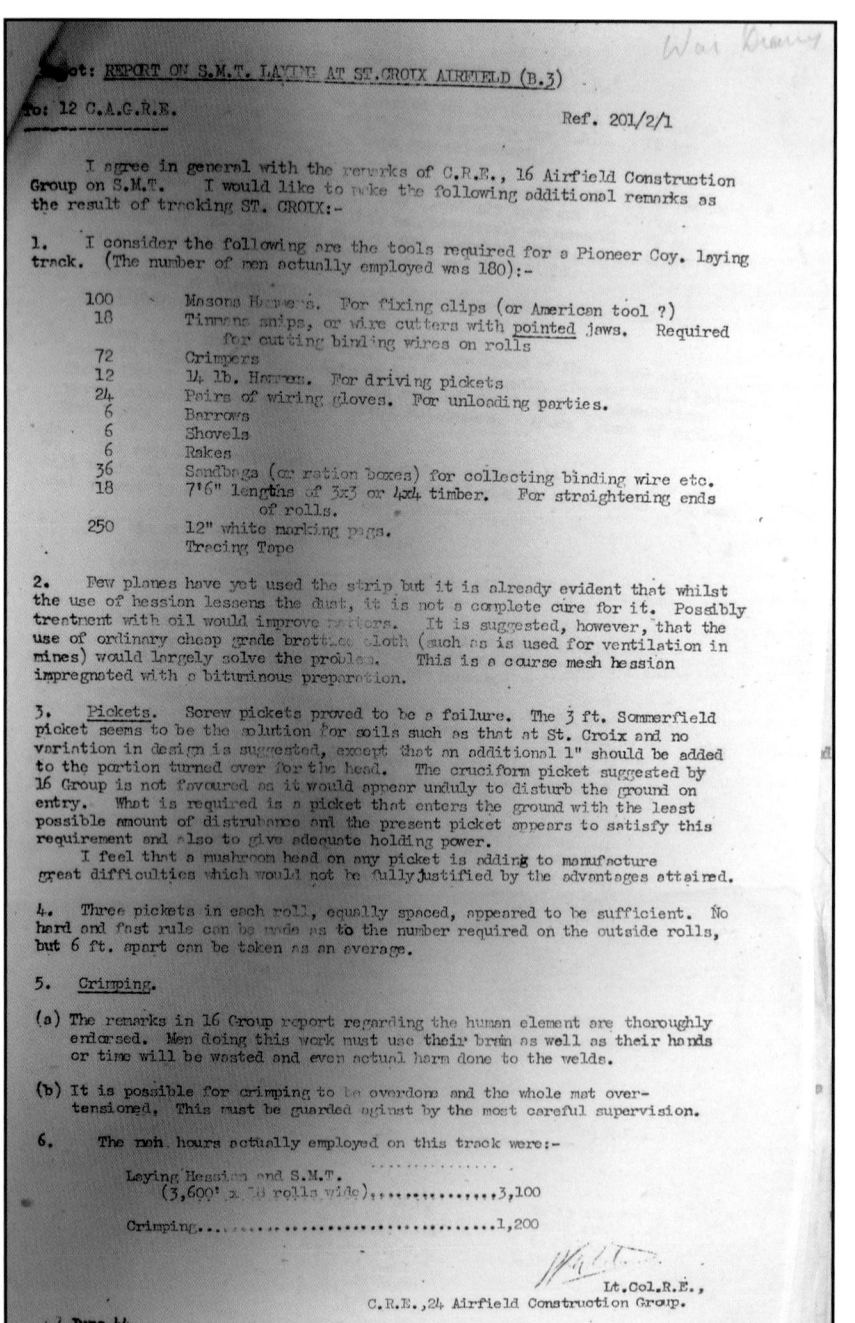

This report covered lessons learned during the construction of the airstrip at Ste Croix.

Another major problem discovered when operating in dry conditions in Normandy was caused by the clouds of dust which were raised by aircraft taking off, and No. 13 Airfield Construction Group produced a detailed analysis of how best to resolve the issue. Their report read as follows: 'The method of oil treatment which has given the best results on the type of ground conditions found in Normandy depends on the soil being consolidated as much as possible. Surface dust and loose material must be brushed off. Naval fuel oil is sprayed at the rate of ¼ gallon per square yard. When this has soaked in (a matter of about two hours) another application of ¼ gallon per square yard is made. No further rolling is done as this makes the surface flaky. The consolidation was to the degree normally given to graded surfaces or airfields. Brushing was done by brooms. This can be done by road sweepers on large-scale work. The above treatment has been given to bare ground and also ground already covered by SMT. It was impossible to brush away loose material from ground covered by SMT. The surface of the ground so treated was hard and the oil had penetrated from three-eighths to half inch. Another application of ¼ gallon per square yard can be made some time after the ½ gallon per square yard is made. This can be done when the surface shows signs of wear. Tests were made on treated ground as follows: (a) on bare ground treated as above and dry; (b) on ground covered with SMT treated and dry; (c) on SMT-covered ground treated and wetted with water. In each test the aircraft used was a Typhoon fighter-bomber. In (a), the aircraft carried no bombs: in (b) and (c) it carried two 1,000lb bombs. The aircraft in each test taxied on the strip, stopped, the engine was revved up with the brakes on and the flaps were raised and lowered alternately. Care must be taken as the propellor on a Typhoon has only about nine inches clearance. The maximum speed obtained from the engine was that at which the aircraft would normally be travelling, at about 50 mph and the aircraft was gradually creeping forward against the brakes. After about ten minutes hard revving with the flaps down, a few flakes of treated soil came away from under the flaps.'

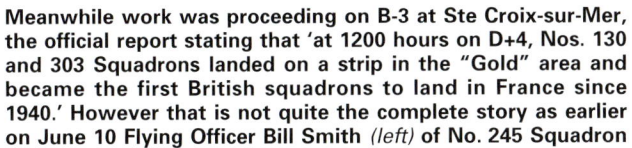

Meanwhile work was proceeding on B-3 at Ste Croix-sur-Mer, the official report stating that 'at 1200 hours on D+4, Nos. 130 and 303 Squadrons landed on a strip in the "Gold" area and became the first British squadrons to land in France since 1940.' However that is not quite the complete story as earlier on June 10 Flying Officer Bill Smith *(left)* of No. 245 Squadron made a precautionary landing in his Typhoon with a badly-vibrating engine. He was surprised to find members of the Press on hand but the welcome was not for him as he had stolen the thunder from Air Vice-Marshal Harry Broadhurst *(above)*, the commander of No. 83 Group, who was about to arrive in his Spitfire to mark the first landing in Normandy!

Above: **The mobile flying control at Ste Croix — the corner of the airfield identification marker 'B3' can just be seen lower right. On June 15, three Canadian squadrons of Spitfires, Nos. 441, 442 and 443 belonging to No. 144 Wing flew in, the first to operate from French soil since Dunkirk. Five days later they were joined by No. 175 Squadron with Typhoons before it moved on to B-5 at Camilly. When the Canadians moved out on July 15 (No. 441 being relocated to B-11 at Longues-sur-Mer, No. 442 to B-4 at Bény-sur-Mer and No. 443 to B-2 at Bazenville), No. 146 Wing arrived, its four squadrons, Nos. 193, 197, 257 and 266, being equipped with Typhoons. No. 263 joined them on August 6. However, by September the usefulness of Ste Croix had passed as the battlefront moved too far away; consequently it was abandoned.**
Right: **This memorial has now been built on the edge of the strip (see page 33) and it would be nice to think that the SMT was a piece rescued from this particular airfield.**

A-3 CARDONVILLE

OPERATIONAL JUNE 16

Latitude: 49°21'N
Longitude: 01°03'W
Grid reference: T-539890
Altitude: 110ft

This airfield was located half a mile north of the main Isigny—Bayeux road, the Route Nationale 13. The task of capturing Isigny was given to the 175th Infantry of the 29th Division, backed up by the armour of the 747th Tank Battalion. They set out on the night of June 7 along the RN13, encountering scattered enemy resistance in villages on either side of the road including Cardonville, losing seven tanks along the way. However they found no organised defence in Isigny itself which was secured on the night of June 8/9.

A-3 at Cardonville was completed as an untracked Emergency Landing Strip by June 14 and upgraded to Advanced Landing Ground status (although still untracked) three days later. As soon as an airfield was usable, units still based in the UK used them for refuelling and this was the case with the 368th Fighter Group based at Chilbolton near Andover in Hampshire. The *Stars and Stripes* newspaper made great play (without identifying either the airfield or unit) that the first American fighter planes to set down in France were from the 397th Squadron at 2015 on June 13. The unnamed staff writer reported that the 'first man down in his P-47 Thunderbolt was Captain Richard E. Leary, of Annapolis, MD, operations officer for the group commanded by Colonel Gilbert Meyers, and as his wheels kicked up the dust of the strip it marked the first planned use of airstrips onto which Allied warplanes have been landing for emergency refueling and re-arming in the last four days. From now on it will be a question of moving fighter units onto newly built strips as fast as the engineers can skin turf and trees from the French fields, level them and put down the long rolls of wire mesh netting.'

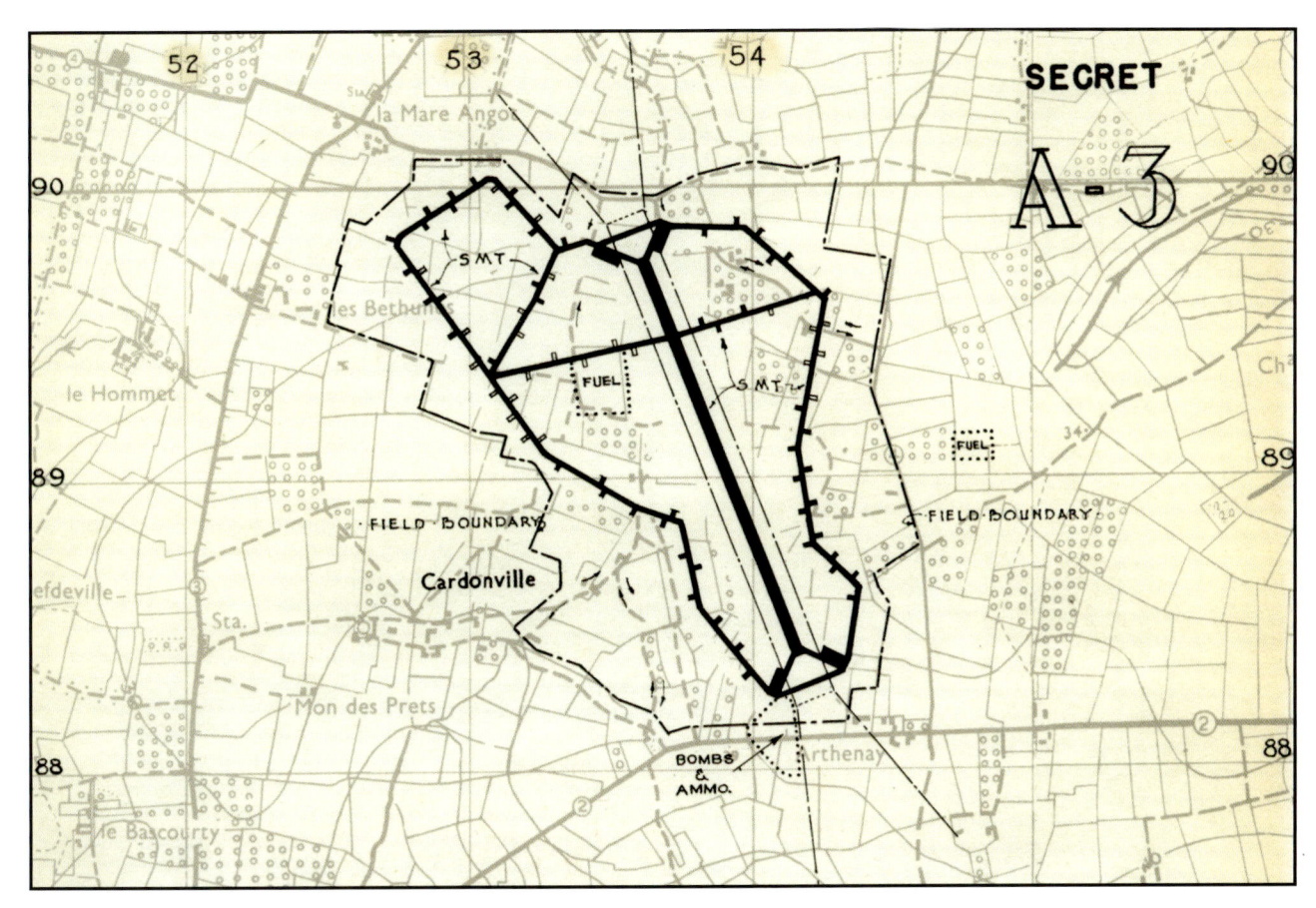

However, our criterion for listing the airfields in operational order is to use the date when the first unit was actually based on the strip which, in the case of Cardonville, was June 16. Even so it was only reported by IX Engineer Command on June 19 that the SMT runway was 80 per cent complete. This is the drawing of A-3 when fully tracked, including the perimeter tracks and dispersals which had been achieved by the 816th Engineers by June 23.

P-47 Thunderbolts of the 368th Fighter Group were based at A-3 from June to late August.

The 816th Engineer Aviation Battalion began work at Cardonville to construct a 5,000ft runway tracked with SMT and provide 75 dispersals, 50 of them being tracked. Facilities included lighting at night and radio homing.

A-3 had been allocated to the P-47-equipped 368th Fighter Group but, before the airfield was finally completed on June 23, the Thunderbolts flew in. First to arrive on June 16 was the 397th, followed four days later by the 395th and 396th.

Then on July 31 the P-38 Lightnings of the 370th Fighter Group (401st, 402nd and 485th Squadrons) joined them for two weeks before moving out to A-19 at La Vieille. Later in August, when Chartres (A-40D) became available, the 368th Fighter Group moved there as it had the benefit of a concrete runway.

Today a memorial at the former airfield remembers the service there by the 368th Fighter Group.

Nice comparison of 'La ferme de la Champagne' bordering the airfield by Stéphane Duchemin.

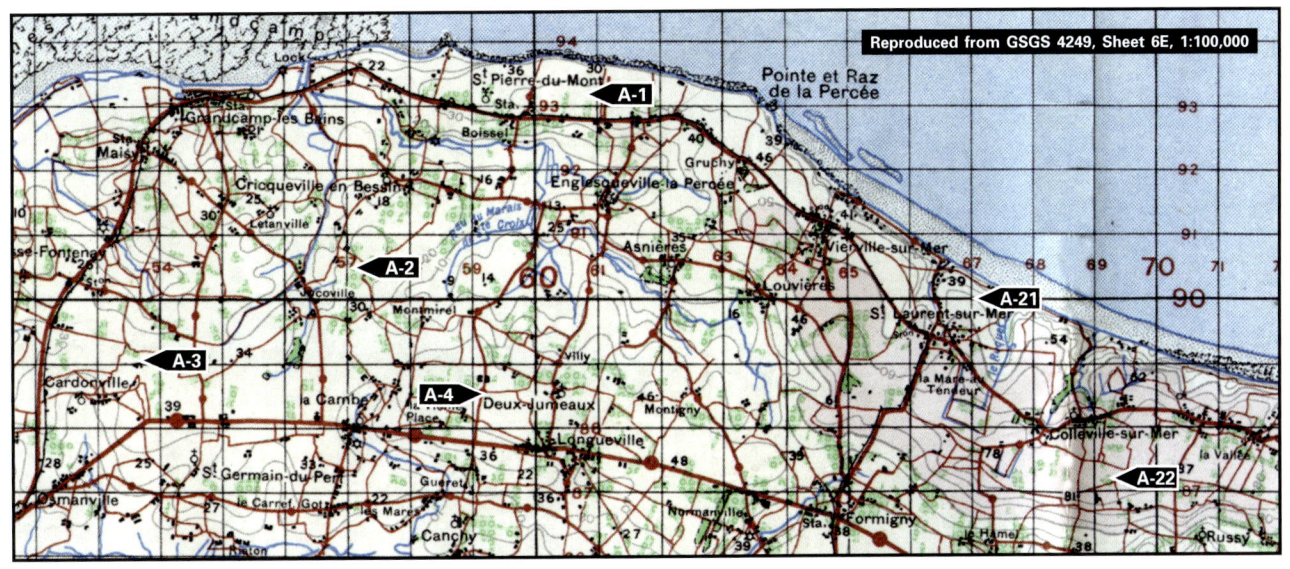

The Ninth Air Force construction programme, worked out by a planning staff under Colonel Herbert W. Ehrgott, called for two emergency landing strips to be prepared on D-Day, one for each of the two landing beaches. By D+3 there were to be two refuelling and re-arming strips on Omaha beach, and by D+8, four advanced landing grounds on Omaha and one on Utah. On D+14 there were to be five advanced landing grounds on Omaha and three on Utah; one runway on each beach was to be 5,000 feet, the others only 3,600 feet because of insufficient shipping for construction materials during the early build-up period. It was estimated that if the planned rate of ground advance was attained, a total of 35 advanced landing grounds would have to be constructed during the first 40 days in order to accommodate all of the Ninth's fighter and reconnaissance groups. Here Stéphane pays his respects at the memorial at Cardonville.

B-2 BAZENVILLE

OPERATIONAL JUNE 16

Latitude: 49°18'N
Longitude: 00°34'W
Grid reference: T-890824
Altitude: 170ft

Situated half a mile south-west of Crépon village, this was designated as a Refuelling and Re-arming Strip and was scheduled to be completed by No. 16 Airfield Construction Group by D+3.

Work began on the arrival of the mechanical equipment but on D+1 pockets of enemy resistance delayed the start. An untracked strip to R&RS standard was planned but as Bazenville was not occupied immediately by the RAF, it was decided to extend it to 5,000ft, 120ft wide, and surface it with SMT. This was completed to Advanced Landing Ground standard by June 13. The taxi-track was 30ft wide of graded earth and marshalling areas for 22 aircraft were also left untracked.

It was not until June 16 that the three Canadian squadrons of No. 127 Wing — Nos. 403, 416 and 421 — flew in with Spitfire IXs. They moved on to B-26 Illiers-l'Évêque in late in August. A Typhoon squadron, No. 174, was also briefly based at B-2 from June 19-24, and No. 443 Squadron with Spitfires from July 15 to August 28.

Pilot Officer Sid Bregman of Toronto, Ontario, a member of No. 403 Squadron (part of No. 127 Wing), pictured on August 2 at Bazenville. Amazingly, this very Spitfire, Mk IX, MJ627, lives on at Biggin Hill today having been converted into a two-seater.

Flying Officer Ross Clarke of Montreal, Quebec, watches an armourer of No. 403 Squadron fits rockets on his Typhoon. The RAF used either a 25lb armour-piercing round or a 60lb high-explosive shell. The rockets were mounted on rails in groups of four and were electrically fired, either in four pairs or in a salvo of eight. A later modification allowed eight rockets to be carried under each wing. However, targeting this firepower was difficult as the weapons were unguided and there was considerable trajectory drop at longer ranges.

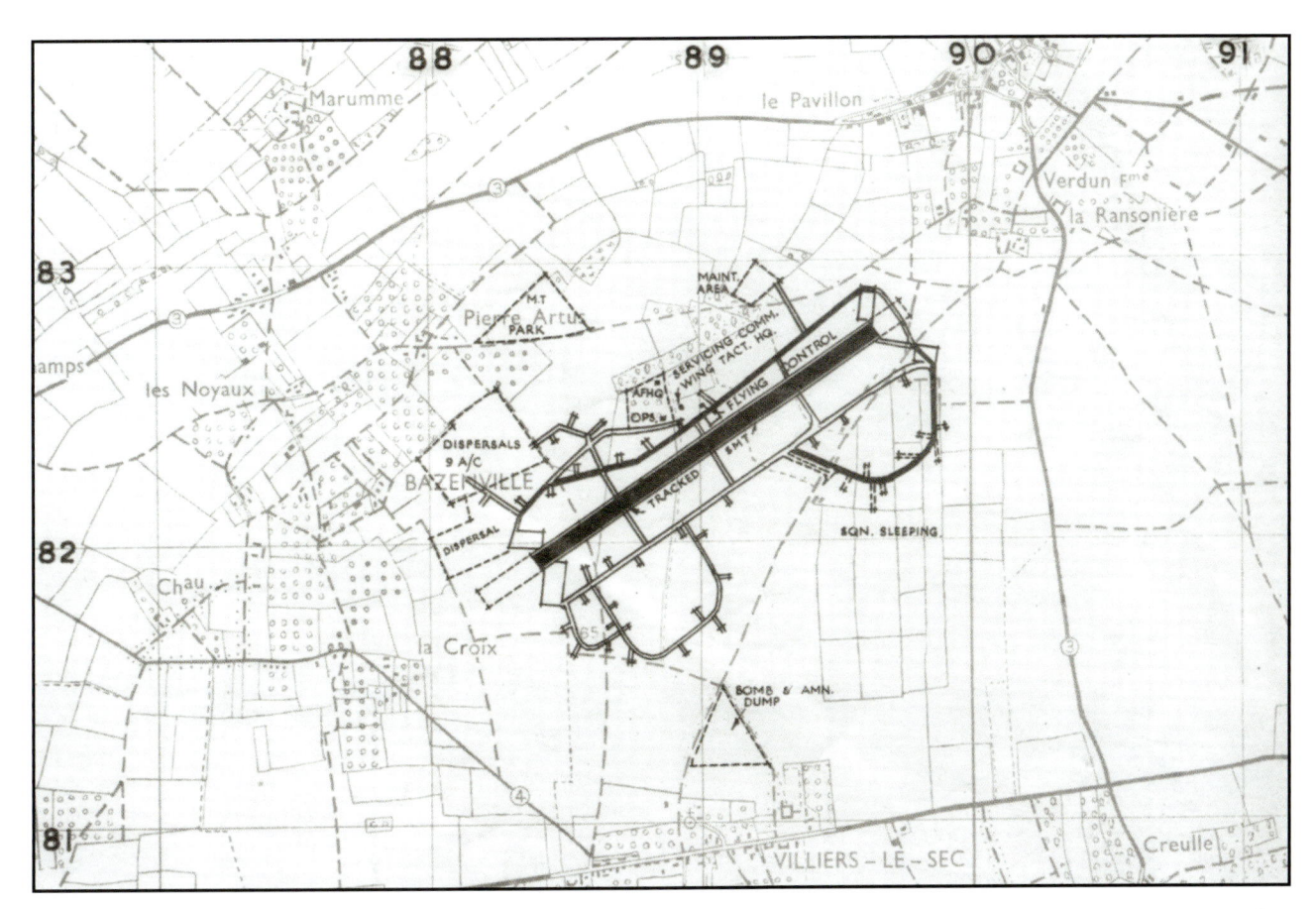

As the second of the Refuelling and Re-armament Strips in the British sector, construction of B-2 at Bazenville (see map page 32) was the responsibility of the Royal Engineers. The target was to complete it to R&RS standard by midday on D+4 and to an ALG by last light on D+5. A reconnaissance of the site was made on D+1 but pockets of enemy resistance held up the start. The untracked strip of 3,600 feet was finished on D+3 but as it was not immediately occupied by the RAF, work continued to extend it to 5,000 feet tracked with SMT. It was completed and handed over at midday on D+6 and as an ALG the following day. (It would have been finished on June 9 if a Liberator had not crash-landed and ripped up much of the SMT.)

Like so many of the airstrips in Normandy, little now remains to mark where they lay, except for the odd memorial.

When B-2 opened for business the front line was just six miles away. The complete Canadian No. 127 Wing arrived on June 16. A primitive Flying Control was set up on the north-western side of the strip and it is understood that the control for No. 83 Group of the Second Tactical Air Force was managed from the local church. A plaque on the memorial records the landing on B-2 by Pierre Closterman *(right)* with No. 602, a cosmopolitan squadron now manned by British, Australian, New Zealand, Canadian and Free French pilots.

June 11, 1944

We were on 'readiness' after tea when suddenly we were informed that we were going to spend the night in France. Jacques and I were distinctly excited at the idea of being the first French pilots to land in France. We decided to don our full regalia and Jacques took his flask of brandy to celebrate the occasion suitably. We took off at 1830 hours and, after a normal patrol — nothing out of the ordinary to report — we met over Bazenville.

Jacques and I, in close formation, landed just behind the Captain in an impenetrable cloud of dust. Christ, what dust! It was white and as fine as flour. Stirred up by the slipstream of the propellers it infiltrated everywhere, darkened the sky, suffocated us, found its way into our eyes and ears. We sank in up to our ankles. For 500 yards round the landing strip all traces of green had disappeared — every growing thing was covered by a thick layer, stirred by the slightest breeze.

Two commandos whose eyes only were visible under a crust of dust and sweat, with Tommy-guns slung on their backs, helped me to jump down from my plane and laughed when they recognised my uniform.

'Well, Frenchie, you're welcome to your blasted country!'

Jacques emerged out of a cloud, a handkerchief over his face, and we shook hands — a moving moment all the same. We were treading French soil after four years' absence.

If the truth must be told, instead of the deep emotion I was expecting, what I felt most was profound regret at having brought my smart new 'best blue' uniform to such a dump. Already I looked much more like a powdered circus clown than an officer of the Armée de l'Air!

A Captain from the Canadian division stopped in his Jeep on his way past to warn us: 'No straying from the airfield. No crossing from one side of the track to the other. Don't touch anything. Avoid areas marked by cloth strips, they are still mined. The Huns have left mines everywhere and only half an hour ago a man was killed and two others wounded by a German sniper hiding in a wood half a mile away who has got telescopic sights.'

We all met again behind a hedge where a mobile canteen gave us tea, biscuits and marmalade (all liberally sprinkled with that blasted dust).

PIERRE CLOSTERMAN,
The Big Show, 1951

Life goes on at Bazenville next to a machine from No. 443 Squadron.

Winston Churchill had first visited Normandy on June 12 when he stepped ashore on D+6 on Mike Sector of Juno Area. The following month, on the eve of the operation to break out of the bridgehead, he returned in a Dakota on July 20 to land at Cherbourg (A-15 Maupertus, which had become serviceable on July 3, see page 110). He toured the port which had been captured in ruins at the end of June (see *After the Battle* No. 147), later motoring to Utah Beach and Arromanches to view the Mulberry harbour in operation. He based himself on HMS *Enterprise* when not visiting sites ashore, including the Caen battle area with General Montgomery on the 23rd. Air Vice-Marshal Harry Broadhurst, the AOC of No. 83 Group, then took the Prime Minster on an aerial tour of the British invasion airfields in a captured German aircraft! When the Air Marshal was the commanding officer of the Western Desert Air Force he had acquired a Fieseler Storch for his personal transport and when he was appointed to the Second Tactical Air Force, the Storch was shipped to the UK.

Around 50 of the Luftwaffe very-short-take-off machines had been captured. Here, Churchill is pictured arriving in the Storch bearing RAF markings at B-3 at Ste Croix-sur-Mer which had just seen the arrival of the Typhoons of No. 146 Wing.

Wing Commander Charles Green greets the Prime Minister at B-5 Camilly (see page 70) where Nos. 174, 175 and 245 Squadrons of No. 121 Wing, also equipped with Typhoons, had been in residence for a month.

Churchill: 'On my last day at Arromanches I visited Montgomery's headquarters, a few miles inland. The Commander-in-Chief was in the best of spirits on the eve of his largest operation, which he explained to me in all detail. He took me into the ruins of Caen and across the river, and we also visited other parts of the British front. Then he placed at my disposal his captured Storch aeroplane, and the Air Commander himself piloted me all over the British positions. This aircraft could land at a pinch almost anywhere, and consequently one could fly at a few hundred feet from the ground, gaining a far better view and knowledge of the scene than by any other method. I also visited several of the air stations, and said a few words to gatherings of officers and men (see pages 24-25). I flew back home that evening, July 23, and arrived before dark.' Here he shakes hands with Wing Commander Michael Judd, the CO of No. 143 Wing at Bazenville. The Air Vice-Marshal stands on the extreme left . . . but what happened to his Storch?

It appears that in April 1945 the plane had an engine failure and the Air Marshal crashed onto one of the hangars at Brussels-Evere (B-56) in Belgium. The Storch went through the roof but fortunately Broadhurst escaped serious injury.

As far back as December 1942, soon after the US 660th Engineer Topographical Battalion arrived in the UK, the selection of airfield sites in France was begun. At that time, there was only the 1:50,000 GSGS map series available (the 1:25,000 maps *(below)* had not yet been produced) but from these, possible locations were selected. Meanwhile, a test was carried out to determine the best height to photograph the chosen areas by taking pictures of a specially-selected location at 6,000, 9,000 and 12,000 feet, where the photogrammetric data could be compared with a known ground survey. From this, it was determined that photography from 12,000 feet would produce the best result for compilation on the Multiplex apparatus at a scale of 1:10,000, overlaid on the 1:50,000 map series *(right)*. The American unit worked in close liaison with the Director of Survey, Home Forces, and upwards of 120 sites were pre-surveyed in this fashion before D-Day.

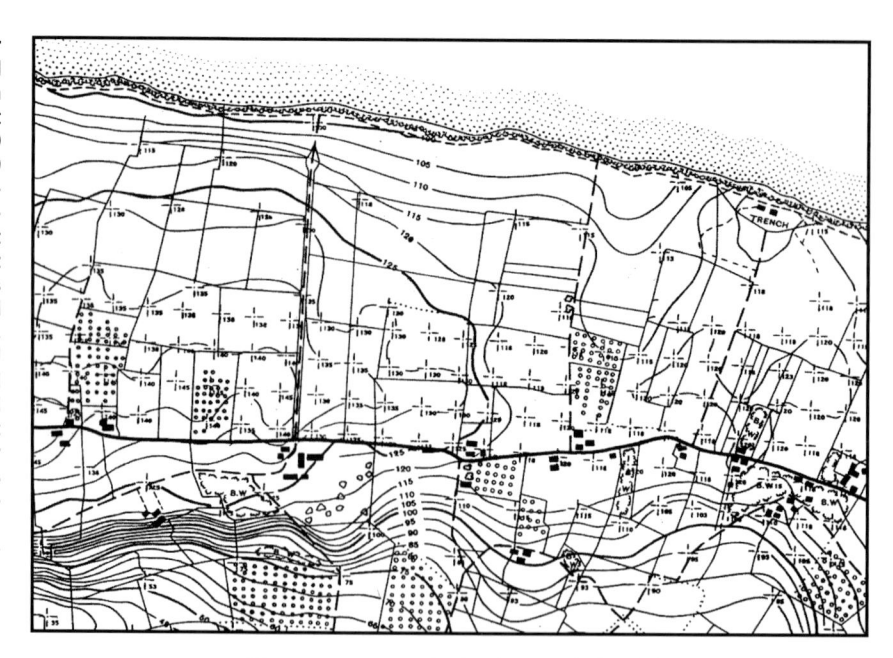

A-1 ST PIERRE-DU-MONT

The contours on the basic map helped the engineers to align the runway to suit the terrain and plot the east-west strip on an alignment of 91 degrees.

OPERATIONAL JUNE 17

Latitude: 49°23'N
Longitude: 00°57'W
Grid reference: T-609931
Altitude: 135ft

This site at St Pierre-du-Mont, which had been pre-chosen for a crash strip, lay just one mile east of Pointe du Hoc, the objective of the 116th Infantry of the 29th Division. To capture the gun battery on the cliff-top, a spearhead assault was to be mounted from the sea by the 2nd Ranger Battalion, while a second Ranger landing was to be made mid-way between it and the western end of Charlie Beach in the Omaha Area.

The 834th Engineer Aviation Battalion was scheduled to land at H+4 hours but due to the intense opposition faced on Omaha, this was not possible. To relieve the 2nd Rangers, on D+1 a column of ten tanks supported by 116th Infantry advanced westward along the coastal road to St Pierre-du-Mont and by noon were a 1,000 yards from Pointe

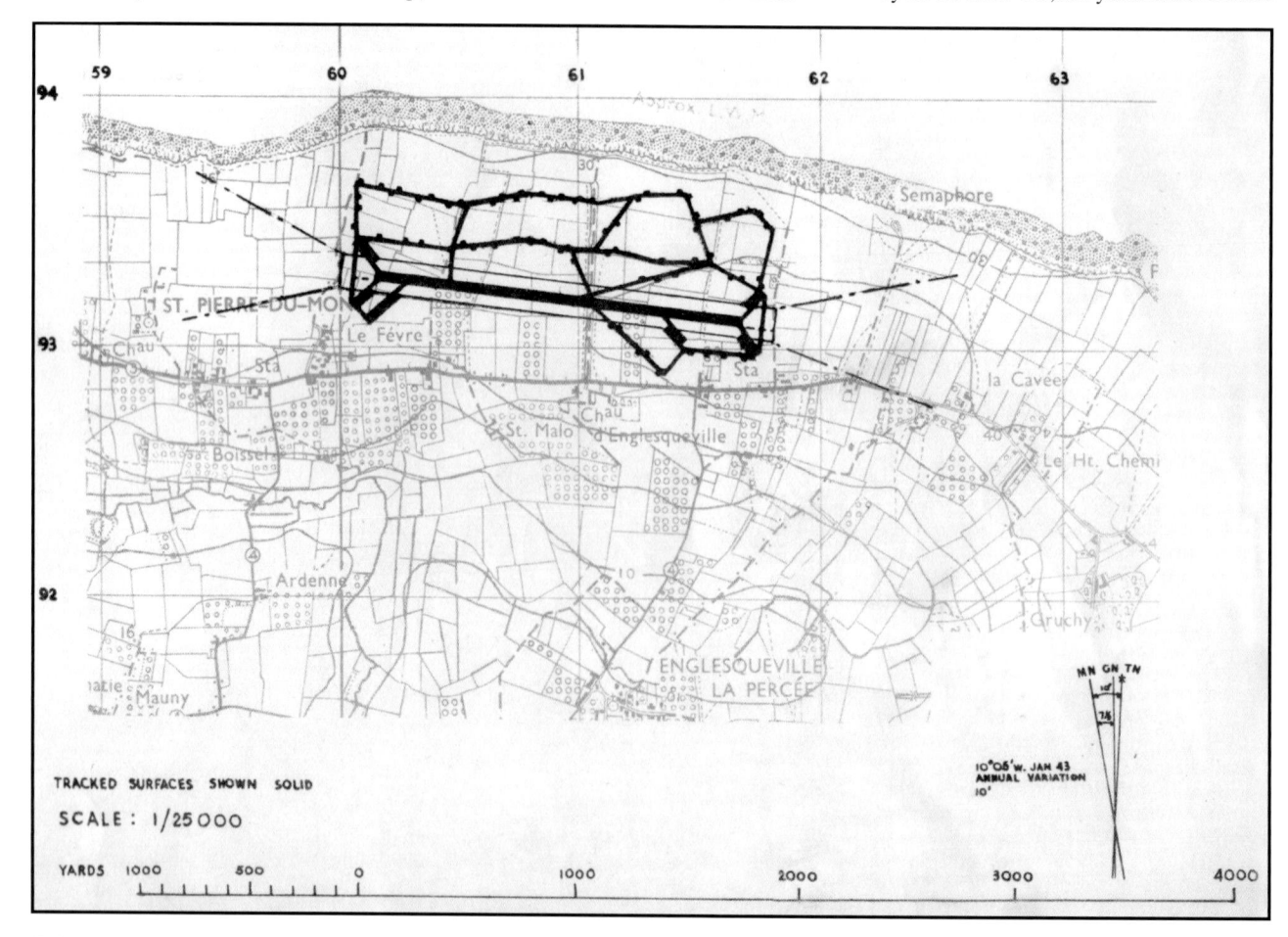

This was the first edition of the plan for A-1 at St Pierre-du-Mont before it was finally developed with the addition of a crash strip.

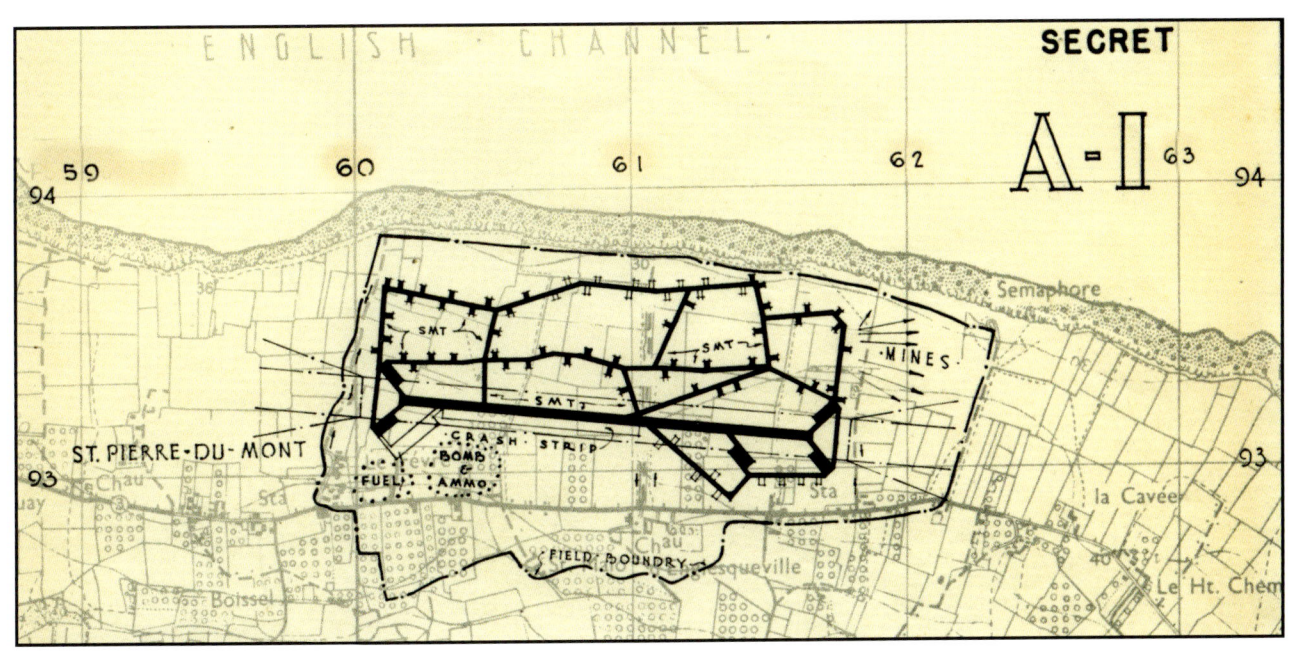

Three stages in the life of an airfield . . . from conception . . . to realisation . . . to oblivion!

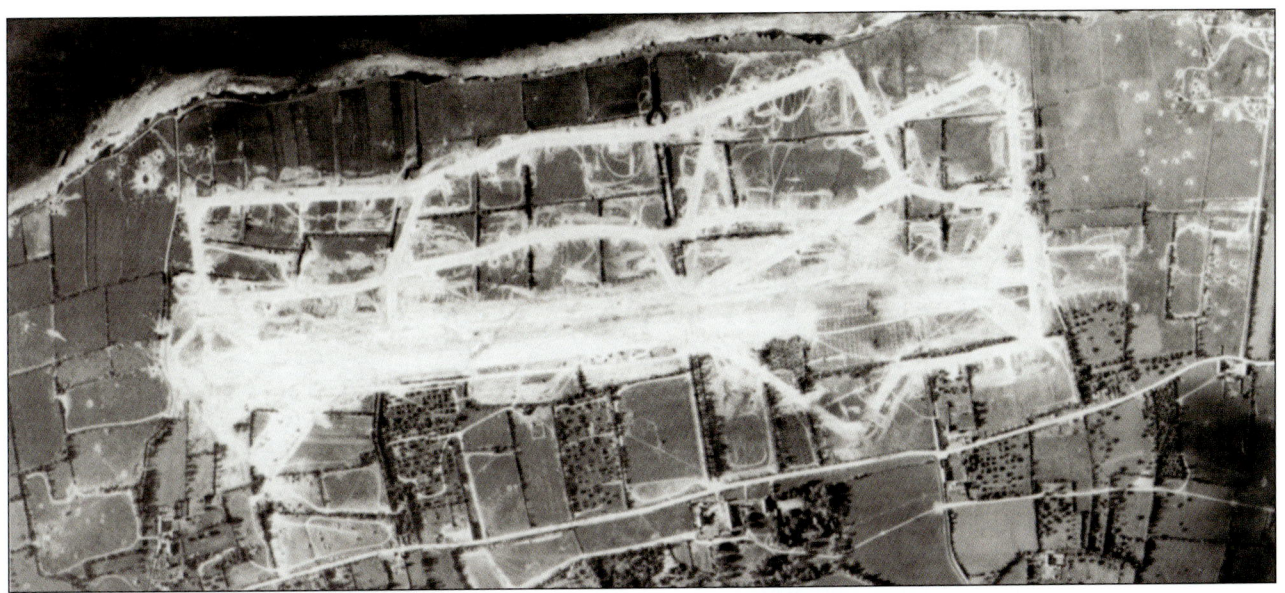

This photo shows the first P-38 to land in France (see pages 2-3) at A-21C, St Laurent-sur-Mer, on June 14. However, according to the record books, P-38 Lightnings — either from the 367th or 370th Fighter Group — were not based in France until the end of July, all three squadrons of the 370th (the 401st, 402nd and 485th) then being at Cardonville. The three squadrons of the 367th Fighter Group, which also arrived in late July, were split over three airfields: the 392nd at A-10 Carentan; the 393rd at A-14 Cretteville and the 394th at A-6 at Beuzeville, often referred to as Ste-Mère-Église. Roger Freeman, renowned historian of the US Eighth and Ninth Air Forces, explained that 'the generally poor standard of aircraft recognition in the Allied fighting services led to special identity markings for those aircraft involved in the support of the cross-Channel invasion of Europe. These took the form of five alternating stripes of white and black around wings and fuselage, which were applied to most fighters on June 4 and 5, 1944 [quite crudely — see the Spitfire on page 40. Ed]. On Lightning wings, each band was 24 inches wide, the first white band being painted immediately outboard of the fuselage boom. The last white band would have extended over the inner bar of the National Insignia had it not been painted around. The stripes on the fuselage booms were also 24 inches wide, commencing at the leading edge of the radiator housing and extending back almost to the tailplane. The stripes on the upper surfaces of the wings compromised camouflage, and from July 4 stripes were removed from the upper surfaces of the wings and from the top of the fuselage booms down to the side centre line. This was followed by another directive in August requiring the stripes to be removed from the under surfaces of the wings between the 25th of that month and September 10.'

du Hoc where less than a hundred Rangers were found to be holding out.

The following day, the engineers who had pushed westward behind the infantry, reached St Pierre where they began work to build their Refuelling and Re-arming Strip (R&RS). Snipers were still active, and the area had first to be swept for mines, but by June 14 a 5,000ft runway of SMT had been finished. Alongside was a crash strip of graded earth, also 5,000ft long. Portable airfield lighting enabled 24-hour operations with VHF homing available. There were 50 tracked dispersals and 25 untracked.

Airfield A-1 was assigned to the P-47 Thunderbolts of the 366th Fighter Group, and the first two squadrons — the 389th and 391st — flew in on June 17 followed by the 390th on the 20th.

A memorial to the memory of the 366th Fighter Group was dedicated on August 25, 1989.

Above: **Composite photograph prepared of St Pierre-du-Mont by the 942nd Engineer Aviation Topographic Battalion in July.** *Below:* **Note the Lightnings dispersed in the south-eastern corner of this striking photo of A-1. In the distance on the left can be seen the promontory of Pointe du Hoc, the capture of which held up the engineers waiting to construct the airstrip.**

On June 16, a Thunderbolt from the 367th Fighter Squadron of the 358th Fighter Group, based at the Advanced Landing Ground at High Halden in Kent, came a cropper while making an emergency landing at Cricqueville. After 1st Lieutenant Jacob C. Blaziek was rescued from the cockpit, the P-47 was ignominiously dragged from the field of battle.

A-2 CRICQUEVILLE

OPERATIONAL JUNE 17

Latitude: 49°21'N
Longitude: 01°00'W
Grid reference: T-571905
Altitude: 100ft

Just over a mile to the south-west of A-1 lay the site for A-2 which was to be constructed by the 820th Engineer Aviation Battalion. There was much concern on D+1 that the two American beach-heads had not joined up and Cricqueville was on the route taken by the 116th Infantry of the 29th Division on the drive to secure a link-up with the forces that had landed on Utah.

Original plans had called for two-thirds of the airstrips to be built to fighter specification with runways of 3,600 feet but by mid-June the Ninth Air Force had decided to use all of its groups as fighter-bombers. This necessitated lengthening runways to 5,000 feet, but a shortage of SMT meant that only 3,600 feet was tracked, the remaining 1,400 feet being left as earth until more materials became available.

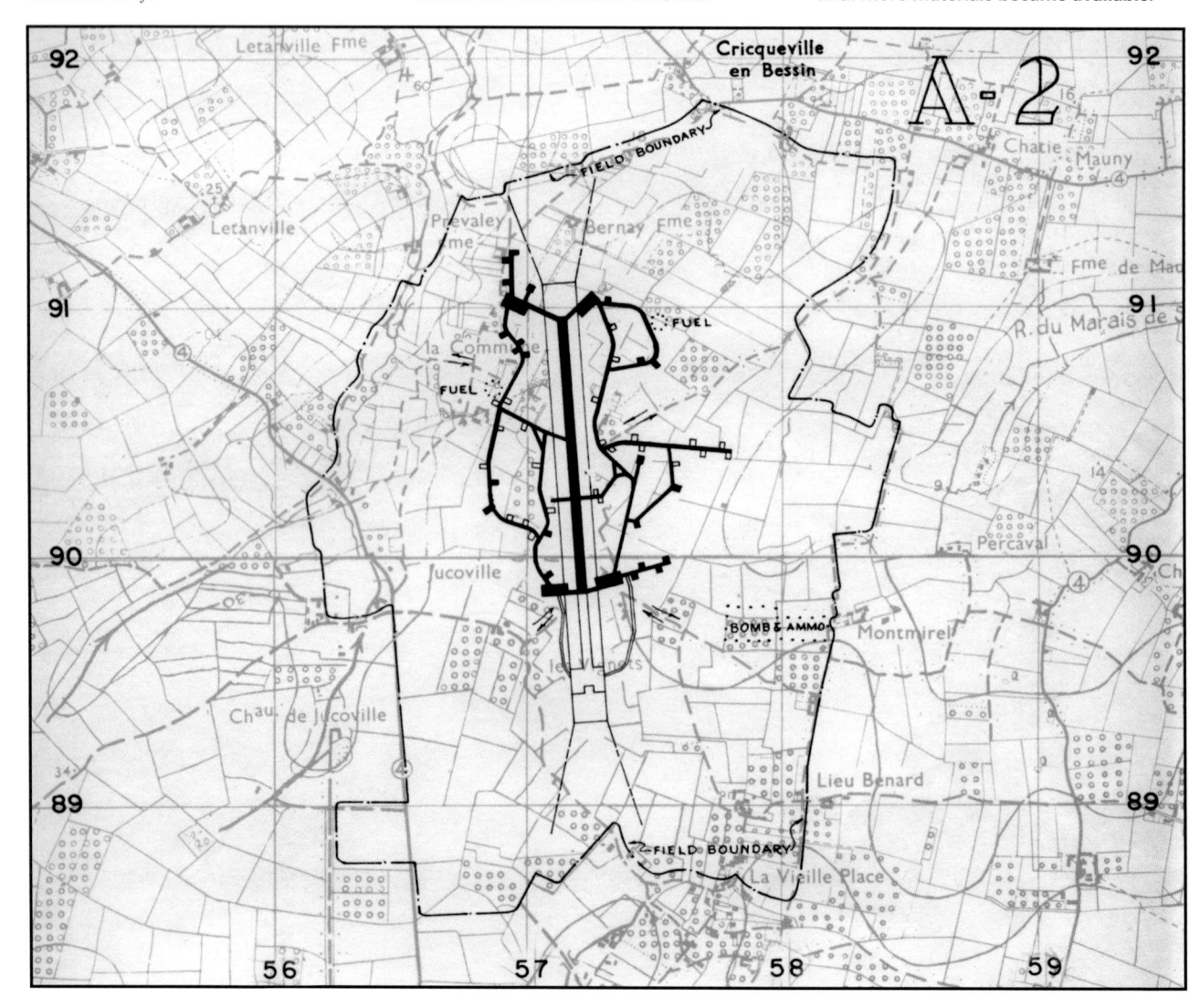

Unusually, Cricqueville has two memorials, one to the 354th Fighter Group, in residence from June 17 to mid-August, and the other to the 367th Fighter Group which arrived at the end of July and remained until early September. This P-38 of the latter group was pictured in August after the D-Day stripes had been removed from the tall booms. A VW Schwimmwagen provides a unique follow-me vehicle.

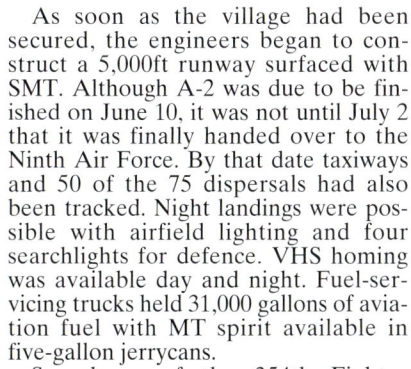

As soon as the village had been secured, the engineers began to construct a 5,000ft runway surfaced with SMT. Although A-2 was due to be finished on June 10, it was not until July 2 that it was finally handed over to the Ninth Air Force. By that date taxiways and 50 of the 75 dispersals had also been tracked. Night landings were possible with airfield lighting and four searchlights for defence. VHS homing was available day and night. Fuel-servicing trucks held 31,000 gallons of aviation fuel with MT spirit available in five-gallon jerrycans.

Squadrons of the 354th Fighter Group began arriving, the 353rd and 356th on June 17 and the 355th the following day. Equipped with P-51 Mustangs, they remained at Criqueville until mid-August. From August 14 they shared the airfield with the P-38 Lightnings of the 367th Fighter Group, their squadrons, the 392nd, 393rd and 394th, moving on to A-44 Peray in September.

A memorial to the 354th Fighter Group was unveiled in August 1990 and another one to the 367th by the commune of La Cambe in September 1988.

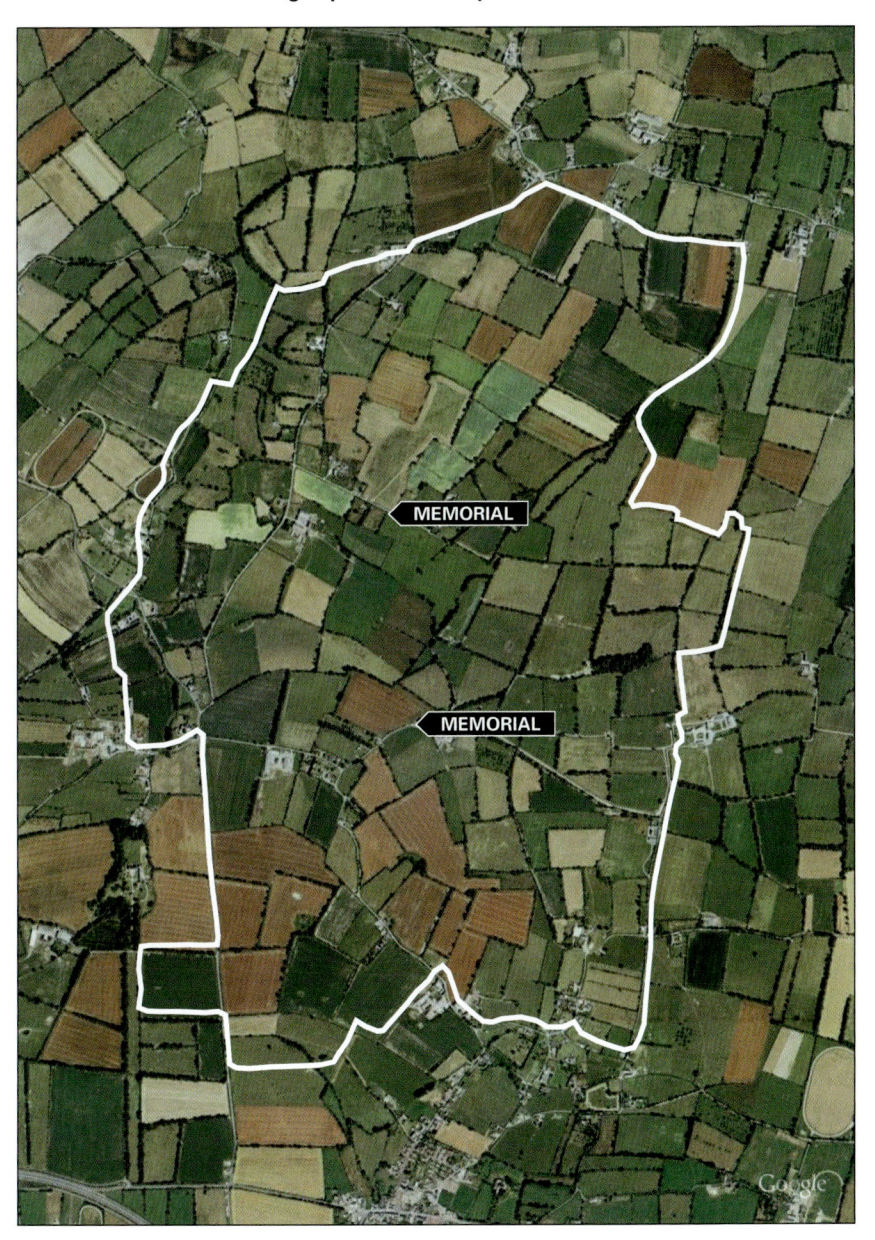

UNDERGROUND OPERATIONS ROOM

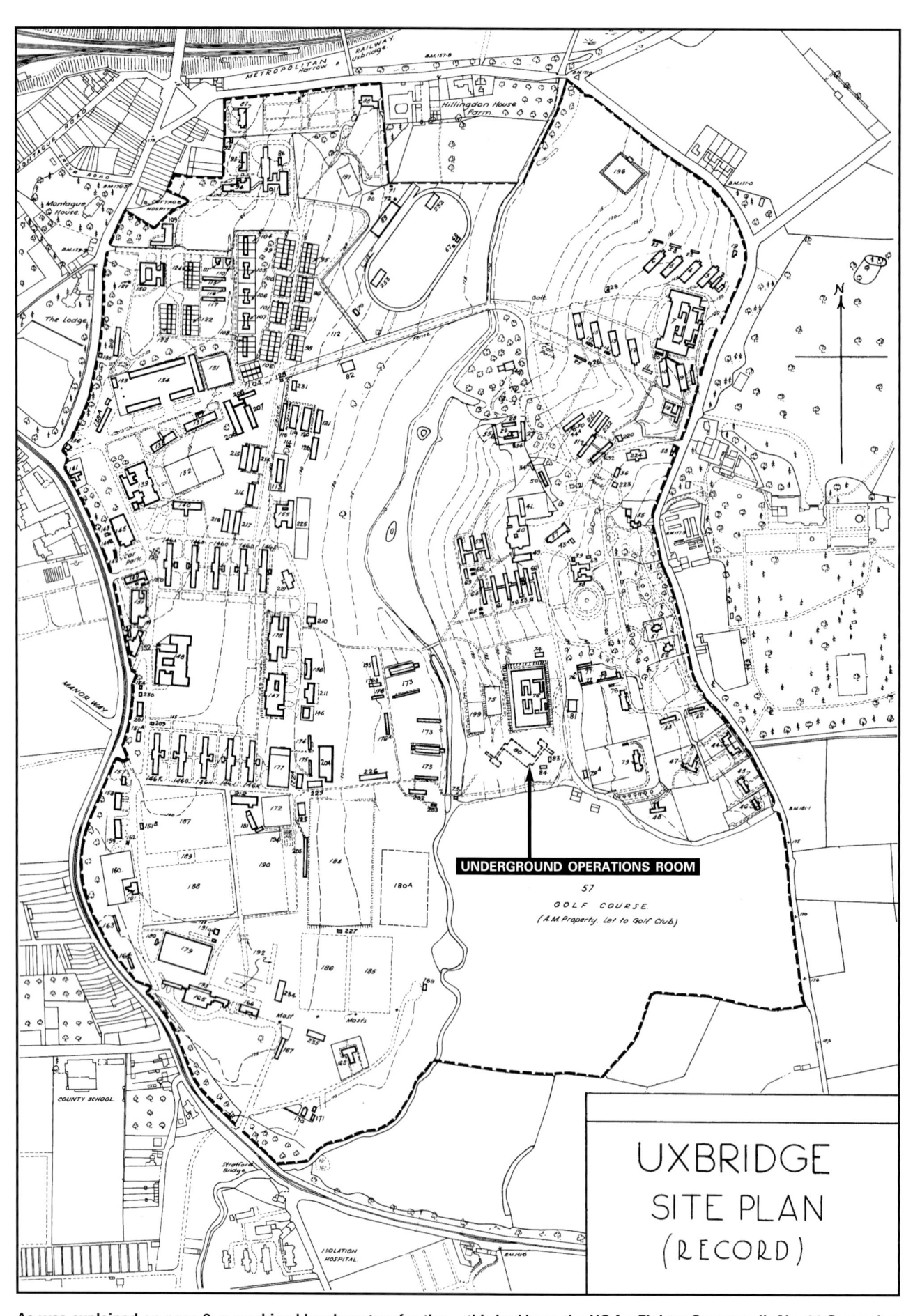

UXBRIDGE SITE PLAN (RECORD)

As was explained on page 8, a combined headquarters for the US Ninth Air Force and the RAF's Second Tactical Air Force was established at RAF Uxbridge in west London. Back in 1940 this had been the HQ for Fighter Command's No. 11 Group, but now it was to serve as the operational headquarters for the Allied Expeditionary Air Force.

The air plan called for what was virtually an air umbrella stretching from England to the beaches. Such a plan envisaged the employment of six squadrons of Spitfires on low cover, and three squadrons of P-47s on high cover throughout the hours of daylight. This commitment embraced the whole area of the five beaches and the area five miles inland and 15 miles seaward. Patrols of the area were necessarily limited to 50 minutes for the low cover squadrons and an hour for the high cover squadrons. However, the first day's experience disclosed that the control mechanism set up at Uxbridge was too involved for speedy provision of air support. So the plan was revised to the extent that squadrons on air alert werre placed at the disposal of the air controller on board the five headquarters ships anchored off the French coast: *Largs* for Sword Beach; *Hilary* for Juno; *Bulolo* for Gold; *Ancon* (below) for Omaha and the *Bayfield* for Utah.

The *Ancon* had been built in 1939 specifically to serve as an amphibious force flagship, commanded by Rear Admiral John L. Hall in Force 'O' Omaha. A fantastically complicated system of communications and signals joined Uxbridge to its operating units and to associated forces on land and sea. The overall air plan provided for ship-to-shore, point-to-point, and ground-to-air signals. On each of the five headquarters ships scheduled to accompany the initial landing force, an air representative would be available to advise assault commanders and to direct Allied aircraft to targets in the Channel or on the beaches. In the shipping lanes three fighter-direction tenders would guide the fighters to their targets and provide necessary radar and signal controls. Until ground-control interception stations would begin operations on the Continent, air, ground, and naval headquarters exchanged liaison officers to assure close contact and understanding. Air support parties would accompany the assault forces to facilitate timely air assistance. Until the Allied forces could be firmly established on the Continent the diverse lines of communication would be tied together chiefly through the combined control centre at Uxbridge.

After the war was over, RAF Uxbridge had a varied history, serving as the Olympic Village in 1948; the home of the Queen's Colour Squadron of the RAF Regiment; the location of the London Air Traffic Control Centre, and even becoming a target for an IRA bomb attack in 1981. *Above:* The station was closed on March 31, 2010 in a Ministry of Defence programme to reduce defence sites in Greater London in favour of concentrating activity at RAF Northolt. *Right:* Today much of the complex has been demolished and redeveloped for housing. Fortunately the underground Ops Block has been retained.

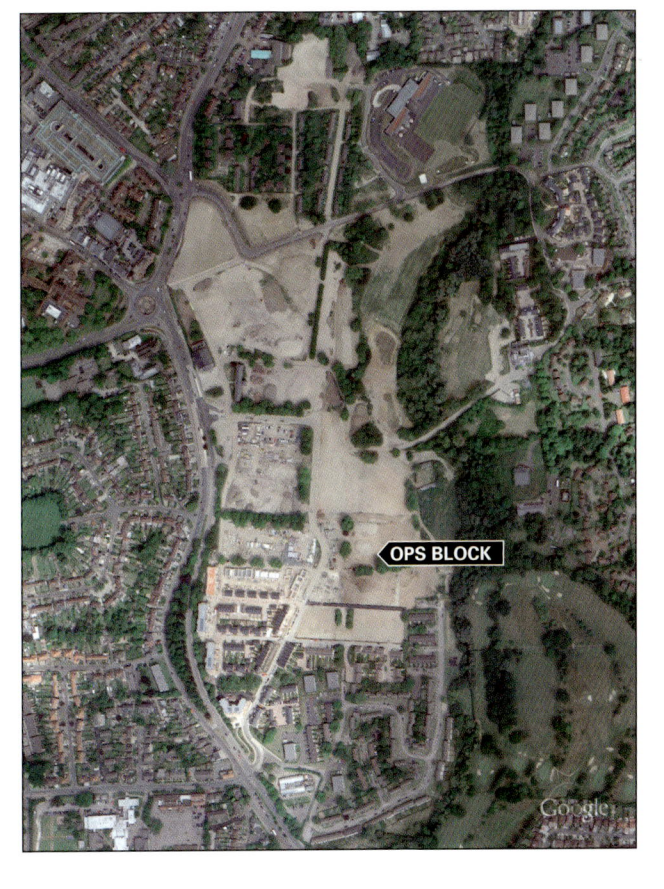

From D-Day until June 10, control of the Ninth Air Force was run from the *Ancon* but this then passed to the IX Tactical Support 70th Fighter Wing which had arrived the day before at A-2 at Cricqueville *(right)* — see map page 39. Back in February, the plan provided for the US First Army's command post in Normandy to be located nearby at Au Gay, west of Omaha, and just inland from Pointe du Hoc *(below)* which had been assaulted by a Provisional Ranger Force under Lieutenant Colonel James E. Rudder. The position mounted six 150mm guns in concrete emplacements and would be a severe threat to the Omaha invasion force. However, unbeknown to the Allied planners, the Germans had pulled the guns back and hidden them in a sunken road along an apple orchard to prevent them being destroyed by the heavy pre-D-Day bombing campaign. Sergeant Leonard Lommel of Company D describes what they found: 'We were up on top of the cliffs around 0730. There were no guns in the positions given so we decided that they must have been moved. I only had about a dozen men left. The road was our next objective where we were supposed to set up a road-block, which we did. Then Jack Kuhn, my platoon sergeant, and I saw these markings in this sunken road that looked like something heavy had been over it. We went down this road and came upon a little draw with camouflage all over it, and lo and behold there were the guns. They were sitting in proper firing condition, with ammunition piled up neatly, everything at the ready, but they were pointed at Utah Beach, not Omaha. There was nobody at the emplacement. We looked around cautiously, and over about a hundred yards away in a corner of a field was a vehicle with what looked like an officer talking to his men. I said, "Jack, you cover me and I'm going in there and destroy them". All I had were two thermite grenades — his and mine — which I put in the traversing mechanism. And then I broke their sights. We ran back to the road and got all the other thermites from the remainder of my guys, and rushed back and put the grenades in traversing mechanisms, elevation mechanisms, and banged the sights. There is no noise to a thermite so no one saw us.'

'*June 9, 1944:* Reconnaissance for the Army CP began although General Bradley is not in a rush to set up on land as V Corps has still not pushed more than four or five miles inland, and a German counter-attack is in the wind. The 2nd Division is coming ashore but without its vehicles; there is still great trouble in bringing the ships in with even flow. Isigny had been taken by the 175th Infantry in the morning.

'*June 10:* The unloading went faster, today and Mulberry is being built up in good time to permit unloading, whatever the condition of the sea. At first it was planned that we should go ashore at 1300, but there is delay with the vehicles, and the Rhino ferries did not get away until 1900. We are scheduled to leave tomorrow at 0800.

'*June 11:* We went ashore on an LCVP at 0900. Despite a message sent to Army CP requesting that we be picked up at General Hoge's headquarters, there was no one to meet us. The First US Army CP is located three kilometres east of Grandcamp-les-Bains, about a mile in from the coast, in an apple orchard which had been badly torn up by heavy naval gunfire. This is in the area bitterly fought over by the Rangers and 32 bodies were removed by the Advance Party before the CP was set up. In the lane which borders the CP on the left are four German 155s, and great piles of ammunition of light and heavy calibre.'

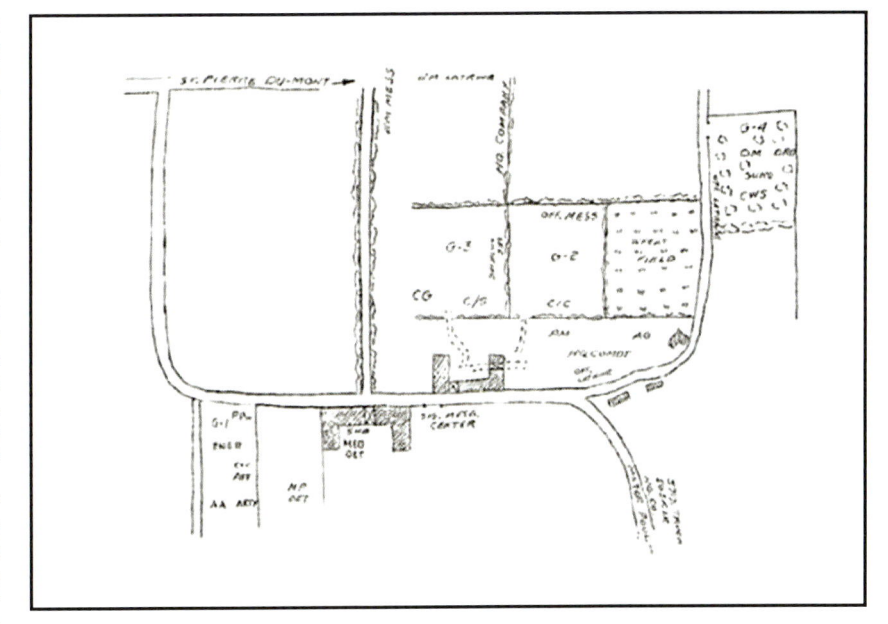

Once Point du Hoc had been secured, General Bradley's staff carried out a reconnaissance and chose a suitable site in an apple orchard and there First Army established a tent camp. By June 10 the 35th Signal Construction Battalion had installed cable communications with V Corps on Omaha, and within three days had established reliable radio communication with Uxbridge and the tactical headquarters of General Montgomery's 21st Army Group on the beach-head. At the same time, IX Tactical Air Command set up their advance headquarters in the next field alongside the First Army HQ. On June 18 this headquarters assumed the major responsibility for the direction of air support. The latter headquarters filtered ground requests for assistance, ordered missions as it saw fit, and transmitted to Uxbridge only such requests as it could not meet with its own resources.

US FIRST ARMY HEADQUARTERS

A-6 BEUZEVILLE

OPERATIONAL JUNE 17

Latitude: 49°25'N
Longitude: 01°17'W
Grid reference T-363976
Altitude 70ft

Before the airstrip A-6 at Beuzeville (often referred to in American accounts as Sainte-Mère-Église) had been tracked, it was used by gliders to bring in men, supplies and equipment from England. This picture is dated June 15.

The capture of Sainte-Mère-Église was the mission of the US 82nd Airborne Division. The 505th Parachute Infantry Regiment landed on and around its drop zone to the north-west; the 3rd Battalion rapidly assembled, and before dawn the town was in American hands. However, it was the 12th Infantry Regiment of the US 4th Division that captured the village of Beuzeville just to the north-east on D+1.

Tracking now well underway. In the far distance over on the left is what appears to be a crash dump with a Thunderbolt and a Spitfire or Mustang sitting on the ground with its undercarriage collapsed.

ALG A-6 was planned to be constructed between the village and Sainte-Mère-Église and the 819th Engineer Aviation Battalion quickly began preparing the site for a 5,000ft strip tracked with SMT. It was completed by June 18 together with the standard 75 dispersals of which 50 were tracked. Facilities included airfield lighting, VHS homing, night-time Darky Watch (enabling aircraft to call for a homing bearing using the call-sign 'Darky'), and 31,000 gallons of aviation fuel in trucks.

First to arrive were the 405th and 406th Squadrons of the 371st Fighter Group on June 17, with the 404th six days later. (Although the official USAAF history states otherwise, some sources say that the 394th Squadron of the 367th Fighter Group was at Beuzeville during the July/August period before moving to A-2 Criqueville.)

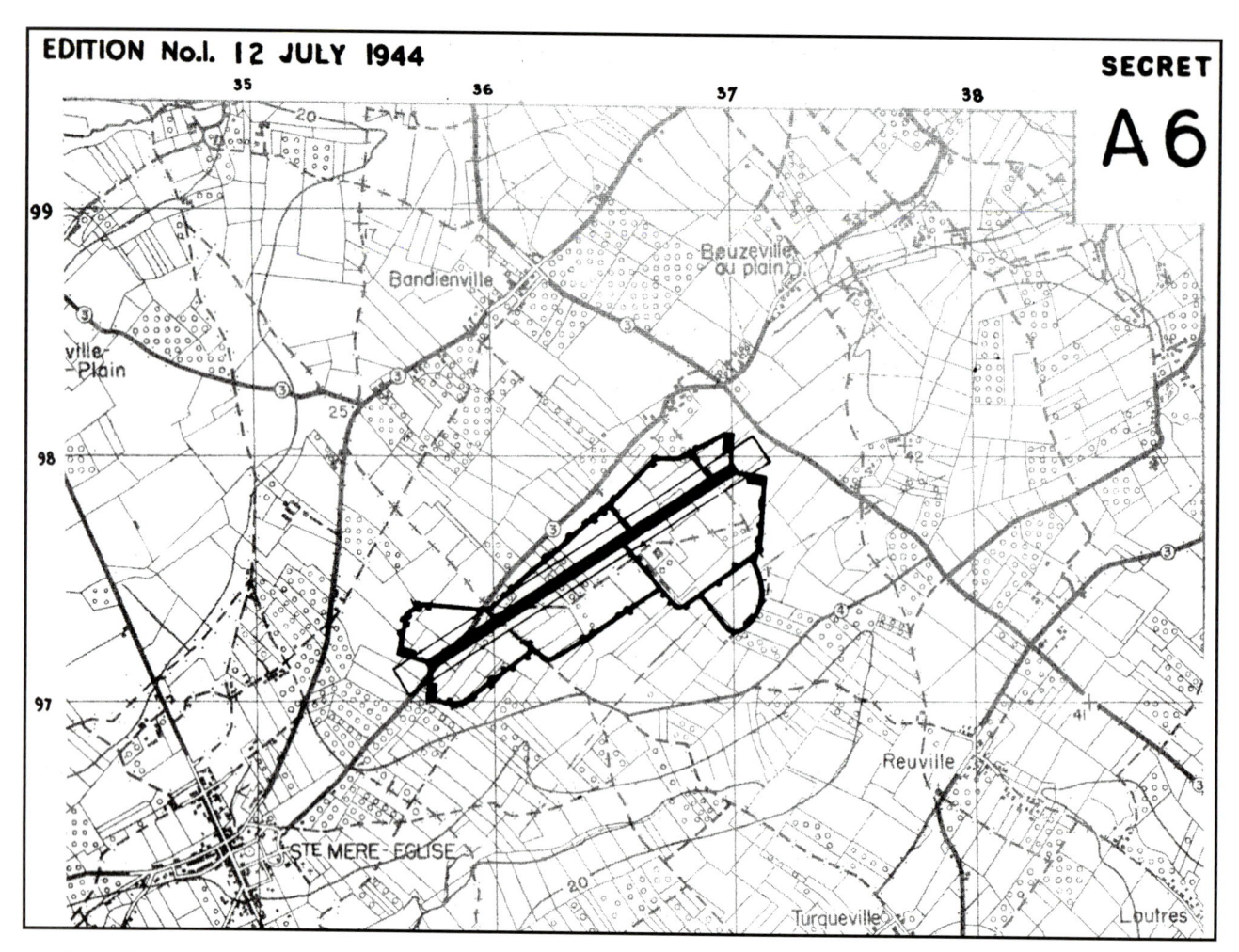

The first edition of the engineering plan did not indicate the extent of the perimeter or the dispersed services.

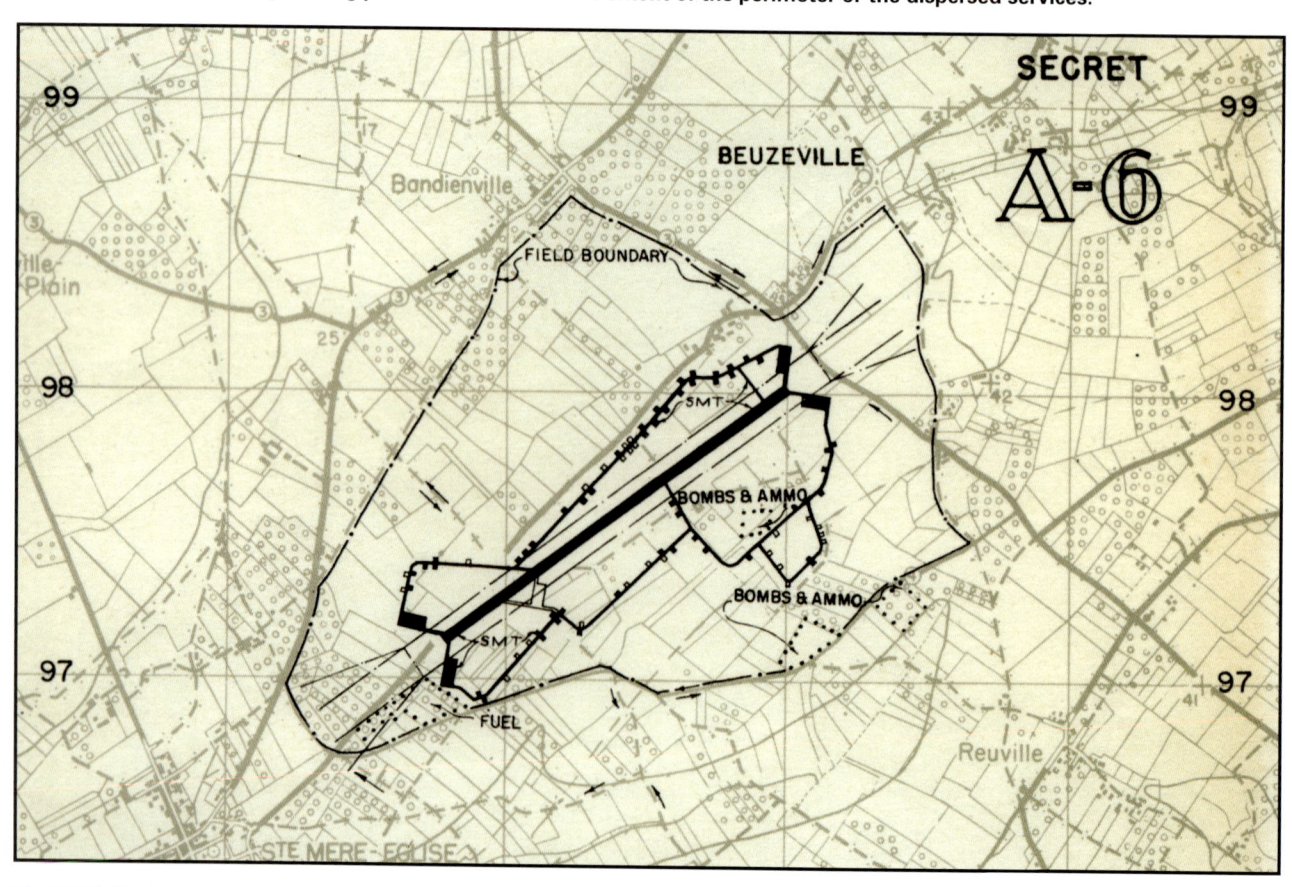

The 819th Engineers reported A-6 finished on June 18 although two squadrons of the 371st Fighter Group had landed the previous day.

A Thunderbolt from the 371st Fighter Group comes to grief. Based at the Advanced Landing Ground at Bisterne in the New Forest, between June 17 and 29 the group used both its British base and its assigned landing ground at Beuzeville. However, even at Bisterne where the two runways were surfaced with the more flimsy Sommerfeld Tracking, blown tyres and bent props were the norm, and three P-47s were lost in accidents. (The unit had to relocate to Ibsley in April while one runway at Bisterne had SMT laid down.) Normandy lay some 150 miles to the south taking the P-47s around 30 minutes to reach the French coast, leaving 90 minutes over the battle area. Throughout the hours of daylight, several missions of 12 to 16 P-47s would be despatched from England to maintain continuous fighter cover over the beach-head. This particular aircraft appears to have crashed on take-off since the bomb-load is still on board.

The memorial, unveiled in June 1979, specifically records that A-6 was 'protected by the 552nd AAA AW Battalion commanded by Lieutenant Colonel Benjamin M. Warfield'.

57

B-4 BENY-SUR-MER

OPERATIONAL JUNE 18

Latitude: 49°18'N
Longitude: 00°25'W
Grid reference: T-993808
Altitude: 180ft

The initial plan was for No. 25 Airfield Construction Group (which comprised HQ No. 25 ACG, Nos. 64 and 681 Road Construction Companies, and Nos. 214 and 217 Pioneer Companies), to work on B-16 at Villons-les-Buissons but should that not be possible they were to start on B-4 at Bény-sur-Mer. In the event the plan did not go as scheduled. Although the road units landed on Mike Beach in Juno Area on D+2, the Group HQ and the main body did not reach dry land until D+3, coming ashore on Nan Beach.

To try to get things moving, the OC of No. 681 Road Construction Company was ordered to reconnoitre the site for B-4 but in the interim some of the party from Group HQ went to the location for B-16 only to be turned back by forward troops as the area was still in close proximity to the enemy. The Commander Royal Engineers finally managed to get ashore two and a half days late to find work in full swing at Bény.

This had entailed the removal of 150 yards of hedging; the lifting of German anti-landing poles; chopping down 30 trees, and cutting and removing 150,000 square yards of crops. The ALG with its untracked 3,600-foot strip was completed on June 14 but work continued clearing a second parallel strip. The first aircraft to touch down long before it was completed was an AOP Auster IV from 'A' Flight of No. 652 Squadron on June 6, which departed the following day for B-10 at Plumetot.

Spitfire IXBs of the Canadian No. 126 Wing began arriving on June 18, Nos. 401, 411 and 412 Squadrons moving out again on August 8. Also leaving on the same date were the Spitfires of No. 442 Squadron which had arrived on July 15. On August 13 the Typhoons of No. 268 were followed the next day by the Mustang IIs of No. 2 Squadron. More Spitfires of No. 4 joined them two days later.

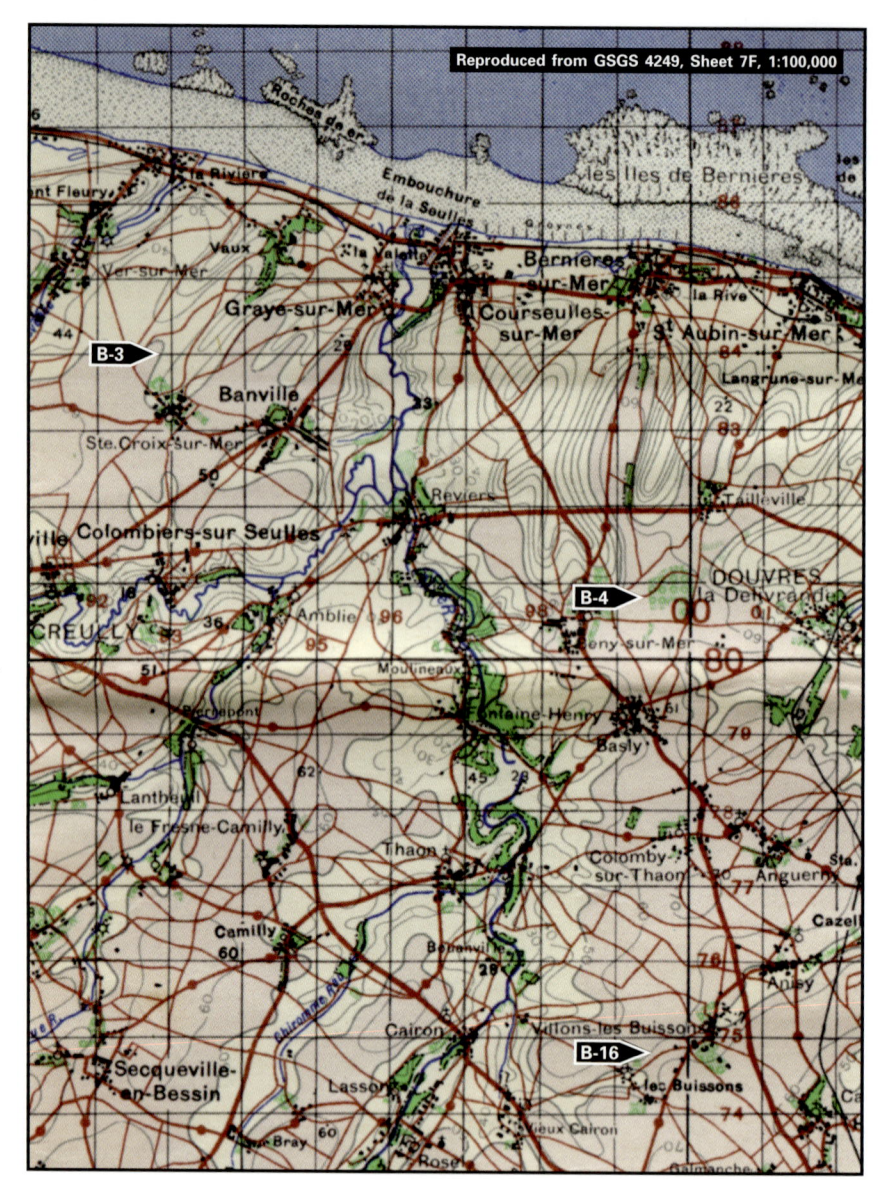

The War Diary of No. 25 Airfield Construction Group reveals that there was confusion on June 7 due to different sets of orders being received. After embarkation, the Commander of the Royal Engineers (CRE) was held on their LST in Portsmouth harbour throughout the following day. The main body sailed at 0500 on June 9 reaching Courseulles-sur-Mer at 1900 hours. Early the next morning they proceeded via Banville to Villons-les-Buissons but the area was still too close to the enemy and the CRE was not at the rendezvous. Instead the unit proceeded to the secondary location of Bény-sur-Mer where airfield B-4 was to be constructed. Meanwhile the CRE had got away at 1515 on June 9, coming ashore at Graye-sur-Mer at 1800 on June 10.

Air observation was paramount and strips for Austers were a priority. Even though Bény was still receiving odd rounds from the enemy, the first resident was 'A' Flight of No. 652 Squadron with Auster IVs on June 6. Then on June 12 while work on B-4 was proceeding, at 1100 hours a Thunderbolt crashed near the strip. The pilot was uninjured and another P-47 promptly landed and took off with the other pilot on board! At 2000 hours another Thunderbolt put down on the airstrip with slight engine trouble but the pilot was quickly redirected to one of the American airstrips. Three-quarters of an hour later, a Typhoon landed with its engine running rough. Then on June 14, a Spitfire crashed on the strip at 1445. Although the pilot was alright, a pioneer from No. 681 Road Construction Company was hit by the aircraft and killed. The Spitfire squadrons of the Canadian No. 126 Wing — Nos. 401, 411 and 412 — began flying into B-4 from Tangmere on June 18.

Accomodation on the airstrips during the early days was mainly in tents. This photo taken on June 23 shows pilots of No. 412 Squadron grouped around their CO, Squadron Leader Jack Sheppard. The Canadians were at Bény until August 8.

This photo was taken on August 1 when the Canadian Air Officer Commander-in-Chief Air Marshal Lloyd Breadnor visited the wing which was then led by one of Canada's top-scoring pilots 'Dal' Russel, nick-named by his ground crew 'Deadeye Dick'. He had commanded No. 411 (RCAF) Squadron at Redhill back in April 1943, being promoted at the age of 25 to command No. 126 Wing. However, at the end of his tour in November that year, he spent the next six months developing tactics at No. 83 Group headquarters, but was anxious to return to operational flying. Following the loss of a Canadian squadron commander, he asked Johnnie Johnson, the RAF's highest-scoring fighter pilot and wing leader of the Canadian Spitfire Wing, for command of No. 442 Squadron. Johnson had a very high regard for the blond, curly-haired Russel, considering him to have 'all the attributes of the popular conception of a fighter pilot', adding that he was 'a great favourite with the ladies'. Russel had to drop a rank to take command immediately. Four days after the Allied landings began, Army and RAF airfield engineers were working on the first British landing strip at Ste Croix-sur-Mer (B-3) and Johnson sent Russel and his wingman to check the airstrip, making them among the first to land in France. Johnson led his three Canadian squadrons to B-6, from which operations deeper into France began. Russel shared in the destruction of a Focke-Wulf fighter and damaged a second fighter, but most of his sorties were against ground targets. (During this hectic period he learned that his younger brother, Hugh, had been shot down nearby and killed flying with another Canadian Spitfire squadron.) In July Russel was once again promoted to Wing Commander and took command of the four Spitfire squadrons of No. 126 Wing. He led them during the devastating attacks in the Falaise pocket and then in support of the advancing Allied armies as they pushed forward through France, Belgium and Holland.

Spitfire IXs (identified as MK464 and MK277) of No. 442 Squadron lift off from Bény-sur-Mer in early August.

The same day that B-2 became operational, June 18, American engineers opened A-4 at Deux-Jumeaux near Vierville-sur-Mer (see map page 39). Now US forces had advanced up the Cotentin peninsula and had reached the outskirts of Cherbourg. The capture of the port was seen as a vital step in bringing in supplies as a storm had completely wiped out the American prefabricated Mulberry harbour and gravely damaged the British one at Arromanches. However, by the time the German garrison in the port surrendered on June 27, 95 per cent of the quays for deep-water vessels had been destroyed. Although repair work began at once, it was not until the end of September that Cherbourg was 75 per cent complete and clearance work was still going on at the end of the year. Bény remained a major airstrip right through August, only to be relinquished when Nos. 2, 4 and 268 Squadrons flew out on September 1 to B-27 at Boisney (see page 203). Being reclaimed for farmland, virtually nothing remains to be seen today from the air, the present-day vertical of Bény showing the same area as in the 1944 photo. *Below:* Now this simple memorial stands to mark its passing.

P-47s of the 48th Fighter Group flew into A-4 from its UK base at Station 347 at Ibsley in Hampshire on June 18.

A-4 DEUX-JUMEAUX

OPERATIONAL JUNE 18

Latitude: 49°20'N
Longitude: 00°59'W
Grid reference: T-591884
Altitude: 139ft

The village of Deux-Jumeaux, just a quarter of a mile north of the RN13, was taken during the advance of the 115th Infantry, 29th Division, on June 8. It was also assigned to the 816th Engineer Aviation Battalion which then had to split their efforts between constructing A-4 and A-3 further down the road.

This airfield had a similar layout of a 5,000ft SMT runway with 54 tracked and 21 untracked dispersals. It had complete airfield lighting, refuelling from trucks and 24-hour radio watch.

Allocated to the 48th Fighter Group, the first squadrons to arrive were the 492nd and the 493rd on June 18 followed on July 4 by the 494th. This group moved to Villacoublay (A-42D) at the end of August.

A memorial, erected by the 493rd Fighter Squadron Association and dedicated to the 48th Fighter Group, now stands to record the brief, yet vital role of A-4 in Operation 'Overlord'.

The 816th Engineers had to split the workforce between A-3 (page 36) and Deux-Jumeaux.

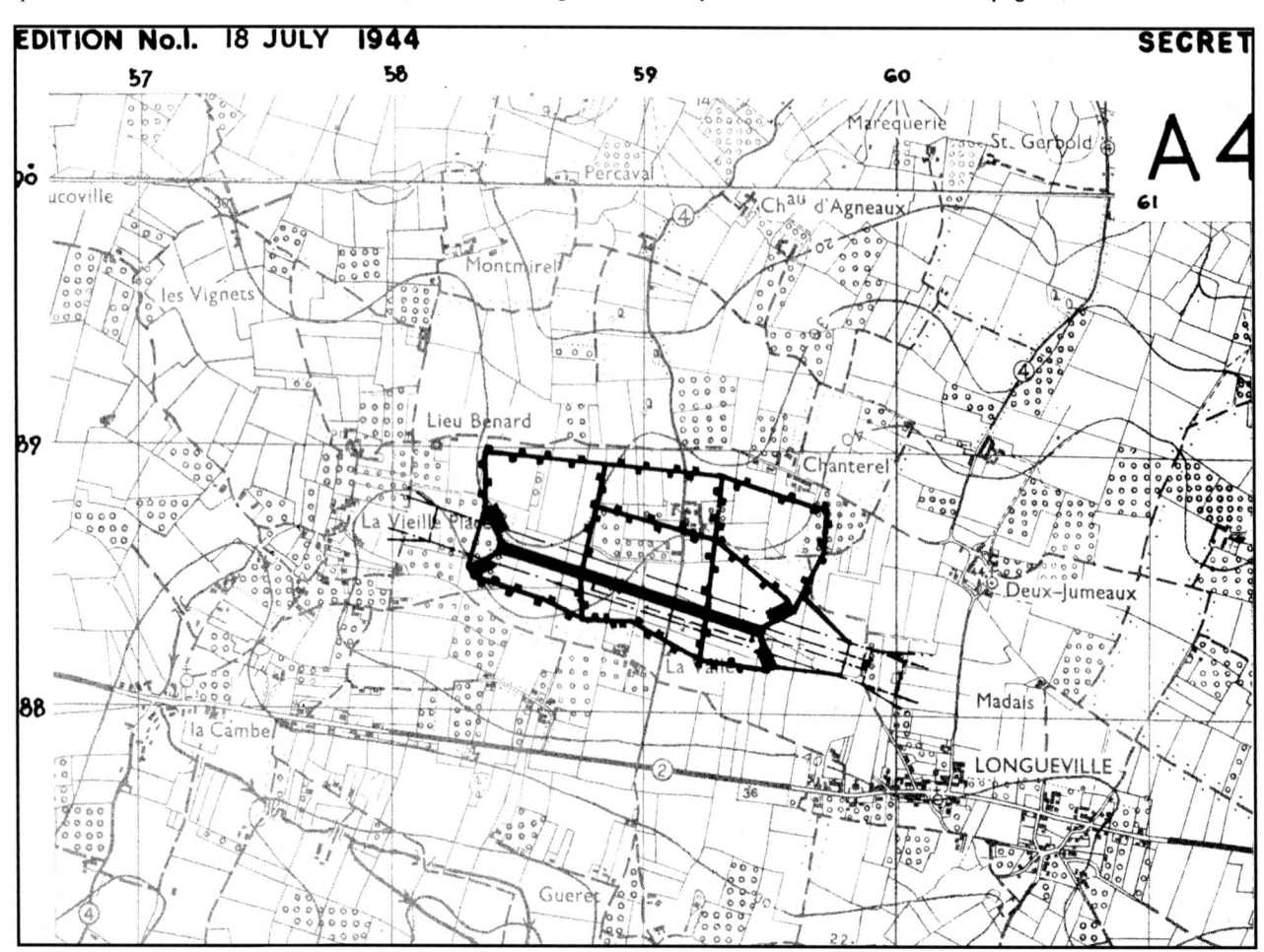

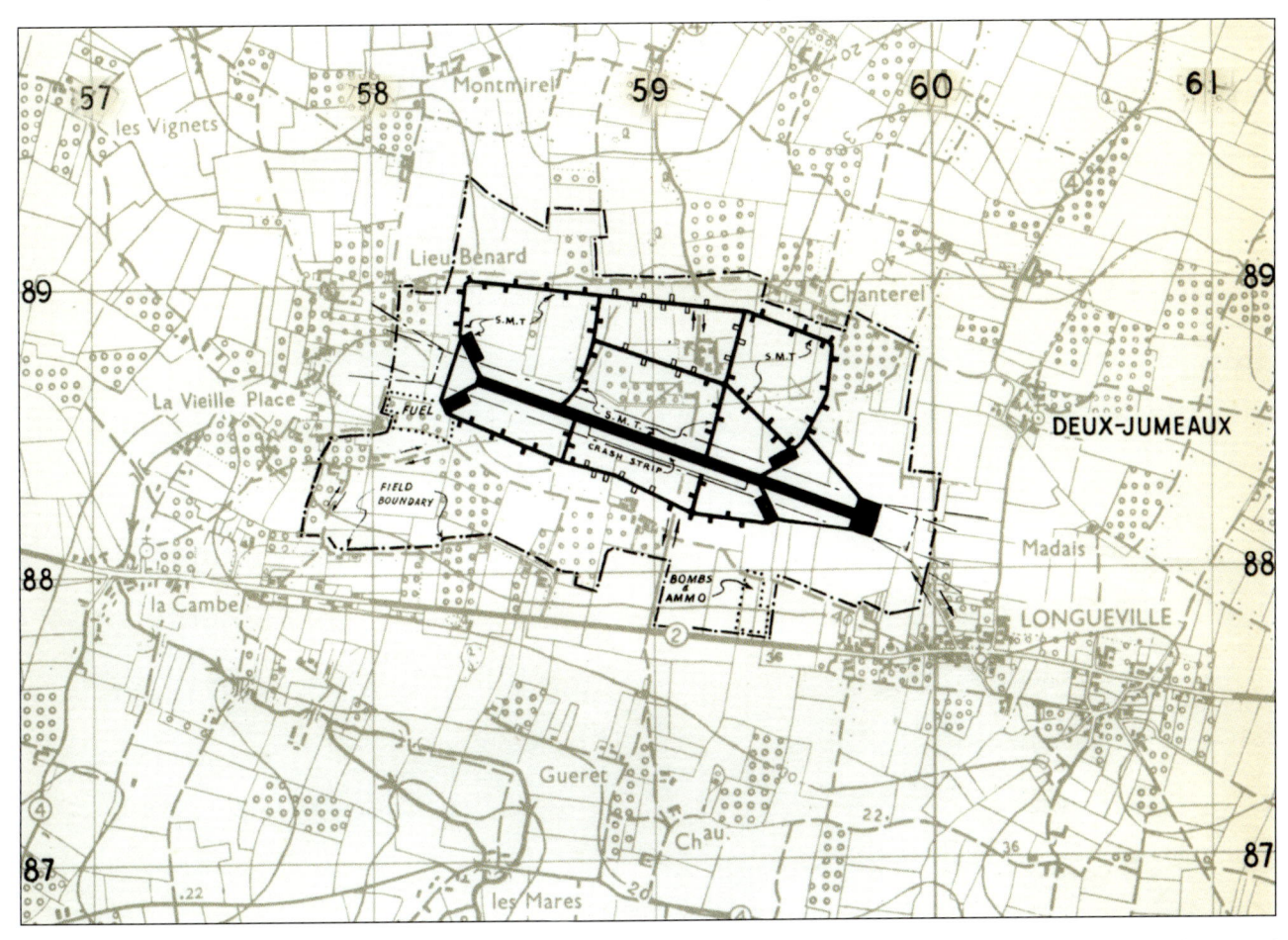

The 48th was one of the first Thunderbolt groups to move to the Normandy bridgehead although Ibsley continued to be used until July 4 when the last of the unit departed. Thereafter the group continued operating from A-4 until the front had moved beyond Paris when they re-located to the former French Air Force airfield south of the capital at Villacoublay (A-42D).

Airfield protection provided by the 18th AAA Group included this water-cooled .50 calibre Browning M2A1. The photo was taken on June 26 looking across to the manor house at Douville. Attacks on the airstrips were fairly infrequent although there were occasions when over-zealous gunners brought down Allied aircraft in spite of the zebra stripes identifying them as friendly.

Survey record photograph prepared by the 942nd Engineer Aviation Topographical Battalion in July 1944.

The French Air Force undertook extensive aerial photography of the country in 1947. This is the same area on August 28 that year.

The memorial to A-4 has been positioned a short distance south of the E-W runway.

B-6 was located mid-way between Ste Croix-Grand-Tonne and Coulombs and is some seven miles inland from Gold Beach (not nine as given in the War Diary of the group earmarked to construct it). The HQ party of No. 13 Airfield Construction Group of the Royal Engineers finally got ashore at Le Hamel at 1430 on June 9 only to find that No. 614 Road Construction Company were already at Coulombs in spite of enemy activity from snipers. However, they found the site covered with standing crops which were then cleared with the help of local farmers. Estimated completion date for the strip was June 16 and two days later for finishing the taxi-track and dispersals.

B-6 COULOMBS

OPERATIONAL JUNE 20

Latitude: 49°14'N
Longitude: 00°33'W
Grid reference: T-896754
Altitude: 200ft

Coulombs, situated some seven miles from the coast and half a mile north of the Route Nationale 13 between Caen and Bayeux, was reached by the 69th Brigade of the 50th (Northumbrian) Division by the evening of D-Day — the deepest thrust achieved on the first day.

This airstrip had been planned as a forward base for No. 124 Wing currently operating Typhoon IBs out of Hurn in Hampshire. A runway of 5,360ft, of which 5,000ft was surfaced with SMT, was completed on June 16 by No. 13 Airfield Construction Group although only the taxi-track on the southern side had SMT.

Nos. 181 and 247 Squadrons arrived on June 20 followed by the wing's third squadron, No. 182, on July 3. They stayed at Coulombs until the end of August when they transferred to B-30 at Créton. During the same month the Typhoons of No. 137 Squadron were also based at B-6 from August 14-28. Finally a Mosquito squadron, No. 264, flew in on September 4 but transferred to Carpiquet (B-17) with its hard runway the following day.

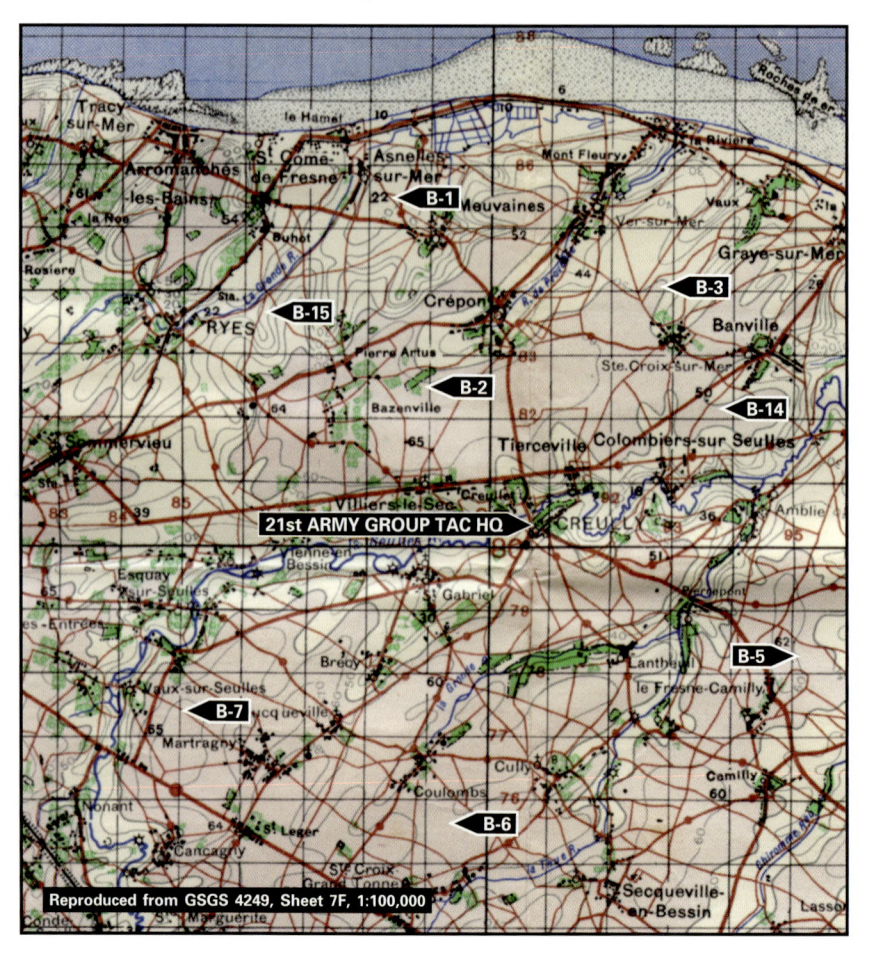

The B-6 memorial which stands in Ste Croix-Grand-Tonne is dedicated not only to the squadrons of No. 124 Wing but is also in remembrance of Squadron Leader (later Air Commodore) Christopher 'Kit' North-Lewis. He had taken over command of No. 181 Squadron in May and on August 15 was promoted to Wing Commander in charge of the wing.

Five Airfield Construction Groups of the Royal Engineers were now in Normandy. No. 16 had been tasked with B-2 at Bazenville and the 3,600ft R&RS there had been completed by D+3 but the RAF did not occupy it immediately as they wanted it upgraded to a 5,000ft tracked runway. No. 24 Group had completed the R&RS at B-3 Ste Croix-sur-Mer by D+4 and worked on developing it to an ALG by D+7. The delayed No. 13 Group were late at Coulombs so the completion of B-6 was behind schedule. No. 23 Group had been sent to Le Fresne-Camilly to build B-5 but this group also landed late and work only began on D+4. No. 25 Group had been earmarked for B-16 at Villons-les-Buissons but, because of enemy activity, had been diverted to B-4 Bény-sur-Mer, completed by D+9. B-6 was due to be finished as a 5,000ft tracked runway by last light on D+7 but, partly due to the group being landed in reverse order with the reconnaissance parties and the Royal Engineers commander being put ashore last, it was not handed over until D+10. (The RAF's Airfield Construction Wings did not build their first airstrip until August when B-19 at Lingèvres became operational.) This photo was taken on August 1, Coulombs being retained until the Mosquitos of No. 264 Squadron departed on September 5.

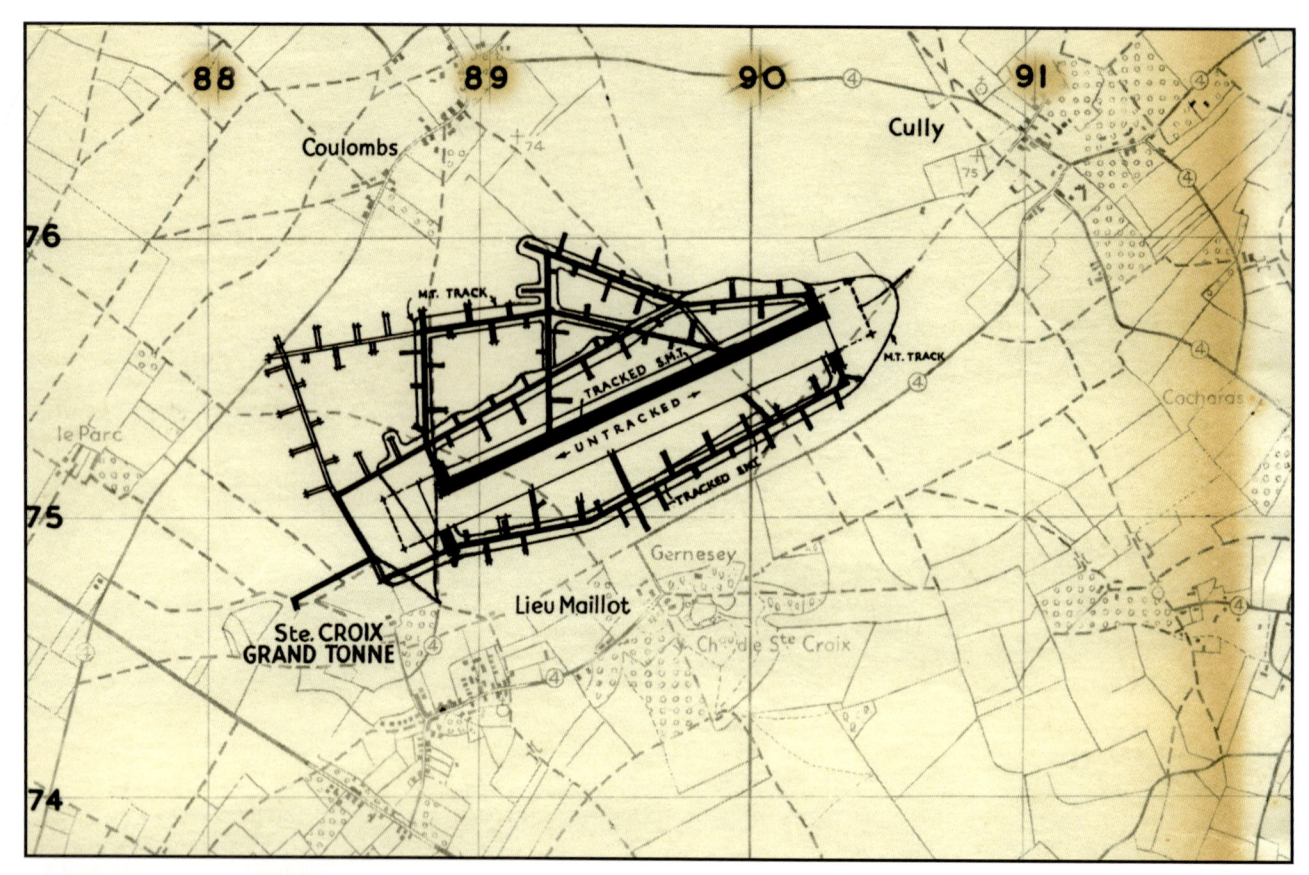

By the end of June, 21st Army Group reported that, excluding the emergency landing strip, ten airfields had been constructed in the British beach-head area and this number had risen to 17 by the end of July (13 of them in the British sector) of which eight had tracked runways and one of bituminised hessian. However, the report is somewhat adrift as there were actually 11 airfields (not 10) operational in the British sector (plus the ELS and nine airfields in the American sector) by the end of June, and by the end of July there were 14 airfields operational in the British sector — not 13 — plus 20 in the American. On the 14 airfields operated by the RAF, the dust problem had generally abated due to the wet weather in July. The years have been kind to B-6 and after the passage of over 70 years, the scars of war have completely disappeared.

Pilot Officer C. E. Benn of No. 182 Squadron pictured beside his Typhoon (JR427) which he brought back to Coulombs with a badly damaged port wing. Intense flak east of Vire smashed a three-foot hole in the wing, put instruments out of commission, and fragments holed the fuselage and canopy, just missing Benn's head. Unfortunately no date is given for this incident.

Although there was no requirement for the commander of a wing to take part in operations, on August 12 Group Captain Charles Appleton, the CO of No. 124 Wing, borrowed this Typhoon (MN928) from No. 247 Squadron to make up the numbers on a late-afternoon patrol from Coulombs. At around 1740, he was hit by ground fire and brought down near Flers.

One significant operation undertaken by the Second Tactical Air Force that had a critical impact on the battle was carried out by No. 124 Wing before they were based in Normandy. On June 9 the code-breakers at Bletchley Park deciphered German signals which indicated that the location of the headquarters of Panzergruppe West was based around the château at La Caine, a hamlet six miles south-east of Villers-Bocage. Although there was always a danger of revealing the fact that Ultra was decoding enemy messages by reacting to the contents, the opportunity to knock out the HQ was too good to miss. On June 10, Mitchells of No. 2 Group based in Britain were over the target at 2119-2121 hours, 61 aircraft dropping over 400 500lb bombs. The crews reported that the area was blanketed by the explosions. Then between 2102 and 2155 hours, 40 Typhoons from the wing attacked with rocket projectiles and guns in three waves. *Left:* This photograph was taken on July 6 but it was not until February 1945 that the Bombing Analysis Unit could investigate the accuracy and effect of the attack. 'Very little structural damage was found in the village, only two buildings being totally destroyed. There was, however, a large amount of blast damage to windows and roofs, and there were signs of considerable fragmentation in many areas. This type of damage is typical of 500lb bombs fused nose instantaneous. The chateau itself had suffered little structurally. Although its windows and roofs were damaged, and its walls heavily pitted by fragments (and possibly also by gun-fire), it was certainly not rendered uninhabitable by the attack. It is not known how many Germans were wounded, but it is certain that 18 of them, including the Chief-of-Staff of the Panzer Group West, were killed. They were buried in a bomb crater in the orchard. The inscription on the grave indicates that the following officers were killed: Generalmajor Ritter und Edler von Dawans; Major i. G. Burgsthaler; Major i. G. von Waldow; Rittmeister Buchheim; Rittmeister Kühl; SS-Hauptsturmführer Beck; Oberleutnant Fugh; Unteroffizier Ziegler. *Right:* La Caine today.

Lieutenant-Colonel Richard Havers, the Commander Royal Engineers (CRE) of No. 23 Airfield Construction Group, explained that 'before entering the concentration area I had visited 121 Airfield Commander and discussed with him in general terms the layout of his airfield. The field was for Typhoon fighter-bombers which are heavier and more stable on the runway than Spitfires, but, when taking off with tail up, there is only six inches ground clearance between the tip of the prop and the ground. Typhoon's do not 'scramble' off the field, but usually take off in pairs so that large marshalling areas at the ends of the runway are not essential. The relative positions of Airfield HQ, Operations and Intelligence and MT maintenance areas, bomb storage areas, etc, are variable according to the desires of each Airfield Commander and, if not agreed in principle beforehand, would certainly have to be adjusted to the satisfaction of the RAF. In the concentration area on June 2, just before embarking, I was fully briefed and given the multiplex map of the area, marked with two possible alignments. Only officers of my recce party and the No. 88 Rd Constr Coy recce party were given the actual airfield site prior to embarkation. My recce party and No. 88 Rd Constr Coy's recce party, who preceded the group, were in different ships but due to arrive together at H+23 hours. They passed peacefully through the Straits of Dover at 1800 hours on D-1 and arrived off Mike Beach on the evening of D-Day. The last two parties to disembark of the total advance party were these two recce parties which landed in different places during the afternoon of D+2. I found Group HQ by a stroke of luck almost at once and went off to contact the commander of I Corps. According to instructions, they should have been at La Délivrande which was found to be in possession of black-faced commandos who had just "cleaned it up". I Corps was found eventually about 800 yards from Group HQ on a parallel road. In the meantime No. 88 Rd Constr Coy's recce party had been to the airfield site, which was occupied by tanks which were expecting an attack at any moment. They were told to keep clear and had not the necessary backing to enable them to get to the site. A proper recce began at first light on D+3 and, after permission from Corps had been obtained, work was started on the morning of D+4, while the laying out of the field was still being done by the No. 88 Rd Constr Coy's recce party with the assistance of the recce party from No. 720 Rd Constr Coy which had since arrived.'

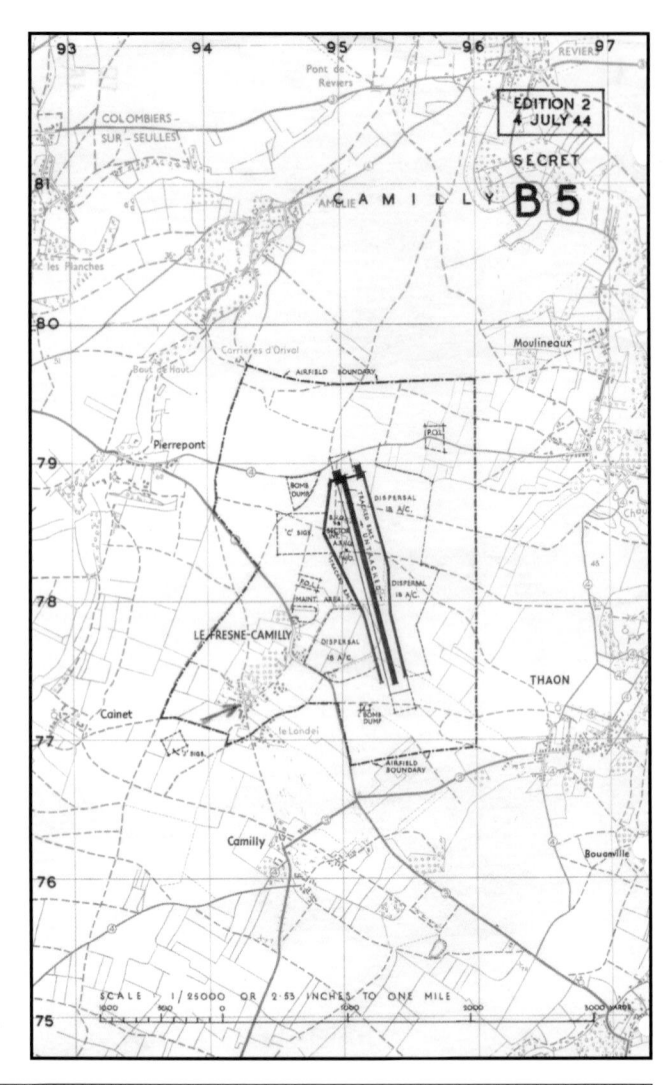

B-5 CAMILLY

OPERATIONAL JUNE 24

Latitude: 49°16'N
Longitude: 00°29'W
Grid reference: T-952782
Altitude: 170ft

Camilly, five miles inland from Courseulles, was scheduled for use by Typhoon fighter-bombers that were much heavier than Spitfires and had only six to nine inches clearance under the tip of the prop and the ground. Thus they needed to operate from a tracked runway.

Landing on the evening of D+2, the Royal Engineer recce party from No. 23 Airfield Construction Group plus No. 88 Road Construction Company found the airfield site occupied by tanks which were expecting an attack at any moment. The first location surveyed was south of Le Fresne-Camilly but this was turned down as a road that was a main advance artery bisected it. Even at the site that was finally chosen, it was thought initially that the lateral road just to the north of the strip might have to be diverted but in the event this proved unnecessary.

Work finally began on D+4 but the lower end of the field was still subjected

To cut or not to cut! Experience at Le Fresne-Camilly showed that it was preferable to roll crops under the tracking rather than cut them as a greater amount of unevenness could be accepted in order to achieve a dust-proof surface. The work at B-5 comprised grubbing out 1,100 yards of hedge; scraping 243,000 square yards; grading 280,000 square yards and rolling 632,000 square yards. For this, the group used four motor graders, four eight-yard scrapers, seven crawlers, six rollers, two blade graders, 16 three-ton tipper lorries, plus other miscellaneous transport. Over 108,000 square yards of SMT was laid at the rate of 90 square feet per man per hour, exclusive of screw picketing. Shelling caused a loss of about 20 working hours filling in over 30 shell-holes and repairing track damaged by shell-fire. This photo was taken at the end of July when wheat was being cleared to enlarge the dispersal area. The Polish Spitfire was from No. 308 Squadron although then still based in Britain at the forward airfield at Ford.

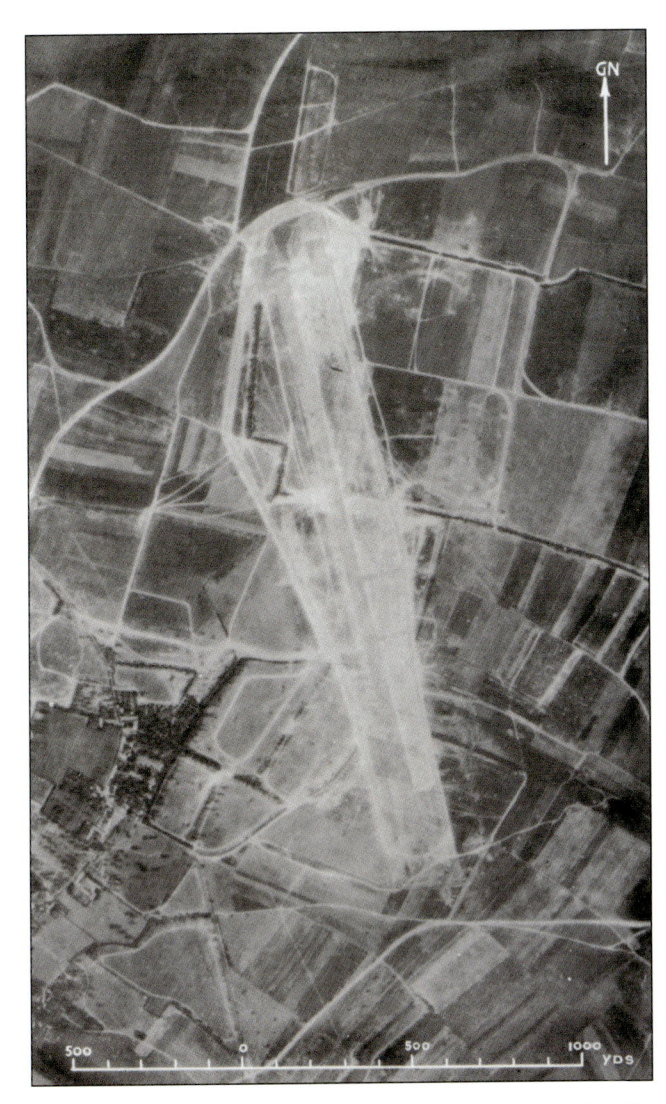

An alternative site crossing the road south of Le Fresne-Camilly was turned down as it would have cut a main advance artery, although it was more into the wind, and the site proposed was approved by the CRE and his RAF adviser. Permission was obtained to divert the lateral road which ran north of the site if necessary but this was found unnecessary in spite of the dip in the ground in front of Flying Control which was graded to the prescribed limits after the removal of the hedge. Initially there was only sufficient SMT available for the runway itself, and the rate of delivery from the beaches prevented the full use of the pioneers and slowed up the progress although it all arrived by the last date in the plan. From D+4 onwards the lower end of the field was subjected to spasmodic 88mm shelling which lost, in all, one and a quarter working days. There were no casualties, except one Mack whose petrol tank was holed by a splinter, and a little damage to the track. Most of the shells fell in the untracked areas. There was considerable misgiving in the group about SMT, which was fairly new to airfields at that time, and much trouble with billowing in front of wheels of landing aircraft had occurred in England. Only a fortnight before the construction, a War Office experiment, carried out by No. 23 Airfield Construction Group and No. 121 RAF Wing, to try and reduce the number of clips and the overlapping of rolls to one square mesh, had proved a failure through excessive billowing.

to spasmodic shelling which delayed completion by over a day. With this airfield it was found that it was better to roll crops rather that cut them as that helped keep the dust down. Initially, there was only enough SMT available for the runway but later tracking arrived to cover the dispersal areas and the 30ft taxiway. B-5, with a tracked 5,000ft runway 120ft wide, was completed at 1820 hours on June 17 (D+11).

First to arrive on June 24 at this exclusively Typhoon base were Nos. 174 and 175 Squadrons of No. 121 Wing, formerly stationed at Holmsley South in Hampshire, with No. 245 joining them three days later. The wing moved forward to B-24 at St André-de-l'Eure on August 28. Other squadrons based at B-5 were No. 198 (July 8-11), No. 609 (July 9-19), and No. 184 (July 16-August 28).

Typhoons usually took off in pairs, these two being from No. 175 Squadron. Meanwhile, armourers work on a machine from No. 245 Squadron in the foreground.

The problem with billowing of the SMT (Typhoons being almost twice as heavy as Spitfires) was only solved by using more securing clips, special screw pickets to pin down the track, and crimping tools to take out waves in the SMT and by stretching the rolls by lorry winch. Also a Thunderbolt belly-landed at Camilly during construction but fortunately without tearing up the tracking that had been laid. The airstrip was passed to the RAF on June 15 as being fit for flying but the first aircraft to land were three Dakotas bringing in more screw pickets. The plan was for them to return with wounded but as soon as the first aircraft touched down, it brought down enemy fire from the 88s. The Dakota kicked up such a cloud of dust that the second machine over-ran and crashed into the first one. Four more touched down safely but further aircraft were turned away to land elsewhere as it was evident that the wounded could not be evacuated from B-5 with any degree of safety. When the Typhoons arrived to the same welcome from the 88s on June 24, they vowed to remove the source of annoyance without delay, but it seemed that as soon as one battery was silenced, another opened up from a different direction.

Top: **Armourers prepare Typhoons of No. 175 Squadron with 3-inch rockets from the armament store** *(above)*, **located off the north-western corner of the airstrip. Lieutenant-Colonel Havers made a special point of collecting data on the achievements of the squadrons using 'his' airfield, and in July alone he recorded 1,365 operational sorties with just under 100 tanks set on fire and over 50 other vehicles destroyed.**

No. 184 Squadron of No. 129 Wing was based at Le Fresne-Camilly (abbreviated to just Camilly) from July 16 to August 28 when they moved, together with the three squadrons of No. 121 Wing, to B-24 at St André-de-l'Eure.

A fine study of an unnamed pilot of No. 175 scrambling to his Typhoon on July 24. Taken by Flying Officer N. S. Clark, one wonders if this was a staged photo for Churchill's visit — see page 43.

The unusual memorial plaque on the right was unveiled on June 10, 1990 by Général Yves Ezanno, the former commanding officer of No. 198 Squadron. It is located beside the D22 which runs on the western perimeter of the airfield boundary, but for some reason, the plan engraved on the plaque is angled with west at the top.

The landscape on the western side of the Normandy battlefield, with many small fields and sunken roads meant suitable sites were limited; also they depended on the advance of the front line. This map, prepared for the official US history, illustrates the progress of the next four American airstrips (after ELS-1 and A-6). Work on A-10 at Carentan had begun on June 15; A-7 at Azeville started June 16; A-8 at Picauville commenced June 20, and A-14 at Crettville began on June 23. Operational dates are given on the map.

The 50th Fighter Group was allocated A-10 and its 313th Fighter Squadron landed with its P-47 on June 24, the other two squadrons — the 10th and 81st — arriving the following day. Lethal Liz II of the latter squadron shares its dispersal with former residents.

A-10 CARENTAN

OPERATIONAL JUNE 24

Latitude: 49°18'N
Longitude: 01°10'W
Grid reference: T-440846
Altitude: 80ft

The failure of the US V Corps (Omaha) and VII Corps (Utah) to link up by D+1 as had been planned was of great concern to the Allied command. The Germans bitterly resisted the capture of Carentan at the base of the Cherbourg peninsula right up to June 12. Even then they mounted a desperate counter-attack on June 13.

The airstrip planned for Carentan was located immediately south of the Route Nationale 13 to Isigny. The latter town had already fallen on the night of June 8/9 so now the 826th Engineer Aviation Battalion could move in (they had been working on A-8 at Picauville). The official date given in the records for the completion of A-10 was July 1 but by that day the 50th Fighter Group had been there for nearly a week as their three P-47 squadrons, the 10th, 81st and 313th, flew over from the UK on June 24-25.

The engineers had laid down a 5,000ft strip, tracked with SMT, and provided 50 tracked dispersals and 25 just of graded earth. Over 20,000 gallons of aviation spirit was on hand in trucks; complete airfield lighting plus searchlights had been installed as well as the usual radio and homing facilities.

The 50th Fighter Group was joined on July 31 by the P-38s Lightnings of the 392nd Fighter Squadron (367th Group) but they switched operations to A-2 at Cricqueville on August 15 and the following day the 50th departed for A-17 at Méautis at which point Carentan had served its purpose and was abandoned.

But that was not the end of the story. In June 2013, the Nerrant family — father Patrick and sons Stéphane and Olivier — opened the Normandy Tank Museum on the western end of A-10, even going so far as to restore part of the original runway. It was a unique creation that recorded and remembered the part played by both armour and aviation in the battle of Normandy but sadly the museum was forced to close in September 2016.

Carentan is unique amongst the invasion airfields due to the fact that it was also the location of the Normandy Tank Museum where over 40 vehicles, aircraft and thousands of artefacts from the Second World War were displayed. Opened in June 2013 by Patrick Nerrant and his two sons Stéphane and Olivier, the museum was the culmination of 35 years spent assembling exhibits. It was also fortunate that it had part of the old runway and five acres of land available for outdoor demonstrations. So one can understand how Patrick was dismayed in April 2015 to find that the farmer had ploughed up the strip, so preventing him from flying his Piper Cub and Boeing Stearman for the commemorations for the anniversary of D-Day that year.

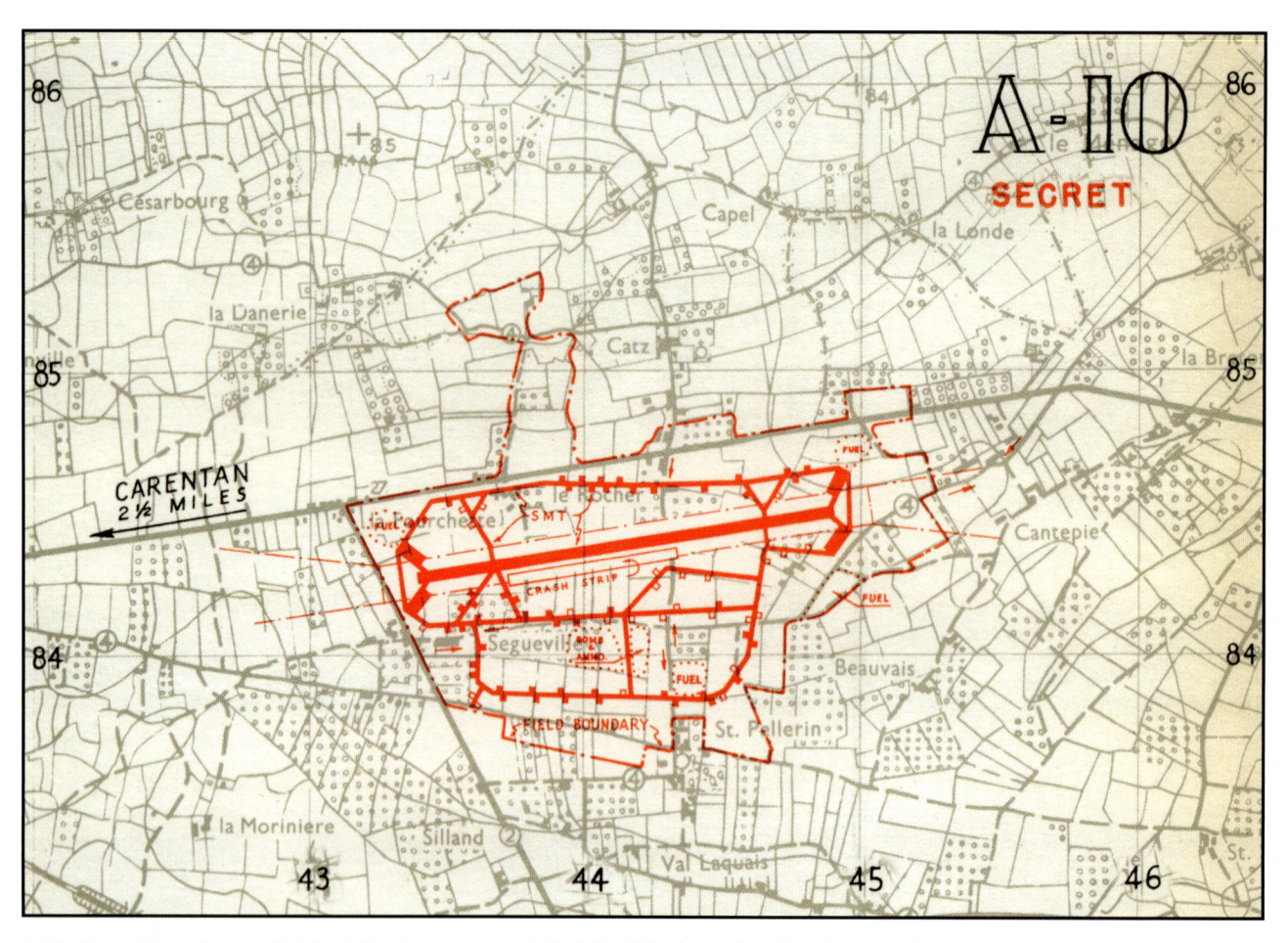

A-10: the outline plan and finished airstrip, courtesy of the 942nd Engineer Aviation Topographical Battalion. Photo taken in July.

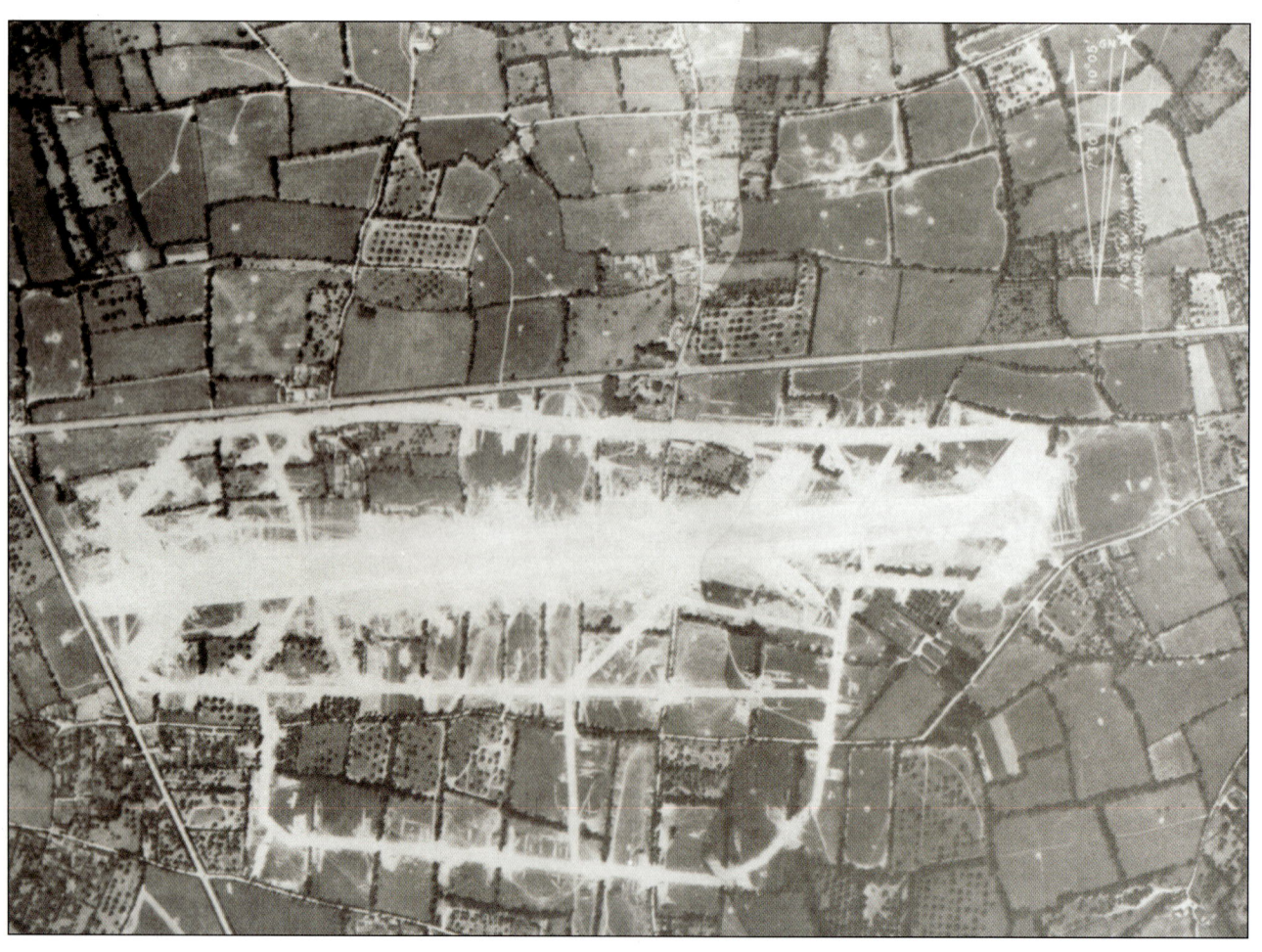

The old Route Nationale 13 has now been bypassed with a new carriageway that completely bisects the A-10 airstrip.

Over 10,000 Stearmans were built by Boeing to serve as the primary trainer for both the United States Army Air Forces and the US Navy. Here Patrick makes a low pass in his machine along the old A-10 airstrip at Carentan. Sadly he was forced to close the museum in September 2016 and disperse all the exhibits. The memorial lies on the line of the old runway.

B-7 MARTRAGNY

OPERATIONAL JUNE 25

Latitude: 49°16'N
Longitude: 00°37'W
Grid reference: T-850777
Altitude: 220ft

Four miles east of Bayeux lay the former French airfield at Martragny, taken by the 56th Brigade of the 50th (Northumbrian) Division from Gold Beach on June 7. The aerodrome was grass but by June 25 a 3,600ft runway had been laid down by No. 16 Airfield Construction Group together with taxi-track and marshalling areas for 54 aircraft, surfaced with SMT.

On D-Day, the Allied Expeditionary Air Forces comprised over 6,600 aircraft composed of ten basic types with a large number of varying marks. Leigh-Mallory complimented the maintenance personnel who managed to keep the aircraft operational, particularly during June and July when most of the squadrons were based on the newly-made airstrips. The dust problem alone was deemed worse than North Africa by participants in that theatre. In July the fuel consumption by the AEAF reached 30 million gallons, almost a million gallons per day. They were also expending 750 tons of bombs and 200,000 rounds of ammunition daily.

Flight Lieutenant Ray Lallemant was a flight commander with No. 198 Squadron, later becoming CO of No. 609. The Typhoons had arrived at Martragny ten days earlier after the Mustang wing had moved out.

The three squadrons of No. 122 Wing flew in from Funtington which was one of the most successful of the temporary advanced landing grounds built in Sussex. Equipped with the North American Mustang III, Nos. 19, 65 and 122 Squadrons left via Ford on June 15 in preparation for the move to the Continent as soon as

Here a Mustang of No. 122 Squadron is being bombed up with a 500-pounder.

No. 16 Airfield Construction Group, Order No. 3: 'HQ 16 Air Con Gp, 609 Rd Con Coy RE and 231 Coy Pnr Corps will move to MARTRAGNY 8676 on June 13 to commence work on MARTRAGNY airfield. HQ will move by MT and march route not before 1000 hrs on route CREUILLY, St GABRIEL 8879, VAUSSIEUX 8478. 609 Rd Con Coy MT convoy will move by same route not before 1100 hrs. 609 Rd Con Coy Mech Eqpt will move on the route CREPON 8983, BAYEUX 7879 and on the BAYEUX-CAEN rd not before 1100 hrs. 231 Coy Pnr Corps will move by march route not before 1300 hrs.' The No. 13 ACG War Diary takes up the story:

'June 14: Work commenced on single strip 3600' long at MARTRAGNY.

June 19: Work stopped at 1200 hrs due to inclement weather prohibiting use of plant on site.

June 20: Progress impeded due to plant being unable to operate on wet site.

June 22: R&RS available 1200 hrs.

June 24: ALG completed 2230 hrs, fully tracked.

June 25: Squadrons landed on strip 0730 hrs.'

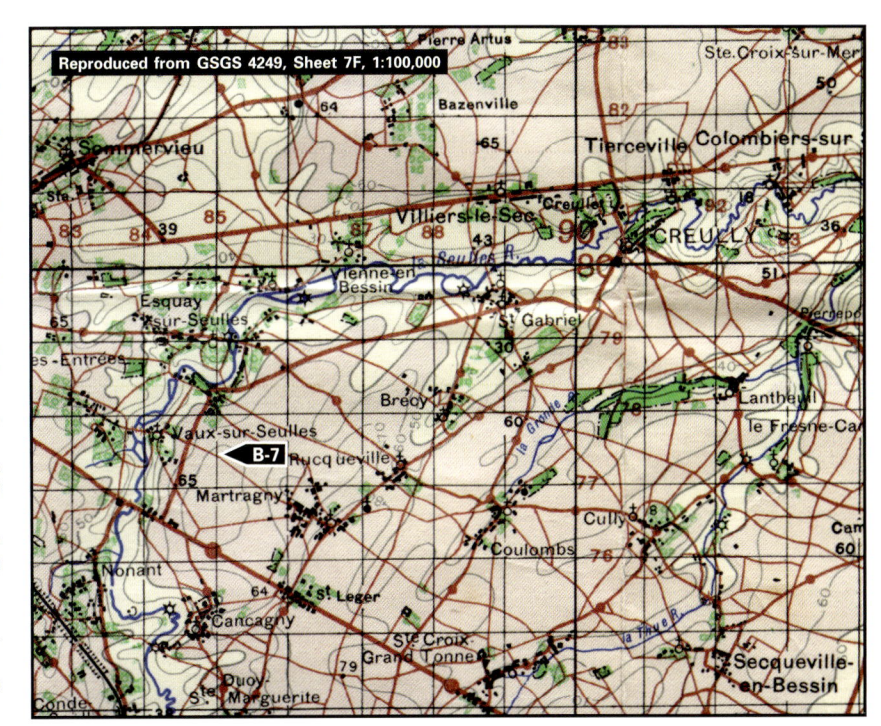

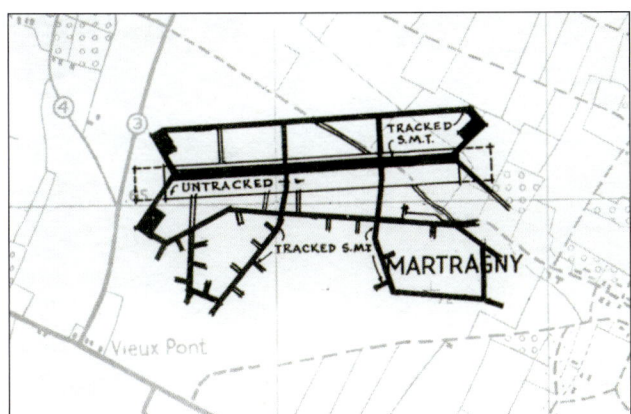

Gone as if it had never existed . . . the airstrip at Martragny . . . but the exploits and sacrifices of its pilots have not been forgotten.

Between June and September three wings operated from B-7 comprising seven squadrons but it was not until 1987 that one of the pilots felt that something should be done to remember those lost in the air battles over Normandy. So Denis Sweeting (right) compiled a list of all the 274 Typhoons lost in which 151 pilots had perished. With Denis at the Martragny memorial are George Hardy, and George Lane who was shot down near Vimoutiers on August 19.

Martragny was finished. They flew in on June 25-26, moving out on July 15-17 to B-12 at Ellon.

They were replaced by the Typhoon IBs of Nos. 123 and 136 Wings. No. 198 Squadron came from B-10 at Plumetot and No. 609 from B-5 at Camilly on July 19; No. 164 from B-8 Sommervieu on July 20 while No. 183 joined them direct from Eastchurch in Kent five days later. All carried out 'cab-rank' standing patrols over the battlefield until they all left Martragny on September 3 bound for B-23 at La Rue Huguenot (also referred to as Morainville).

There are today three memorials marking the site of the airfield.

Denis broached the idea for a Typhoon memorial with the former CO of No. 198 Squadron, Général Yves Ezanno. He gave the proposal his blessing and Jacques Bréhin, President of the Association pour le Souvenir des Ailes de la Victoire de Normandie, brought the project to a successful conclusion. It was unveiled at Noyers-Bocage (on the N175 from Caen to Villers-Bocage) on June 9, 1990 by Général Ezanno (above) and the local Mayor (see *After the Battle* No. 69). The Martragny Memorial at the top of the page has since been relocated and a second memorial added to all the RAF airfields in Normandy (see page 224).

TYPHOON PILOTS KILLED IN THE BATTLE FOR NORMANDY: MAY–AUGUST 1944

No. 124 Wing
G/Capt. C. H. Appleton
DSO, DFC — 12.08.44

No. 136 Wing
Wing Cmdr J. M. Bryan
DFC and Bar — 10.06.44

No. 146 Wing
Wing Cmdr E. R. Baker DFC — 17.06.44

No. 137 Squadron
F/O I. C. Hutcheson — 27.08.44
F/Lt M. Wood — 18.08.44

No. 164 Squadron
F/Sgt G. M. Fisher — 06.07.44
F/Sgt G. D. Fowell — 06.07.44
F/Lt A. E. Napier DFC — 14.08.44
F/O A. E. Roberts — 06.06.44
F/O G. R. Trafford — 25.08.44
F/Sgt R. A. E. White — 25.08.44

No. 174 Squadron
P/O E. G. Boucher — 05.08.44
F/Lt F. A. Grantham DFC — 14.08.44
F/Lt L. McNeill — 12.06.44
F/Sgt H. J. Somerville — 29.07.44
F/Sgt E. W. J. Taylor — 10.08.44
F/O W. C. Vatcher DFC — 26.07.44

No. 175 Squadron
F/O J. M. Cowie — 30.05.44
F/Sgt R. C. Dale — 09.07.44
P/O S. S. Finlayson — 21.05.44
W/O K. M. Hopley — 30.07.44
P/O O. D. Leitch — 15.06.44
F/O P. S. G. Moran — 14.08.44
W/O J. H. Pugh — 05.06.44

No. 181 Squadron
W/O R. D. Gilbert — 19.08.44
F/Sgt G. J. Howard — 06.06.44
F/Lt G. J. Jones — 16.06.44
P/O G. E. Rendle — 07.06.44

No. 182 Squadron
F/Lt A. J. Hay — 18.08.44
Lt H. G. Jennings — 19.08.44
F/O W. J. Kasubeck — 09.08.44
Capt. G. H. Kaufman DFC — 18.07.44
W/O H. C. B. Talalla — 29.07.44

No. 183 Squadron
F/O R. D. Ackers — 18.08.44
F/Lt G. C. Campbell-Brown — 17.08.44
F/Lt H. W. Evans — 06.06.44
F/O M. H. Gee — 06.06.44
P/O G. F. Humphrey — 17.08.44
S/Ldr The Hon. F. H. L. Scarlett — 12.07.44
F/Sgt T. W. Stokoe — 01.08.44
F/O A. R. Taylor — 06.06.44
W/O W. F. Tollworthy — 09.08.44
F/O J. Ralph — 23.05.44

No. 184 Squadron
F/O R. J. Currie — 18.08.44
F/Lt D. H. Gross — 18.08.44
F/Lt H. M. LaFlamme — 30.07.44
W/O G. C. Polkey — 25.05.44
F/Sgt J. J. Rowland — 07.06.44

No. 193 Squadron
F/Sgt K. G. Hodnett — 25.06.44
F/O J. A. Inglis — 12.06.44
W/O J. MacCartney — 10.08.44
S/Ldr D. G. Ross DFC — 05.06.44

No. 197 Squadron
F/Lt L. S. Bell — 18.08.44
P/O L. S. Clark — 05.07.44
F/O H. W. Coles — 24.05.44
F/O D. E. F. Potter — 07.06.44
F/Sgt D. J. A. W. Price — 17.08.44
F/Sgt M. C. Richards — 13.06.44
P/O J. Watson — 17.06.44

No. 198 Squadron
F/Sgt E. L. Bartley — 15.06.44
F/Sgt P. S. Barton — 23.06.44
F/Sgt F. Bonnet — 19.08.44
F/Lt J. G. Champion — 31.07.44
P/O R. Crouch — 14.06.44
S/Ldr I. J. Davies DFC — 22.06.44
P/O J. S. Fraser-Petherbridge — 20.06.44
F/O H. Freeman — 24.05.44
F/O J. T. N. Frost — 20.08.44
P/O D. W. Mason — 18.06.44
F/Sgt J. Milne — 08.06.44
S/Ldr J. Niblett DFC — 02.06.44
W/O G. J. Stokes — 07.06.44
W/O C. E. Stratford — 22.08.44
F/Sgt R. A. Thursby — 09.08.44
P/O E. Vallely — 24.05.44

No. 245 Squadron
S/Ldr J. H. Collins DFC — 11.08.44
Lt W. A. Gale — 17.08.44
F/Lt L. J. Greenhalgh — 07.06.44
Sgt D. J. Lush — 02.06.44
F/Lt A. E. Miron — 17.08.44
F/Lt W. E. Reynolds — 13.07.44
F/Sgt L. A. Ryan — 18.08.44
F/O R. E. Temple — 07.08.44

No. 247 Squadron
F/Lt W. F. Anderson — 20.06.44
W/O D. L. Burke — 15.07.44
F/O A. E. Diggins — 18.08.44
F/Lt R. Guthrie — 18.08.44
P/O R. B. Hemmings — 08.08.44
F/Sgt L. B. Morgan — 25.07.44
F/Sgt G. C. Robinson — 15.07.44
Sgt S. R. Ryen — 18.07.44

No. 257 Squadron
S/Ldr W. C. Ahrens — 16.07.44
F/Sgt R. R. Blair — 06.06.44
S/Ldr R. H. Fokes DFC, DFM — 12.06.44
P/O G. Turton — 22.06.44
F/Lt J. F. Williams DFC — 26.07.44

No. 263 Squadron
F/Lt P. M. Bell — 18.08.44
F/O A. W. Campbell — 25.08.44
F/Sgt J. Charlton — 24.06.44
S/Ldr H. A. C. Gonay — 14.06.44
F/O W. W. Heaton — 09.06.44
F/O J. A. Hodgson — 07.07.44
F/O L. Parent — 07.06.44
F/Lt H. M. Proctor DFC — 24.08.44
W/O A. J. Ryan — 24.06.44
P/O S. D. Thyagarajan — 25.08.44

No. 266 Squadron
P/O I. H. Forrester — 28.07.44
F/Sgt J. C. Harrold — 19.07.44
F/Sgt W. R. Love — 17.08.44
F/Sgt R. McElroy — 19.07.44
P/O J. H. Meyer — 19.07.44
F/Lt R. W. Nesbitt — 12.06.44
F/Sgt A. O. Holland — 19.05.44

No. 438 Squadron
F/Lt T. A. Bugg — 12.08.44
F/Lt R. M. McKenzie — 18.07.44
F/O D. K. Moores — 03.08.44
F/O W. H. Morrison — 15.08.44
F/Lt L. E. Park — 27.06.44
F/O G. H. Sharpe — 18.08.44

No. 439 Squadron
F/O E. J. Allen — 12.08.44
F/O J. Kalen — 18.07.44
F/O R. O. Moen — 12.08.44
F/O R. A. Porrit — 19.08.44
F/Lt J. W. Saville — 05.06.44
F/Lt W. K. Scharff — 19.08.44
F/O F. M. Thomas — 08.07.44

No. 440 Squadron
F/O L. R. Allman — 06.06.44
F/O J. S. Colville — 18.08.44
F/O J. F. Dewar — 12.08.44
F/O S. V. Garside — 07.06.44
F/Lt J. G. Gohe — 12.06.44
F/Lt G. W. Hicks — 08.08.44
F/O J. Lippert — 30.07.44
W/O C. J. McConvey — 16.07.44
F/O R. B. M. McCurdy — 13.08.44
F/O W. J. Mahagan — 07.06.44

No. 609 Squadron
P/O R. K. Adam — 31.07.44
F/Sgt R. Ashworth — 29.07.44
F/Sgt L. E. Bliss — 11.07.44
P/O J. D. Buchanan — 27.07.44
F/Lt M. L. Carrick — 18.08.44
F/Sgt L. P. Fidgin — 13.05.44
F/O R. H. Holmes — 27.06.44
P/O P. M. Price — 27.07.44
F/Lt R. J. H. Roelandt — 26.08.44
F/O G. A. Rowland — 29.06.44
F/O D. L. Soesman — 11.05.44
P/O J. K. Stellin — 19.08.44
W/O F. L. Taylor — 15.08.44
F/Lt R. L. Wood — 11.05.44

In September 1984, Jacques Bréhin was instrumental in the recovery of the remains of Flight Sergeant Reg Thursby from his crash site at Ste Marguerite-de-Viette (see *After the Battle* No. 51). He has also found a number of other Typhoon crashes: MN125 of Flight Lieutenant Peter Roper of No. 198 Squadron who baled out wounded at Monts-en-Bessin; Typhoon MN667 which was being flown by Flight Lieutenant Frank Holland of No. 184 Squadron. He was shot down at Croissanville but survived and escaped. Also MP137 (Flight Lieutenant Arthur Miron killed) of No. 245 Squadron at Hôtels-Sainte-Bazille; JP656 (Flight Sergeant John Rowland killed) from No. 184 Squadron at Biéville-Quétiéville; MN464 (Flying Officer Frank Thomas killed) of No. 439 Squadron at Vienne-en-Bessin; and MN809 (Flight Lieutenant William Anderson killed) of No. 247 Squadron near Cheux.

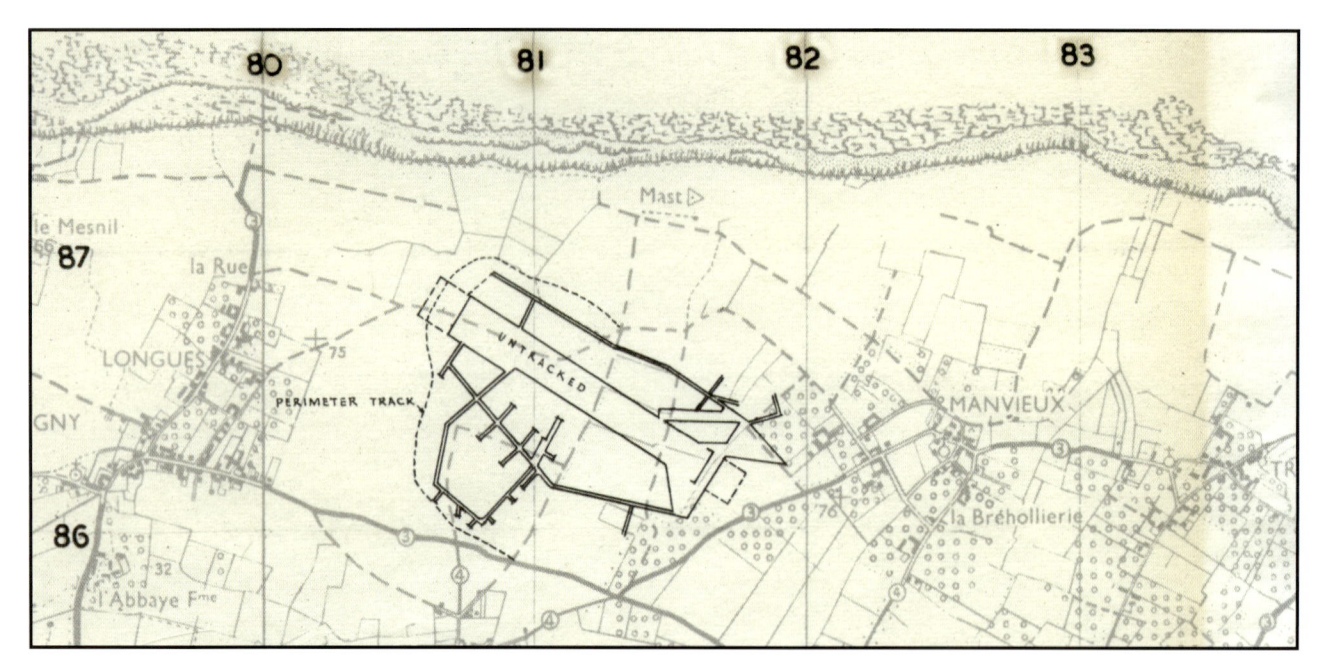

B-11 LONGUES

OPERATIONAL JUNE 25

Latitude: 49°20'N
Longitude: 00°41'W
Grid reference: T-810862
Altitude: 180ft

A fighter strip, 3,600ft by 240ft angled NW-SE had been planned for a cliff-top site half a mile inland at Longues-sur-Mer, some 4½ miles north of Bayeux. However the Germans had built a four-gun battery nearby which had survived the pre-landing bombardment and at 0555 hours it opened fire on the ships off Gold Area. The *Bulolo* replied, silencing it for a time, but it came to life again later, being then engaged and put out of action by *Ajax* and *Argonaut*. The battery was finally captured by C Company of the 1st Hampshires (231st Brigade, 50th (Northumbrian) Division) on D+1.

The site for B-11 on the cliffs at Longues-sur-Mer was initially surveyed by No. 24 Airfield Construction Group on June 10 and a strip selected on a bearing of 293 degrees magnetic but, owing to the balloon barrage being flown around Arromanches some two miles to the east, a recce party from No. 720 Road Construction Company was briefed to instead select a strip with a bearing of not less than 310 magnetic. This was carried out on June 18 and work commenced at 0600 hours on June 20.

Here on August 5, Squadron Leader Tommy Brannagan, the CO of the Canadian No. 441 Squadron, undertakes a little target practice on the clifftop.

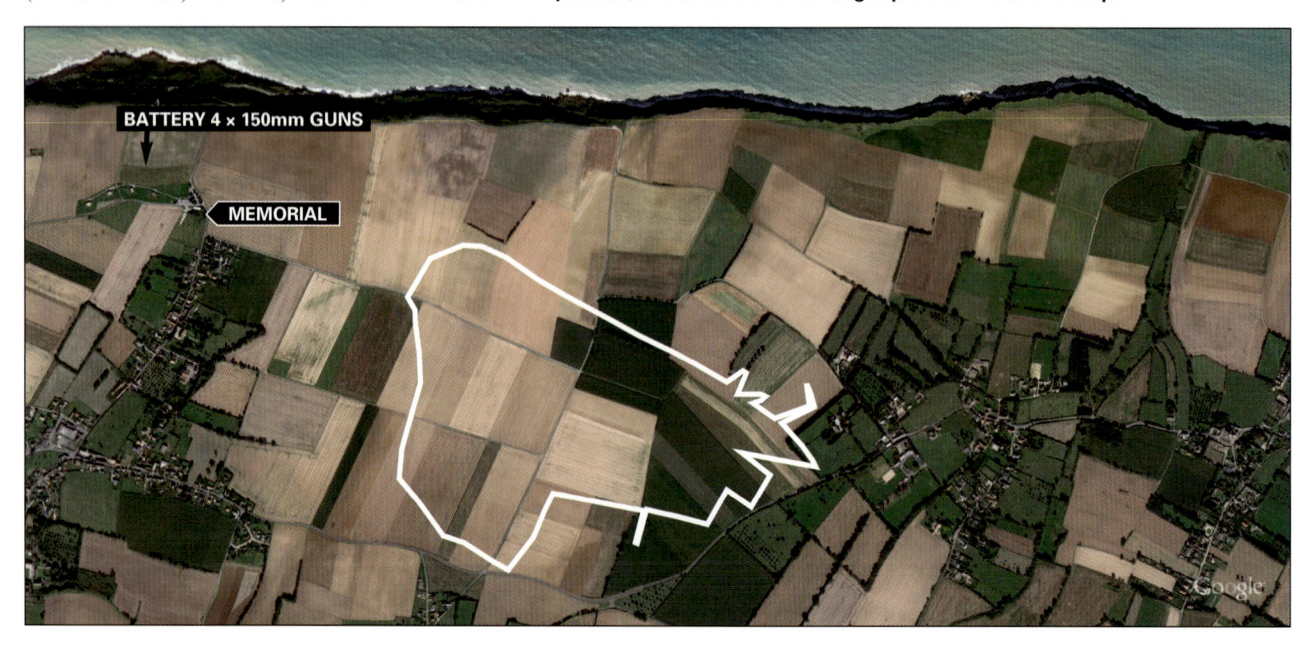

Most of the crops were cut by local labour while the airfield was being set out. Anti-landing posts had to be removed and the area checked for mines before work could begin. Working in two shifts (0600 to 1400 and 1400 to 2200), over a quarter of a milllion square yards had to be graded and levelled. Hedge clearance totalled 1,500 yards and 400 tons of hardcore was brought in to infil 700 cubic yards of ditches. The first aircraft landed at 1530 hours on June 25 and by 2000 hours B-11 was occupied by three squadrons. It was officially handed over to No. 125 Wing at 1700 hours on June 26. Here the wing commander, Geoffrey Page, is pictured about to take off on a sortie. His Spitfire is armed with a 250lb bomb under each wing and a 500lb below the fuselage.

The airfield was completed by No. 23 Airfield Construction Group on June 21 and occupied by the Spitfire IXs of No. 125 Wing on the 25th. Its three squadrons — Nos. 132, 453 (RAAF) and 602 — had been previously operating over the battlefield from Ford in Sussex. On July 17, the CO of No. 602, Squadron Leader 'Chris' Le Roux, was leading 12 aircraft on an armed recce patrol, shooting up transport. In the Operations Record Book he is credited with a claim for a motor cyclist and staff car and it was believed that he was responsible for having put Generalfeldmarschall Erwin Rommel out of action. The German's car crashed off the road south of Livarot (see *After the Battle* No. 8).

The wing departed for B-19 at Lingèvres on August 13. No. 441 (RCAF) Squadron from No. 144 Wing was also based at B-11 from July 15 to August 13 when they also moved to B-19.

The airfield memorial lies 300 yards to the west, and specifically mentions three French pilots of No. 602 Squadron: Capitaine Pierre Aubertin; and Sous-Lieutenants Pierre Clostermann and Jacques Remlinger. The latter is also credited with the attack on Rommel.

In this picture, Australian pilots from No. 453 Squadron use a Jeep to pull a roller, weighed down with two 500-pounders, to help flatten imperfections on the strip. Aircraft control is being handled from the checkerboard sentry box.

Longues appeared to attract VIPs. On August 5, Marshal of the Royal Air Force Lord Trenchard (with the cane) — the first officer to hold that rank — was pictured chatting with members of No. 441 Squadron. His role was that of an unofficial 'Inspector-General' for the RAF. Air Vice-Marshal Harry Broadhurst, the AOC-in-C, stands with his hand on the muzzle of the cannon.

Broadhurst flew in with the Chief of the Air Staff, Marshal of the RAF Sir Charles Portal, in his Storch. We saw it earlier on page 43.

Longues had two other claims to fame when B-11 became the home of No. 602 Squadron with its famed French aviator, Sous-Lieutenant Pierre Clostermann. He is seen here congratulating Flight Lieutenant Ken Charney after their return from an evening sortie on which they both claimed an FW 190. Clostermann's autobiography *Le Grand Cirque* was published in English as *The Big Show* in 1951.

Also his commanding officer, South African Chris Le Roux, flying from Longues, was credited by the official RAF historian for incapacitating Generalfeldmarschal Erwin Rommel on July 17 by shooting up his staff car on the road from Livarot to Vimoutiers (see *After the Battle* No. 8.) Six weeks later Le Roux went missing over the Channel when he took off in bad weather to fly to England to collect beer for his unit.

The memorial to the squadrons that operated from B-11 is now rather overshadowed by the tourist office alongside to cater for visitors to the nearby gun battery. It includes the names of the three French pilots of No. 602 Squadron. In post-war years there has been much speculation over the attribution of the attack on Rommel to Le Roux — even Jacques Remlinger being named as the pilot responsible at one stage. Then in 2003 a Canadian artist produced a painting depicting Charley Fox, a Canadian Flight Lieutenant with No. 412 Squadron, based at B-4 at Bény-sur-Mer, carrying out the attack. A thorough examination of the claim by the Tangmere Aviation Museum, including detailed analysis of the timing of the attack, appears to prove beyond reasonable doubt that Fox and his wingman Edward Prizer were at the correct place at the correct time.

85

B-10 PLUMETOT

OPERATIONAL JUNE 27

Latitude: 49°17'N
Longitude: 00°22'W
Grid reference: U-033785
Altitude: 173ft

With work continuing on B-4 at Bény, orders were given to No. 25 Airfield Construction Group to reconnoitre a site for a second ALG (a 3,600ft fighter strip) at Plumetot, 1½ miles south-east of Douvres-la-Délivrande. The site was covered in growing corn but the main difficulty was to obtain an area clear of troops as Lieutenant-Colonel George Clark, the CRE 25 ACG, explains: 'In the congestion which existed at that time in that part of the beach-head, it appeared difficult to convince other people that an airfield really did require the space it does. Supply points and medical units littered the ground and it was only after much argument, some of it regrettably acrimonious, that we were able to get on with the job.'

Another problem was that the German radar station to the north-west, which was a D-Day objective, had still not been silenced, and it was only with the liquidation of that position on June 17 — and the completion of the strip at Bény — that work could begin. However, Plumetot was still under observation from a factory at Colombelles and intermittent shelling caused some casualties.

It was the proximity of the German radar station-cum-strongpoint named Hindenburg at Douvres-la-Délivrande that delayed the commencement of B-10 at Plumetot. The garrison did not surrender until June 17.

The plan was to construct the earth runway first for one wing of fighters (completed June 25) and then add an all-weather strip covered with PBS (Prefabricated Bituminous Surfacing) alongside. This was not completed until July 8. The CRE commented that he was surprised that once Typhoons started to operate from Plumetot he could not understand why the Germans did not take advantage and shell the field more vigorously.

Clearing B-10 of mines was still in progress when the Typhoons of No. 198 Squadron arrived on July 11.

No. 25 Airfield Construction Group under Lieutenant-Colonel George Clark was composed of Nos. 64 and 681 Road Construction Companies and Nos. 214 and 217 Companies of the Pioneer Corps. They were briefed to lay down a 1,200-yard ALG for a fighter wing at Villons-les-Buissons but when that site was found still to be in the hands of the enemy, the group was transferred to Bény (see page 58). Their next task was to build an ALG of 1,200 yards near Plumetot to become airfield B-10. The site comprised excellent farmland and once the earth strip had been completed, the unit were to lay down an all-weather strip surfaced with PBS. The weather delayed completion of the ALG until D+15, the PBS strip not being ready until D+32.

As work continues laying the PBS for the all-weather runway, a Typhoon of No. 198 Squadron takes off from the adjacent earth strip.

B-10 hosted both Czech and Polish squadrons but unfortunately there does not appear to be any photographs of the Czech Spitfires in Normandy as they only spent one day at Plumetot at the end of June. Here a machine of No. 312 Squadron (code DU) is pictured at their UK base at Tangmere.

B-10 became a very active base. First to arrive long before it was completed were the AOP Austers of No. 652 Squadron on June 7; they remained until July 8. The initial fighters were the Spitfire XIs of No. 4 Squadron and the Typhoons of No. 184, both landing at Plumetot on June 27. They lost no time in retaliating against the positions that had been shelling the strip. The latter left for B-5 Camilly on July 16 and the Spits for Bény B-4 on August 16.

The Czech Spitfire IXs of No. 134 Wing (Nos. 310, 312 and 313 Squadrons) came for a flying visit on June 28-29 before returning to Tangmere. From July 1-9, No. 609 Squadron was in residence before they moved their Typhoons to B-5, and No. 198 replaced them on July 11 until they transferred to B-7 at Martragny on the 19th.

From July 29 to August 14 the Mustangs of No. 2 Squadron moved in, joined on August 4 by the Polish Spitfires of Nos. 302, 308 and 317 (No. 131 Wing). They stayed until September when the latter two went to B-31 at Fresnoy while No. 302 flew back to the UK. Finally, the Typhoons of No. 268 Squadron had a brief stay from August 10-13 before switching to Bény, and No. 33 Squadron spent an overnight stop in Normandy on August 19-20 with their Spitfire LF IXEs.

Above: **The Poles are well represented at Plumetot with this Spitfire IX of No. 302 Squadron (code WX) and that** *(below)* **of No. 317 Squadron (JH).**

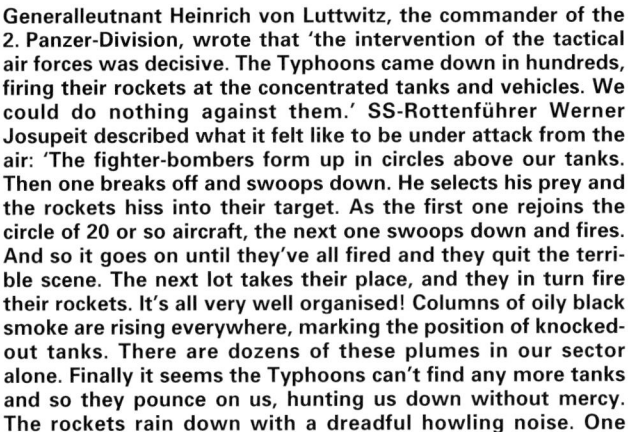

Generalleutnant Heinrich von Luttwitz, the commander of the 2. Panzer-Division, wrote that 'the intervention of the tactical air forces was decisive. The Typhoons came down in hundreds, firing their rockets at the concentrated tanks and vehicles. We could do nothing against them.' SS-Rottenführer Werner Josupeit described what it felt like to be under attack from the air: 'The fighter-bombers form up in circles above our tanks. Then one breaks off and swoops down. He selects his prey and the rockets hiss into their target. As the first one rejoins the circle of 20 or so aircraft, the next one swoops down and fires. And so it goes on until they've all fired and they quit the terrible scene. The next lot takes their place, and they in turn fire their rockets. It's all very well organised! Columns of oily black smoke are rising everywhere, marking the position of knocked-out tanks. There are dozens of these plumes in our sector alone. Finally it seems the Typhoons can't find any more tanks and so they pounce on us, hunting us down without mercy. The rockets rain down with a dreadful howling noise. One lands right next to a comrade. But he's not injured. Fortunately the rockets fragment into a few large splinters and so there's a chance you won't get hit.' In an analysis of destroyed tanks in Operation 'Goodwood' (July 18-21), the Second Tactical Air Force claimed 257 tanks destroyed, 222 by Typhoon pilots using rockets, but investigation by the Operational Research Section after the battle confirmed only ten of the 456 knocked-out AFVs were attributable to Typhoons using rocket projectiles. Similarly, the German counter-attack at Mortain, on August 7, which was attacked by both the Second TAF and Ninth Air Force, led to claims of 252 tanks destroyed but of the 177 Panzers and assault guns that took part in the battle, only 46 were lost, of which nine were verified as being hit by rockets from Typhoons — some four per cent of the total claimed. However spectacular on film, the figures illustrate the limitations of Allied air-to-ground weapons against heavy armour. Nevertheless, those facing aircraft repeatedly mounting 'cab-rank' attacks were extremely demoralised.

One interesting comment in the War Diary of No. 25 Airfield Construction Group for June 24 was the appearance of a low-flying German aircraft (type not given): 'Everything in the neighbourhood opened up but no hostile action by the aircraft.' Then, during the heavy bombing of Caen on July 7 in preparation for the assault on the city, one of the Lancasters was hit by flak and belly-landed on the strip, fortunately without damaging the runway. As the PBS was still being laid, one presumes that the plane landed on the earth strip. Laying PBS was still reported to be continuing on July 13. On July 22 a flying bomb passed over Plumetot at 1,000 feet, flying south, so obviously it must have been a rogue V1 with a mind of its own. In this picture, an Allied convoy is passing B-10 as it moves south along the main road to Caen.

B-9 LANTHEUIL

OPERATIONAL JUNE 27

Latitude: 49°16'N
Longitude: 00°32'W
Grid reference: T-905786
Altitude: 157ft

General Sir Bernard Montgomery, the commander of the Allied land forces, came ashore in France on Mike Beach in Juno Area at 8.45 a.m. on D+2. The headquarters for 21st Army Group was located just over four miles inland in the park of the Château de Creullet at Creully and the airstrip of Lantheuil was constructed by No. 13 Airfield Construction Group of the Royal Engineers just a mile to the south.

A runway — 3,600ft by 120ft — had been laid down by June 22, the Typhoons of Canadian No. 143 Wing arriving five days later. On July 5 an order to track the runway was given, the work being carried out from July 6-8. The three squadrons, Nos. 438, 439 and 440, departed for B-24 at St André-de-l'Eure on August 31.

Also from June 23 into July Lantheuil was the base for the Austers of No. 659 (AOP) Squadron.

No. 13 Airfield Construction Group had the joint task of constructing B-6 at Coulombs (see page 66) and B-9 at Lantheuil. The latter site lay between the village of that name and the larger town of Creully where General Montgomery had set up his Tactical HQ in the château grounds on June 8.

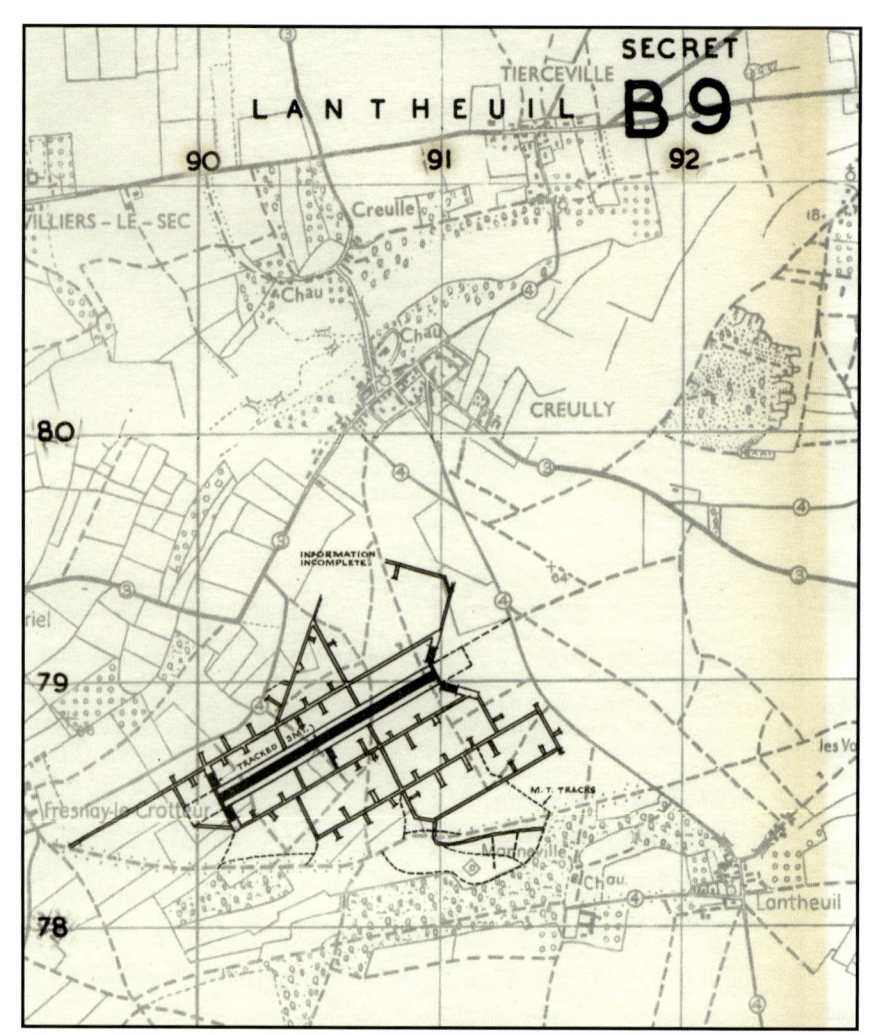

Three days later No. 13 Airfield Construction Group sent a recce party to see if the site would be suitable for a three-squadron airstrip.

By the evening of June 11 the airstrip had been marked out ready for construction to begin the following day. With the labour force split between B-6 and B-9, on the 13th the crops were being cut and cleared and trees removed where necessary. Work then began harrowing and grading and, for some unexplained reason but most probably to try to eliminate the dust problem, 84,000 square yards were sown with grass seed. Tracking the runway involved laying SMT, 18 rolls wide, over 1,200 yards plus four assembly areas which required a total of 1,034 rolls of tracking weighing 258 tons. Stores were unloaded at 25-yard intervals together with clips and pickets. Four parties, each of 66 men, were to begin at zero, 300, 600 and 900-yard intervals laying the SMT, first putting down a central pilot strip to act as a guide. As time was of the essence, all available officers from No. 653 Road Construction Company and from Nos. 164 and 222 Companies of the Pioneer Corps, were present because with a rushed job, the commander of No. 13 ACG deemed officer supervision absolutely necessary. Track-laying began at 0500 hours on July 7 and was completed by 2300 hours. An inspection and crimping party had the track ready for flying by 0745 hours on July 8 — a really remarkable achievement. And, as the unit report states, only 2½ hours time had been lost: 30 minutes each for breakfast and tea, an hour for dinner, plus half an hour for watching a raid on Caen!

Flight Lieutenant N. Gordon of No. 440 Squadron had to make a wheels-up landing at Lantheuil on August 1. This photograph shows his Typhoon being wheeled rather ignominiously from the field of battle.

Difficult to believe but a salvage crew spent a risky day near the front line recovering a Typhoon wreck from which the monocoque could be mated with another aircraft that had been badly damaged by flak. 'F3' denotes a machine from No. 438 Squadron.

According to the caption, Typhoons of No. 143 Wing fired more than 53,000 cannon shells in the course of one day's close ground support. The wing was led by Group Captain Paul Davoud, one of Canada's renowned airmen.

On Sunday, August 13, a service conducted by the wing padre, Squadron Leader Herbert Ashford, was held at one of the dispersals at Lantheuil. It also marked the simultaneous decoration of three squadron commanders.

Group Captain Davoud, already the holder of the Distinguished Service Order and Distinguished Flying Cross, reads the lesson.

The memorial which today looks out across the airfield stands to remember days now consigned to history.

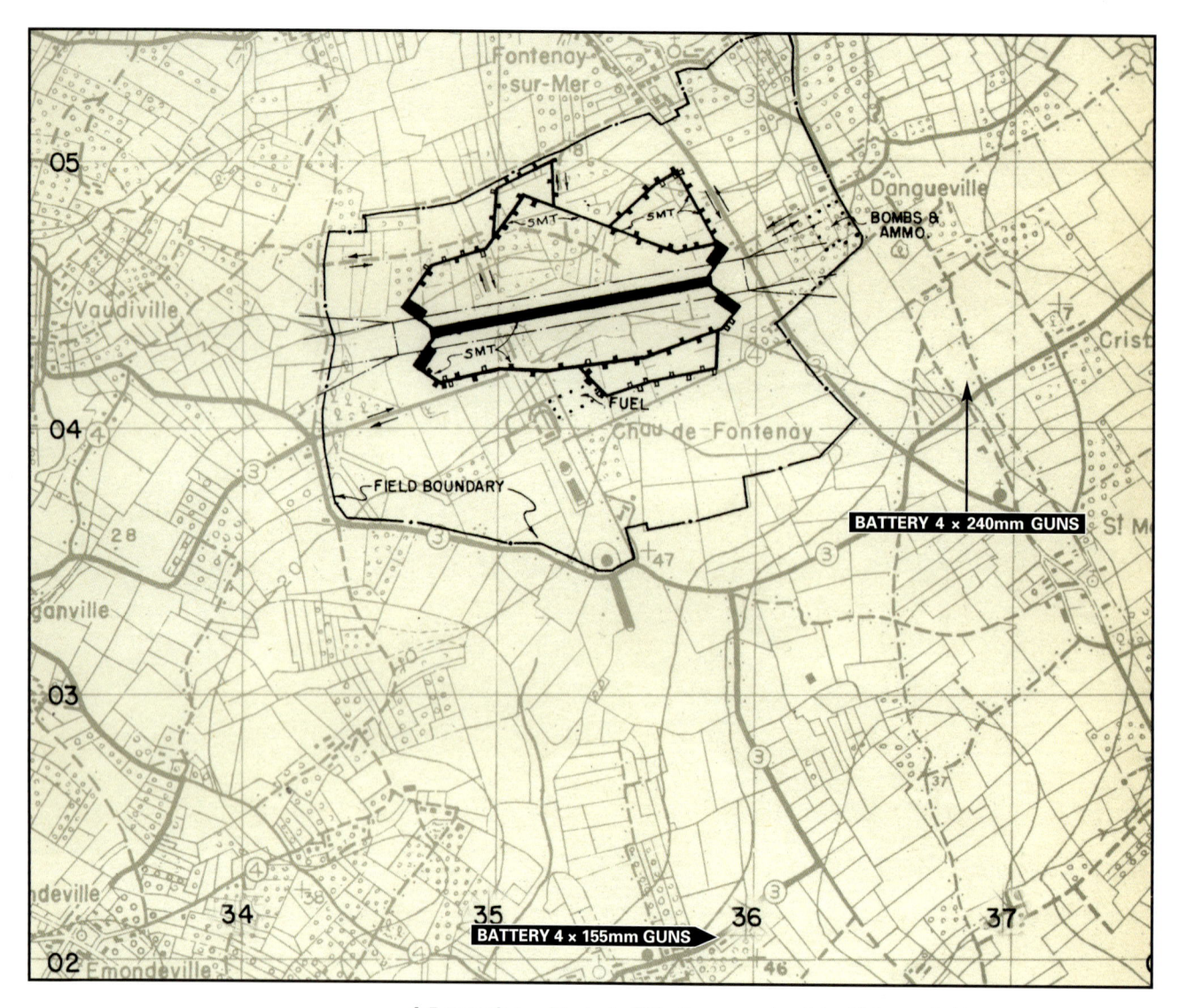

A-7 AZEVILLE

OPERATIONAL JUNE 27

Latitude: 49°28'N
Longitude: 01°18'W
Grid reference: O-352044
Height: 90ft

The site earmarked for A-7 lay just west of two powerful German coastal batteries sited on the Cherbourg peninsula. The fort at Azeville consisted of four large casemates on the eastern edge of the village containing 155mm guns, with 240mm guns emplaced a mile to the east in the second battery at Crisbecq. Both batteries were protected by pillboxes, trenches, machine guns, barbed-wire entanglements and mines.

These strong points were barring the advance to the north by the 22nd Infantry Regiment of the US 4th Division but the first attack to capture them on D+1 failed. On the following morning its 1st and 2nd Battalions tried again but a counter-attack drove both back with considerable losses.

A-7 was planned to be built in the grounds of the Château de Fontenay, a mile and a half to the north of Azeville, but two four-gun batteries barred the way and it was not until June 16 that the 819th Engineer Aviation Battalion were able to start work.

On June 9, a third attack on Azeville was assigned to the 3rd Battalion. Picking their way through the minefields, they advanced with the support of a single tank, and the combined effect of satchel charges and a flame-thrower finally encouraged the fortress commander to surrender.

For the time being, Crisbecq was bypassed although the troops were still held up by defences in the area of another strong point at the Château de Fontenay which was situated right on

A panorama of the battery and strong point at Azeville today, courtesy of Adrian Farwell.

94

Photo mosaic prepared by the 942nd Engineer Aviation Topographic Battalion in July.

the edge of the site for the airfield. For three days (June 10-12) there was little progress so on the 12th the 39th Infantry Regiment was brought into the fight. Its 2nd Battalion pushed patrols to Crisbecq but to their surprise they found that it had since been abandoned. Now that the area was clear, the 819th Engineer Aviation Battalion, engaged on A-6 at Beuzeville, could begin work.

The plan was to lay down a 5,000ft runway but as it was found that this length would involve extensive earth works, instead they settled for a 3,600ft fighter strip topped with SMT. There was room for 50 tracked and 25 untracked dispersals, plus the usual radio, lighting and fuel facilities.

This survey photograph taken by the French Air Force in 1947 still shows traces of the abandoned airstrip.

This dispersal on the southern side of the strip appears to have been a popular venue for photographs. Here *Miss Warrior* is pictured with the ruined château as a backdrop.

Although it was not finally finished until July 2, the 365th Fighter Group stole a march on the engineers and the Thunderbolts of the 386th and 387th squadrons flew in on June 27. The 388th followed on July 6. Spending the next two months at Azeville, they departed for A-12 at Lignerolles at the end of August.

During their tenure they had been joined by the 363rd Fighter Group (380th, 381st and 382nd Squadrons) which arrived on August 23. However, in September it was re-designated the 363rd Tactical Reconnaissance Group as there was a pressing need for battlefield intelligence. The same month they moved on to Le Mans.

Left: **Colonel Ray Stecker, the CO of the 365th Fighter Group that began arriving with P-47s in late June.** *Right:* **The château today.**

The Mustangs of the 363rd Fighter Group under its Commanding Officer, Colonel James B. Tipton, arrived in late August.

By the end of June, the Ninth Air Force had seven fighter groups using airstrips in Normandy: the 368th at Cardonville, the 366th at St Pierre-du-Mont, the 371st at Beuzeville, the 354th at Cricqueville, the 50th at Carentan, the 48th at Deux-Jumeaux and the 365th at Azeville. The code A9 on this Mustang denotes it belongs to the 380th Fighter Squadron based at A-7 in August, later redesignated as part of the 363rd Tactical Reconnaissance Group.

POTENTIAL AIRFIELD SITES.

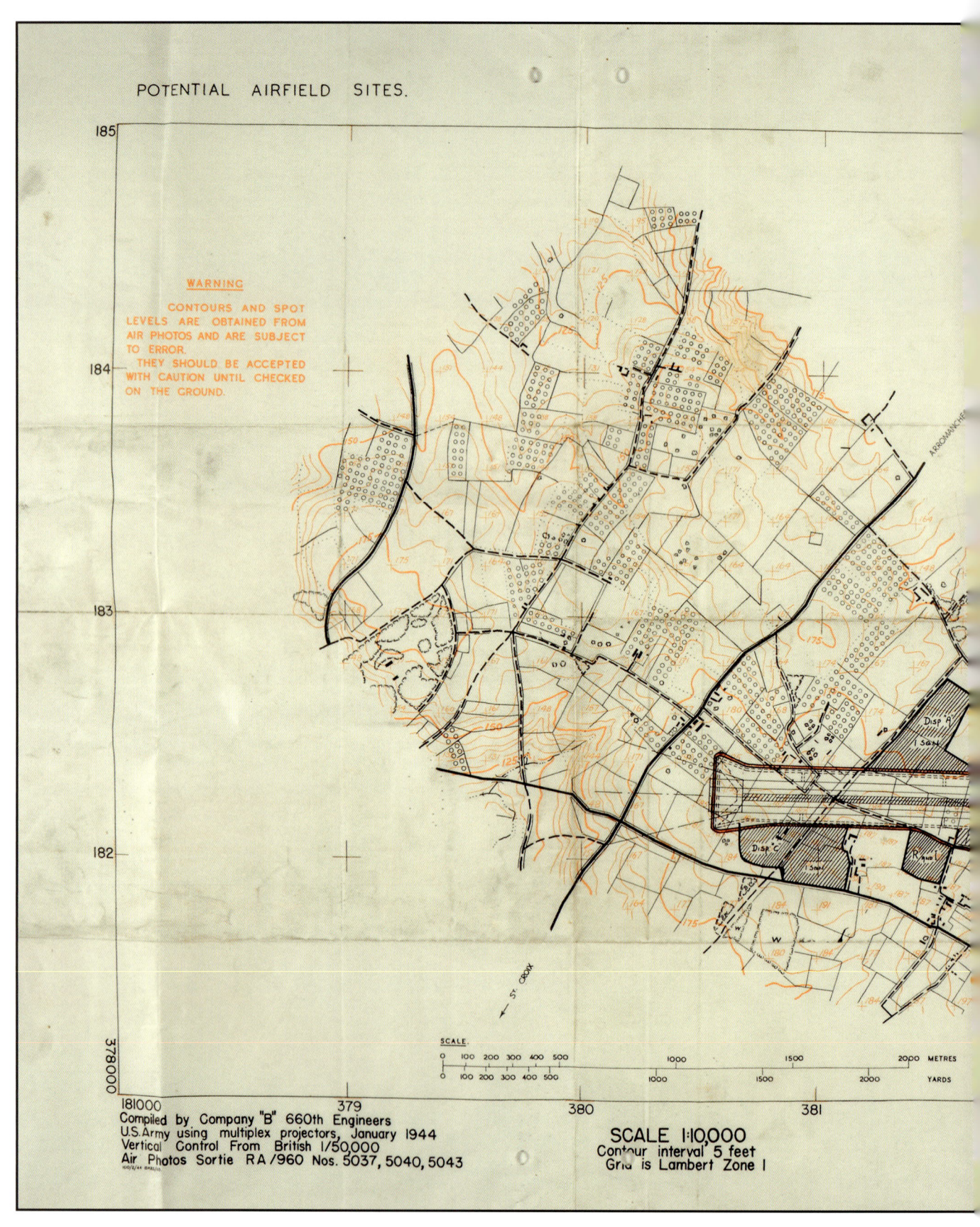

WARNING

CONTOURS AND SPOT LEVELS ARE OBTAINED FROM AIR PHOTOS AND ARE SUBJECT TO ERROR. THEY SHOULD BE ACCEPTED WITH CAUTION UNTIL CHECKED ON THE GROUND.

Compiled by Company "B" 660th Engineers
U.S. Army using multiplex projectors, January 1944
Vertical Control From British 1/50,000
Air Photos Sortie R.A./960 Nos. 5037, 5040, 5043

SCALE 1:10,000
Contour interval 5 feet
Grid is Lambert Zone 1

Having worked on B-3 at Ste Croix and finished it to ALG standard by dusk on D+3, the men of No. 75 Road Construction Company and No. 135 Company of the Pioneer Corps of No. 24 Airfield Construction Group moved to Sommervieu to build B-8. This is the plan they used to set out the airstrip. Compared to B-3, the new site was very difficult as it was covered by small fields and orchards, with hedges, ditches and banks, so Royal Engineers from XXX Corps had to be called in to help. In the end, Sommervieu took 11 days to complete compared with two for Ste Croix. Lieutenant-Colonel Peter White, the commander of No. 24 ACG, reported that 'the French were very helpful. Although we were ruining their orchards, crops and pasture and pulling down several thousand trees, they raised not a word of dissent and helped by loaning mowers. Their attitude was that it was all for the benefit of France.' Colonel White added a note of complaint to his report 'as the credit for building the airfield was given in almost all the papers, including *The Times*, to the RAF Servicing Commandos who, of course, had no hand in it whatsoever. These inaccuracies in the press do a great deal of harm.'

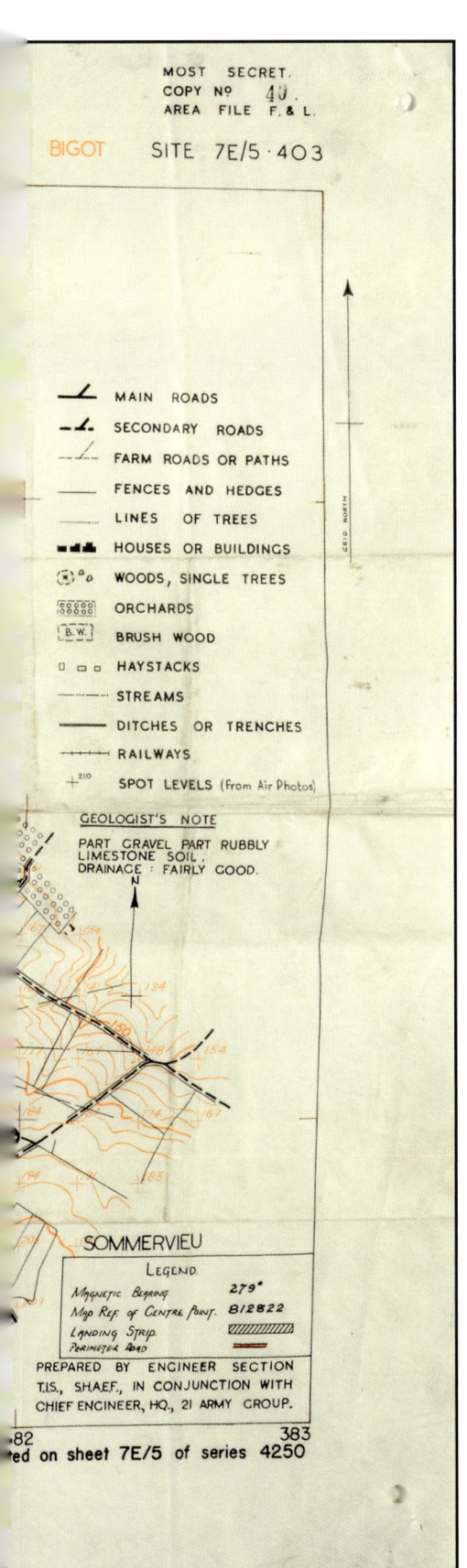

In spite of the impression given by these Mustang pilots of No. 168 Squadron (at B-8 from June 29 to August 14), Sommervieu was one of the busiest bases in the sector with British, French and Canadian squadrons in residence.

B-8 SOMMERVIEU

OPERATIONAL JUNE 29

Latitude: 49°18'N
Longitude: 00°40'W
Grid reference: T-812822
Altitude: 191ft

Two miles north-east of Bayeux, Sommervieu could be considered as true Free French property as it became home to three of their squadrons. It had been captured by the 9th Durham Light Infantry (151st Brigade, 50th Division) on D-Day.

The airfield was prepared with a runway of graded earth, 3,600ft by 120ft, and was completed by No. 24 Airfield Construction Group on June 22.

On July 28, these pilots of No. 266 Squadron, recently arrived, were about to take part in an attack on 'the largest German tank concentration reported since the opening of the campaign'. L-R: Pilot Officer Sam Bennet, Flying Officer George Wharry, Warrant Officer Chester West and Pilot Officer John Thompson. The squadron was the last to leave Sommervieu on September 6.

On the outbreak of the Second World War, Basil Dean became the head of the Entertainments National Service Association (ENSA), the organisation set up to provide entertainment for the British armed forces. Dean had produced 11 films featuring George Formby, the dearly-loved, ukelele-playing singer who joined ENSA in February 1940. He toured factories, theatres and concert halls performing for the troops and also served as a dispatch rider in the Home Guard as well as starring in several films. He had married Beryl Ingham in 1924 and she performed with him, his memorable songs including *Chinese Laundry Blues*, *When I'm Cleaning Windows*, *Leaning on a Lamp-Post* and not forgetting *Bless 'Em All*. In July 1944, he and Beryl travelled to Normandy for a four-week tour, performing his first scheduled concert aboard HMS *Ambitious* (right). He then embarked on impromptu performances on the back of Army lorries and behind sandbags near the front line. During dinner with Montgomery, the General asked Formby to visit the men of the 6th Airborne Division who had been holding several bridges without relief for 56 days. On August 17 he spent a day visiting the front-line troops, giving nine shows.

On August 10 George and Beryl had visited No. 400 Squadron at Sommervieu, being pictured here with the Commanding Officer, Squadron Leader Dick Ellis, Group Captain Ernest Moncrieff, commanding No. 39 Recce Wing, and Squadron Leader Frank Chesters, the CO of No. 430 Squadron. Greg Clark, a Canadian war correspondent, has just presented Beryl with a silver Mustang broach on behalf of his daughter who was an ardent admirer of George. By the end of the war it was estimated that he had performed in front of three million service personnel. (Beryl died on December 24, 1960 and George on March 6 the following year.)

B-8 Sommervieu was used by No. 39 Reconnaissance Wing (Nos. 168 and RCAF 400, 414 and 430 Squadrons equipped with a mixture of Mustangs and Spitfires) from June 29 to August 14-15 when they flew to B-21 at Ste Honorine. No. 266 Squadron, a member of No. 146 Wing, arrived from B-3 at Ste Croix on July 25, departing to B-23 at La Rue Huguenot (Morainville) on September 6.

Next to arrive on August 19 was No. 145 Wing comprising the three Spitfire-equipped Free French squadrons: Nos. 329, 340 and 341. They moved to B-29 at Bernay/Valailles on September 2. Sommervieu was also used briefly by No. 164 Squadron from July 17-20 with their Typhoons and from August 20-September 2 by No. 74 Squadron with Spitfire LF IXEs.

Colonel White of No. 24 ACG explained that 'some 3,000 trees were removed. About one third of these were apple trees in orchards and the remainder tall oak, acacia, elm and ash in hedges. Bulldozers dealt with most of the trees but a demolition party helped as there were not enough bulldozers. About two tons of explosives were used. The most difficult obstacle consisted of a bank with a double row of tall trees on it and a ditch three feet deep by about six feet wide on either side. It was most awkward to get a bulldozer at these trees. The big problem with the trees was their removal once they were felled. All the group transport was used fully in dragging them away and finding sufficient fields round about in which to dump them. They were dragged near to hedges, their limbs lopped off and then the whole bulldozed into the hedges.'

A-8 PICAUVILLE

OPERATIONAL JUNE 29

Latitude: 49°22'N
Longitude: 01°24'W
Grid reference: T-284951
Altitude: 70ft

Picauville lies just over a mile west of the RN13 between Carentan and Sainte-Mère-Église. In the 'Overlord' planning, it was located within the objective area that was hoped could be secured on D-Day. However, the delay was caused principally by the scattered airborne drops, the strength of the German resistance, and difficulties in subsequent attempts to cross the inundations either side of the Merderet river. A crossing was finally achieved on June 9 at which point two regiments of the 90th Division, the 357th and 358th, were tasked with exploiting the bridgehead, the latter managing to advance to Picauville on the 10th.

The airfield was laid out by the 826th Engineers but not fully completed until July 16 although the squadrons of the 405th Fighter Group arrived as soon as the runway had been finished. This was the second airfield to be operational using Prefabricated Bituminous Surfacing (after B-10 at Plumetot). PBS was impregnated jute with gave a dust-free base, SMT tracking sometimes being laid on top. The landing strip measured 5,000ft with over 100 dispersals, 86 of which had been surfaced with SMT. Complete airfield lighting had been installed with VHS and Darky Watch homing (see page 55).

The 509th and 511th Squadrons arrived on June 29 with the 510th coming in on the following day. All departed for St Dizier (A-64) in the second week of September.

A-8 at Picauville was the second American airfield to be constructed using PBS. The 826th Engineer Aviation Battalion was not able to start until June 20 but progress thereafter moved ahead speedily and the 5,000ft by 120ft runway was completed in six days.

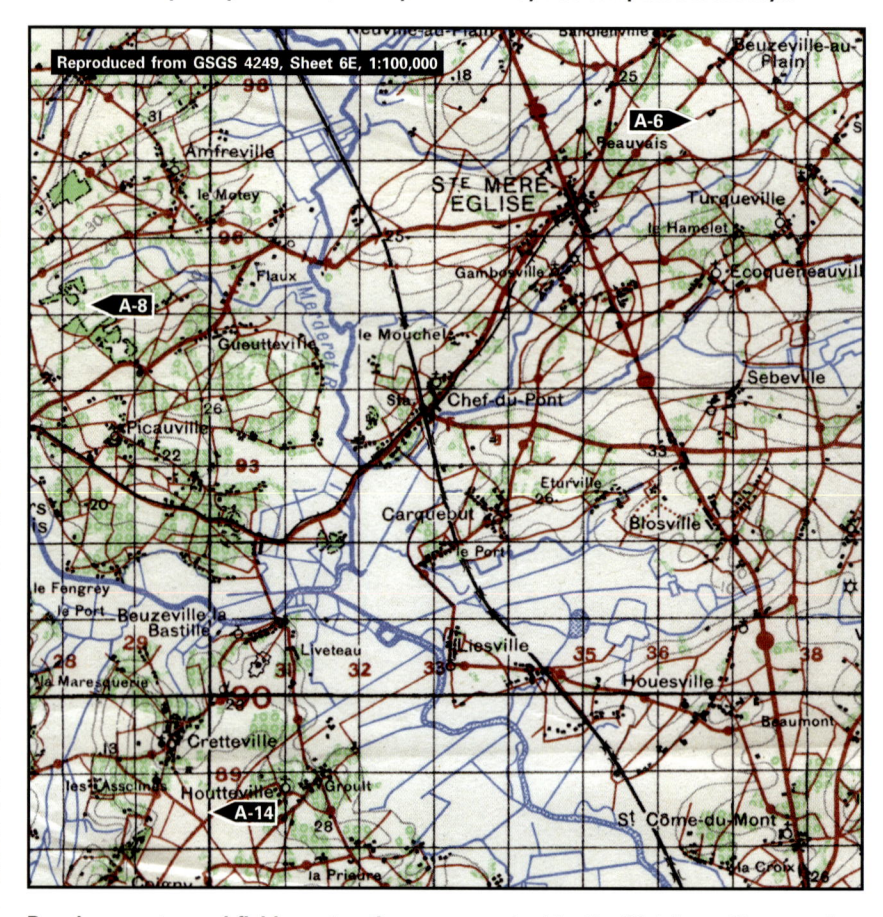

Regular reports on airfield construction were required by the 21st Army Group and on June 14 the US IX Engineer Command listed progress in its sector. However, its report mis-identifies four of the ALGs already completed, stating that St Pierre-du-Mont was A-2 (instead of A-1); Couqueville (*sic*) was A-2, not A-3; Cardonville was given as A-4 when it was A-3, and it gave A-5 for Deux-Jumeaux, not A-4. The report stated that a recce had been completed at Picauville for A-8, the next to finish being A-14 at Cretteville. (Perhaps it would be helpful to remind readers that our listing is in the order that each ALG received its first operational unit, not the date when completed.)

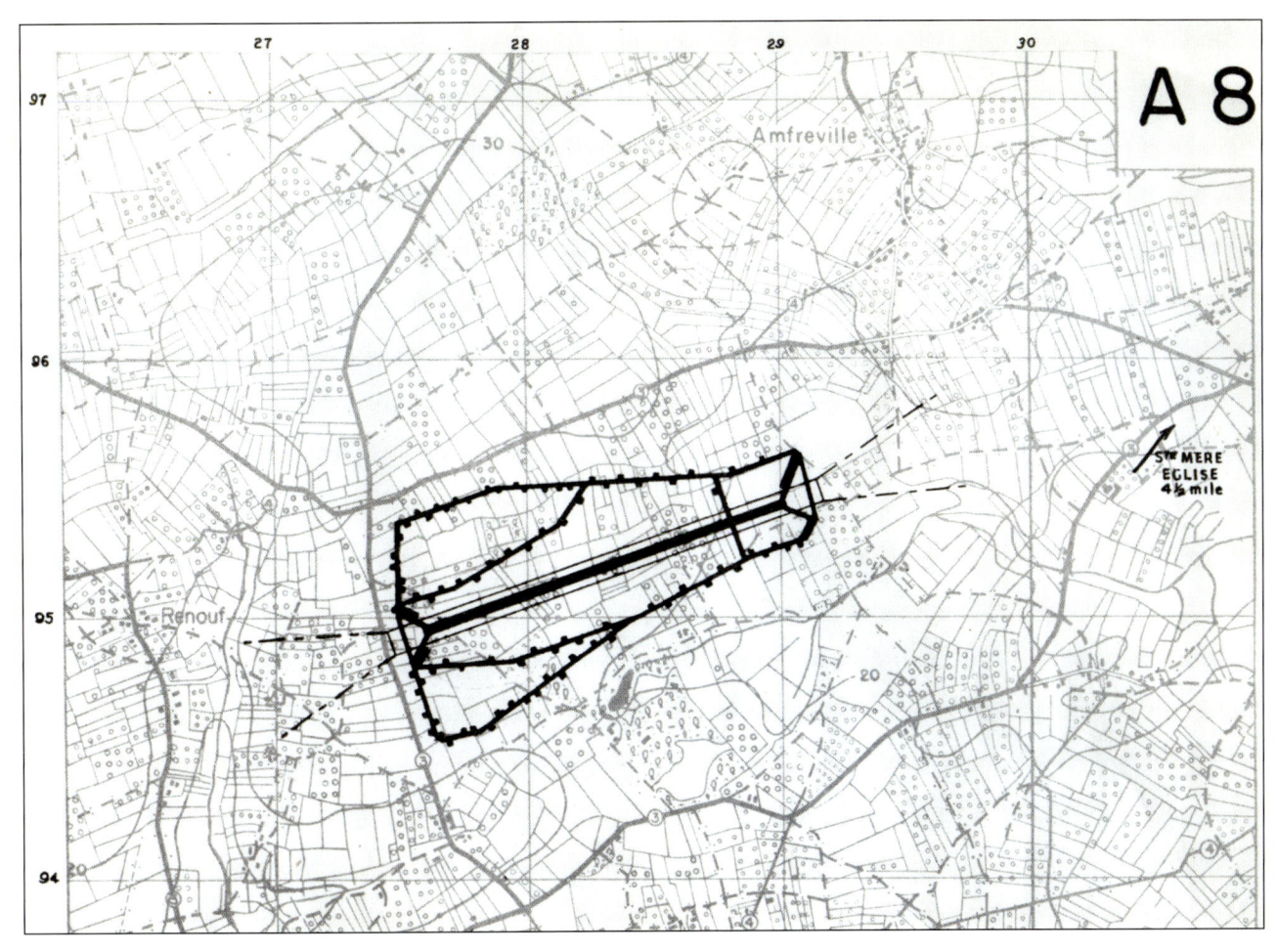

Above: **The basic outline for A-8 as planned, and** *(below)* **as completed on July 16 with the obligatory crash strip.**

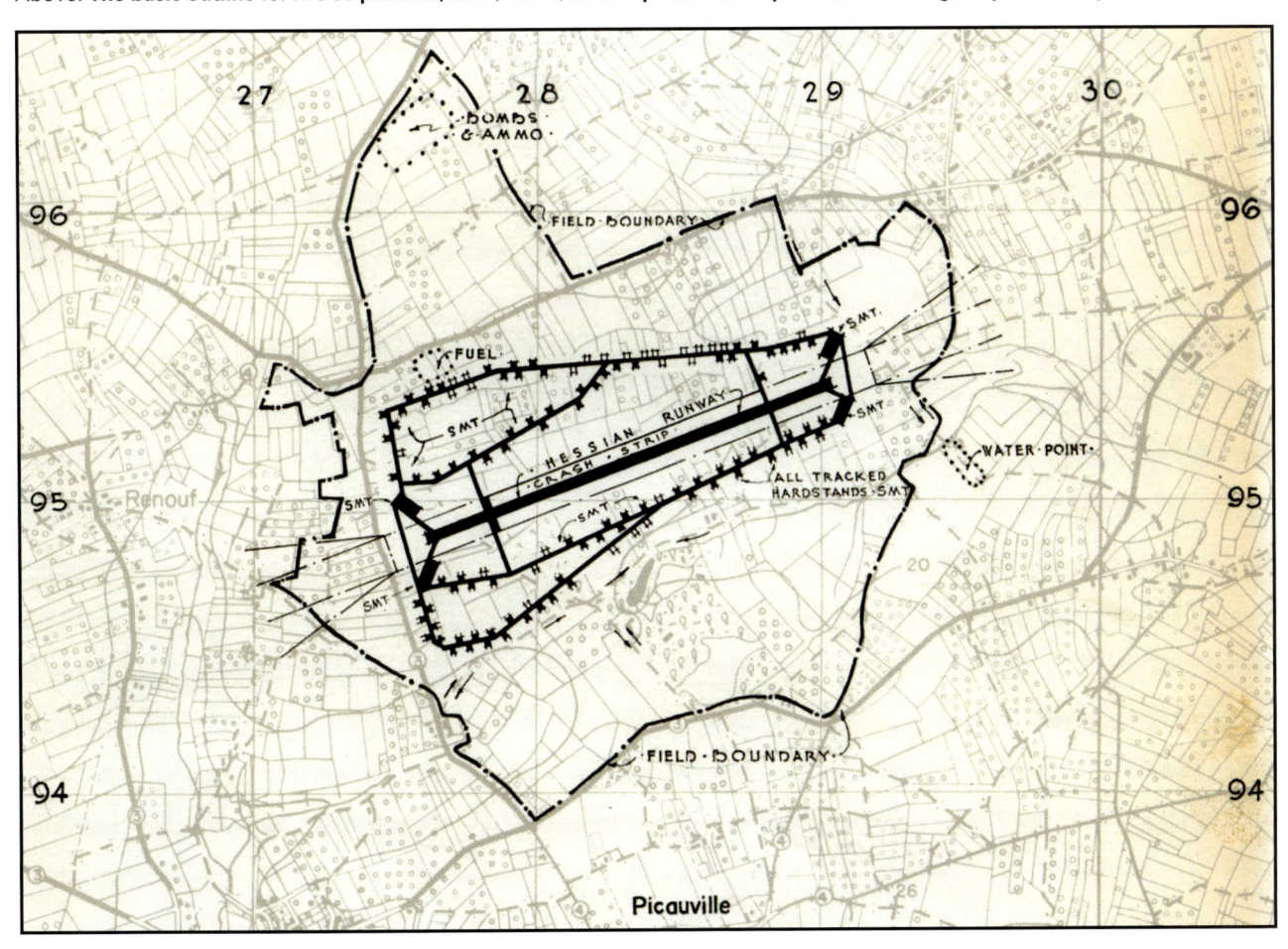

The additional dispersals were useful as in August two RAF squadrons, Nos. 264 and 604, of the Second Tactical Air Force were brought in. They were equipped with the Mosquito XIII and deployed in the night-fighter role over the battlefield. A-8, however, was not really ideal for their operation so they moved to B-17 at Carpiquet as soon as that airfield with its concrete runway became available.

Above: Following the landings, Nos. 264 and 604 Squadrons began carrying out night patrols over the beach-head, the latter being the first night-fighter unit to be based in France. When the Americans required night cover over their sector, on August 6 the first British aircraft flew into A-8, Squadron Leader Bastian Maitland-Thompson's Mosquito being suitably adorned US-style for the occasion! *Below:* In late June, the 422nd Night Fighter Squadron received the Northrup P-61 and on July 25 was transferred from Ford in the UK to Maupertus in France, the airfield on the outskirts of Cherbourg (see page 110), coded A-15. Named after the venomous North American spider, the Black Widows were painted all black with a crew of three. The 425th Night Fighter Squadron went to A-33 at Vannes on August 18. This photo is said to show one of their Black Widows, flown by Lieutenant Colonel Severson, an exchange pilot from the US Marine Corps, at A-8 in September.

The capture of Cherbourg completed a distinct phase of operations in the cross-Channel attack. Nevertheless, the Allied armies occupied a lodgement area considerably smaller than planned. The slow advance southward, and especially the failure to push out into open country south and south-east of Caen, which was still in German hands despite every effort to capture it, meant a reduction in the planned programme of airfield construction. This was, however, much less serious than planners had anticipated. By dint of improvisation, Ninth Air Force engineers were able to lay out fields in countryside that planners had considered unsuitable for airstrips. In early July about one-third of the Ninth Air Force fighters and fighter-bombers were based on the Continent. Yet the available space for airfields in Normandy was now virtually all used up and the strips constructed on a temporary basis were requiring an ever-increasing proportion of engineer labour to maintain them. From an air force point of view, the lodgement secured at the end of June was relatively satisfactory but would not long remain so.

Two years after the war the remains of A-8 still scarred the landscape at Picauville but 70 years later all has reverted to nature.

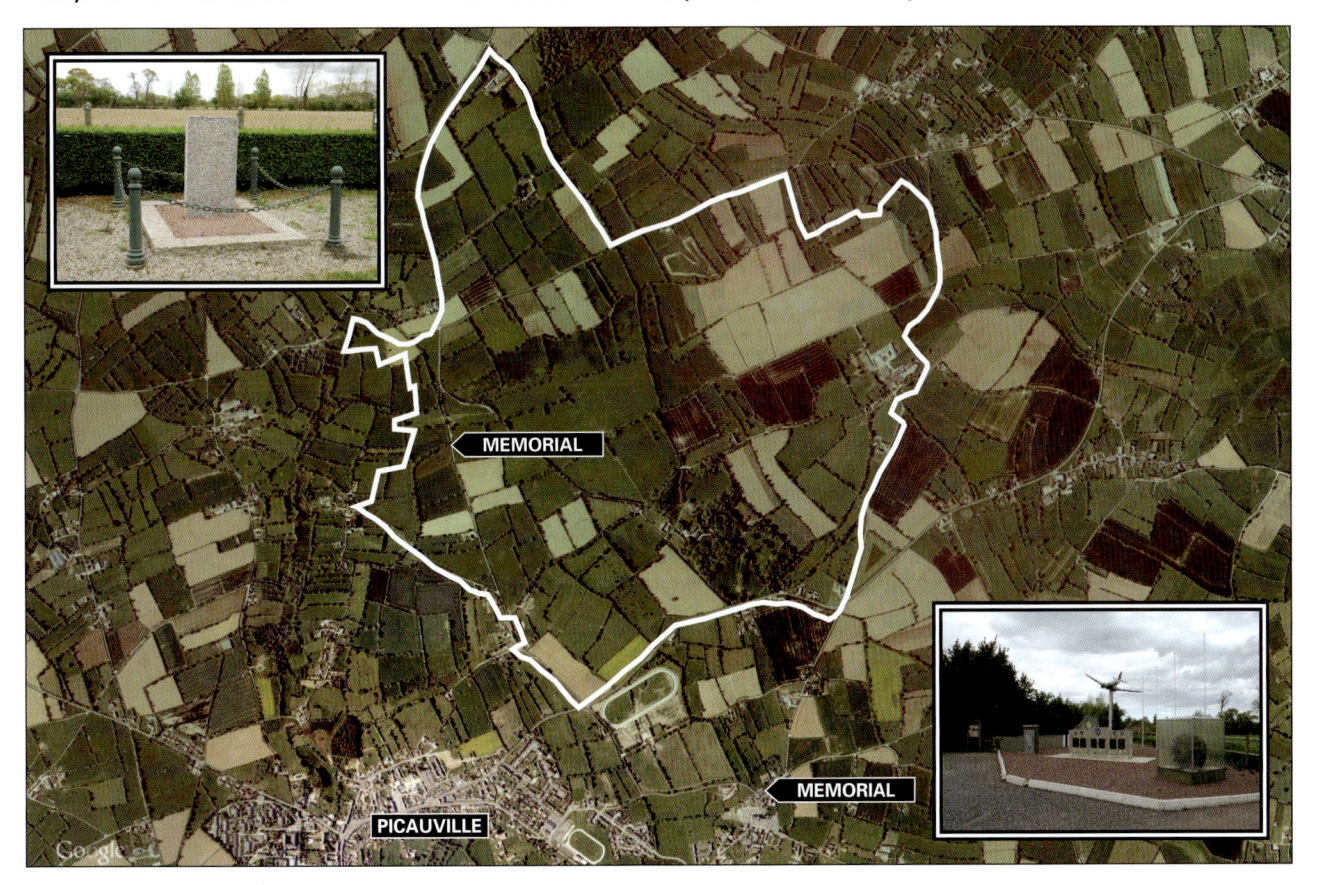

There are two memorials to A-8, one along the D69 at the western end of the former runway and another across the street from the village church at Picauville. The latter also commemorates the five C-47 carrier planes that crashed around here on D-Day and D+1.

105

A-14 CRETTEVILLE

OPERATIONAL JULY 3

Latitude: 49°20'N
Longitude: 01°22'W
Grid reference: T-300885
Altitude: 90ft

Cretteville, eight miles north-west of Carentan, was overrun by the 508th Parachute Infantry of the 82nd Airborne Division on June 13. The 819th Engineer Aviation Battalion laid down a NE-SW runway 5,000ft long of graded earth, of which 3,600ft was surfaced with PBS hessian, with a crash strip alongside.

First unit to be based there was the 358th Fighter Group, its P-47 squadrons (the 365th, 366th and 367th) arriving on July 3-4. Then on the 27th the P-38 Lightnings of the 393rd Fighter Squadron (367th Group) joined them. They stayed until August 15 when they departed for A-2 at Cricqueville, while the previous day the 358th Group had moved 60 miles south to A-28 at Pontorson.

On August 17 the three squadrons (the 512th, 513th and 514th) of the 406th Fighter Group arrived from Tour-en-Bessin, remaining at A-14 until September 4 when they relocated to St Léonard (A-36) south-west of Le Mans.

By the beginning of July the British had constructed 11 airfields (although three or four were still subject to shell-fire), and the Americans had another ten in use. Altogether they represented about three-quarters of the programme scheduled for this date. [1] ELS-1 Pouppeville. [2] B-1 Asnelles. [3] A-21C St Laurent-sur-Mer. [4] B-3 Ste Croix-sur-Mer. [5] A-3 Cardonville. [6] B-2 Bazenville. [7] A-1 St Pierre-du-Mont. [8] A-2 Cricqueville. [9] A-6 Beuzeville. [10] B-4 Bény-sur-Mer. [11] A-4 Deux-Jumeaux. [12] B-6 Coulombs. [13] B-5 Camilly. [14] A-10 Carentan. [15] B-7 Martragny. [16] B-11 Longues-sur-Mer. [17] B-10 Plumetot. [18] B-9 Lantheuil. [19] A-7 Azeville. [20] B-8 Sommervieu. [21] A-8 Picauville. [22] Although the site for A-13 at Tour-en-Bessin had been captured on June 7, it was not operational until July 19. The extract in the panels below and opposite has been taken from records of the US First Army.

AIRFIELD CONSTRUCTION REQUIREMENTS

Priorities in Airfield Construction.
1. The following priorities are to be accorded the various types of airfield construction in meeting operational requirements on the Continent:
PRIORITY I ELSs for emergency landing of aircraft operating over the area.
PRIORITY II R & R strips for refuelling and re-arming fighter aircraft.
PRIORITY III ALGs (later airfields).

Specifications.
2. The following specifications are to be used in the construction of ELSs, R & R strips, ALGs and airfields as shown:

ELS. Minimum length 1,800ft.

R & R strip. Minimum length 3,600ft with two marshalling areas 100 yards by 50 yards at each end.

ALG (or airfield). For fighters: minimum length 3,600 ft with dispersal facilities for 54 aircraft. For fighter-bombers: as for fighters above, except that minimum length is to be 5,000ft.

3. There will be no tracking requirements for ELSs. R & R strips are to be tracked as shown in the airfield construction programme. The amount of tracking required for ALGs and airfields will depend upon local conditions, but for planning purposes it is to be assumed that all ALGs and airfields in the United States Sector will require 75 per cent tracking and those in the British Sector 50 per cent tracking.

Airfield Construction Programme.
7. The following is the airfield construction programme required to meet operational requirements. Totals shown are accumulative with the exception of the Item (i), ELSs, which have not been carried forward:

NORMANDY FRONT
2 July 1944

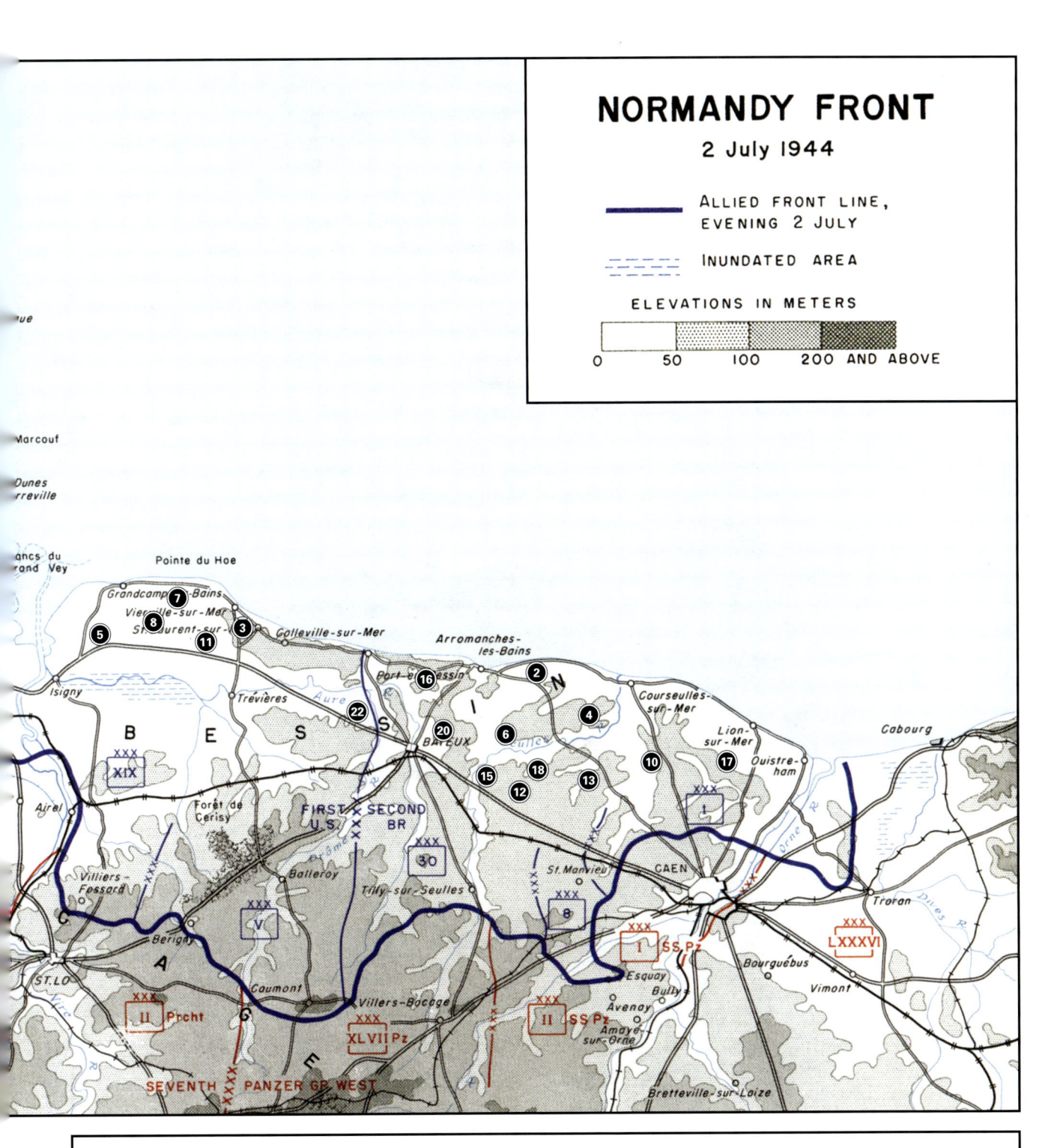

— ALLIED FRONT LINE, EVENING 2 JULY

--- INUNDATED AREA

ELEVATIONS IN METERS
0 50 100 200 AND ABOVE

US SECTOR

D-Day: One ELS West, One ELS Centre.

a.m. D+4: Two 3,600ft R & R strips both 100 per cent tracked.

a.m. D+8: Five ALGs (includes two R&R strips brought up to ALG standard). Two of these ALGs to be 5,000ft and three 3,600ft in length.

a.m. D+14: Eight airfields. Three of these airfields to be 5,000ft and five 3,600ft in length.

a.m. D+24: Twelve airfields. Five of these airfields to be 5,000ft and seven 3,600ft in length.

a.m. D+40: Eighteen airfields. Five of these airfields to be 5,000ft and thirteen 3,600ft in length.

BRITISH SECTOR

D-Day: One ELS.

a.m. D+3: One 3,600ft R & R strip, patched with tracking as necessary.

D+3/4: One 3,600ft R & R strip, patched with tracking as necessary, and one 3,600ft R & R strip 100 per cent tracked.

a.m. D+4: One 3,600ft R & R strip, patched with tracking as necessary, and one 3,600ft R & R strip 100 per cent tracked.

a.m. D+8: Five ALGs (includes the R&R strips above brought up to ALG standard). Two of these ALGs to be 5,000ft and three 3,600ft in length.

a.m. D+14: Ten airfields. Three of these airfields to be 5,000ft and seven 3,600ft in length.

a.m. D+24: Fifteen airfields. Five of these airfields to be 5,000ft and ten 3,600ft in length.

a.m. D+40: Twenty-five airfields. Five of these airfields to be 5,000ft and twenty 3,600ft in length.

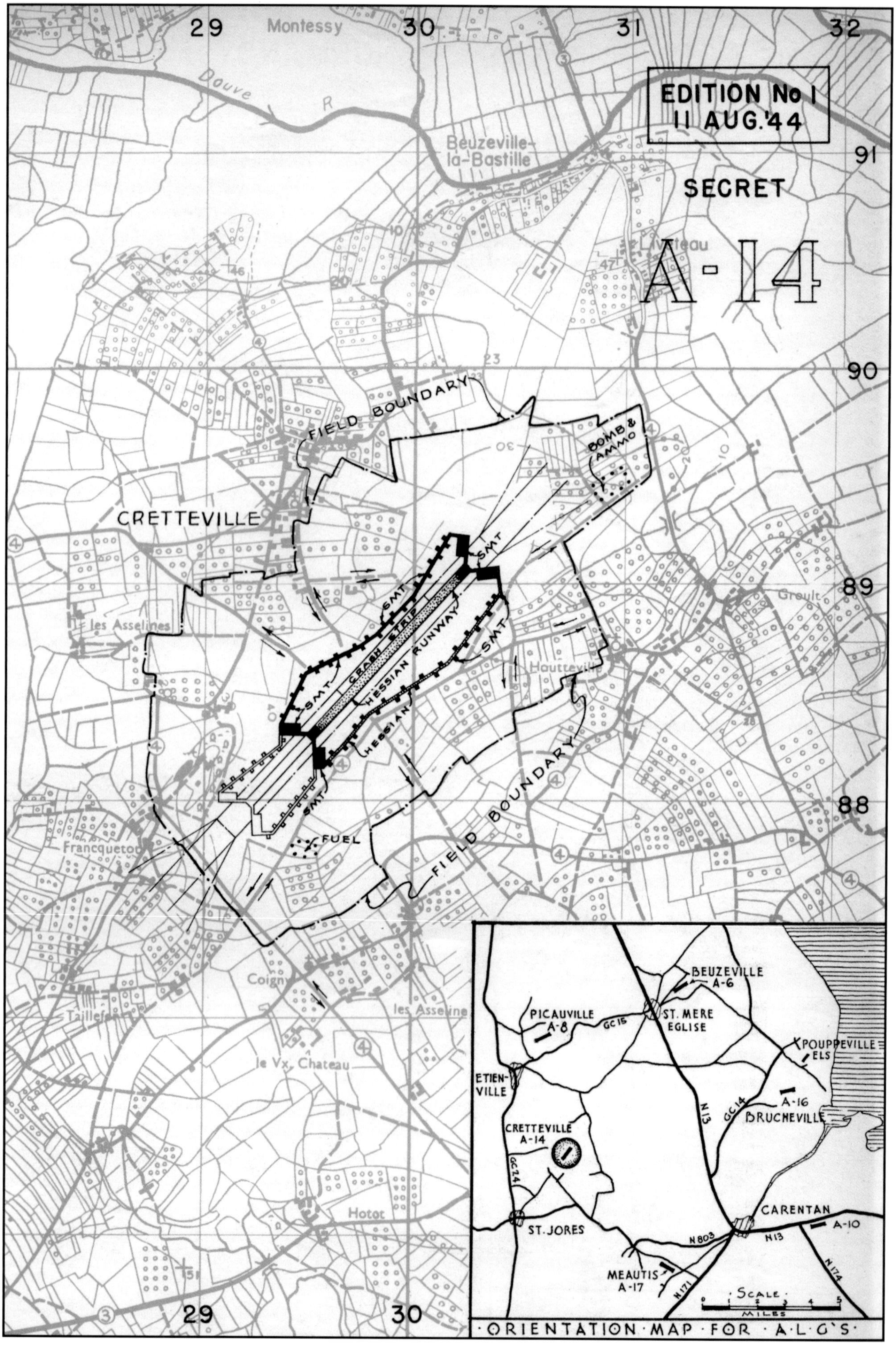
EDITION No I
11 AUG.'44
SECRET
A-14
29
30
31
32
91
90
89
88
Montessy
Douve R
Beuzeville-la-Bastille
Le Livateau
FIELD BOUNDARY
BOMB & AMMO
CRETTEVILLE
SMT
CRASH STRIP
HESSIAN RUNWAY
HESSIAN
FUEL
les Asselines
Hautteville
Groult
Francquetot
Coigny
Taillefer
les Asselines
le Vx. Chateau
Hotot
BEUZEVILLE
A-6
PICAUVILLE
A-8
GC15
ST. MERE
EGLISE
POUPPEVILLE
ELS
ETIEN-
VILLE
N13
GC14
A-16
BRUCHEVILLE
CRETTEVILLE
A-14
GC24
ST. JORES
CARENTAN
A-10
N803
N13
N174
MEAUTIS
A-17
N171
SCALE
MILES
ORIENTATION MAP FOR A.L.G'S.

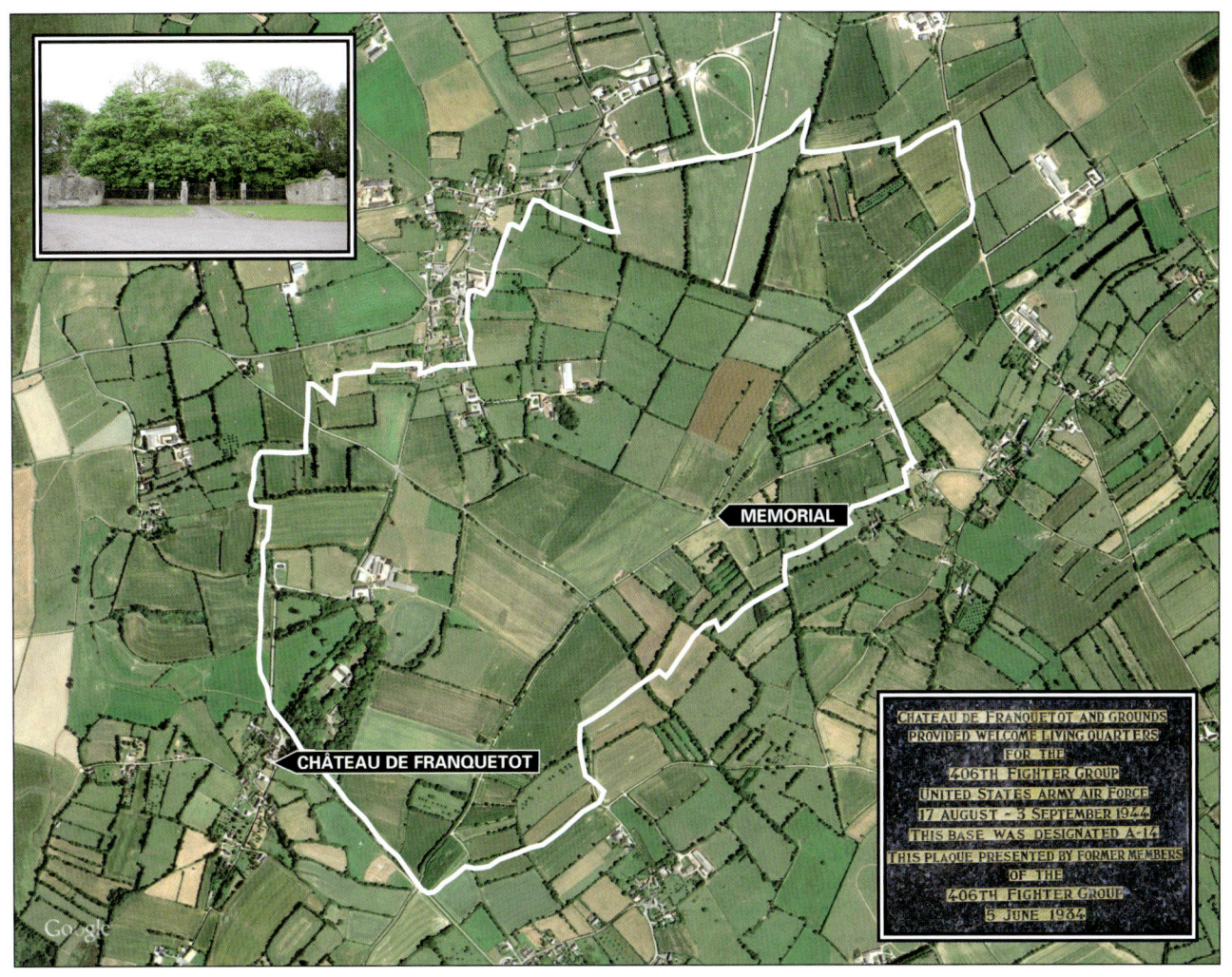

CHÂTEAU DE FRANQUETOT AND GROUNDS
PROVIDED WELCOME LIVING QUARTERS
FOR THE
406TH FIGHTER GROUP
UNITED STATES ARMY AIR FORCE
17 AUGUST – 3 SEPTEMBER 1944
THIS BASE WAS DESIGNATED A-14
THIS PLAQUE PRESENTED BY FORMER MEMBERS
OF THE
406TH FIGHTER GROUP
5 JUNE 1984

In June 1984, the 406th Fighter Group unveiled a plaque at the entrance to the Château de Franquetot at Cretteville which had been their quarters in 1944. A plaque commemorating the presence of the 358th Fighter Group was added in June 2014. Before that, on the 50th anniversary of D-Day, this memorial had been dedicated at the site of the old airfield.

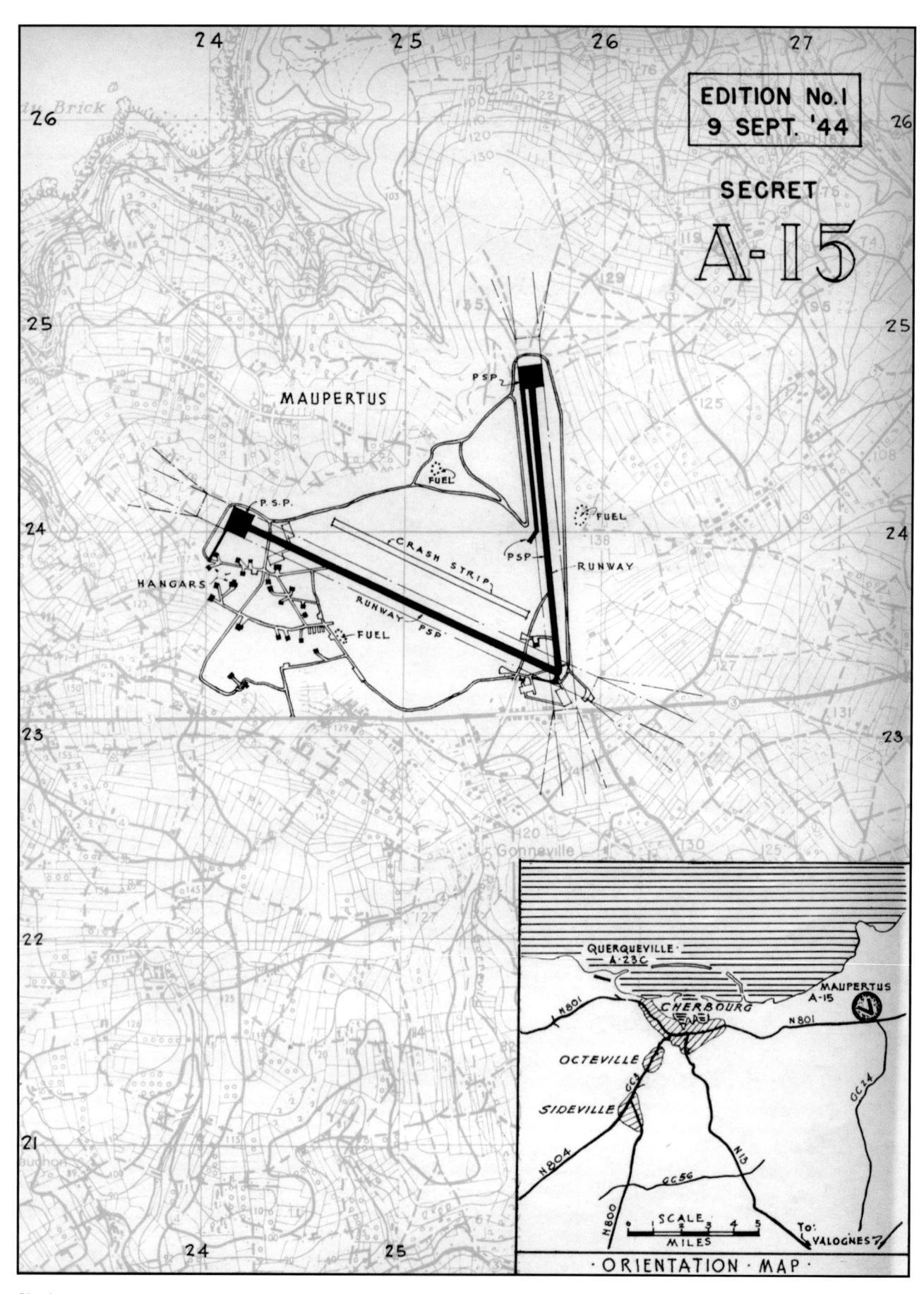

Cherbourg — which had played a prominent part in the evacuation of Allied forces from France to England in 1940 — was one of the greatest transatlantic ports in France. Although third in tonnages handled after Marseilles and Le Havre, the capture of both the latter ports was still in the future, so the acquisition of Cherbourg to help supply the US zone of operations was urgent following the destruction of the American Mulberry harbour. All organised resistance north-east of Cherbourg ceased on June 28, which also gave the Allies the use of the pre-war airfield at Maupertus.

A-15 MAUPERTUS

OPERATIONAL JULY 3

Latitude: 49°38'N
Longitude: 01°28'W
Grid reference: O-250239
Altitude: 459ft

Originally known as Cherbourg-Théville, with the fall of France in 1940, the aerodrome just east of Cherbourg at Maupertus became a forward Luftwaffe base for operations against England. Both I. and III./JG27 operated from there throughout July and August 1940 and from December III./JG77.

On June 18, 1944, US troops advancing from Utah reached the west coast of the peninsula, thus cutting it in half, and for the next ten days they concentrated their efforts in a drive northwards to capture the important port of Cherbourg, deemed essential for the re-supply of American forces. When on June 21 a storm in the Channel severely damaged the prefabricated Mulberry ports off Omaha and Utah, the capture of Cherbourg became even more pressing. By June 26 German resistance in the city was waning so the 22nd Infantry of the 4th Division turned to capture the airfield. After a stiff battle, the 1st Battalion had taken positions south of the airfield; the 2nd Battalion the western edge while the 3rd Battalion took Maupertus itself and eliminated the defences on the northern side. The following day the airfield was in American hands.

A-15 was the first location to be brought into use using runways prepared using pierced steel planks (PSP). Two engineer aviation battalions — the 850th and 877th — were brought in to speedily bring Maupertus into operation.

The first runway on a N-S axis was ready on July 3 followed by the secondary on a NW-SE axis. First unit to arrive was the 382nd Fighter Squadron of the 363rd Fighter Group, illustrated here by *Fools Paradise IV* — the P-51 (44-13309) of Major Evan McCall.

111

The 850th and 877th Engineer Aviation Battalions had been standing by in the wings ready to begin work to rehabilitate Maupertus and within 48 hours 5,000 feet of PSP had been rolled out to create a N-S strip. A second runway was laid down measuring 6,000ft on a NW-SE axis.

By July 3 the airfield was ready for use, the 382nd Squadron of the 363rd Fighter Group being first to land with its P-51s. The 381st followed on the 4th with the 380th joining them the next day. The group stayed until August 23 when it moved to A-7 at Azeville.

The P-61 Black Widows of the 422nd Night Fighter Squadron arrived on July 25, departing for A-39 at Châteaudun, north-west of Orléans, on August 28. Then on September 1 the 387th Bomb Group brought its Marauders in from the UK, its four squadrons (the 556th, 557th, 558th and 559th) remaining until they also all moved to Châteaudun on the 18th.

Follow-up units were the 422nd Night Fighter Squadron later in July with their P-61 Black Widows *(above)* **and the B-26 Marauders of the 387th Bomb Group** *(below)* **which relocated from Stoney Cross in Hampshire at the beginning of September.**

On the 70th anniversary of D-Day in 2014, Maupertus hosted a unique event when ten C-47s flew in to assemble at what is now Cherbourg Airport. Two actually parked close to the line of the wartime N-S runway.

In the mid-'fifties Cherbourg airfield had a single 6,050ft runway with a grass area for light aircraft to the south of it, and in the flight guide for 1956 there was a warning to pilots to make a preliminary circuit as cattle and sheep graze on the landing area!

The airfield was then earmarked for a NATO base and a new 8,000ft runway was laid down by the United States using French contractors. Today the remains of the wartime runway can be detected alongside the present runway.

A memorial obelisk now stands in front of the terminal building dedicated to the Ninth Air Force in general, specifically listing 26 of the advanced landing airstrips.

113

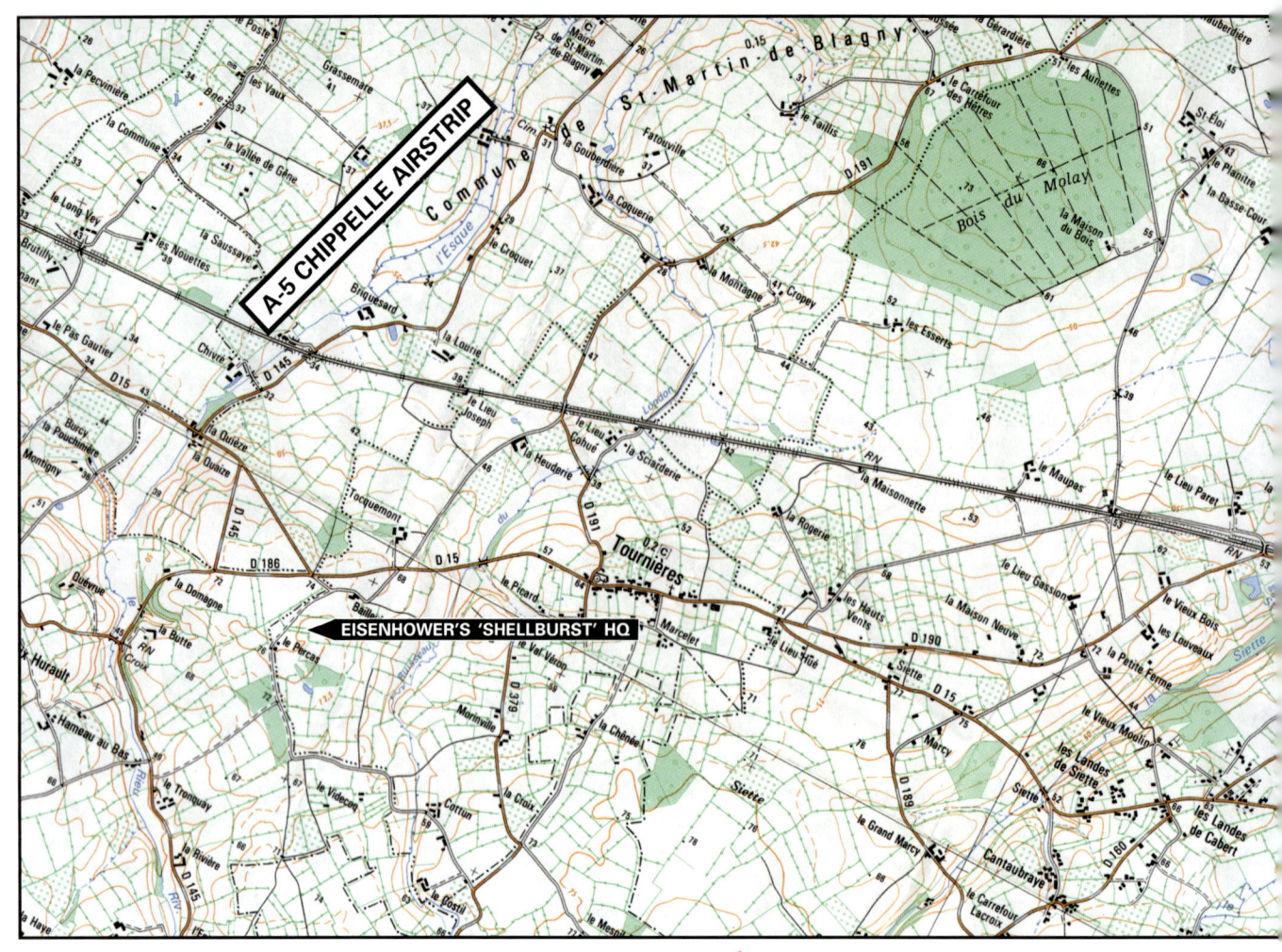

A-9 LE MOLAY

OPERATIONAL JULY 5

Latitude: 49°15'N
Longitude: 00°52'W
Grid reference: T-656788
Altitude: 150ft

Le Molay lies just over seven miles west of Bayeux and, as part of the opening phase to capture St Lô, the 38th Infantry Regiment (US 2nd Division) captured the village on June 10.

Construction of the airstrip was allocated to the 834th Engineer Aviation Battalion which had been working St Pierre-du-Mont on A-1. They completed a 4,000ft by 120ft runway tracked with SMT by July 8. There were 50 tracked and 25 untracked dispersals.

The 12th Tactical Reconnaissance Squadron (67th TR Group) flew in from Middle Wallop on July 5 and stayed until August 11 before they transferred to Rennes (A-27). Also on July 5 the 107th and 109th TR Squadrons arrived at Le Molay, moving on to Toussus-le-Noble (A-46), just south of Paris, on August 29. However up to October it continued to be used as an air depot and for the evacuation of casualties to the UK.

Exactly two months after D-Day, General Eisenhower moved his Advance Command Post, code-named 'Shellburst', to Normandy. Until then,

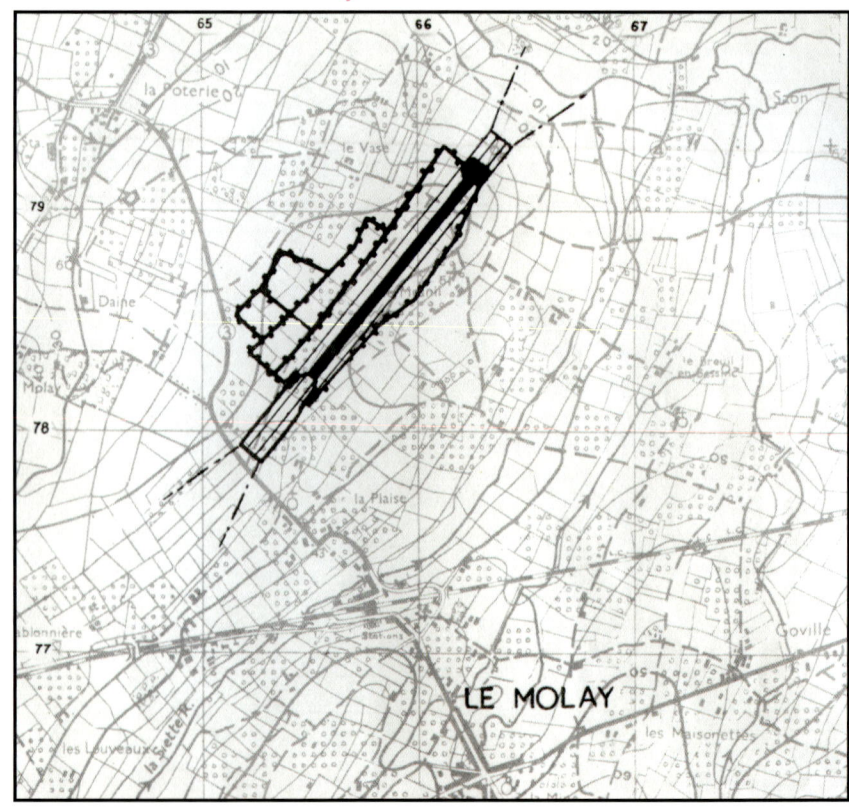

The initial plan for A-9, just north of Le Molay, was issued on July 18, providing a 4,000ft runway tracked with SMT (see page 13). Later a NE-SW crash strip was prepared on the eastern side, parallel to the runway, see the drawing of July 30 on page 116.

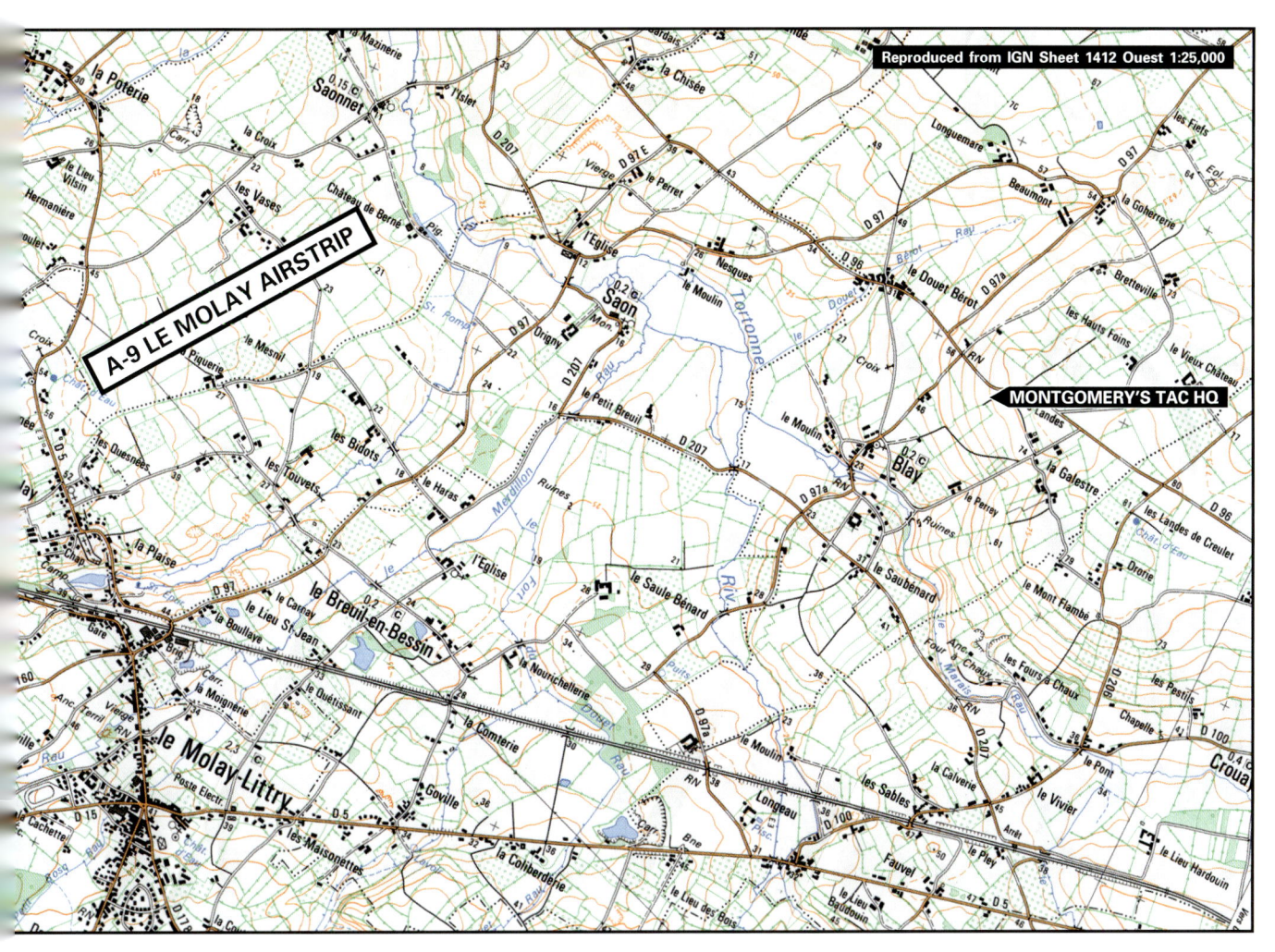

On June 16, King George VI set foot in France, being met by General Montgomery on Mike Beach from where he took his Majesty to the forward headquarters of 21st Army Group which had been set up in the grounds of the castle at Creully (see page 90). Naturally the Press made a big thing of the event in the national papers, so much so that it identified the location of the HQ to the Germans who began shelling the area. Consequently, on June 24, Montgomery had to move to Blay, a village just over the boundary line with American forces. An airstrip was located nearby, suitable for single-engine observation aircraft and convenient in case Monty wanted to use his Miles Messenger. Meanwhile, General Eisenhower was still based in the UK but exactly two months after D-Day he moved his Advance Command Post, now re-named 'Shellburst', to Normandy. Although he had been commuting regularly from 'Sharpener' to France, Tedder had been pressing the Supreme Commander to establish a tactical headquarters on the Continent to permit closer liaison with the forces on the battlefield. On August 16 Eisenhower held his first press conference at his new headquarters, set up 12 miles south-west of Bayeux at Tournières, and in reasonable proximity to Montgomery's TAC HQ. The 834th Engineer Aviation Battalion had already built an airfield at Le Molay-Littry which was available from July 8. This Dakota bears the insignia of the 21st Army Group.

Le Molay was unique as it was the only airstrip constructed in Normandy with covered shelter for aircraft comprising two steel-framed hangars from the Butler Manufacturing Company, established in Kansas City, Missouri, in 1901 and still the world's largest manufacture of steel-framed buildings.

The hangars at A-9 were clad in canvas and are believed to have been used for storage of supplies. As the primary units based at Le Molay were photo-reconnaissance aircraft — F-4/P-38 Lightnings and F-6/P-51 Mustangs — cameras and photographic development obviously needed sheltered facilities.

Ike had been commuting regularly to France but his deputy, Air Chief Marshal Sir Arthur Tedder, was pressing him to relocate to a tactical headquarters on the Continent to be nearer the front. On August 7 it was advised that the SHAEF Advance Command Post was now at Tournières, a mile or so west of Le Molay, where A-9 was ideally situated to service the HQ, a special dispersal area even being set aside for important visitors.

A fine memorial now stands to record A-9's wartime use, including its role as a VIP airfield.

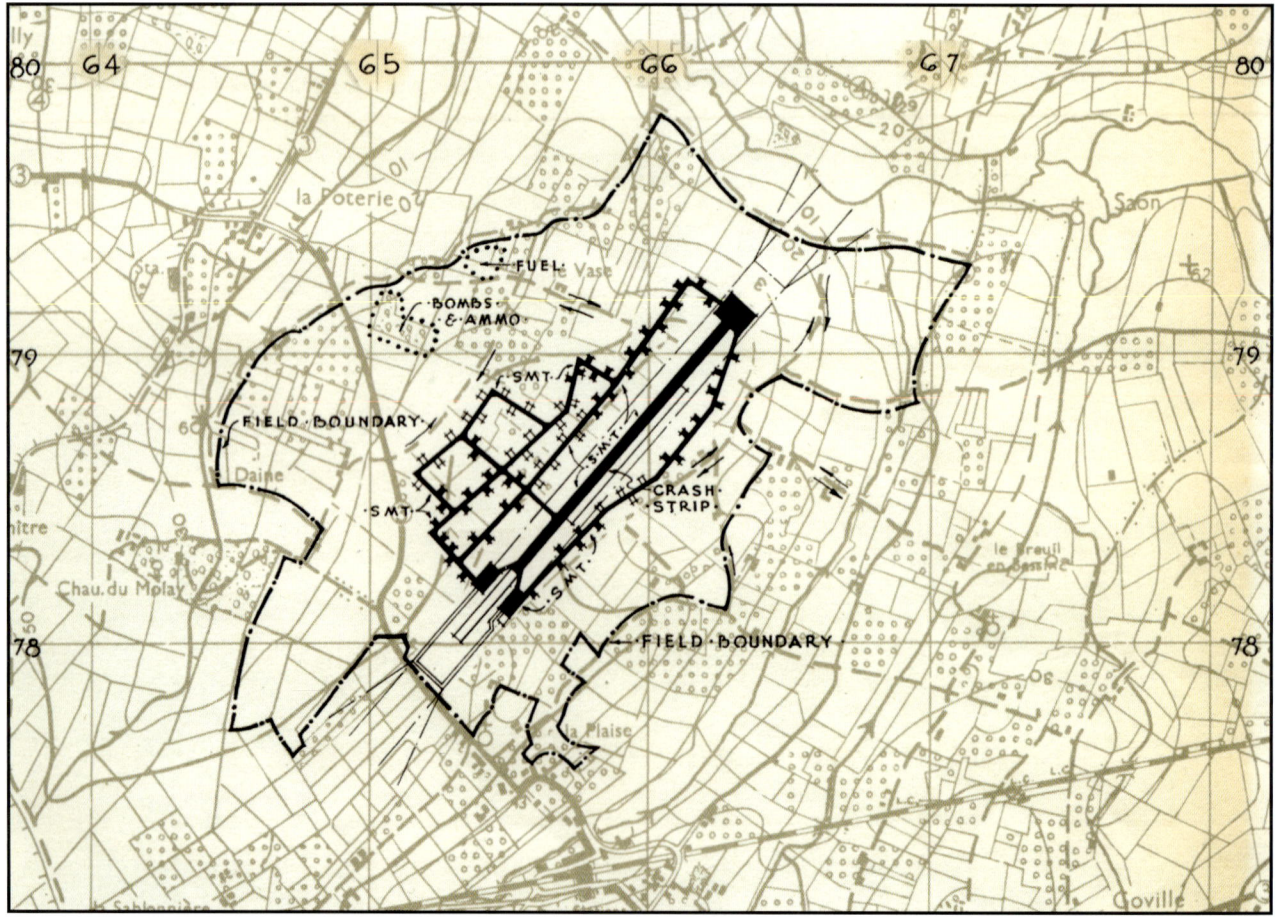

Apart from the memorial at Le Molay, the location of Montgomery's Tactical Headquarters has also been marked at Blay *(inset)*.

A-5 CHIPPELLE

OPERATIONAL JULY 6

Latitude: 49°14'N
Longitude: 00°58'W
Grid reference: T-591767
Altitude: 105ft

By the evening of June 10, American forces had advanced to the Bayeux—St Lô highway (RN 172), the boundary between the 29th and 2nd Divisions running almost directly through the site for the 820th Engineer Aviation Battalion's airfield A-5. This was located a mile north-west of Tournières on the road leading west to Périers, the site being captured by the 115th Infantry Regiment of the 29th on June 10.

An SMT-surfaced runway, 5,000ft long, was completed by July 5 ready for the 404th Fighter Group. Fifty tracked dispersals were available, and another 25 just of graded earth. Full radio and homing was provided.

Its three squadrons — the 506th, 507th and 508th — flew in with their P-47s the next day, remaining at Chippelle until the end of August when they transferred to A-48 at Brétigny.

A memorial listing the casualties suffered by the 404th now stands nearby.

When Eisenhower's Advanced Command Post opened near Tournières on August 6 Montgomery, in order to be nearer Eisenhower, had already relocated his own TAC HQ from Blay to a new location at the Forêt de Cerisy on August 3 (see map page 158). With the urgency to build more airfields, on July 4 Ike was photographed speaking with Sergeant Clide W. Smith concerning the progress of those being built in the Cherbourg peninsula. The caption claims it shows an 'airstrip under construction near Montebourg and Carentan', but as these two towns are over 20 kilometres apart, it is difficult to say whether it refers to A-7 or A-10.

On June 16, the 820th Engineers began work on a fighter strip at Chippelle, four miles west of Le Molay. A 5,000ft runway and dispersals had been finished by July 5 and the Thunderbolts of the 404th Fighter Group flew in the following day.

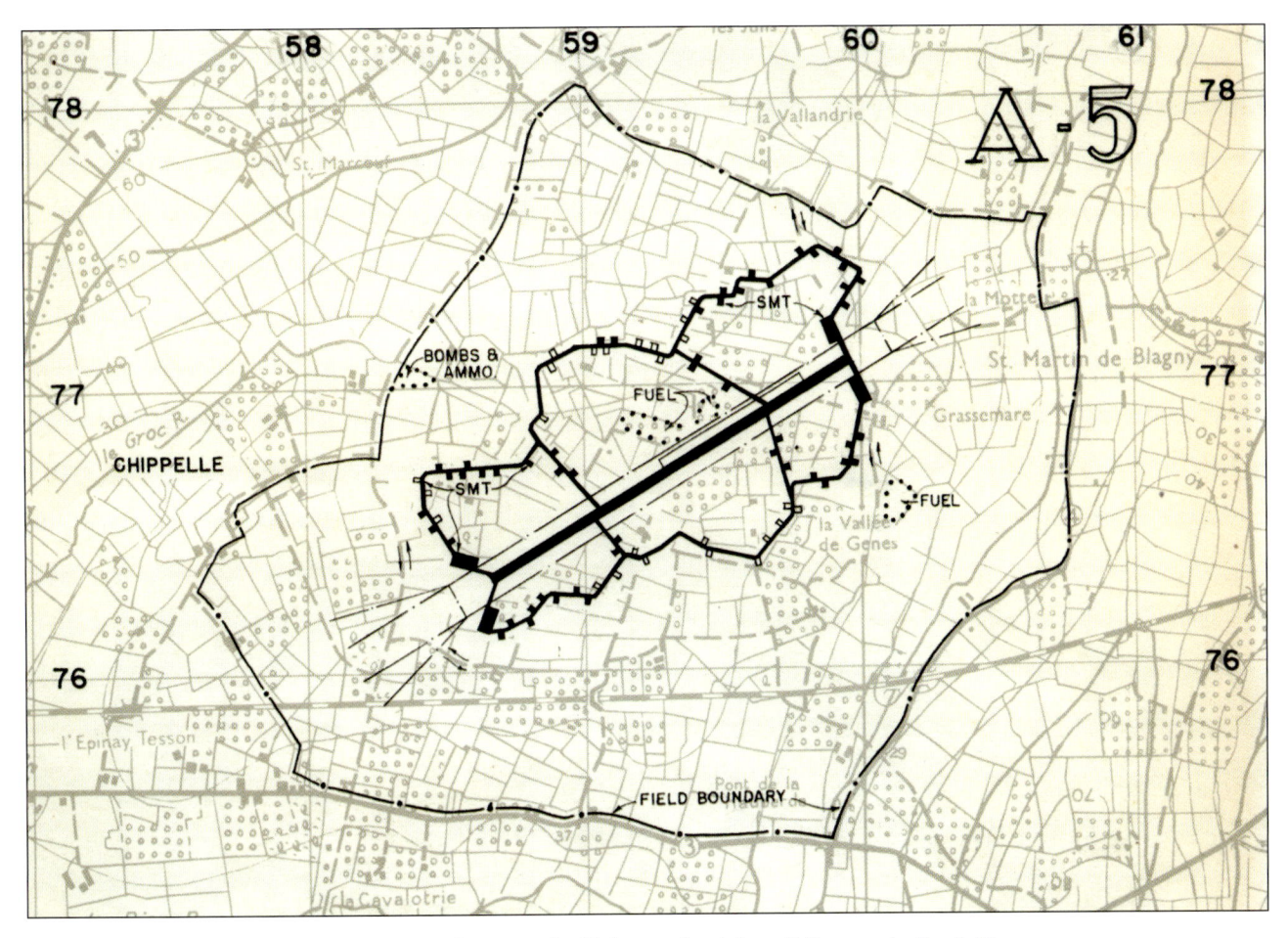

The railway is the main line from Bayeux to Carentan, Le Molay station lying off the map to the right.

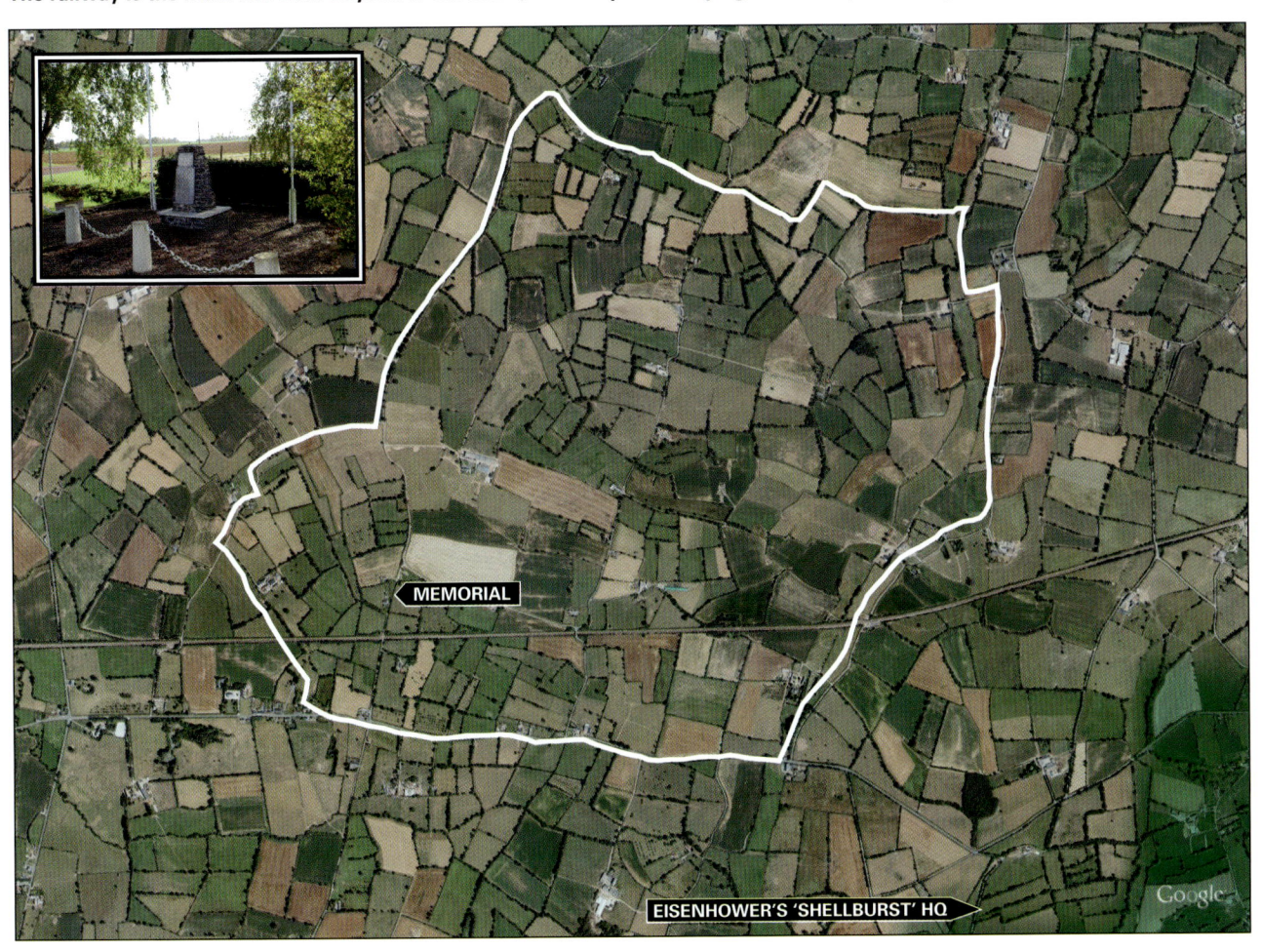

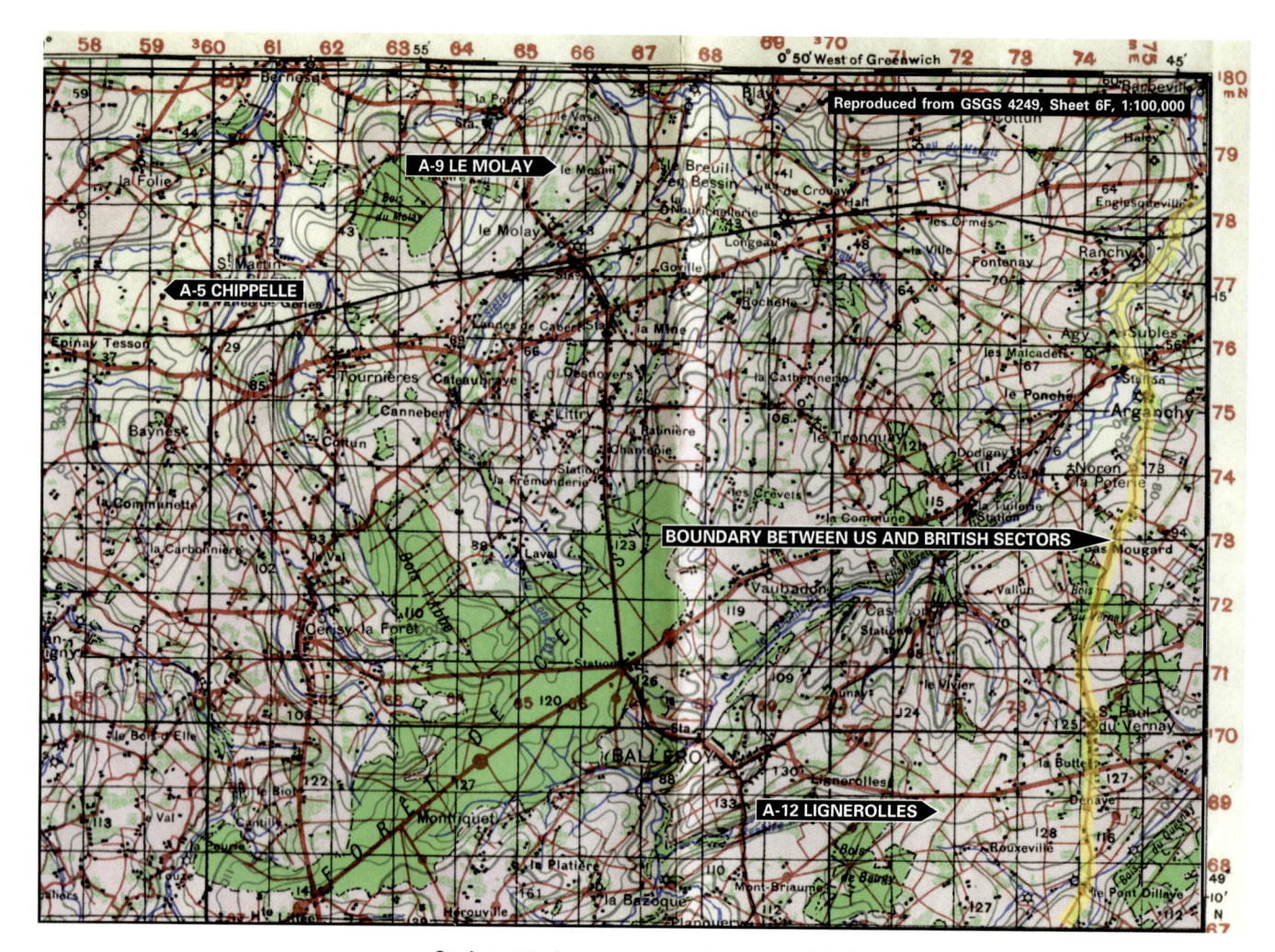

A-12 LIGNEROLLES

OPERATIONAL JULY 7

Latitude: 49°10'N
Longitude: 00°47'W
Grid reference: T-718688
Altitude: 440ft

Lying 1½ miles south-east of Balleroy (just off the Bayeux—St Lô road), its site captured by the 26th Infantry, 1st Division, on June 11, the task of building A-12 was given to one of the busiest Engineer Aviation Battalions, the 820th, which had already prepared A-2 at Cricqueville and A-5 at Chippelle. And after finishing A-12, they moved on to Rennes to work on A-27 followed by A-38 at Montreuil.

The runway at Lignerolles was to be 5,000ft surfaced with PBS hessian. Work began as soon as the area was clear and the P-47 Thunderbolts of the 362nd Fighter Group flew in from Headcorn in Kent on July 6. Its three squadrons, the 377th, 378th and 379th, remained at A-12 until August 10.

Meanwhile, the American break-out was gathering pace and 80 miles to the south-west Rennes was entered by the 13th Infantry, 8th Division, on August 3. As there was now an airfield available just outside the city with two concrete runways, the 362nd Group was transferred there to support the American advance into Brittany, the squadrons leaving for A-27 on August 10-13.

On June 10 a huge gap, some ten miles wide, had opened up in the German defences south of Balleroy, just where the 820th Engineers were due to build A-12 near the village of Lignerolles, south-east of the Forêt de Cerisy.

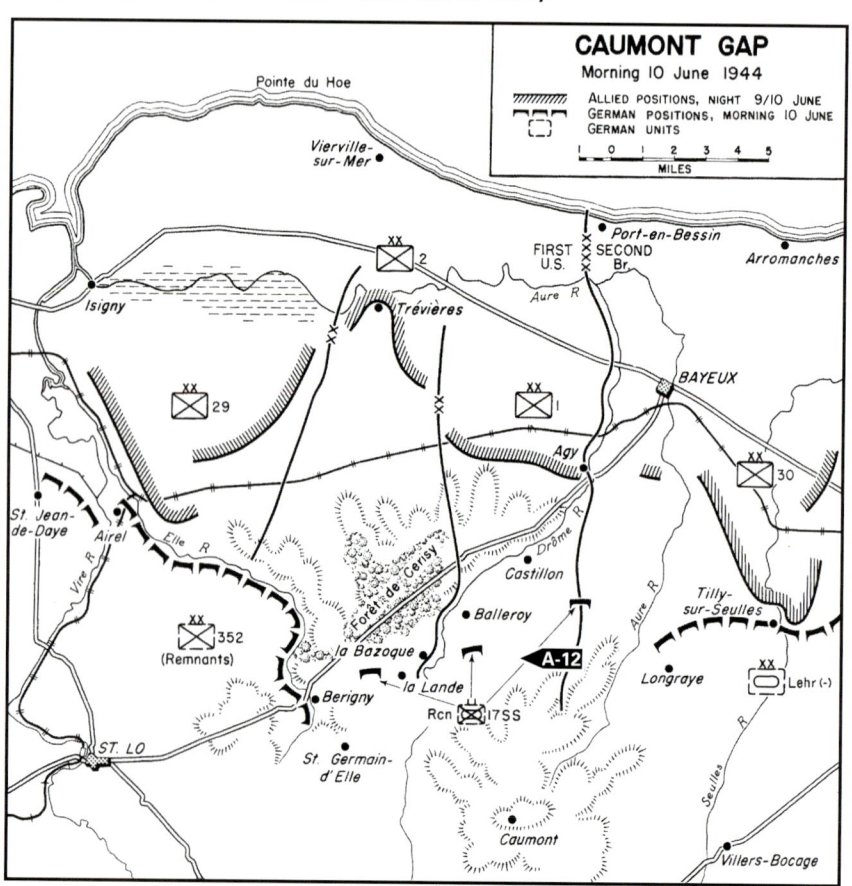

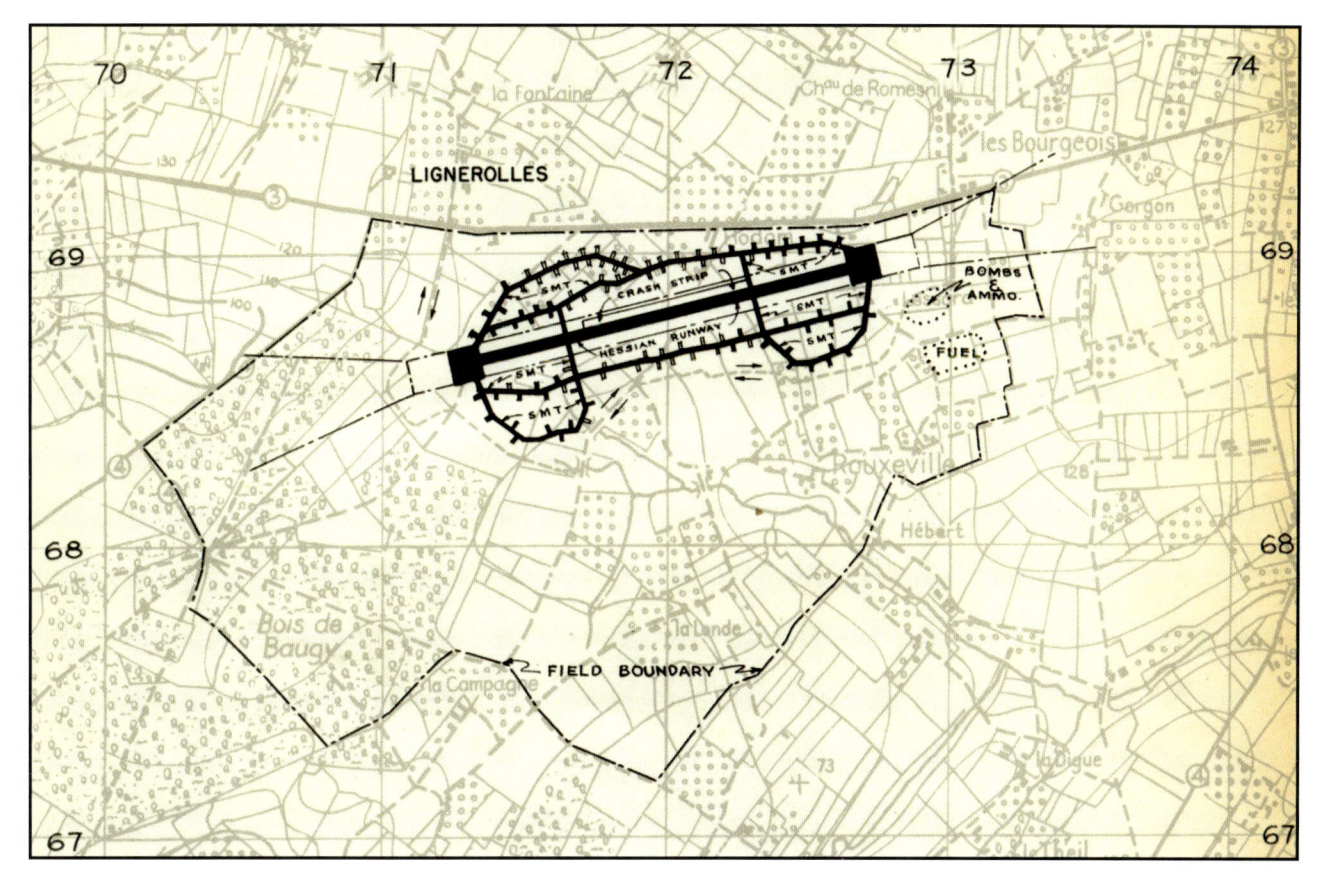

The inter-army boundary between the US First and British Second ran right through the opening in the German defences which then came under attack by both armies on June 12. **However, the following day the push was called off to avoid the Allied flanks to be exposed to the threat of an enemy armoured counter-attack.**

In their place at A-12 came the 365th Fighter Group. Its 386th, 387th and 388th Squadrons arrived on August 31 but so swift was the advance across France that they moved forward on September 3 to A-48 at Brétigny. This was a French aerodrome with two concrete runways situated on the southern outskirts of Paris, the capital having been entered on August 25.

A memorial has been erected virtually in the centre of the airfield right on the line of the PBS runway along a road that starts from the D13 at a place called Le Hodam.

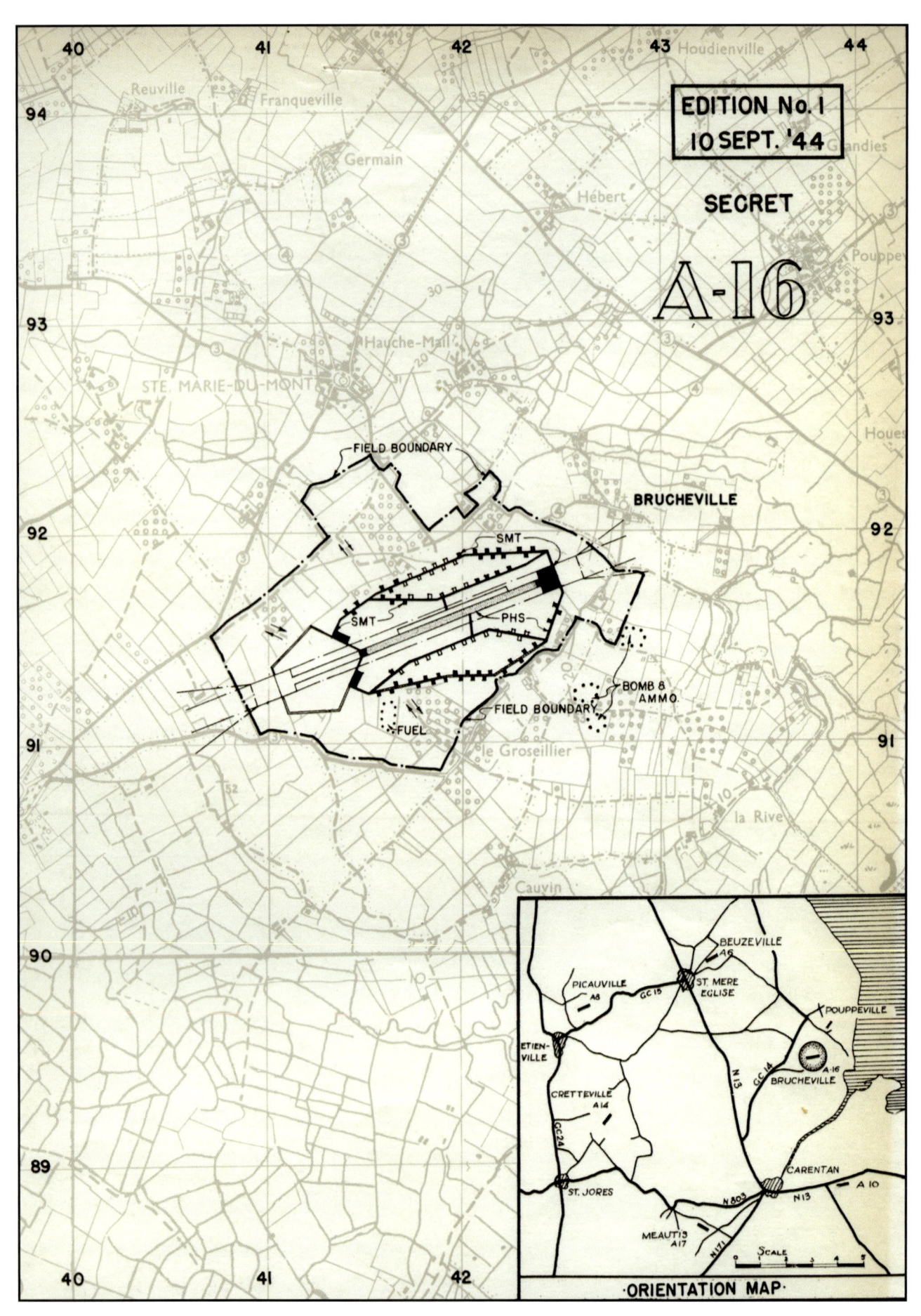

The orientation map shows the location for the first airstrip laid down in Normandy by the 843rd Engineers. They began A-16 at Brucheville on July 6, the first aircraft touching down on the earth strip the following day. Official operational date was August 2. The other airstrips shown were all operational by then save for A-17 at Méautis which was available by August 17.

A-16 BRUCHEVILLE

OPERATIONAL JULY 7

Latitude: 49°22'N
Longitude: 01°13'W
Grid reference: T-418917
Altitude: 60ft

Even while work was under way, the P-47s of the 36th Fighter Group, then operating from Kingsnorth, the closest of the Ninth Air Force's bases in Kent, moved to A-16 on July 7 as their forward base in Normandy.

Situated just over a mile inland from Utah Beach, A-16 was built by the 843rd Engineer Aviation Battalion and saw the first P-47s from the 53rd Fighter Squadron land on July 7.

The flying strip was 5,000ft of graded earth covered with Prefabricated Bituminous Surfacing. Taxiways and dispersals were tracked with SMT.

The other two squadrons of the 36th Fighter Group, the 22nd and 23rd, flew in from the UK on August 3. By the end of August a PBS strip had become available at Le Mans (A-35) so the 53rd moved there on the 29th, the other two squadrons following on September 5-6. The A-16 memorial was dedicated in 1990.

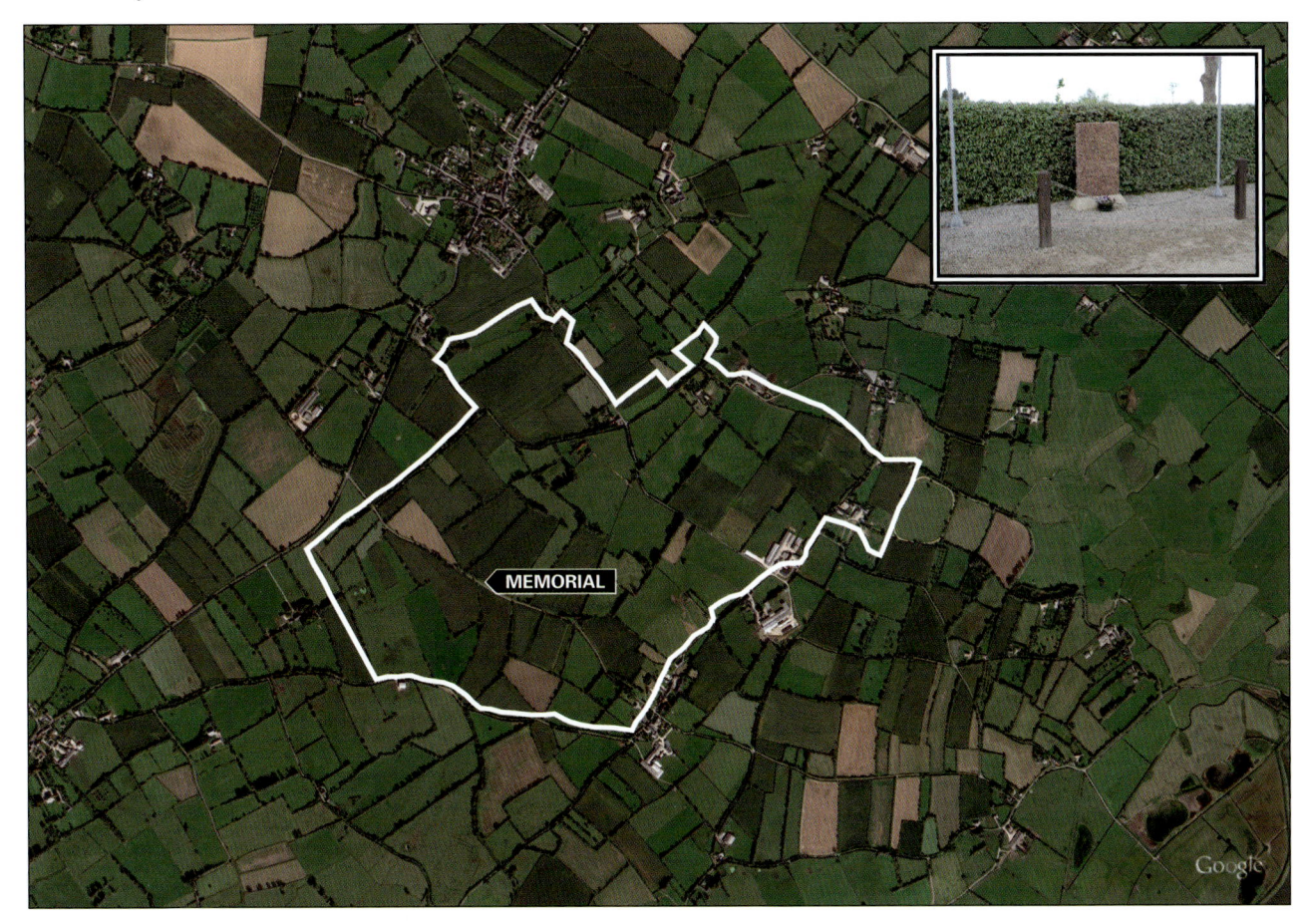

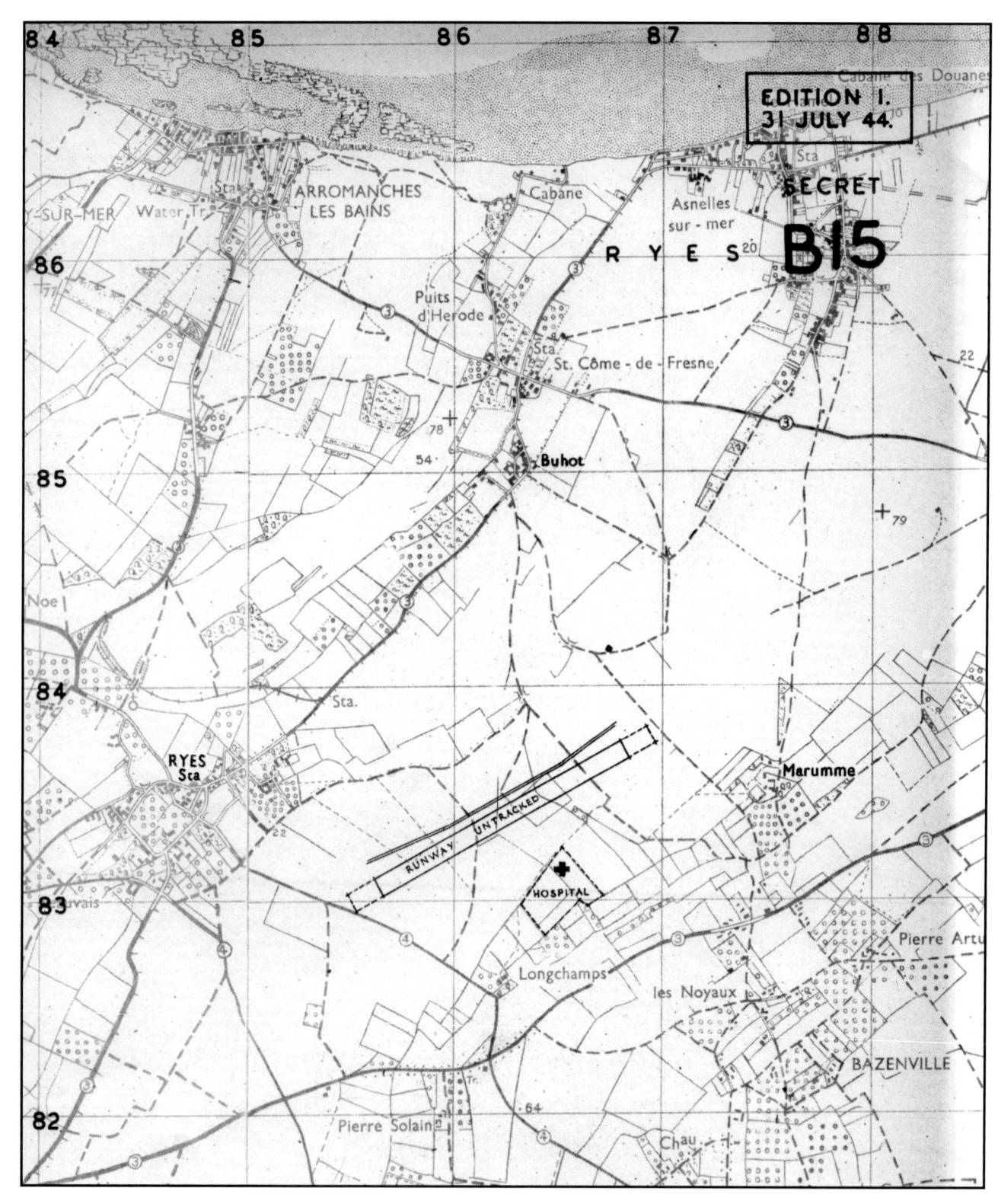

The Refuelling and Re-armament Strip at Ryes was not a good site as it was extremely restricted because almost all the ground in the bridgehead was now occupied or allocated. The site was bounded by two roads, a stream, a hospital and an ammunition dump. However, it was urgently needed and No. 24 Airfield Construction Group were given a target of completing its 3,600-foot earth runway in just 72 hours. A recce was carried out on July 1 but the first site had to be rejected as it was intersected by one of the main traffic routes being used by Second Army which could not be diverted. Nevertheless, by 1800 on July 2, an alternative strip had been agreed and marked out, although it was only just within the limits of undulation. Work began at dawn on July 3. The ground was mainly grass with some corn and two patches of potatoes. Flags of different colours, each 18 inches square and made up locally, were used to mark out the strip. Yellow were to indicate areas to be worked on and green flags at the side of the cleared areas. Red flags denoting holes, ditches or other obstructions were placed by a party which walked the area. Ten French farmers were brought in to rake the ground with horse-drawn machines. To keep the dust down because of the adjacent hospital, only the potatoes and those parts of the strip which had to be graded were scraped. Sheepsfoot rollers and a bulldozer were used to level the strip. Black and white flags indicated the line of the taxi tracks while blue flags marked the inside of the MT road. On the afternoon of July 5 a Spitfire came over and made three trial landings and take-offs which indicated that additional grading was necessary to iron out dangerous undulations. Altogether 2,654 man hours and 757 machine hours were logged on the construction.

By the time this photo was taken on August 26 the runway was barely visible.

B-15 RYES

OPERATIONAL JULY 8

Latitude: 49°19'N
Longitude: 00°36'W
Grid reference: T-862834
Altitude: 70ft

Another untracked strip of graded earth, Ryes's 3,600ft runway was situated two miles south of Arromanches. Another R&R airfield completed by No. 24 Airfield Construction Group by July 5, it was made available for use by the Typhoons of Nos. 193 and 257 Squadrons of No. 146 Wing. They stayed briefly from July 8 before moving to B-3 at Ste Croix on the 15th where they were joined by the other two squadrons belonging to the wing — Nos. 197 and 266 — from the UK.

Pilots were particularly warned that the balloon barrage lay two miles to the north.

In the event, B-15 was only used briefly by two squadrons of No. 146 Wing — No. 257 from July 8-15 and No. 193 from July 11-16. It was then abandoned as unsuitable for heavy Typhoons. We have angled the present day aerial to match the 1944 shot.

A-22C COLLEVILLE

OPERATIONAL JULY 13

Latitude: 49°20'N
Longitude: 00°51'W
Grid reference: T-695870
Altitude: 152ft

Colleville, as the suffix 'C' indicates, was built as a courier airstrip. Having finished A-3 and A-4 at Cardonville and Deux-Jumeaux, the 816th Engineer Aviation Battalion moved to the Omaha Beach area to construct A-22C. Work began on June 30 and, as it was to be used by C-47 transports, the 3,600ft strip was surfaced with PBS and then part covered with SMT. There was also a marshalling area and unloading apron 2,000ft x 600ft.

The airfield was open for business on July 13 and remained in use until November 4.

Six of the airstrips laid down to support the invasion were designated as 'courier' airfields. A-21C at St Laurent-sur-Mer opened on June 7; A-22C at Colleville on July 13 (see map pages 30-31); A-24C at Biniville opened on July 17; A-23C at Querqueville became available on July 29; A-25C at Bolleville on August 7, and A-30C at Courtils on August 13.

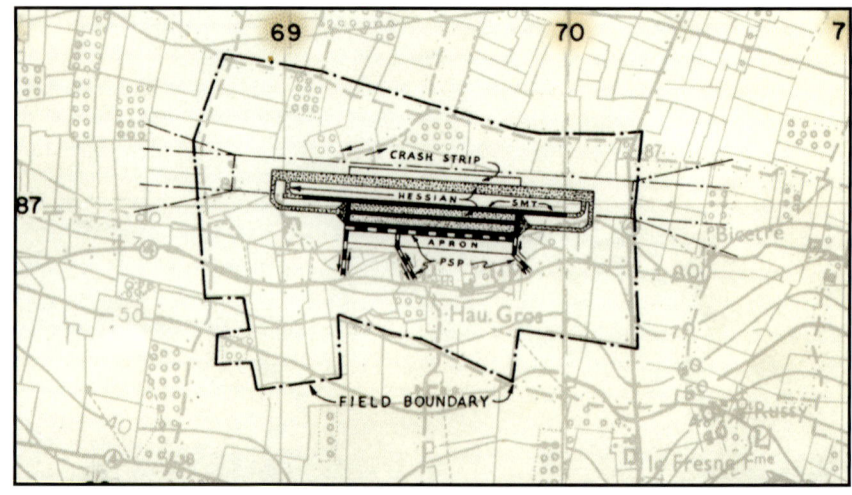

These photos were released by the Field Press Censor on August 26 for a feature in the US Services magazine *Yank* to illustrate the distribution of mail for GIs on the Continent. Without revealing the location, other than 'somewhere in France', it also described how C-47s were arriving daily from England with mail for onward carriage by road. Colleville, which had been surfaced with PBS, performed a vital link in the operation until it ceased to be used in November.

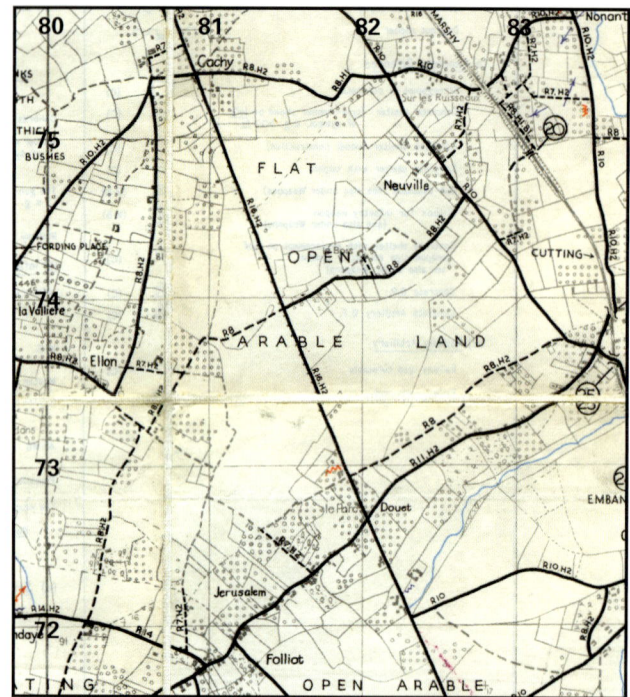

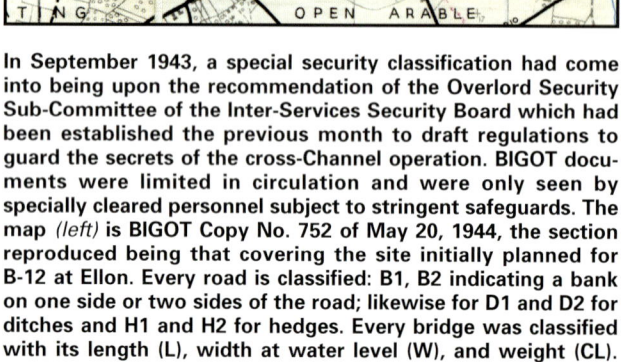

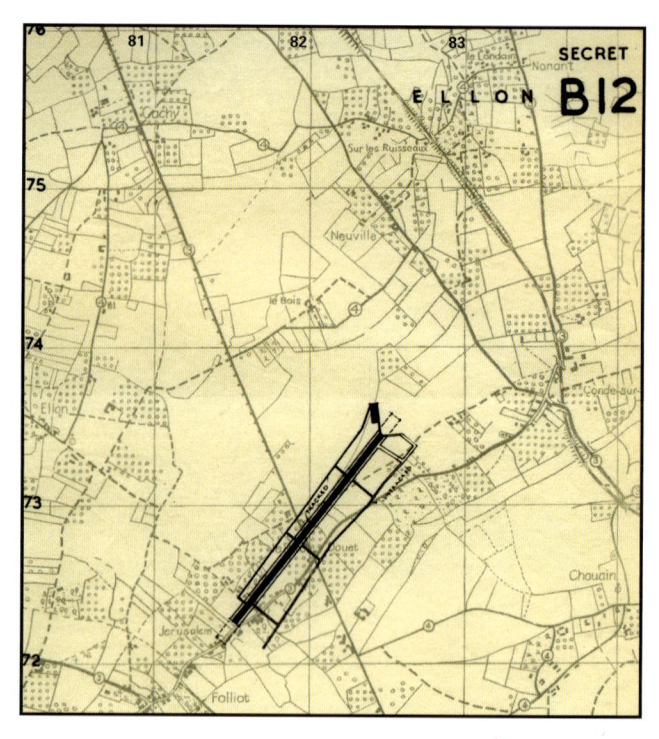

In September 1943, a special security classification had come into being upon the recommendation of the Overlord Security Sub-Committee of the Inter-Services Security Board which had been established the previous month to draft regulations to guard the secrets of the cross-Channel operation. BIGOT documents were limited in circulation and were only seen by specially cleared personnel subject to stringent safeguards. The map (left) is BIGOT Copy No. 752 of May 20, 1944, the section reproduced being that covering the site initially planned for B-12 at Ellon. Every road is classified: B1, B2 indicating a bank on one side or two sides of the road; likewise for D1 and D2 for ditches and H1 and H2 for hedges. Every bridge was classified with its length (L), width at water level (W), and weight (CL).

A movement order was issued by HQ No. 16 Airfield Construction Group for the force to move on June 27 to the vicinity of Ellon (map square 8073) to construct a 5,000ft Advanced Landing Ground. This plan shows B-12 in the first proposed location straddling the main D6 highway. Moved to avoid the road, the airfield was completed to R&RS standard by the evening of July 14 and to ALG standard four days later, save for the stop-butt for testing the guns and the petrol installation. During this period the unit lost two of its officers. On July 12, Lieutenant-Colonel Leslie Hancock was killed by an enemy mine and Lieutenant-Colonel William McDowell by the explosion of an ammunition truck on July 31. Both were laid to rest in Bayeux Cemetery (Plot II, Row G, Grave 26 and Plot III, Row B, Grave 1 respectively).

B-12 ELLON

OPERATIONAL JULY 16

Latitude: 49°13'N
Longitude: 00°40'W
Grid reference: T-811730
Altitude: 310ft

On June 10 the 7th Armoured Division, with the 22nd Armoured Brigade in the lead, began its advance south along the road from Bayeux to Tilly-sur-Seulles, sweeping past Ellon which had been earmarked for airfield B-12. The Austers of No. 658 Squadron began using the site on June 25, moving out on July 13.

A strip 3,600ft long surfaced with SMT was provided by No. 16 Airfield Construction Group, initially for No. 136 Wing with Typhoons, but the short strip was better suited to fighters so Nos. 19, 65 and 122 Squadrons of No. 122 Wing were transferred in on July 16 with their Mustangs from B-7 at Martragny. They stayed until September 2 when they moved to B-24 at St André-de-l'Eure.

An impressive memorial has now been built on land donated by M. Robert Renault. It also remembers Lieutenant-Colonel Leslie Hancock, the commander of No. 16 Airfield Construction Group, who was killed on July 7.

To avoid bisecting the main highway (D6) from Bayeux—Villers-Bocage, the airstrip was moved to the western side of the road (see plan on page 131).

On August 9 a sortie was carried out to photograph B-12 and fortunately the cover included B-19 at Lingèvres, located three miles to the south, which was the first advanced landing ground constructed in Normandy by the RAF Airfield Construction Service (see page 154). Nevertheless, the RAF had already been involved in making Carpiquet serviceable as No. 5352 Airfield Construction Wing had been working on it from mid-July, getting it operational on July 25 (see page 139).

Mustangs from B-7 at Martragny arrived on July 15-17, the three squadrons, Nos. 19, 65 and 122, remaining at Ellon until the beginning of September. This particular machine, FZ190 of No. 19 Squadron, is being attended to by Flying Officer F. H. Price; LAC L. Polley, Corporals F. Hughes and J. Lee and Sergeant W. G. Ward. This aircraft turned out to have an incredibly charmed life as it survived throughout the war only to be scrapped in December 1946.

A timeless comparison — fighting men may fade away but the fabric of Normandy lives on.

See the plan on page 149 for the location of B-12 Ellon, B-18 Cristot and B-19 Lingèvres.

One of the finest memorials to any of the invasion airfields in France is that at Ellon, located beside the old runway. Multiple marble panels describe the different aspects of the RAF's service there (unfortunately in rather poor English). The memorial was built at the instigation of Vince Ashworth whose brother, Flying Officer Corran Ashworth of the Royal New Zealand Air Force, failed to return to Ellon on August 3. As a member of No. 65 Squadron, he had taken off that morning to attack barges evacuating German troops across the Seine and was shot down near Oissel. He remains missing in action and commemorated on the Runnymede Memorial. Vince visited Ellon in June 2006, met the landowner Robert Renault, and this magnificent memorial was the result.

Air observation using L-4 Piper Cubs and L-5 Sentinels performed a vital role in spotting for artillery and liaison duties between the various headquarters. Normally 32 aircraft (four flights of eight) were assigned to each squadron although the actual number based on an airstrip like A-24C would have been between two and ten. Normally ten aircraft were assigned to each infantry and airborne division with two serving the artillery HQ and two each to its four field artillery battalions.

A-24C BINIVILLE

OPERATIONAL JULY 17

Latitude: 49°25'N
Longitude: 01°27'W
Grid reference: O-240000
Altitude: 55ft

On June 16, as part of the operation to capture St Sauveur-le-Vicomte, Colonel George Smythe of the 47th Infantry Regiment (US 9th Division) was assigned the task of capturing the high ground just east of Ste Colombe. The regiment had a hard fight in the area of Biniville but managed to reach the main road to the west on June 16.

Biniville was marked out quickly by the 830th Engineer Aviation Battalion with a 3,600ft earth strip, aligned NE-SW, basically for light liaison aircraft. Even the taxi-track was left as just undefined earth. It was ready on July 17 but was only used occasionally by the 125th Liaison Squadron until they moved to Rennes on September 3.

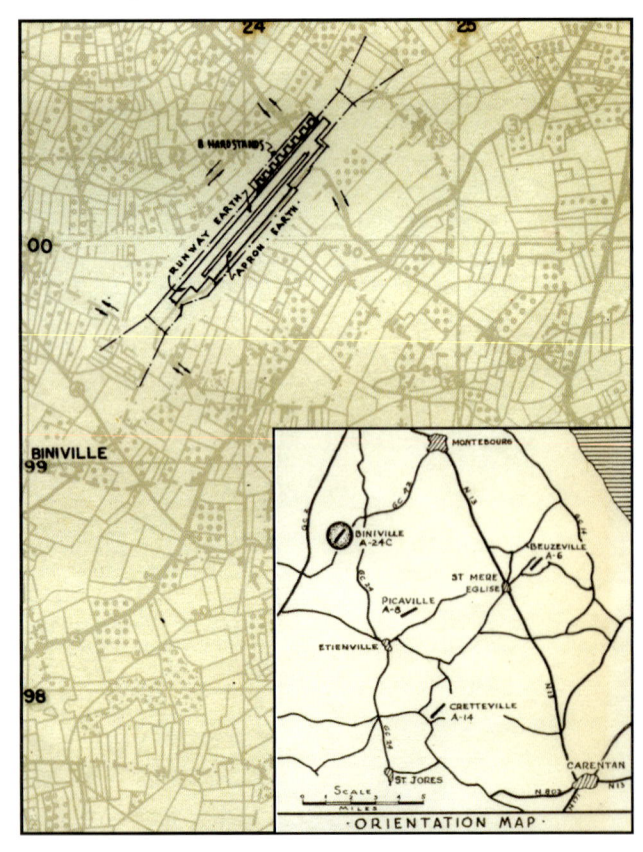

On July 25 Eisenhower announced that US ground forces were to be regrouped under General Bradley commanding the 12th Army Group which was to become active on August 1. That same day General George S. Patton's Third Army became operational to begin the break-out. His headquarters were situated at Néhou (see map opposite) just a mile or so west of A-24C. (This airstrip, laid down primarily for liaison aircraft, is referred to in some records as St Sauveur.)

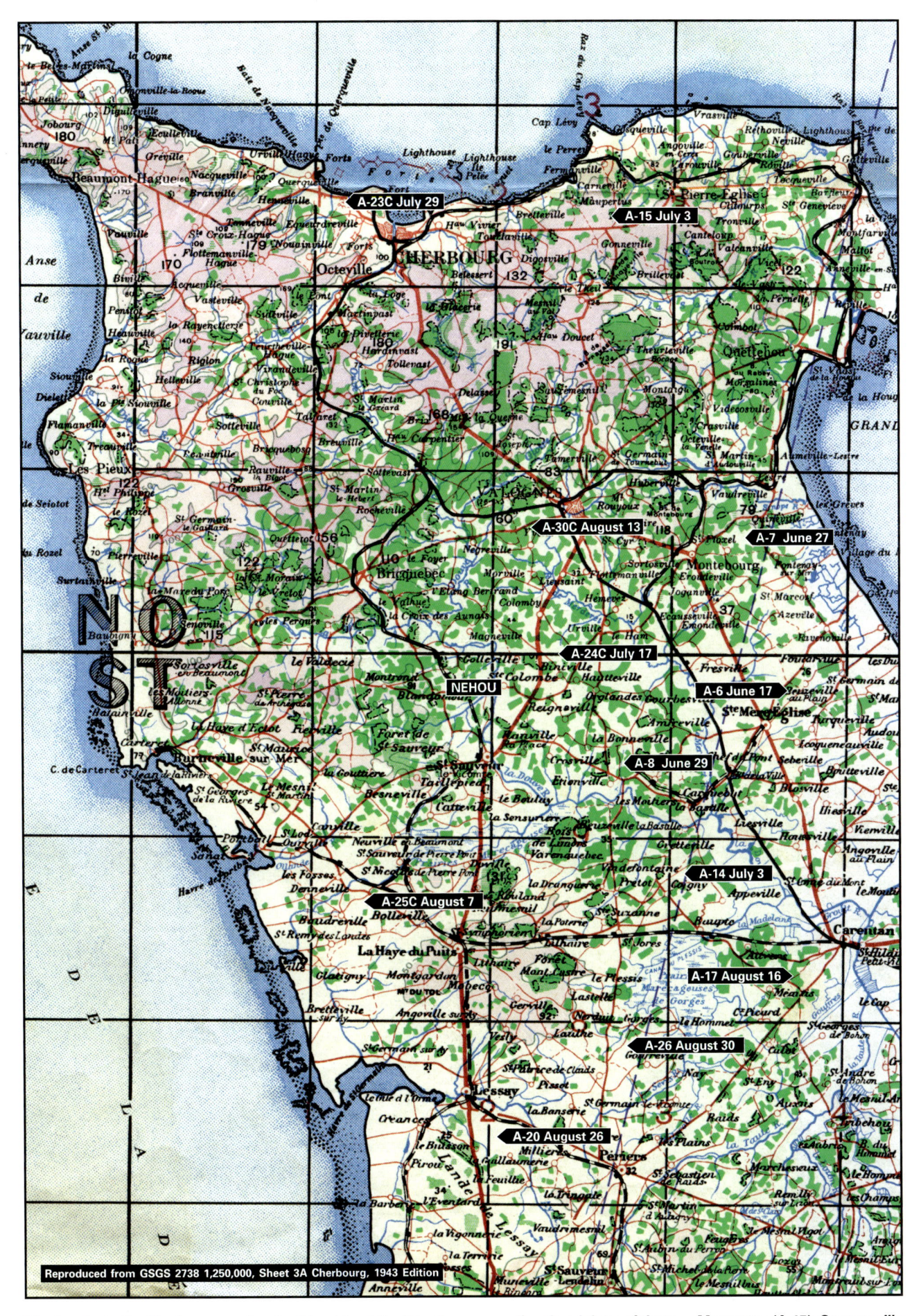

The terrain in the Cherbourg peninsula did not lend itself to the construction of airfields. These dates are when each became operational and three of them — Maupertus (A-15), Querqueville (A-23C) and Lessay (A-20) — were all former French aerodromes.

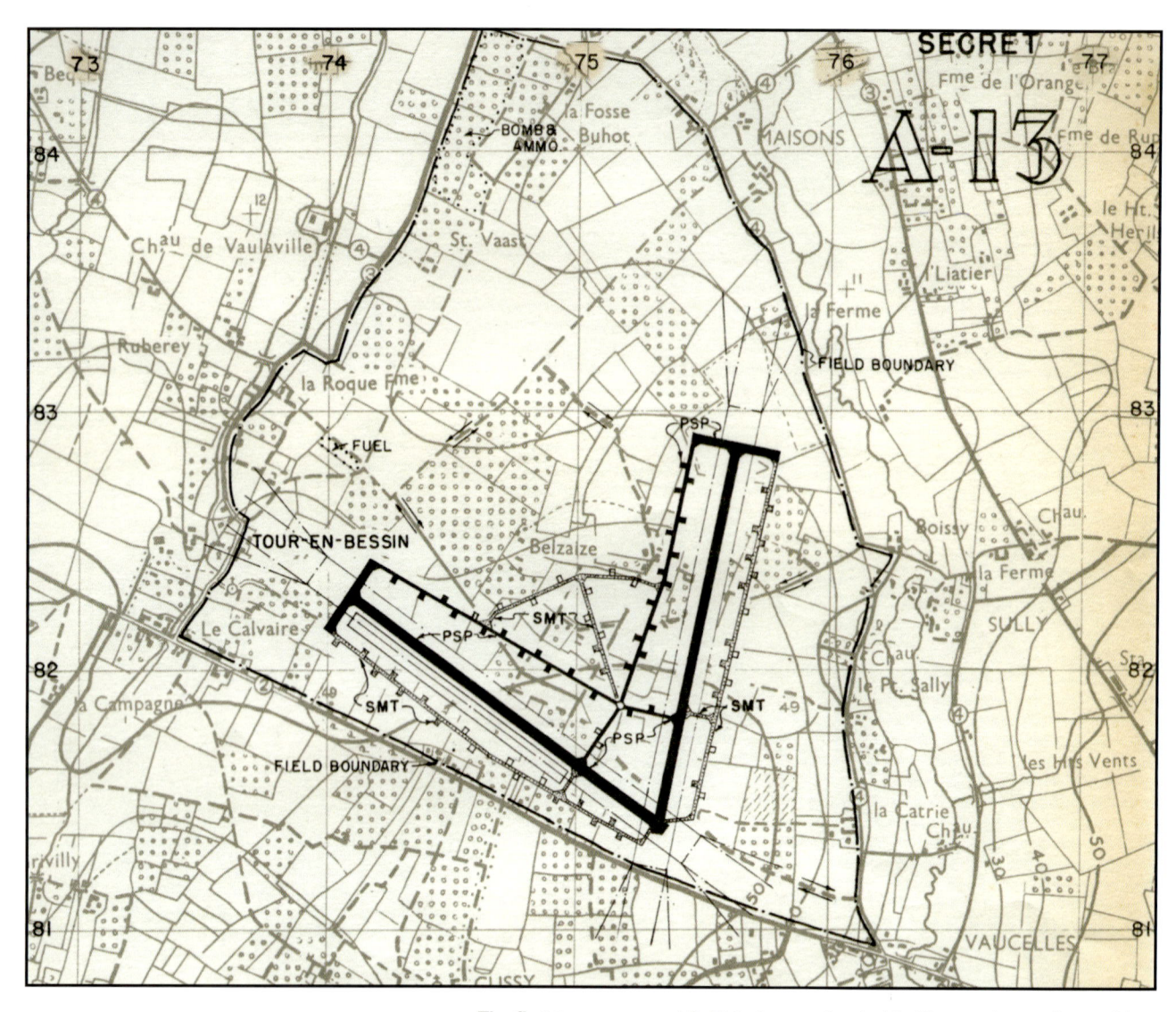

A-13 TOUR-EN-BESSIN

The first two-runway airfield to be constructed in Normandy was located just west of the boundary between the US First and British Second Armies, the site being just north of the N13 from Bayeux to Isigny (see map pages 106-107).

OPERATIONAL JULY 19

Latitude: 49°17'N
Longitude: 00°45'W
Grid reference: T-753813
Altitude: 75-145ft

This airfield was located 2½ miles north-west of Bayeux. It was intended to use it for medium bombers of the Ninth Air Force as well as fighters so it was constructed by the 833rd and 846th Engineer Aviation Battalions with two 5,000ft runways, aligned N-S and NW-SE, surfaced with Pierced Steel Planking (PSP). Taxiways and dispersals were also tracked with PSP.

First to arrive on July 19 were the P-47s of the 513th Squadron of the 406th Fighter Group, followed on the 27th by its other two squadrons, the 512th and 514th. Three days later the 373rd Fighter Group joined them with its three squadrons — the 410th, 411th and 412th.

The 406th Group departed for A-14 at Cretteville, 28 miles to the west, on August 17 and three days later the 373rd Group also moved out to A-29 at St James, 60 miles to the south at the base of the Cherbourg peninsula.

Tour-en-Bessin had been overrun by the 2nd Battalion of the 26th Infantry, 1st Division, on the night of June 7/8 but it was not until July 12 that the 833rd and 846th Engineers arrived to begin work. Over the next 16 days, two 5,000ft runways, surfaced with PSP, were constructed on bearings of 11 and 125 degrees.

This left the airfield clear to receive the B-26 Marauders of the 394th Bomb Group from the 98th Combat Bomb Wing. The first two squadrons, the 584th and 585th, arrived from Holmsley South in Hampshire as soon as the last Thunderbolt had left on the 20th, with the 586th Squadron following on the 29th and the 587th on the 31st. The B-26s remained on ops at Tour-en-Bessin until September 25 when they were relocated further east to A-50 Bricy, just north-west of Orléans.

A memorial was unveiled on the anniversary of D-Day in 1989.

Although intended as a medium bomber base, the first residents were the Thunderbolts of the 373rd and 406th Fighter Groups. The Marauders did not arrive until late in August.

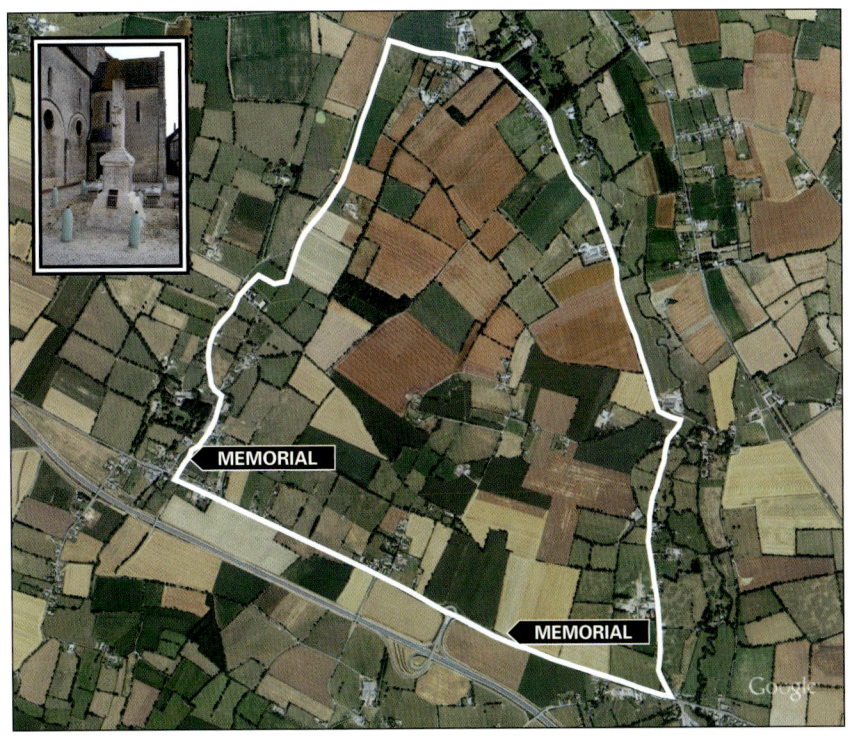

135

B-17 CARPIQUET

After its capture in 1940, Carpiquet airfield became a major Luftwaffe base for its operations against Britain. This FW190 of 13. Staffel of Schnellkampfgeschwader 10 was pictured after the attack on Bournemouth on May 23, 1943.

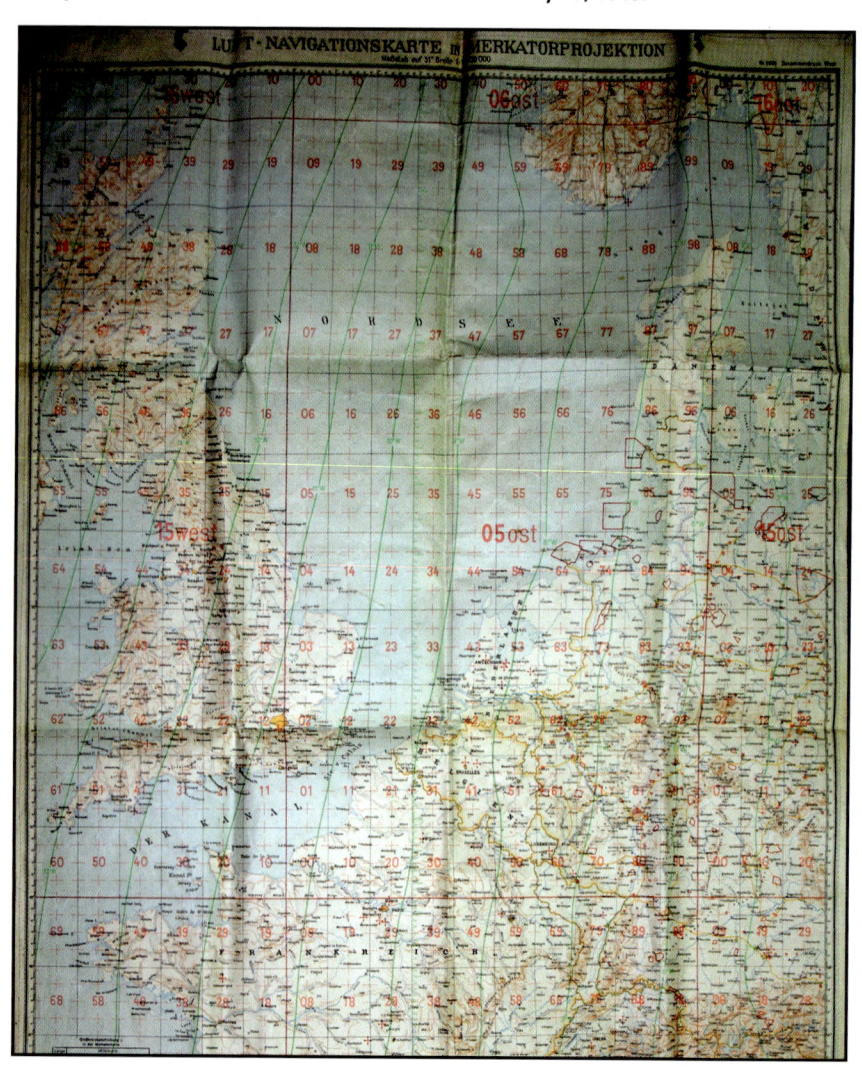

OPERATIONAL JULY 25

Latitude: 49°10'N
Longitude: 00°27'W
Grid reference: T-966677
Altitude: 233ft

Built in 1937 four miles WSW of Caen as a long-range bomber base for the French Air Force, it was used by several of their units during the German invasion. The Luftwaffe installed one concrete runway and the Bf110s of I./ZG2 and Ju88s of KG806 were based there during the summer of 1940. It was also later employed by the fighter-bombers from 10./JG2 and 10./JG26 during the 'tip-and-run' campaign against southern England during 1942, and by SKG10 in 1943.

It had been the intention of the D-Day planners to capture it by the end of the first day but the operation (code-named 'Windsor') to take the airfield could not be launched until July 4. A bitter battle between elements of the 3rd Canadian Infantry Division and the 12. SS-Panzer-Division 'Hitlerjugend' was fought in the area over the next two days, supported by rocket attacks from No. 181 Squadron based at B-6 Coulombs, but this attempt to capture the airfield failed. It was only finally taken by the Canadian 8th Infantry Brigade on July 9 although all opposition in the area was still not extinguished until the 18th.

This map, displayed on the wall of the operations headquarters, was used when planning the raids . . . that is until Chris Smith, who landed on Sword Beach, removed it for a souvenir!

136

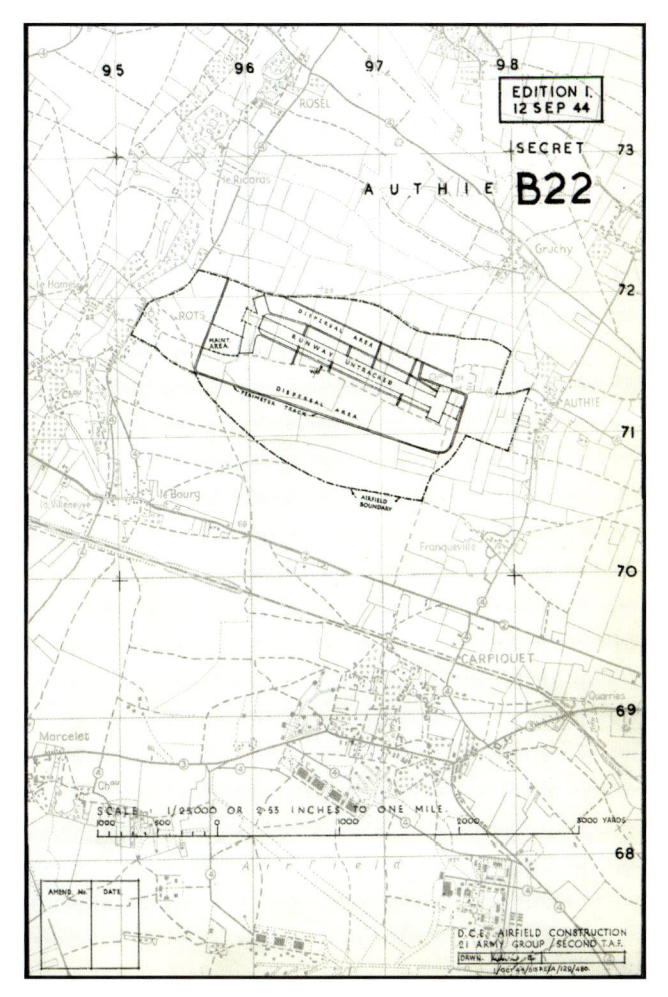

Before the invasion, Allied planners had decided to lay down an untracked runway a mile to the north of Carpiquet. Given the code B-22 Authie, construction was started but then later abandoned, possibly after the aerodrome at Carpiquet became available. This photo shows the progress of the work as at September 12.

At Carpiquet airfield the Germans had laid down a 4,200ft concrete runway.

The Allied need for additional airfields ensured that the capture of Carpiquet was a priority but, as it lay on the direct route for Caen, it was equally an important defensive position for the Germans. The battle which began on July 4 was bloody, and Canadian casualties for Operation 'Windsor' totalled 377 of which 127 men had been killed, most on the first day. The assault comprised infantry attacks, flame-throwers, Churchill tanks firing 11-inch Petard mortars plus the support of two squadrons of Typhoons. Yet, as the ground had been bombed, shelled and fought over, before the airfield could be used it had to be checked for mines. The whole area was covered with metal splinters which made the task of searching with mine detectors very laborious and slow. No. 1 Dog Platoon was brought in, their help being reported by the CO of No. 24 Airfield Construction Group as invaluable. 'They have not found any mines, but they have found a number of unexploded bombs and shells. As they do not bother about splinters they are very much quicker than a mine detector party. Also they can work in and about an area which is covered with broken metal. The Platoon has searched 200,000 square yards between 22 and 31 July, i.e. an average of 20,000 square yards a day. This includes wet days and rest days. It has been found that as there was so little for them to find on the airfield, the dogs were inclined to get uninterested after a bit. They were then taken away for a day onto a specially laid field and their interest revived at once. It is now the practice to keep a few unprimed Tellermines and to plant them at intervals. The finding of these keeps up the dog's interest. I recommended that the Royal Engineers' Dog Platoon could well be employed the whole time by the six airfield construction groups and wings. I could employ them on Carpiquet for at least another three weeks.'

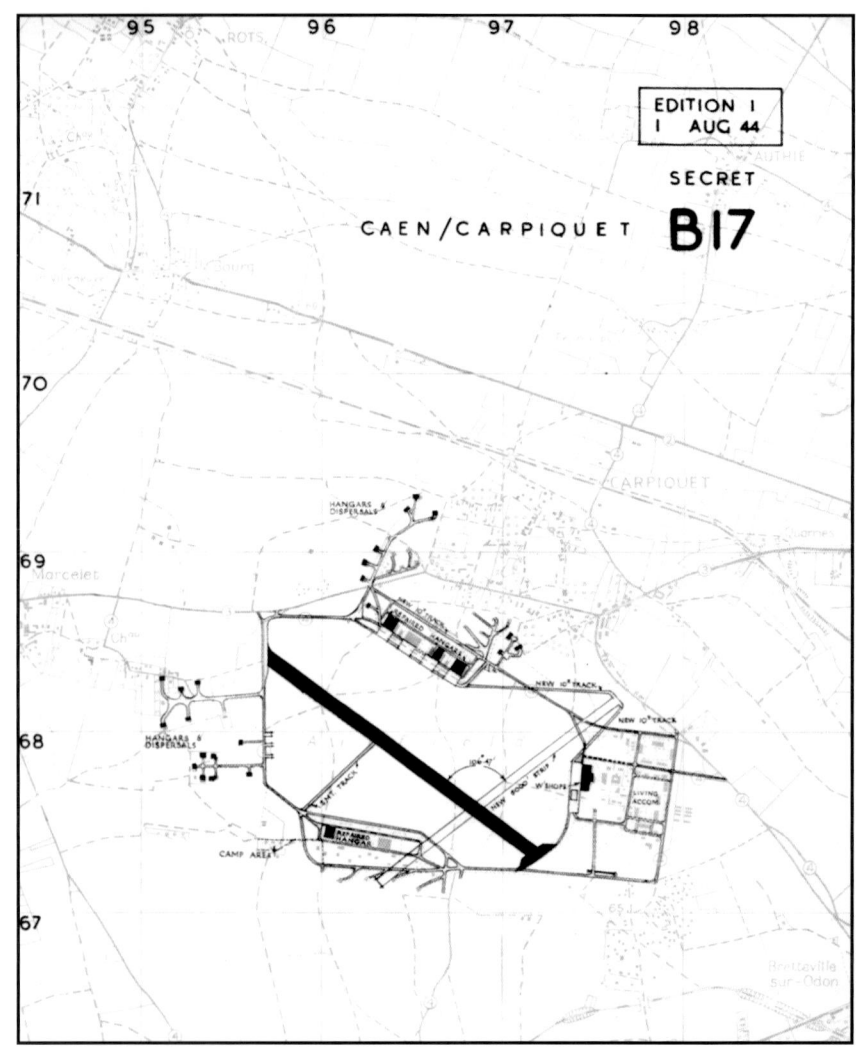

Apart from lengthening the existing runway to 6,000 feet, it was planned to add a second PSP runway of 5,900 feet, so No. 5352 Wing of the RAF's Airfield Construction Service were brought in to help No. 24 Airfield Construction Group with the work.

Once Carpiquet was in Allied hands, No. 24 Airfield Construction Group and the RAF's No. 5352 Airfield Construction Wing began work to bring it back to operable condition but first the bomb disposal section had to check for mines and booby traps.

On August 25, No. 409 Squadron equipped with Mosquito XIIIs arrived at Carpiquet from Hunsdon in Hertfordshire to become the first night fighter unit of the Second Tactical Air Force to be based in France. It was joined on September 5 by the Mosquitos of No. 264, previously based at B-6 Coulombs, and four days later No. 604 that had been operating from the American strip A-8 at Picauville.

At the end of August (26th-31st), Nos. 33, 222, 349 and 485 Squadrons had moved in with Spitfires, but by the end of September all units had moved out.

After the war the airfield became Caen Airport with the secondary runway at 4,130ft by 160ft and still surfaced with PSP as late as 1956. Then, the main concrete runway was 5,050ft but today it has been resurfaced with asphalt and extended to 6,233ft. Meanwhile the secondary has since been reduced to 3,871ft, also in asphalt.

As soon as Carpiquet was serviceable, Mosquito squadrons were brought in, No. 409 from the UK on August 25, No. 264 from B-6 at Coulombs on September 5, while No. 604 relocated from A-8 at Picauville on September 9.

Now the principal airport in Normandy, the two runways are 13-31 at 6,233ft and the secondary 06-24 of 3,871ft, both of asphalt.

A-23C QUERQUEVILLE

After it fell into German hands, Fliegerhorst Querqueville became a forward Luftwaffe base for operations against England in the summer of 1940.

OPERATIONAL JULY 29

Latitude: 49°40'N
Longitude: 01°41'W
Grid reference: O-092267
Altitude: 13-26ft

Located three miles north-west of Cherbourg, Querqueville had been established for the French Navy in 1925 for training and research operations when it was known as Cherbourg-West. It became a Luftwaffe forward base after the fall of France for Bf109s of I. and III./JG27 during the Battle of Britain and it was also used by III./JG54 in March 1941. It was bombed on several occasions by both the RAF and USAAF.

After Maupertus (A-15) was captured, Querqueville was taken by the 47th Infantry of the 9th Division as it advanced up the coast towards Cap de la Hague which was reached on June 30.

Stab JG27 were stationed there from July 14 to August 28 with other elements of Jagdgeschwader 27 being detached there from Plumetot and Carpiquet.

Four years later it was in American hands and the 850th Engineers moved in on June 29 to prepare a stable runway as A-23C had been designated as a transport base. The 826th Battalion had to be called in to help as it was found that the airfield had been heavily mined. Over 4,500 mines were cleared for which several of the men were awarded Bronze Stars.

With all fighting in the Cotentin at an end, the airfield was designated as a transport field but first several thousand land mines had to be cleared. The runway of 4,450ft, surfaced with PBS hessian, was laid down by the 850th Engineer Aviation Battalion, and completed by July 6.

From then until the end of the war A-23C was in continual use, first by the 302nd Transport Wing. After hostilities ended, it had an interesting role as an assembly point for German aircraft ready for despatch to the UK and USA.

A-23C closed on August 8, 1945. The French Navy took it back and used it as an airfield until 1948 but later a naval academy was built on the site.

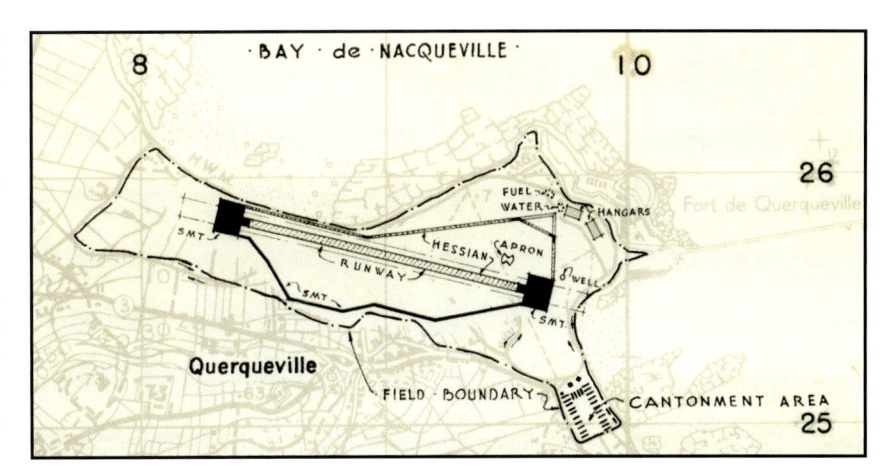

In 1944, air intelligence experts in the US prepared lists of German aviation equipment that they wanted for examination, including one example of every Luftwaffe aircraft under the code-name Operation 'Lusty' (standing for <u>Lu</u>ftwaffe <u>S</u>ecret <u>T</u>echnology). The material was delivered to Querqueville as the harbour at Cherbourg would make shipment easier. All the aircraft were cocooned against the salt air and delivered to Newark Army Airfield from where they were distributed to various centres for evaluation and testing. Altogether the 'Lusty' teams assembled 16,280 items weighing 6,200 tons from which 2,398 were selected for technical analysis at the flight centre at Wilbur Wright Field. When that location became overloaded, aircraft were sent to Freeman Field in Indiana, but after that facility closed in 1946, the large aircraft went to Davis-Monthan Field in Arizona while the fighters were sent to Park Ridge, Illinois, which later became Chicago's O'Hare Airport. Inevitably storage space there ran out and in 1953 many types were scrapped, reputedly being used as fill for the O'Hare runways.

A-23C was released by the USAAF to the French Aeronavale in August 1945, but they ceased to use it in 1948. Finally closed in 1966, it became the location of the École des Fourriers of the French Navy.

141

With Eisenhower's re-organisation of US forces (see page 132), it was essential that the Ninth Air Force headquarters, in charge of the IX Tactical Air Command (supporting the First Army) and the XIX Tactical Air Command (supporting the newly-created Third Army), was bought into immediate contact with its land army counterpart: the 12th Army Group.

General Bradley had established his new army group HQ in the Château des Mares at St Sauveur-Lendelin, north of Coutances, so it was here that the new Ninth HQ was opened at 0001 hours on August 6. Army and air force signal organisations had set up the many communication facilities necessary in a huge circus tent with attendant trailers.

On August 5 Churchill flew by Dakota from Northolt to Cherbourg which was found to be fog-bound so his aircraft had to turn back as the preceeding plane had crashed killing all its occupants. He tried again to reach Normandy two days later and this time, although his departure had been delayed for more than three hours because of bad weather, he landed at Maupertus shortly after lunch. After visiting Montgomery at 21st Army Group headquarters, he proceeded to Saint-Sauveur where Bradley was expecting him. However, the battle was then at a very critical stage as Patton had just launched his armoured columns into Brittany; the First Canadian Army were about to begin Operation 'Totalize' to capture Falaise, and early that morning the Germans had counter-attacked at Mortain. Churchill sensed the tension and so cut short his visit. Eisenhower arrived from Britain just before Churchill left, so the two men were able to have a brief conversation before the Prime Minister flew back to Northolt. Here, Eisenhower is pictured with Bradley at the Château des Mares on August 8.

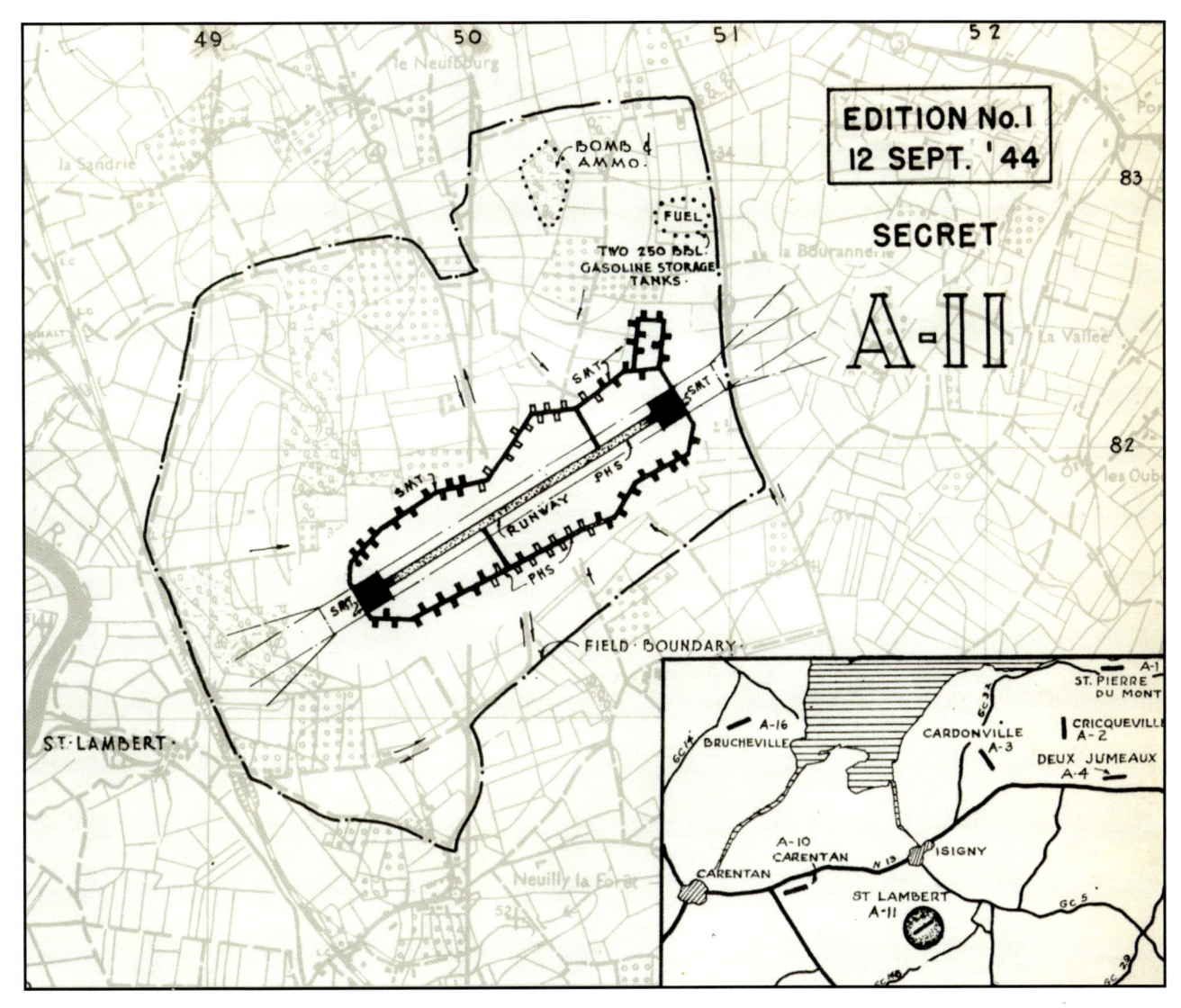

A-11 ST LAMBERT

OPERATIONAL AUGUST 6

Latitude: 49°17'N
Longitude: 01°05'W
Grid reference: T-502818
Altitude: 125ft

In the official USAAF history, this airfield, 2½ miles south of Isigny, is named after the village of Neuilly-la-Forêt which lies to the south of it although the more accepted name is St Lambert which is the closer village to the west.

The strip was constructed by the 832nd Engineer Aviation Battalion for the P-38 Lightnings of the 474th Fighter Group. The runway was 5,000ft surfaced with PBS hessian.

The three squadrons, the 428th, 429th and 430th, began operations on August 6, remaining at A-11 until a move was ordered to relocate to A-43 at St Marceau, nine miles north of Le Mans, on September 2.

A memorial dedicated to the 474th Group now stands at the roadside.

Official records also refer to A-11 as Neuilly after the village of Neuilly-la-Forêt just off the southern boundary.

The same day that the new Ninth Air Force headquarters was opened at Saint-Sauveur-Lendelin, the airfield at St Lambert became operational. Work had begun here on July 22 for the P-38 Lightnings of the 474th Fighter Group, then based at Warmwell in Dorset.

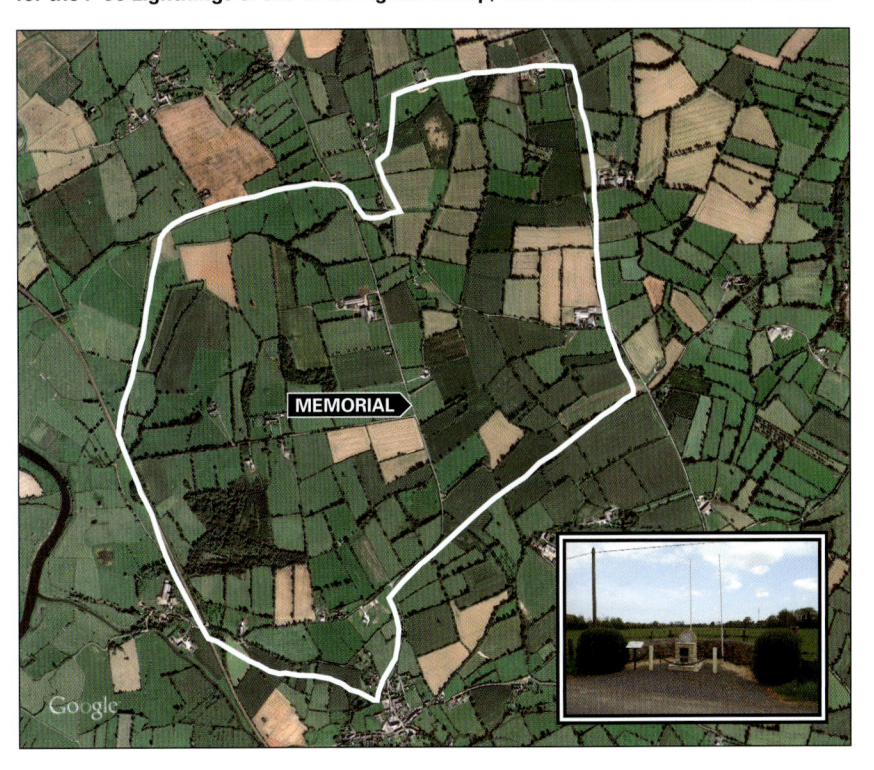

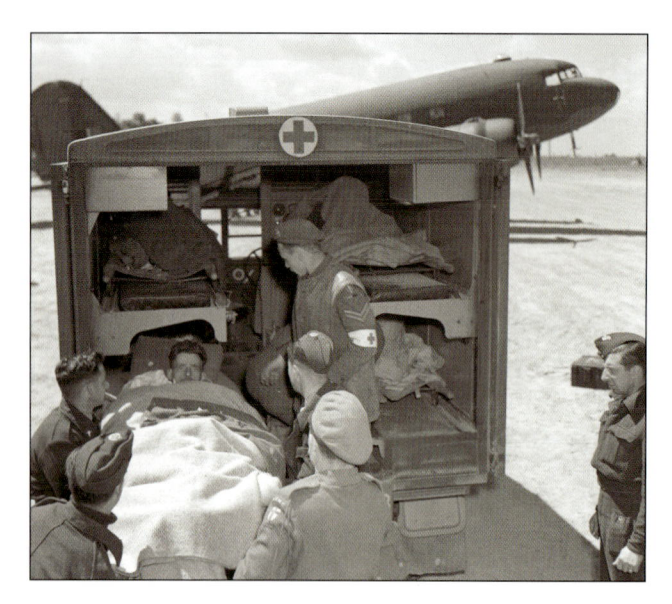

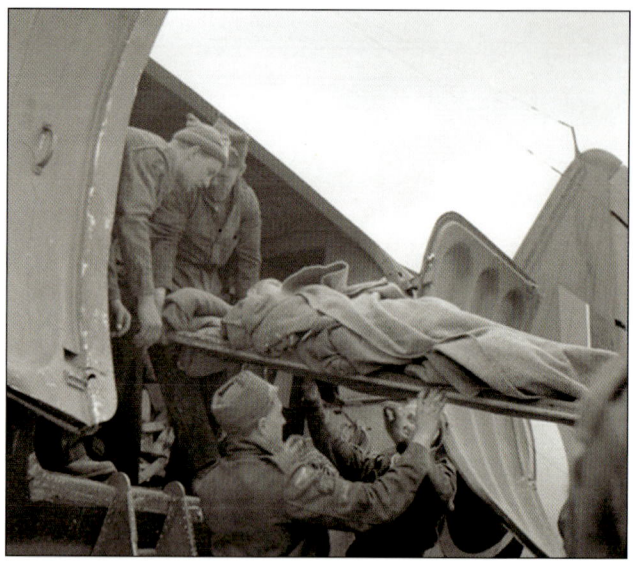

Although the airstrip is not identified, this series of Canadian photos shows 'the first mass air evacuation from France'. The date is given as June 15 'when ten Dakotas landed in France and took off again for England carrying more than 100 patients'.

B-14 AMBLIE

OPERATIONAL AUGUST 7

Latitude: 49°18'N
Longitude: 00°30'W
Grid reference: T-938821
Altitude 155ft

Although this untracked airstrip was called Amblie, it lay just south-west of Banville village, some two miles inland from Graye-sur-Mer in Juno Area. The Canadian 7th Infantry Brigade assaulted Mike Beach and Banville fell easily on D-Day to C Company of the Royal Winnipeg Rifles.

Construction work on B-14 by No. 23 ACG began on June 30, being completed initially for Refuelling and Re-arming on July 3, but it appears that it was seldom

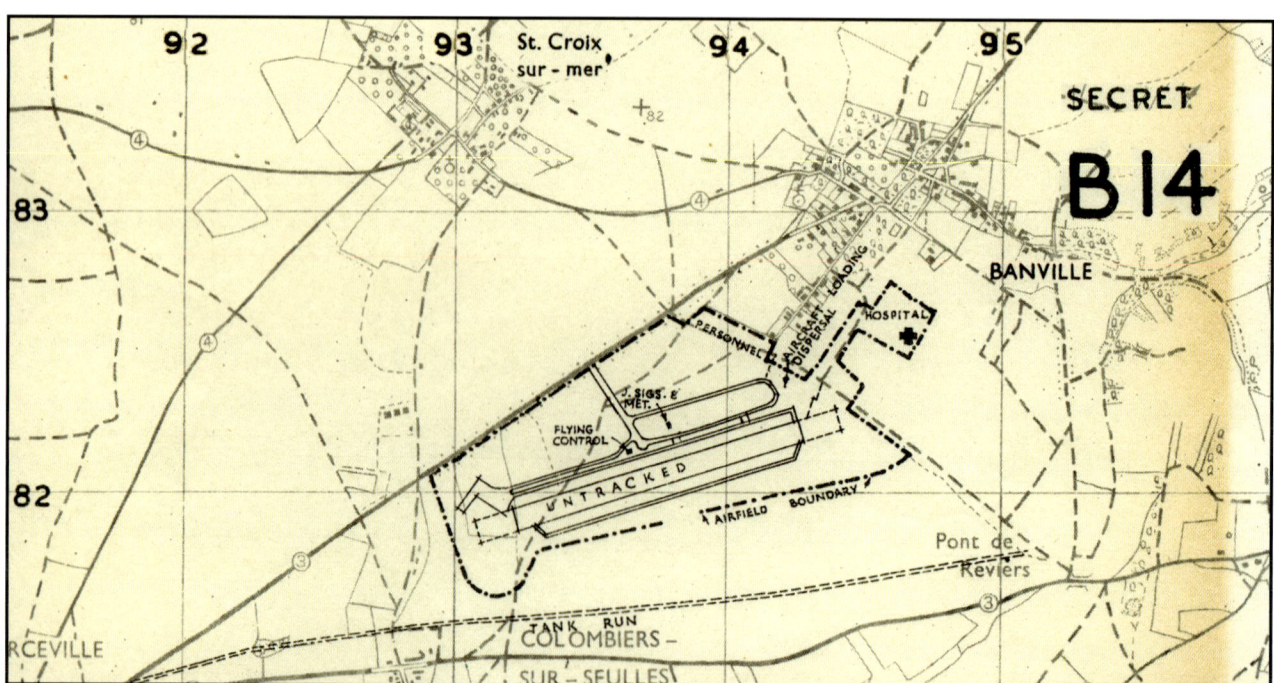

The detailed reconnaissance and setting out of the strip to be constructed at Amblie by 23 Airfield Construction Group was completed on June 29, ready for an 0830 start the following morning. Then on July 6, instructions were received to convert it to a transport field. This work was carried out by July 11.

In the British sector, evacuation of casualties by air began on June 13, which was a week earlier than had been anticipated in planning. Air evacuation was more uncertain than sea evacuation because the airfields on which suitable aircraft arrived changed constantly and there was always uncertainty as to the number of aircraft available. The problem was also complicated because no facilities existed on the airstrip for holding casualties. Consequently no preparations could be made for evacuation until the aircraft had landed and, in a congested beach-head, it was not always possible to deliver casualties at the airstrip on time. On June 18, however, the whole evacuation scheme was centralised under a Medical Air Liaison Officer attached to No. 83 Group, RAF, No. 81 General Hospital. Later, No. 77 General Hospital at Reviers was made the principal collecting centre for casualties to be evacuated by air, and B-14 at nearby Amblie was selected for evacuation purposes. RAF Casualty Air Evacuation Units began to arrive at this time and assisted in holding casualties on the airfield until aircraft were available. However, the holding capacity of these units was not large enough to deal with the numbers to be evacuated. The number dispatched by air up to July 26 was 7,719. Most probably the Press were invited to picture this event at B-2 Bazenville as Amblie, which became the main base for evacuation by air, did not open until August. However, as the photographs depict the role undertaken by B-14, we have chosen to include them in this chapter.

used as such and there were no resident fighter squadrons. Instead it became an Air Staging Post for casualty evacuation by No. 46 Transport Group's Dakotas. The Auster IVs of No. 661 Squadron also used the strip from August 7-17.

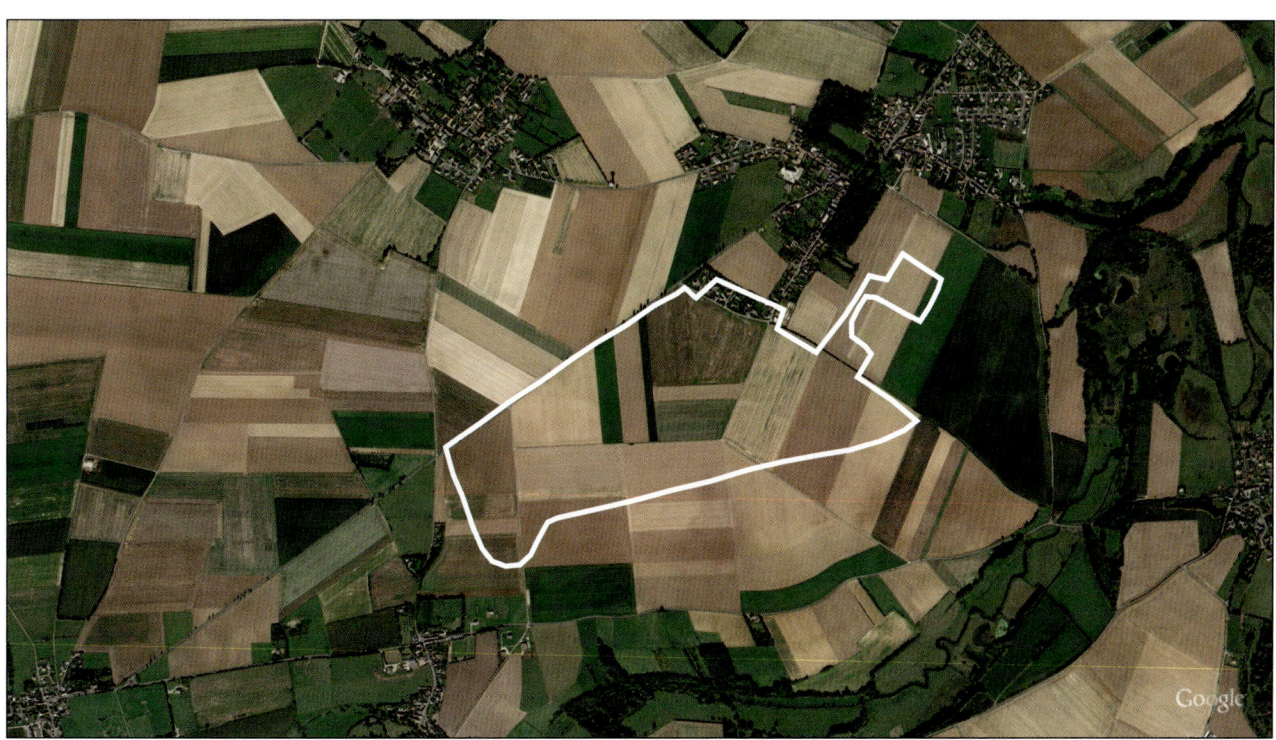

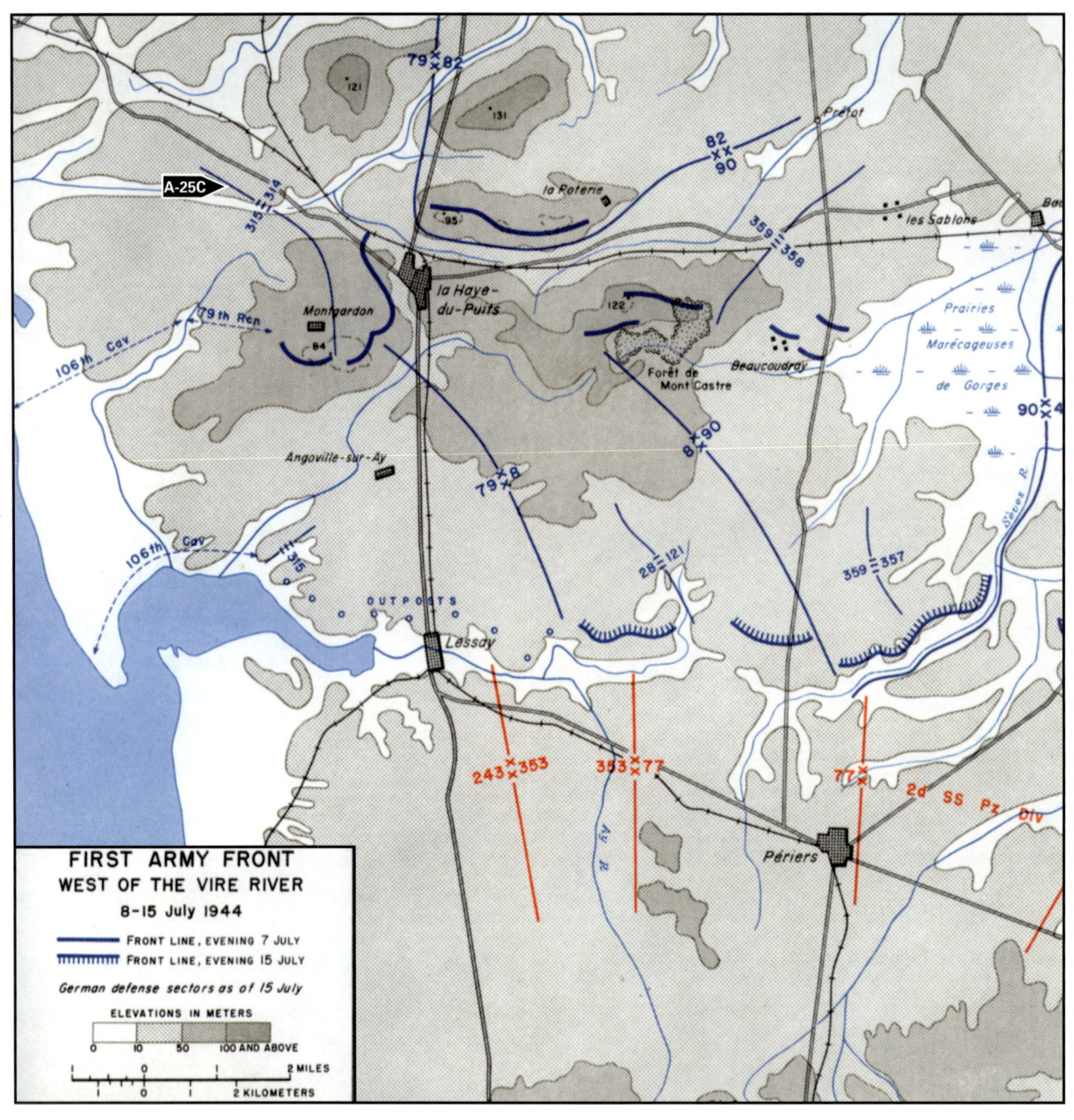

FIRST ARMY FRONT WEST OF THE VIRE RIVER 8-15 July 1944

― Front line, evening 7 July
⊥⊥⊥⊥ Front line, evening 15 July
German defense sectors as of 15 July

ELEVATIONS IN METERS
0 — 10 — 50 — 100 AND ABOVE

By June 18, American forces had cut off the Cherbourg peninsula from the rest of Normandy, having reached the west coast near Barneville-sur-Mer (see map pages 106-107). From here the main road ran south-eastward to La Haye-du-Puits, passing the site chosen for A-25C on the way. The offensive here by the US First Army was begun by VIII Corps on July 3 but the Germans put up such stubborn resistance that it took five days for the 79th Division to finally capture La Haye-du-Puits.

La Haye-du-Puits has fallen but it is not clear from the wartime caption if these men are from the 79th or 8th Division.

The 833rd Engineers were reported to have constructed the transport base at Bolleville with PBS hessien overlaid with Square Mesh Track — just as illustrated in this photograph, which unfortunately is uncaptioned as to the location, but could well have been taken during work on A-25C. (The Route Nationale 803 of the wartime years was downgraded in 1972 to D903.)

A-25C BOLLEVILLE

OPERATIONAL AUGUST 7

Latitude: 49°18'N
Longitude: 01°36'W
Grid reference: T-135864
Altitude: 109ft

The small village of Bolleville lay on the Route Nationale 803 (re-numbered D903 in 1972) running north-west from Carentan to Barneville. It was on the path of the advance of the US 79th Division and was captured by the 314th Infantry Regiment on July 5.

The airstrip had already been scheduled for a transport base — hence the suffix 'C' — and the 833rd Engineer Aviation Battalion began work on July 30 to lay down a 3,300ft runway of Prefabricated Bituminous Surfacing topped with SMT to keep the hessian down.

A-25C was open for business on August 7 for the 31st Transport Group of the 302nd Transport Wing. Unfortunately there was a fatal crash there on September 4 when a Douglas C-47 (41-18513) attempted to take off with a control lock still in place, killing all on board.

The airfield remained in American hands until the end of the war.

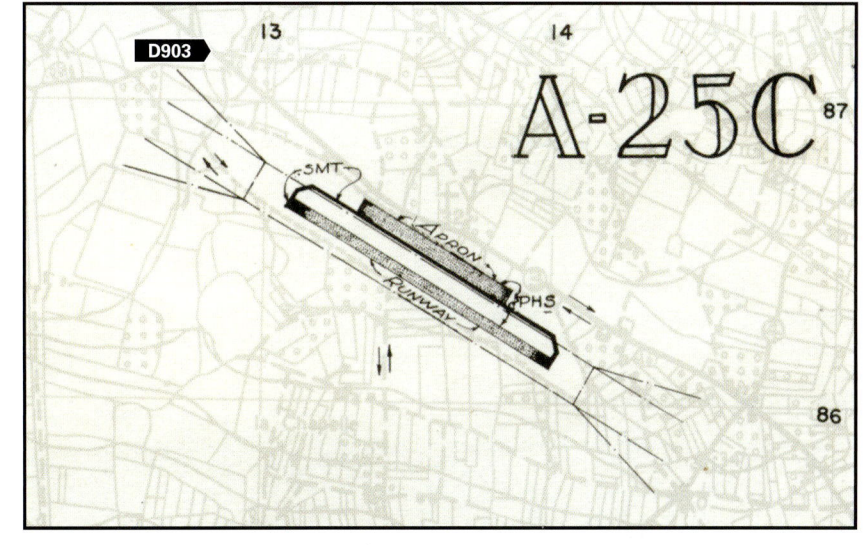

No. 13 Airfield Construction Group were completing taxi-tracks and dispersals at B-6 at Coulombs when orders were received to carry out a reconnaisance of the site chosen near Cristot for B-18. This was carried out by No. 614 Road Construction Company and submitted on June 30, raising the problem of possible mines amongst the standing crops. As a result, two armoured bulldozers were released for work at Cristot. On July 1 permission that had been given at 2130 to begin work was rescinded 30 minutes later due to the tactical situation. Instead work began to lay SMT at B-9 Lantheuil. A further survey was made on July 11 and the cutting of corn began the following day. A bomb disposal section arrived on July 13 and, with a start date for construction on July 18 or 19, a suggestion was put forward that sheep's-foot rollers could be used for detecting mines. The green light was finally given by the 59th (Staffordshire) Division that the area was clear of the enemy and work could begin on July 20. The airfield was to be completely tracked including 63 dispersals. However, rain prevented the heavy plant from being used until the 24th.

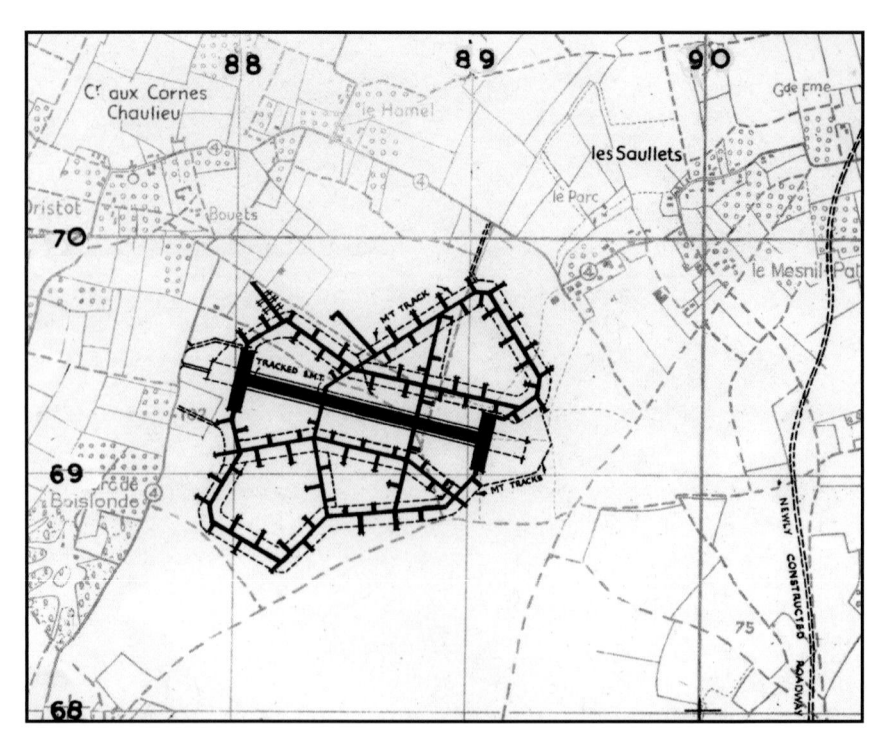

An experiment was carried out by laying straw under the SMT. Although it was more labour-intensive, it was successful in keeping the dust down while the taxi-tracks and dispersals were treated with oil. This photograph shows Cristot on August 9, the day after it had become operational. As well as constructing airfields, the Royal Engineers were also busy at this time with building roads, one of which shows up clearly to the east of the airstrip.

B-18 CRISTOT

OPERATIONAL AUGUST 8

Latitude: 49°11'N
Longitude: 00°34'W
Grid reference: T-885693
Altitude: 330ft

From the evening of June 8, German armour began to mount fierce counter-attacks in the eastern end of the bridgehead towards Bayeux but by June 12 British and Canadian forces had regained the initiative, the British XXX Corps pushing towards Tilly-sur-Seulles while the 3rd Canadian Division aimed for Carpiquet. The little village of Cristot was right in the middle of the battle for Tilly and it was not captured by the 1st/4th King's Own Yorkshire Light Infantry, part of the 49th (West Riding) Division, until June 16.

The terrain for B-18 was recced by No. 13 Airfield Construction Group on June 24 but work did not begin until first light on July 20. Deadline for completion was 0600 on July 27 but the weather with torrential rain delayed progress and the 3,600ft strip was not finished until August 4. A flight of No. 5022 Squadron of the RAF's No. 5357 Construction Wing was brought in on July 28 to help laying tracking. The runway was 240ft wide although only 120ft of the width was surfaced with SMT.

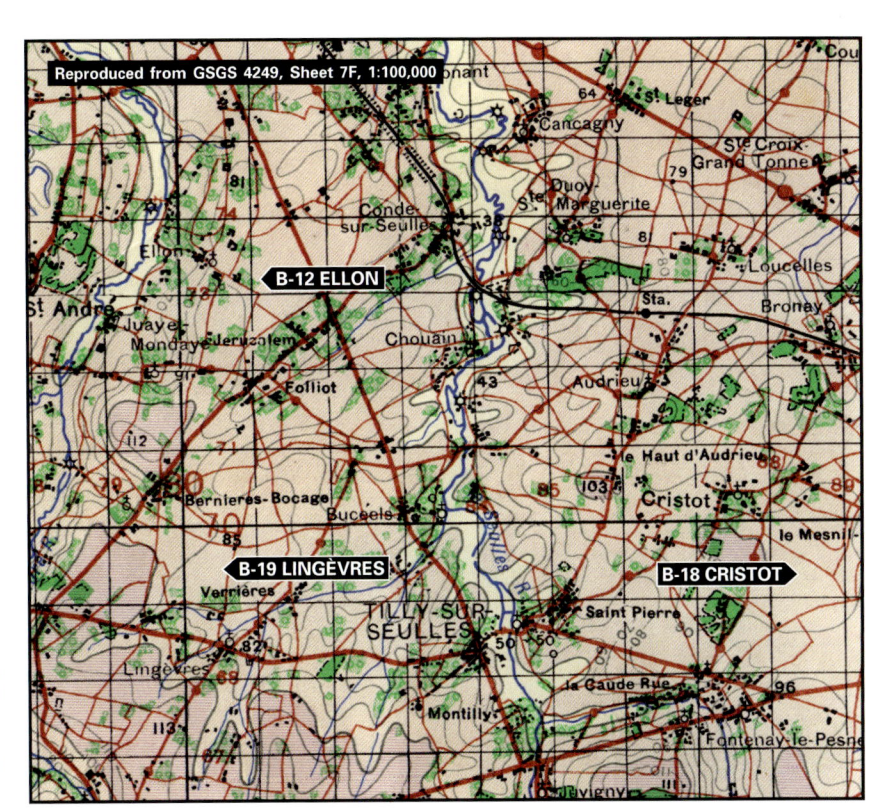

It was operational from August 8 when the Canadian Spitfire squadrons of No. 126 Wing arrived. No. 401 (which started life as No. 1 Canadian Squadron until re-numbered in March 1941) flew in from B-4 at Bény together with Nos. 411 and 412. Also from Bény came No. 442 that also had Canadian roots. They moved out to B-28 at Évreux on September 1 save that No. 411 went to B-24 St André-de-l'Eure.

The position of the airstrip is shown in white on the present-day aerial photograph. Absolutely no trace remains today of the numerous shell-holes from the battle or of the airfield which was abandoned on September 4.

Unteroffizier Willi Ghesla of 1. Staffel, Jagdgeschwader 53, pictured in his Bf109 at Rennes early in August 1940. At the end of the month his unit moved to the Pas de Calais area but on October 5 his war was over when he made a forced landing near Aldington, Kent, and was taken prisoner.

A-27 RENNES

OPERATIONAL AUGUST 10

Latitude: 48°04'N
Longitude: 01°44'W
Grid reference: X-965493
Altitude: 131ft

The airport at Rennes was opened in July 1933 and used by the Luftwaffe throughout the war —first by JG53 and KG27 in the summer of 1940; then KG26 and KG77 in 1942, and by the FW190s of SKG10 and JG11 in 1943-44.

It was regularly attacked by the Eighth Air Force and by the Ninth in the run-up to the invasion. The airfield was captured on August 4 by the 13th Infantry of the US 8th Division, the 820th Engineer Aviation Battalion arriving on the scene three days later.

The airfield had to be swept for mines and the two concrete runways — one of 4,360ft by 125ft and the other 5,535ft by 250ft — repaired, the work being completed by August 10. The same day the Thunderbolts of the 379th Squadron of the 362nd Fighter Group based at A-12 at Lignerolles arrived, followed by the 377th on August 12 with the 378th flying in the next day.

Also arriving on August 11-15 was the 10th Photo-Recon Group (31st and 34th Photo, 155th Night Photo and 12th and 15th Tactical Recon Squadrons) from Chalgrove, Oxfordshire. However, as the war progressed away from Brittany,

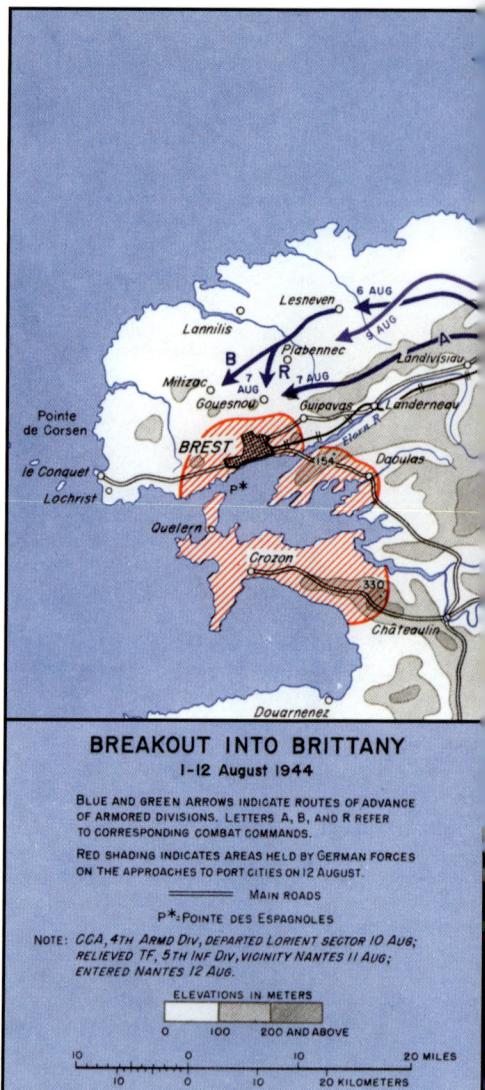

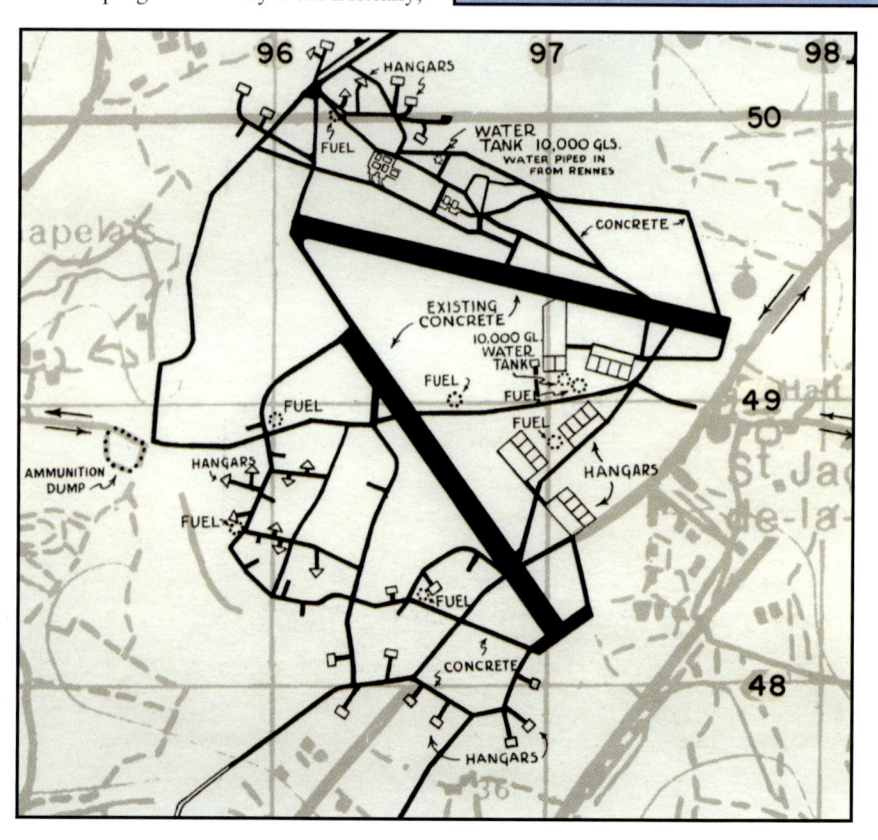

In July 1944, American engineers had begun the construction of airfields within the beach-head for the 98th Bombardment Wing comprising the 323rd, 387th, 394th and 397th Bomb Groups. However, on completion, this had used up all of the pierced steel plank sent to France as a stockpile for the construction of bomber fields in the Paris area and for the 'winterisation' of fighter-bomber fields. To meet this new demand it was necessary to devote much effort to the rehabilitation of captured hard-surfaced aerodromes like Rennes. The break-out in late July, came at an opportune moment for the Ninth Air Force. Not only were the engineers running out of airfield sites for development, but the older fields (none more than seven or eight weeks' old) were steadily deteriorating under constant use and required a great deal of maintenance, especially those covered with square mesh track. Before the end of July more than half of the IX Engineer Command's battalions were engaged in airfield maintenance, a task originally assigned to IX Air Force Service Command. Therefore, on August 8, the IX Engineer Command organised out of its own resources the 1st Airfield Maintenance Regiment (Provisional) to maintain the airfields in the rear areas while the other regiments forged ahead and constructed new fields.

BREAKOUT INTO BRITTANY
1-12 August 1944

BLUE AND GREEN ARROWS INDICATE ROUTES OF ADVANCE OF ARMORED DIVISIONS. LETTERS A, B, AND R REFER TO CORRESPONDING COMBAT COMMANDS.

RED SHADING INDICATES AREAS HELD BY GERMAN FORCES ON THE APPROACHES TO PORT CITIES ON 12 AUGUST.

━━━━ MAIN ROADS
P*: POINTE DES ESPAGNOLES

NOTE: CCA, 4TH ARMD DIV, DEPARTED LORIENT SECTOR 10 AUG; RELIEVED TF, 5TH INF DIV, VICINITY NANTES 11 AUG; ENTERED NANTES 12 AUG.

ELEVATIONS IN METERS
0   100   200 AND ABOVE

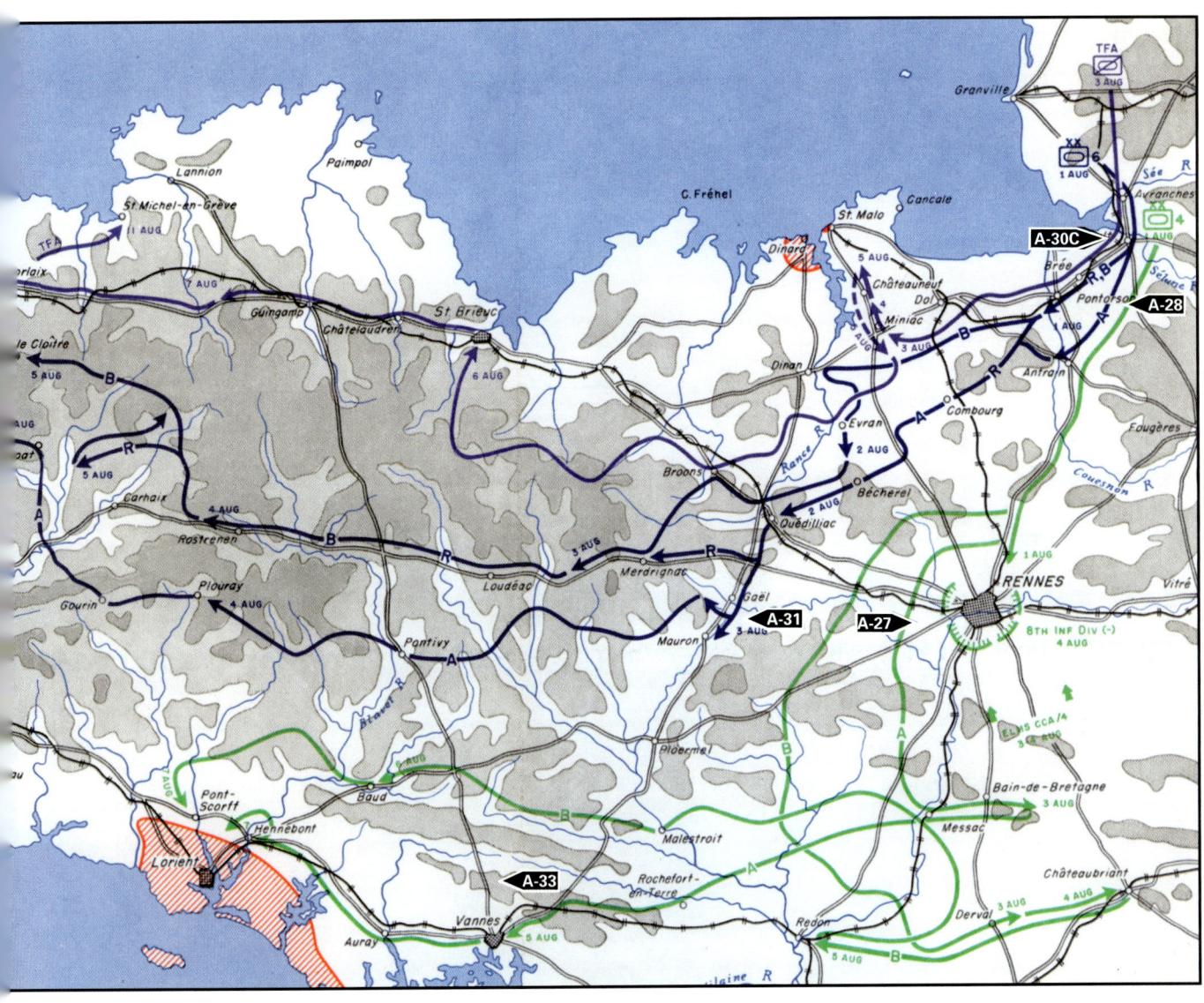

they departed for aerodromes nearer the front, the 10th Photo Group moving to Châteaudun (A-39) on August 26 and the 362nd Fighter Group to Prosnes (A-79) on September 19. The 125th Liaison Squadron operated from A-27 from September 3 to October 1 and the airfield was also used for supply and maintenance. On November 30 the Americans quit the base.

After the war the runways were completely reconstructed as befitting a regional airport catering for medium-range aircraft, the main runway now being just under 6,000ft with the secondary 2,422ft.

The Brittany peninsula became the first major region of France to be liberated after the break-out from Normandy, but the eastward advance proceeded so quickly that Brittany, like the original beach-head area, soon lay far behind the ground spearheads. Accordingly, only a few airfields for the IX TAC were developed on that peninsula. By August 5, when all but one of the engineer battalions were at work in Normandy, 17 fighter-bomber fields had been surfaced with square mesh track or prefabricated hessian surfacing and two medium bomber fields with pierced steel plank — Maupertus (A-15) and Tour-en-Bessin (A-13) — with work underway on Lessay (A-20). Seven additional fields were under construction in Normandy, but once these had been completed, the engineers would reach the saturation point for landing grounds there. The Brittanny airfields were A-27 Rennes, today Saint Jacques Airport, A-28 Pontorson, A-30C Courtils, A-31 Gaël and A-33 at Vannes.

A-31 GAËL

OPERATIONAL AUGUST 11

Latitude: 48°05'N
Longitude: 02°11'W
Grid reference: K629529
Altitude: 419ft

In the pre-D-Day bombing of Luftwaffe bases, the airfield located 3½ miles south of Gaël (see map on previous pages) was targeted by Mosquitos of No. 21 Squadron in one of the low-level raids for which they were famous. This photo was brought back by one of the attacking aircraft. It was bombed again by 12 B-17s on June 15.

The 850th Aviation Engineers utilised the former French Air Force grass aerodrome at Gaël (20 miles west of Rennes) for A-31 where they prepared an E-W strip of 4,500ft.

The airfield had been overrun by Combat Command A of the US 6th Armored Division on August 3 and it was occupied by the 354th Fighter Group from August 10 to September 28. Its three squadrons had been based at A-2 at Cricqueville and, after their service at Gaël, the 353rd, 355th and 356th moved on to A-66 at Orconte, 300 miles away near Vitry-le-François in north-eastern France.

Today a memorial bears plaques denoting its use by the Armée de l'Air and RAF in 1940, the Luftwaffe and the USAAF.

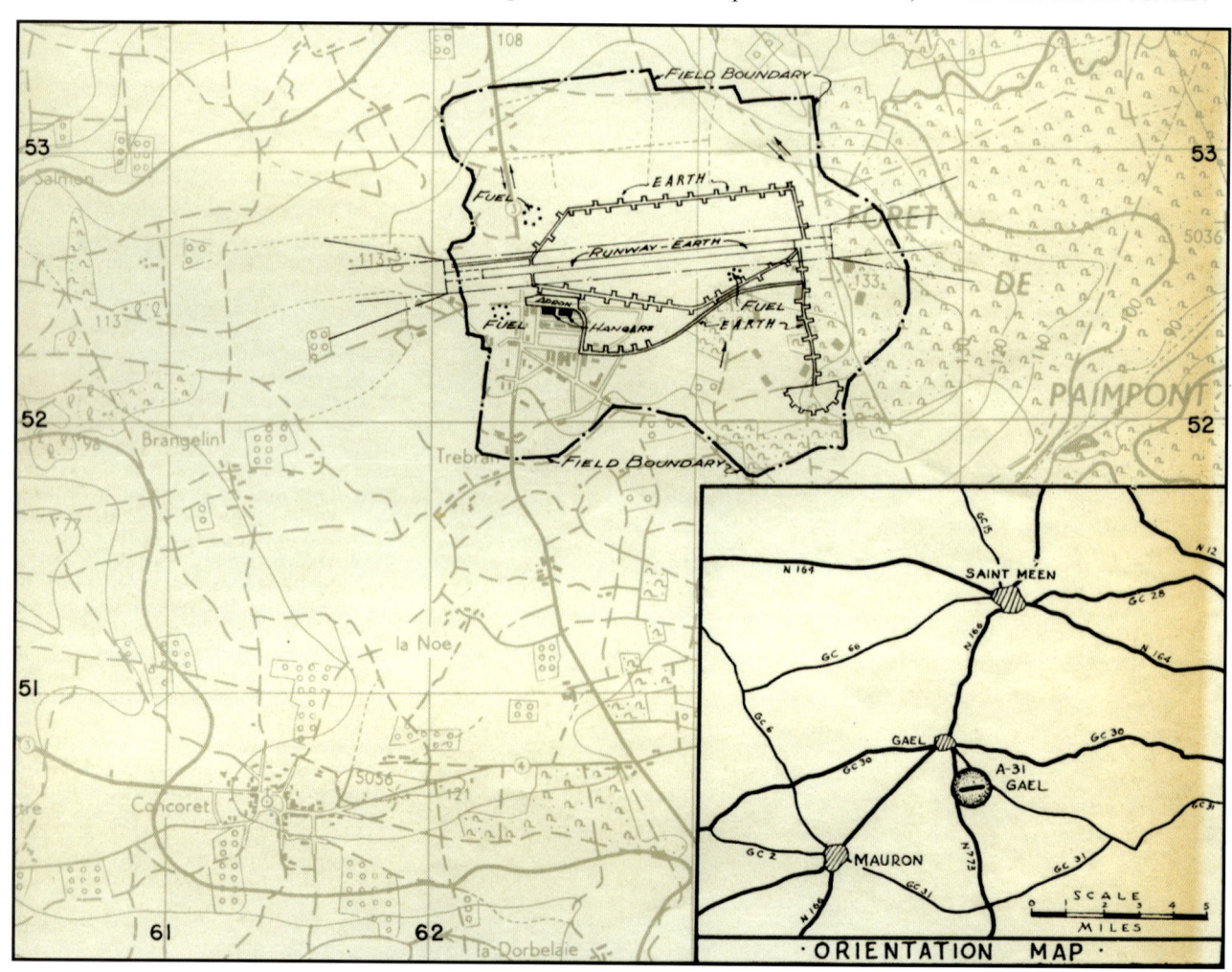

It is difficult to believe that aerodrome A-31 — with its chequered history having been used by the air forces of Britain, France, Germany and the United States — has virtually been swallowed up beneath Paimpont forest. A memorial plaque in a clearing beside the D773 is dedicated to the 354th Fighter Group.

B-19 LINGÈVRES

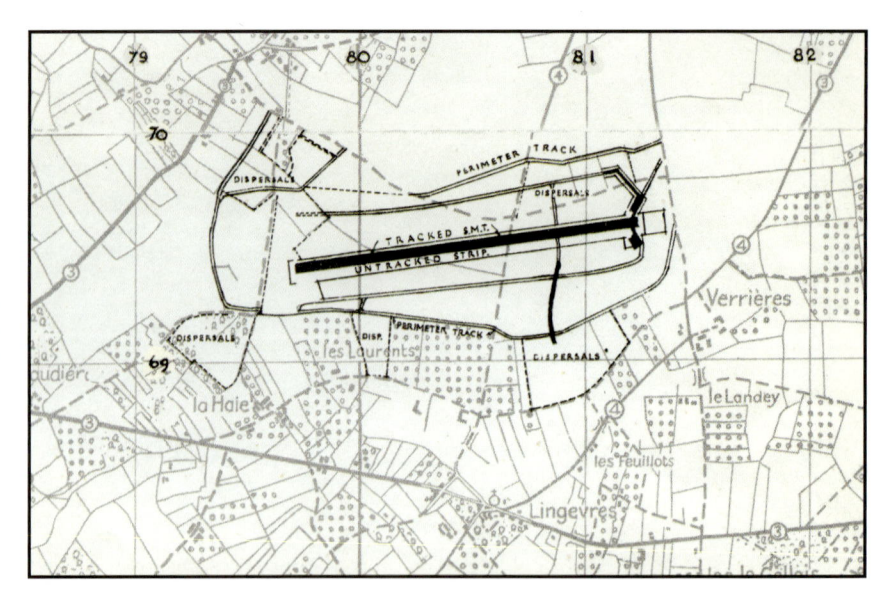

OPERATIONAL AUGUST 13

Latitude: 49°11'N
Longitude: 00°41'W
Grid reference: T-805695
Altitude: 240ft

The flying strip at Lingèvres was located a mile north of the village which had been badly damaged in tank battles on June 11 and again on the 15th.

The 5,000ft strip tracked with SMT was laid down by No. 5357 Wing of the RAF's Airfield Construction Service and for the last two weeks of August it became the home of No. 125 Wing comprising Nos. 132, 453 (RAAF), and 602 Squadrons. They flew in with their Spitfire IXs on the 13th together with No. 441 Squadron. They had all been operating together from B-11 Longues and all moved on to B-40 at Beauvais on September 2.

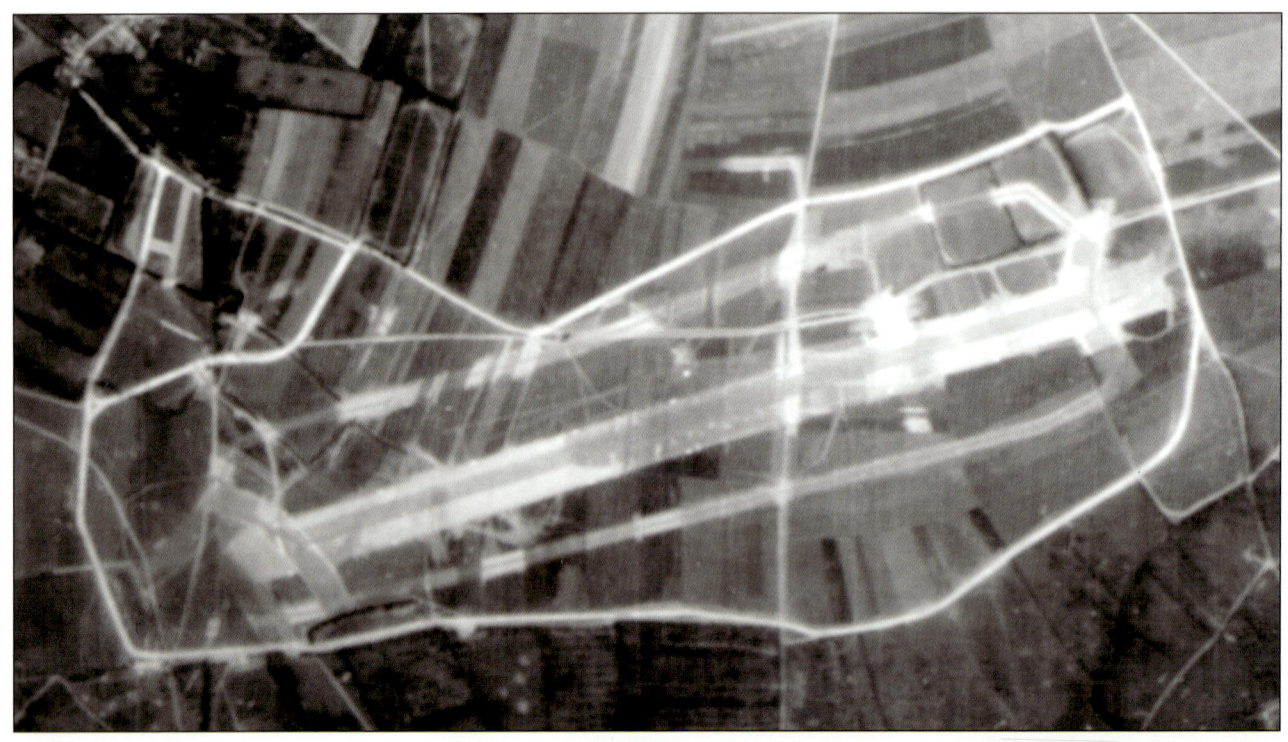

The 21st Army Group reported that during the phase from July 26 onward, the construction and maintenance of airfields became a serious problem. Although the five RE Groups and one RAF Group moved forward with the armies, it was only by maintaining close liaison that they could keep up once the pace of the advance quickened. In some cases airfields were constructed and occupied but were discovered almost at once to be of little operational value as the armies had advanced out of range of fighter aircraft. The airstrip at Lingèvres (see map page 149) was the first to be constructed by the RAF, No. 5357 Airfield Construction Wing having been held in reserve until required. Coming ashore at Courseulles-sur-Mer on July 18, they built B-19 for No. 125 Wing but it was occupied for only 20 days before its squadrons jumped over 120 miles to B-40 at Beauvais.

Each RAF Airfield Construction Wing had a Plant Squadron containing the heavy machinery seen here used at Lingèvres.

Square Mesh Track was available either as 12 feet by 6 feet sheets or rolls 7 feet 3 inches wide containing 77 feet of track. With the latter, 175 square feet per man hour could be laid down but only 80 square feet if panels were used. The tracking then had to be tensioned before stakes were driven in to hold it taut.

LAC Blackett checks that the runway width is 240 feet. The finishing touch was the identification code in white-painted concrete.

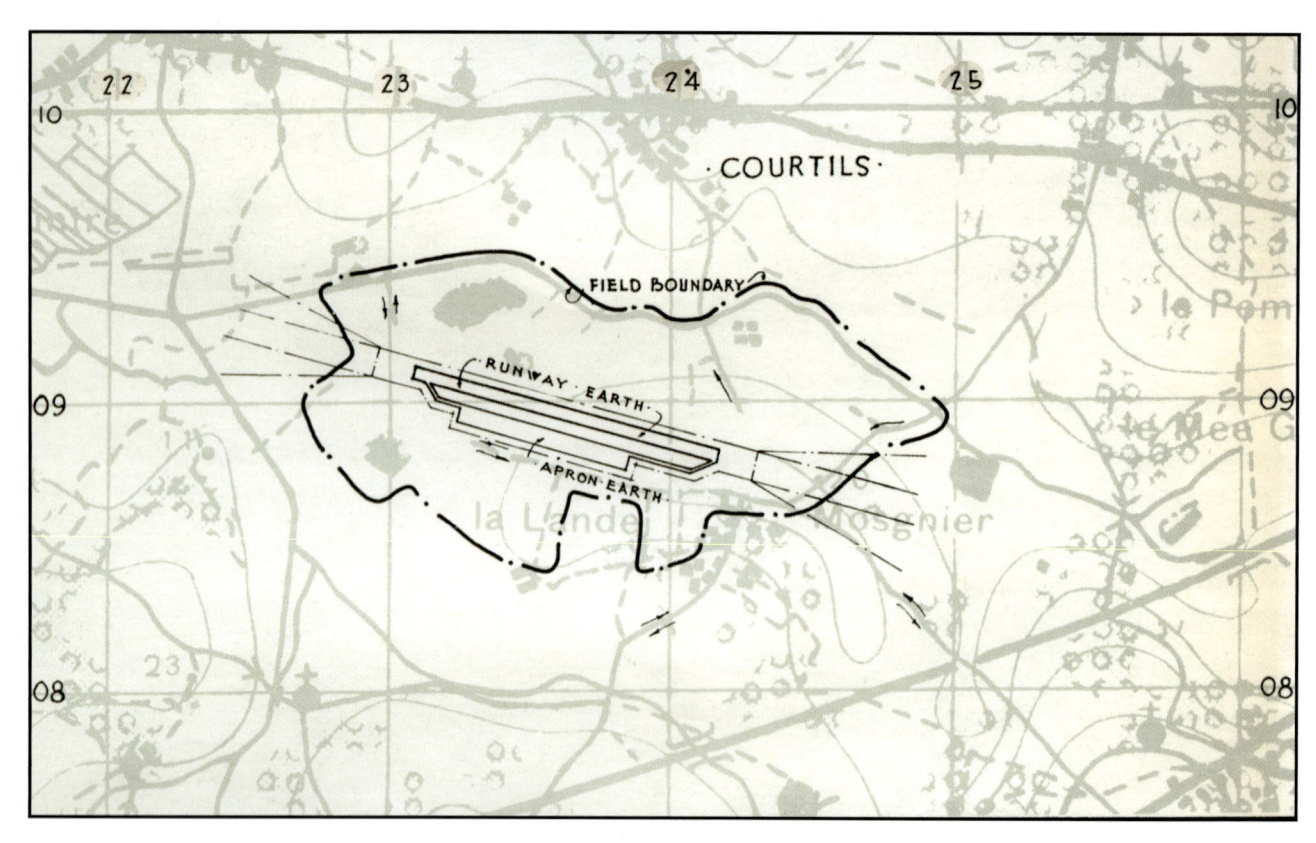

A-30C COURTILS

OPERATIONAL AUGUST 13

Latitude: 48°37'N
Longitude: 01°24'W
Grid reference: T-237089
Altitude: 65ft

The Engineer Aviation Battalions had their work cut out to keep up with the demand for combat bases but in August and September the demand increased due to the requirement for supply and evacuation airstrips behind the fast-moving armies. A-30C was earmarked as an airstrip for transport aircraft and the 834th Engineers began work on August 9 to prepare a simple earth runway (see orientation map opposite).

The village of Courtils was captured by Combat Command R of the US 6th Armored Division on August 1 and from August 13 to September 5 it was used as a communications and transport field. The 3,600ft earth strip was prepared by the 834th Engineer Aviation Battalion.

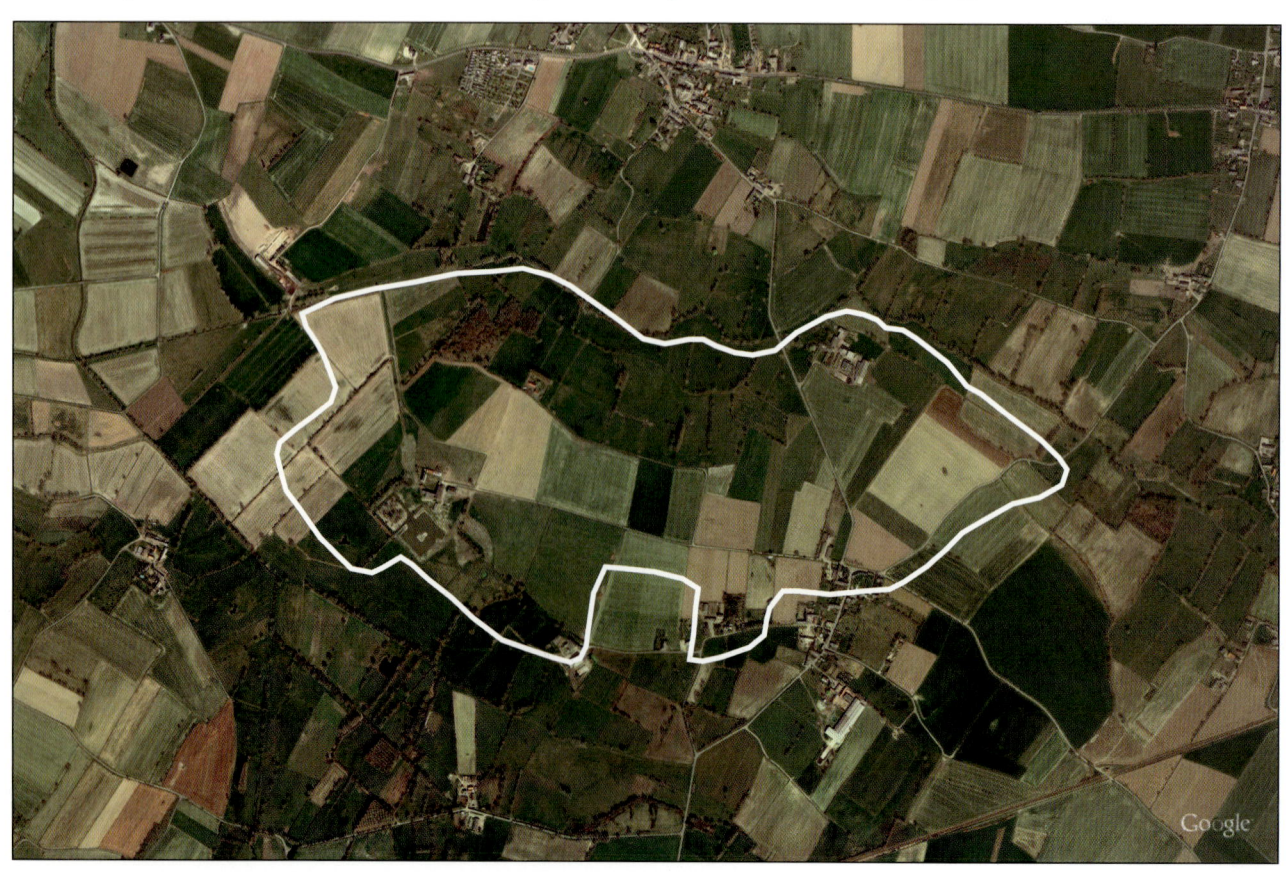

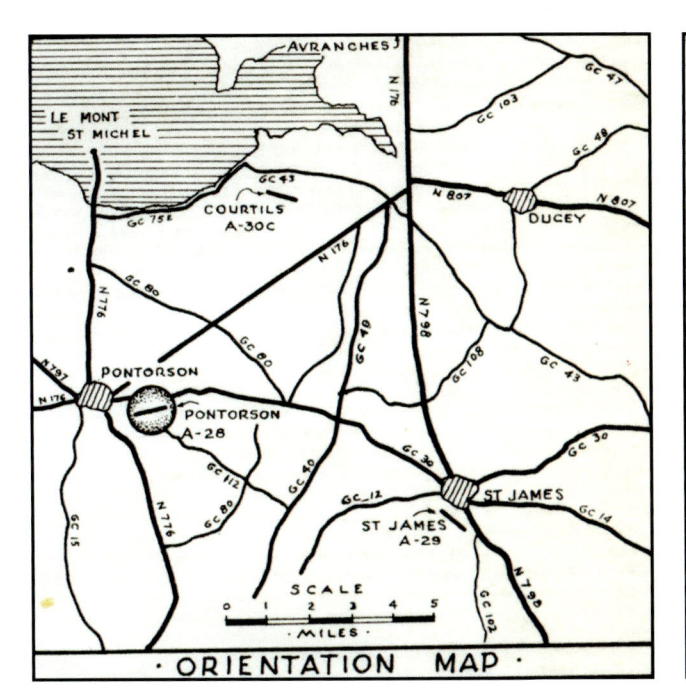

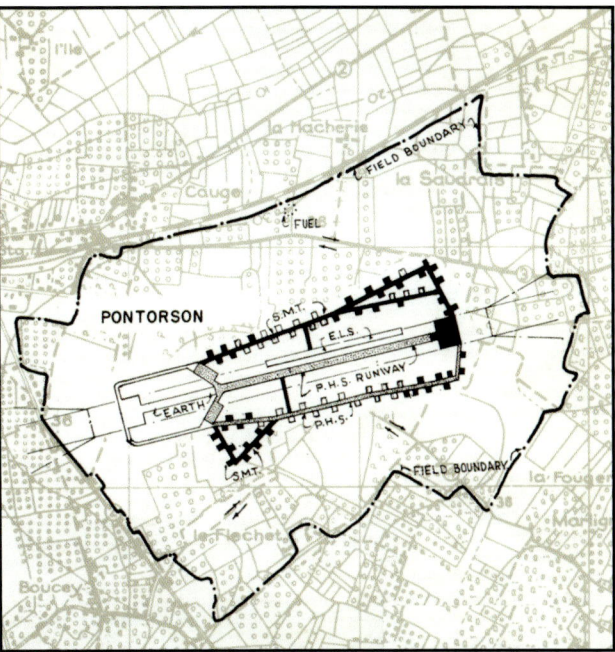

A-28 was opened on August 10 and closed September 28 when the 358th Fighter Group moved to A-67 at Vitry-le-François.

A-28 PONTORSON

OPERATIONAL AUGUST 14

Latitude: 48°33'N
Longitude: 01°29'W
Grid reference: T-177015
Altitude: 131ft

Lying just east of the town of Pontorson, the airfield site was captured on August 1 by CCR of the US 6th Armored Division, the same unit that had secured the site for A-30C six miles to the north. By now, the armour was moving so fast that it hardly met any resistance, leaving whole areas to be mopped up by the infantry.

The 819th Aviation Engineers moved in on August 7, having marked out a 5,000ft E-W strip. This comprised 3,600ft covered with Prefabricated Bituminous Surfacing with the remaining 1,400ft being just graded and compressed earth. There was also an emergency landing strip alongside to preserve the PBS from being damaged in crash landings.

The three P-47 squadrons of the 358th Fighter Group (the 365th, 366th and 367th) all arrived together on August 14 from their previous airfield, A-14 at Cretteville, but within a month they had to move forward 275 miles to Vitry-le-François where they occupied airfield A-67 on September 15.

By then the US First Army had advanced across Luxembourg and the Third almost to Metz. With all of north-eastern France in Allied hands, the border with Germany was first crossed on September 11, the same day that the US Seventh Army advancing from the Riviera linked up with the forces which had landed in Normandy. To the west the First Canadian Army and Second British had cleared Belgium and had now crossed into Holland.

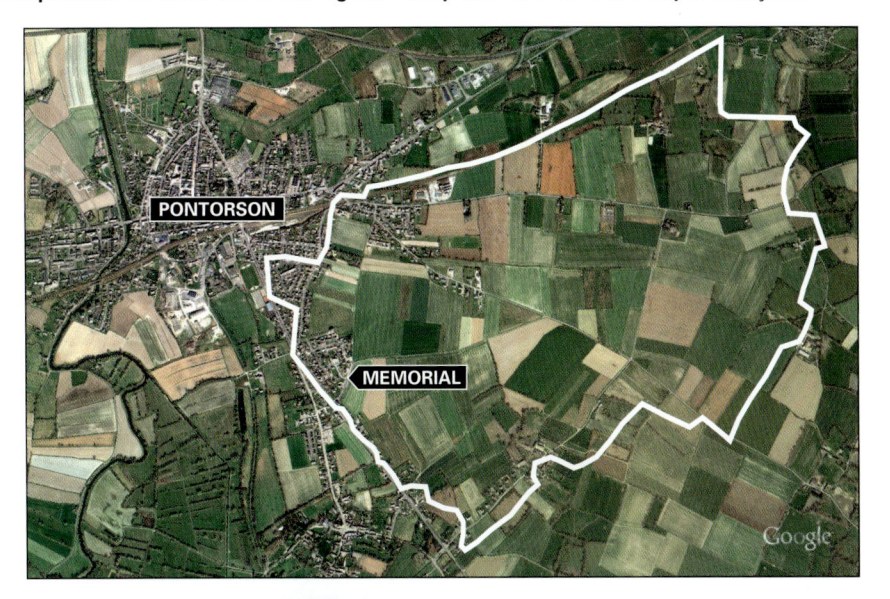

Almost certainly pictured at its British forward base of High Halden in Kent because Sommerfield Tracking was not used on the Normandy airfields, *Chunky* belonged to the 365th Fighter Squadron of the 358th Fighter Group which was based at Pontorson from August 14 to September 15.

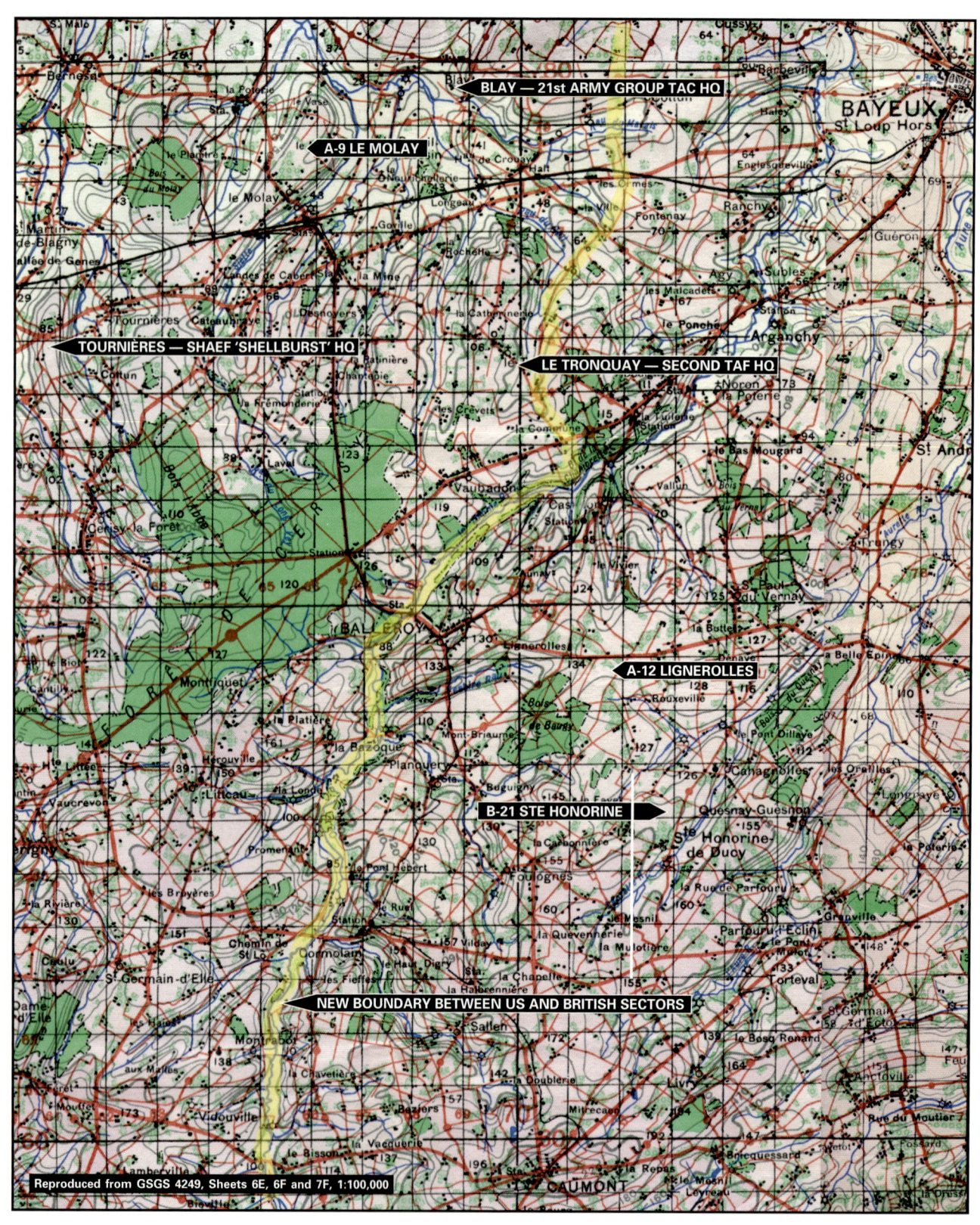

Map labels:
- BLAY — 21st ARMY GROUP TAC HQ
- A-9 LE MOLAY
- TOURNIÈRES — SHAEF 'SHELLBURST' HQ
- LE TRONQUAY — SECOND TAF HQ
- A-12 LIGNEROLLES
- B-21 STE HONORINE
- NEW BOUNDARY BETWEEN US AND BRITISH SECTORS

Reproduced from GSGS 4249, Sheets 6E, 6F and 7F, 1:100,000

With the re-organisation of the American air-ground command on August 6 (see page 142), Air Marshal Coningham moved the headquarters of the Second Tactical Air Force to Le Tronquay, six miles south-west of Bayeux, to where Montgomery had relocated the 21st Army Group HQ three days earlier. The new location was only six miles from Eisenhower's Forward HQ at Tournières. Although Le Molay lay mid-way between the two headquarters, No. 13 Airfield Construction Group received a request on August 2 that HQ TAF would like two 600ft strips, tracked with SMT, at Le Tronquay. Two officers were despatched to get details of their camp layout and requirements in respect of the distance of the strip from the HQ. However, no one could be found at Second TAF who could give any assistance and at 21st Army Group the camp commandant informed them that a strip was already being constructed by No. 575 Army Troops Company of the Royal Engineers, the No. 13 ACG War Diary commenting that the strip bore no relation to the standards previously specified! On August 4, another recce of the area determined that there was only one site that fulfilled the conditions of the Second TAF but this was turned down as being three miles from the camp and next to a hospital. No other site could be found so presumably A-9 at Le Molay was used instead although this was also three miles away. At the beginning of August the Second Tactical Air Force said that they did not require any further fighter airstrips in the beach-head area and that, depending on the speed of the advance, more would be needed 30 miles nearer the Seine.

B-21 STE HONORINE

OPERATIONAL AUGUST 14

Latitude: 49°09'N
Longitude: 00°46'W
Grid reference: T-729661
Altitude: 165ft

The Allied plan for the break-out from Normandy (Operation 'Cobra'), relied on the US First Army pivoting on its left at Caumont while the British Second Army drove south between there and Caen, 20 miles to the east. The little village of Sainte Honorine-de-Ducy, four miles north of Caumont, was entered by the US 26th Infantry (1st Division) on June 12, and units from the British 7th Armoured Division also passed through the village the very same day en route to Villers-Bocage.

However it was not until the end of July that the boundary separating the US V Corps and the British Second Army was moved to the west giving the British responsibility for the Caumont area. This gave No. 16 Airfield Construction Group of the Royal Engineers the opportunity to lay down a 5,000ft untracked ALG just west of Sainte Honorine-de-Ducy. It was also just two miles south of A-12.

On August 14 the Mustangs of Nos. 168 and 430 Squadrons from No. 39 (Recce) Wing flew in to B-21 from Sommervieu (B-8), followed the next day by the Spitfires of Nos. 400 and 414 although the latter squadron came direct from the UK. However, within two weeks they had moved 100 miles to the east to support the swift advance into northern France. On August 29, No. 414 went to a small airfield close to the Seine south of Evreux at Illiers-l'Évêque (B-26), while the other three squadrons went to nearby B-34 at Avrilly at the beginning of September.

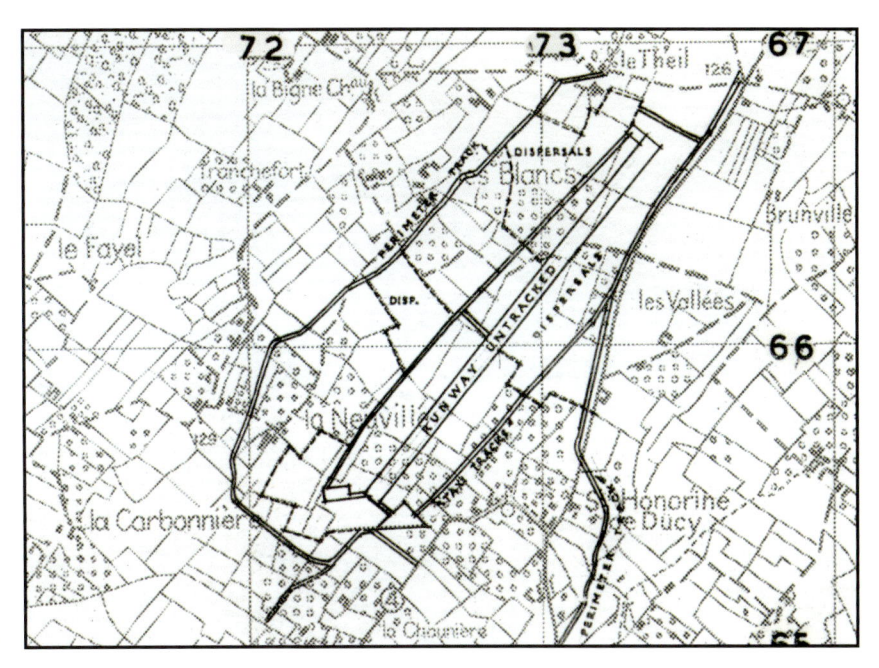

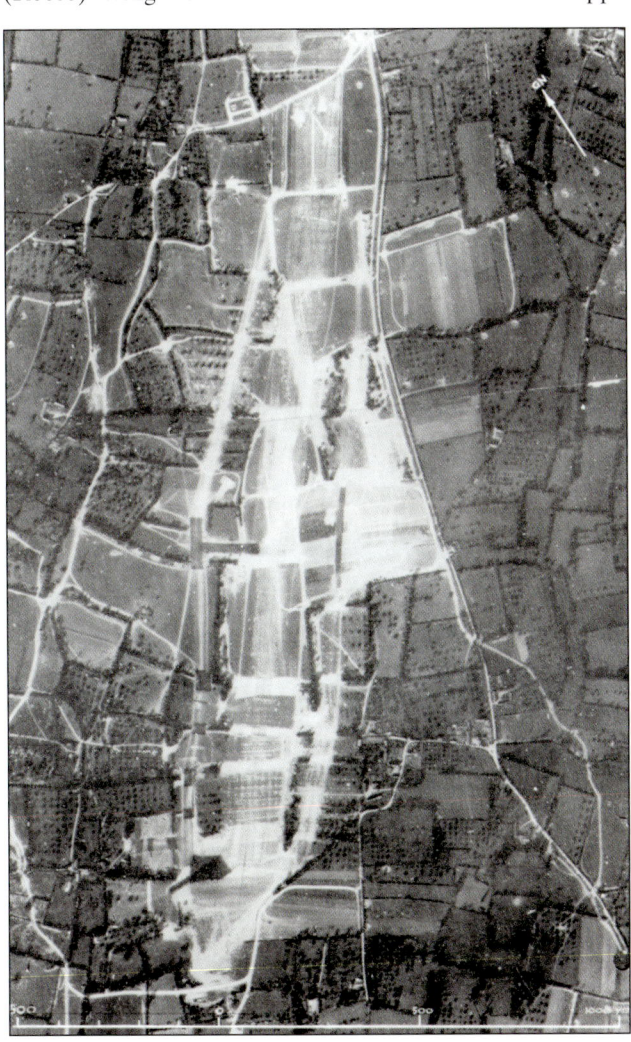

Then, on August 4, 16 Airfield Construction Group received orders to prepare a 5,000ft untracked runway for three squadrons at Ste Honorine-de-Ducy and it had to be completed within five days to be able to move squadrons in from B-8 at Sommervieu.

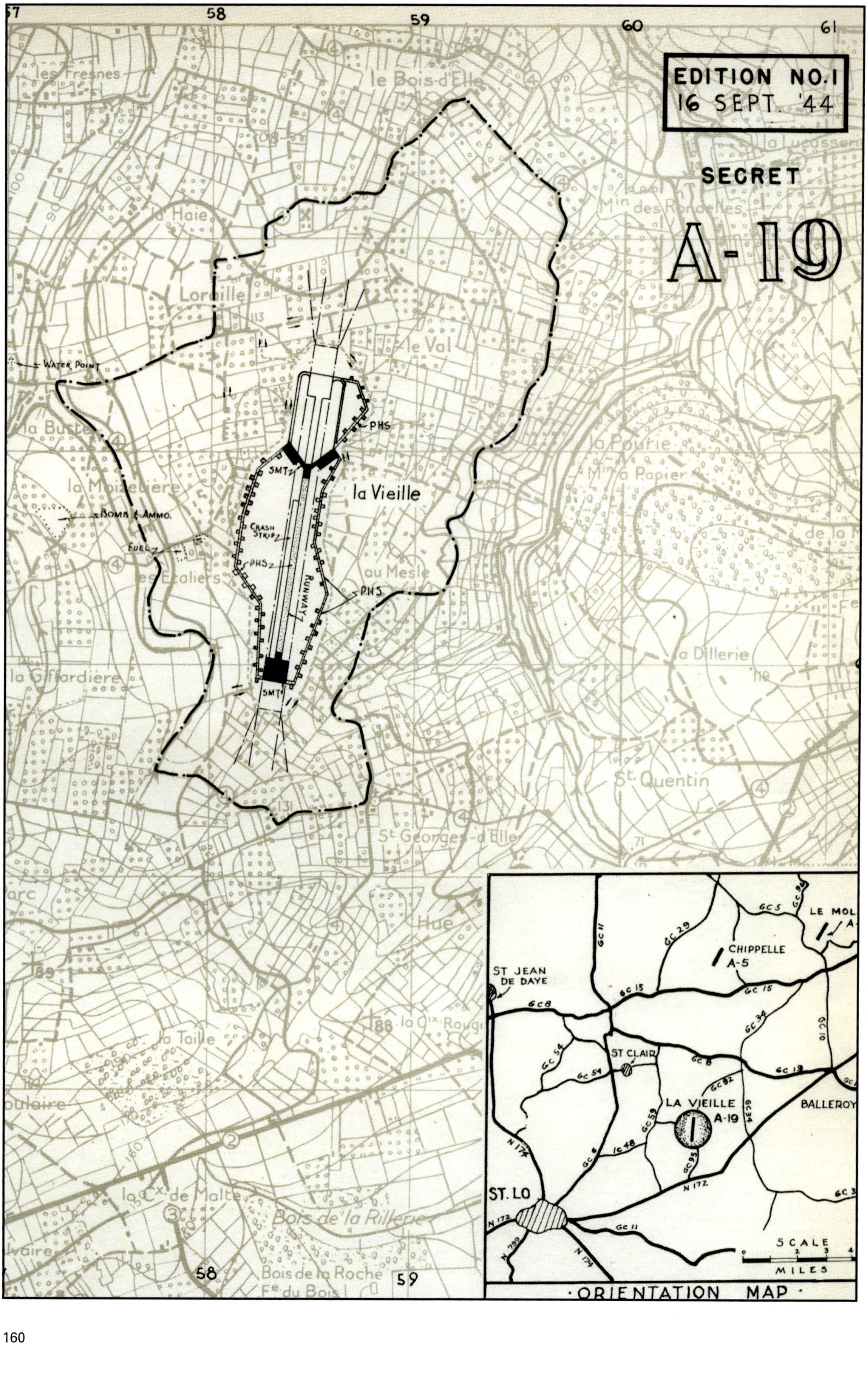
EDITION NO.1
16 SEPT. '44
SECRET
A-19
WATER POINT
BOMB & AMMO.
FUEL
PHS
SMT
CRASH STRIP
RUNWAY
la Vieille
ORIENTATION MAP
ST JEAN DE DAYE
CHIPPELLE A-5
ST CLAIR
LA VIEILLE A-19
BALLEROY
ST. LO
SCALE
MILES

A-19 LA VIEILLE

OPERATIONAL AUGUST 15

*Latitude: 49°09'N
Longitude: 00°58'W
Grid reference: T-584675
Altitude: 400ft*

The P-38 Lightnings of the 370th Fighter Group had been stationed at A-3 Cardonville since the end of July but now they moved their base further south to La Vieille, five miles north-east of St Lô. The area had been first reached on June 18 by the 23rd Infantry of the US 2nd Division, but the front line here was embattled for over a month and not finally cleared by the regiment until July 12.

The 3,600ft PBS strip, with a 1,400ft compressed earth extension, had been finished by the 818th Engineer Aviation Battalion on August 14 and the three

On the day that La Vieille became operational, Allied forces landed in southern France and Patton's Third Army continued its spectacular drive east towards the Seine led by the 5th Armored and 79th Infantry Divisions. However, the speed of the advance was outstripping the capacity of the logistics to keep up and on August 15 Bradley was forced to limit the Third Army to Dreux, Chartres and Orléans. Two days later the restriction was lifted and the leaders of XV Corps were within five kilometres of the river (see map overleaf). Because there was a possibility that German troops on the River Loire might launch attacks against the flank of the Third Army and 12th Army Group, and interfere with US lines of communication, the IX Tactical Air Command was asked to mount 24-hour patrols over the Loire river valley, being provided with a squadron of night fighters to augment daylight operations by fighter-bombers. Meanwhile, further north, Allied ground forces were closing on a gap at Falaise-Argentan through which German forces were attempting to escape. With the area very restricted, attacks on the enemy were left to the RAF's Second Tactical Air Force.

From August 15, A-19 was the base for the P-38 Lightnings of the 370th Fighter Group. The unit progressed through A-3 Cardonville, A-19 La Vieille, A-45 Lonray, A-73 Roye/Amy, A-78 Florennes and Y-29 Zwartberg/Asch in Belgium before ending up in Germany. This shot shows a machine of the 485th Squadron.

squadrons of the 370th Group — the 401st, 402nd and 485th — touched down the following day. They remained at A-19 until September 6 before being moved 70 miles nearer the front to A-45 that had been built at Lonray near Alençon.

THE ADVANCE TO THE RIVER SEINE

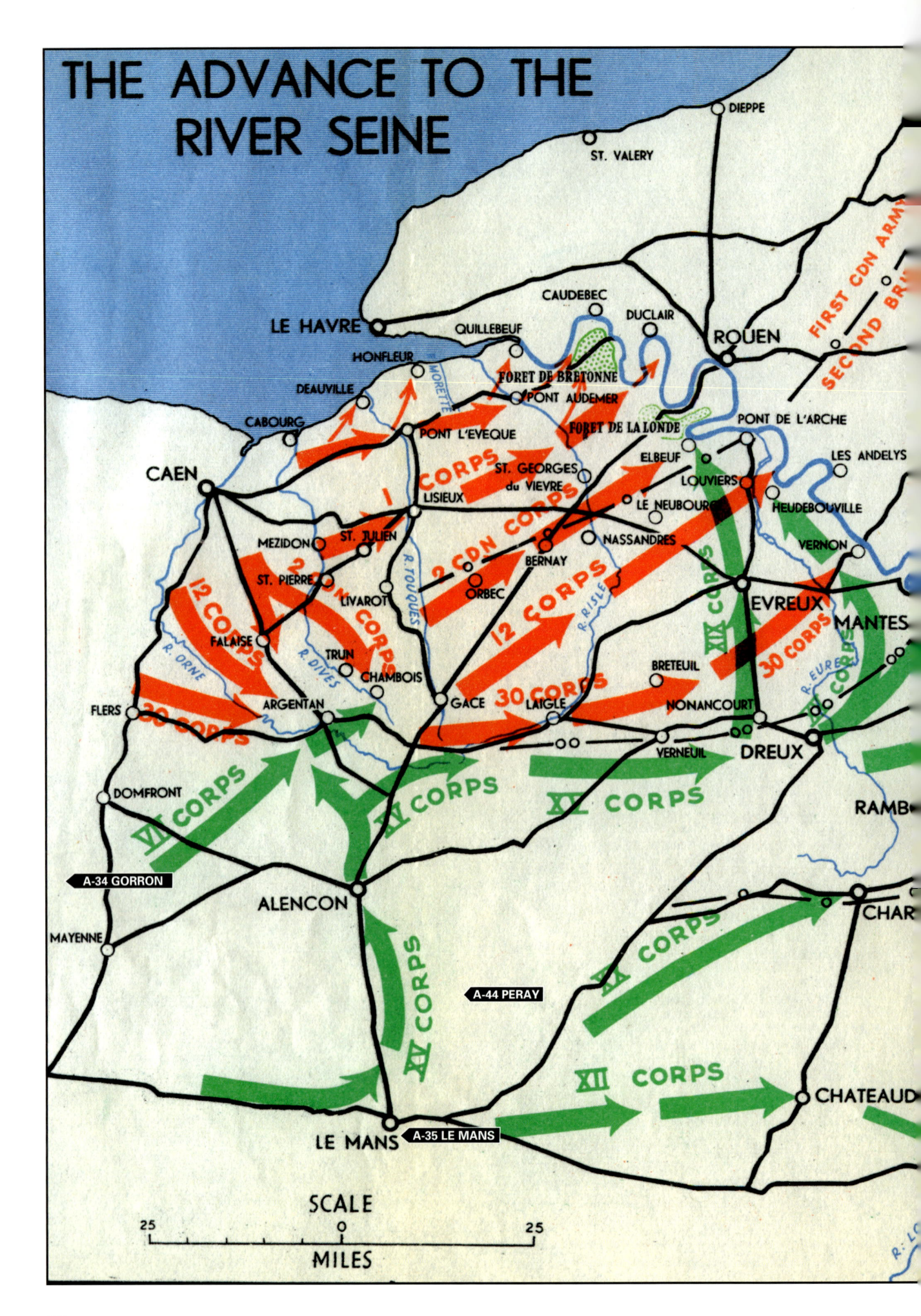

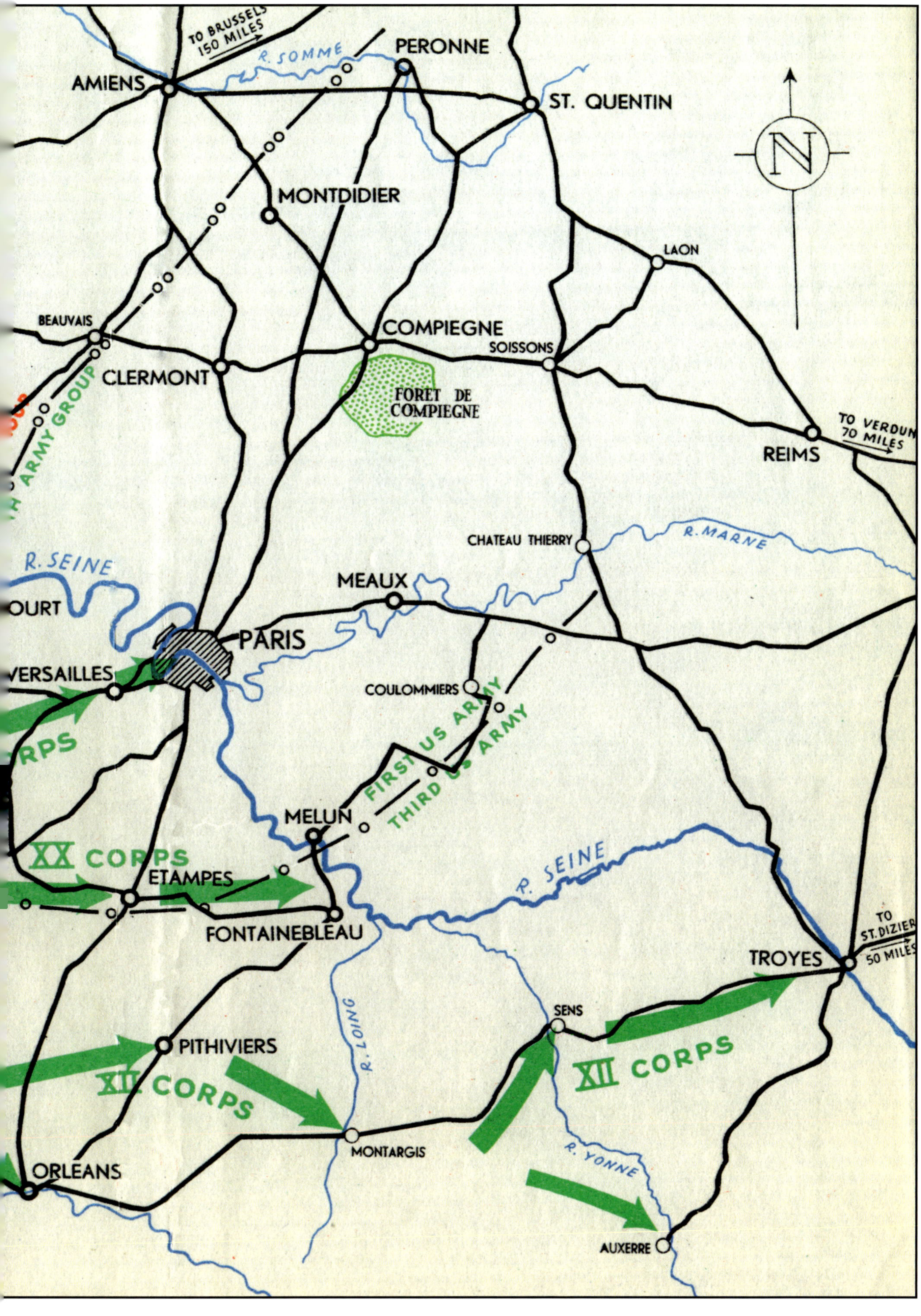
TO BRUSSELS
150 MILES
R. SOMME
PERONNE
AMIENS
ST. QUENTIN
N
MONTDIDIER
LAON
BEAUVAIS
COMPIEGNE
SOISSONS
CLERMONT
FORET DE
COMPIEGNE
ARMY GROUP
TO VERDUN
70 MILES
REIMS
CHATEAU THIERRY
R. MARNE
R. SEINE
MEAUX
OURT
PARIS
VERSAILLES
COULOMMIERS
FIRST US ARMY
THIRD US ARMY
RPS
MELUN
XX CORPS
ETAMPES
R. SEINE
FONTAINEBLEAU
TO
ST. DIZIER
50 MILES
TROYES
R. LOING
SENS
PITHIVIERS
XII CORPS
XII CORPS
MONTARGIS
R. YONNE
ORLEANS
AUXERRE

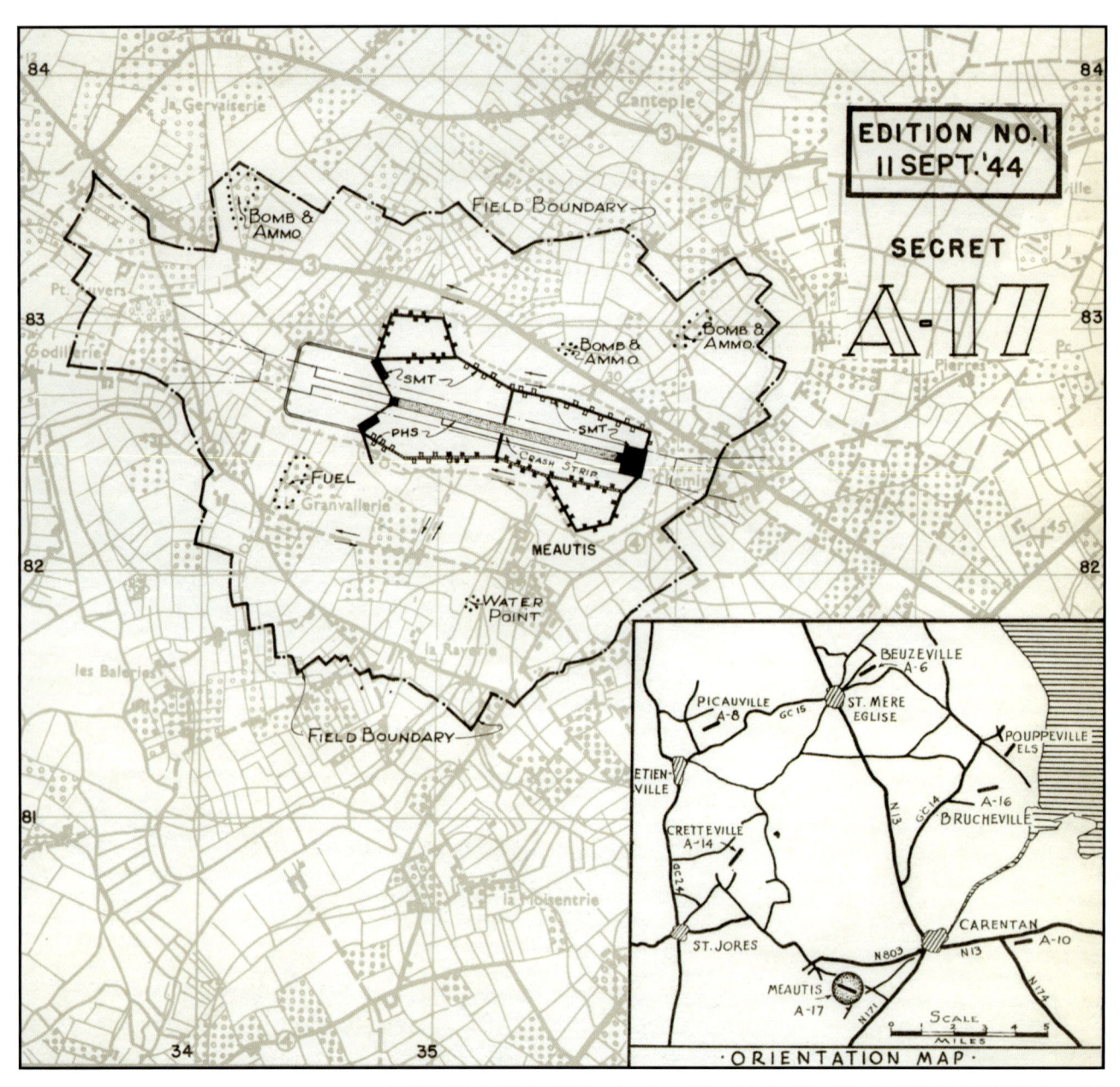

A-17 MEAUTIS

OPERATIONAL AUGUST 16

Latitude: 49°17'N
Longitude: 01°18'W
Grid reference: T-352826
Altitude: 65ft

Méautis lies a mile south-west of Carentan and was built as a fighter strip by the 840th Engineer Aviation Battalion for the 50th Fighter Group, then based on the other side of Carentan on A-10. PBS was used to surface a 3,600ft strip with taxi-tracks and dispersals with SMT.

The three squadrons, the 10th, 81st and 313th, had arrived at A-10 on June 24-25, transferring to A-17 on August 16. The last squadron finally quit the ALG on September 5 when the group moved east to the French airport at Orly (A-47), nine miles south of Paris.

The memorial to the wartime role of A-17 was dedicated on June 7, 1989.

The work to construct Méautis, just ten miles west of A-10 at Carentan, was begun by the 840th Engineer Aviation Battalion on July 24. Using PBS hessian to surface the runway obviously took longer as it was not ready for occupation until the second week of August when the demand for beach-head airfields was over. The three squadrons of the 50th Fighter Group flew in on August 16, this particular machine belonging to the 81st Fighter Squadron.

The life of A-17 was a mere three weeks, the 313th Fighter Squadron departing for Orly, the pre-war Paris airport, on August 30, the other two squadrons, the 10th and 81st, following on September 5. After the break-out from the beachhead it became American policy to develop airfields in clusters of four or five which together could provide for the needs of all the groups of a tactical air command or a medium bombardment wing plus an air depot group. Such 'clutches' were greatly desired by the combat commands, for they permitted a high degree of control with a minimum of communications. Early in August, the 1st Engineer Aviation Brigade, under Colonel Karl B. Schilling, was charged with the construction of airfields in the First Army zone of advance. They moved eastward into the Le Mans area followed by the 2nd Brigade, under Colonel Rudolph E. Smyser, which performed a similar function in the Third Army area.

By 1947 only the ghostly outline remained . . .

. . . and today A-17 is completely lost to history, save for a memorial which has been set up beside the D443.

A-33 VANNES

OPERATIONAL AUGUST 18

Latitude: 47°43'N
Longitude: 02°43'W
Grid reference: vH-206144
Altitude: 455ft

When captured by the Germans in 1940 the Luftwaffe used Vannes as a base for KGr100 from August to June 1941. JG53 stationed its Bf109s there between June and August 1941 and those of JG51 were there from October 1941 to January 1942. JG2 based its FW190s there from November 1942 to October 1943 but they had to be pulled back in the face of increasing Allied attacks on Luftwaffe bases prior to the invasion.

It was Combat Command A of the US 4th Armored Division that first reached the aerodrome with its two concrete runways on August 5. Five days later the 850th Aviation Engineers were on site, repairing a 6,000ft runway ready for the arrival of the 425th Night Fighter Squadron. They flew in with their P-61 Black Widows direct from the UK on August 18.

The Americans held on to A-33 using it for re-supply and evacuation of casualties until June 20, 1945. Once back under French civil control, a programme of reconstruction was begun, with the main runway resurfaced with asphalt. The secondary is now used as an aircraft parking apron. Vannes is now better known as Meucon Airport.

Fast forward from 1940 to 1944 when this unnamed mechanic of the 425th Night Fighter Squadron was pictured servicing an engine of a P-61.

Vannes under new management. The Heinkels of Kampfgruppe 100 with the X-Verfahren radio navigation system which was designed to bring a bomber to within 1,000 feet of its target at a range of 180 miles. Hauptmann Kurd Aschenbreuner, the group commander, is facing the camera with the white-topped cap.

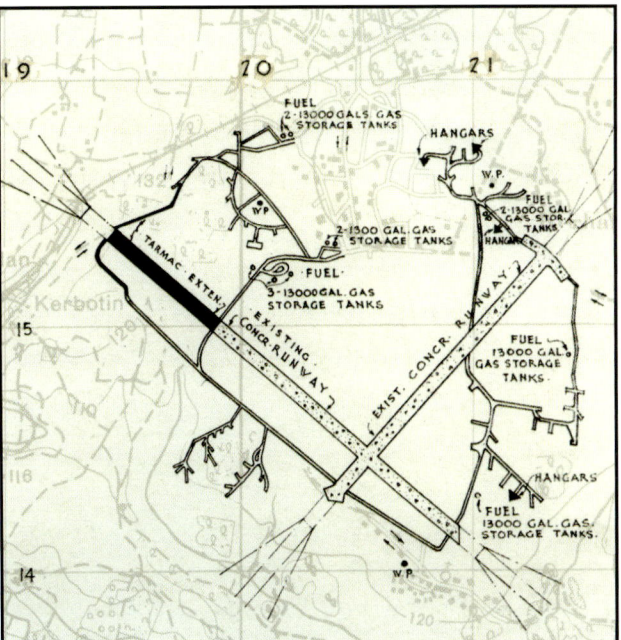

Poor soil, rainy weather, and an inadequate supply of surfacing materials prevented the completion of the airfields in the Le Mans sector until early September, by which time the battle area had been carried so far beyond that it lay at the extreme limit of effective fighter-bomber radius. Also the unavailability of the railways to move up supplies, and the virtual monopoly of road transportation by the ground armies, had forced the aviation engineers to depend on their own inadequate truck resources and whatever facilities the IX Service Command could spare for the transport of surfacing materials from Cherbourg and the beaches to the airfields under construction. The resulting shortage of surfacing was destined to remain a chronic problem throughout the rest of the campaign, thus the capture of ready-made aerodromes like Vannes in Brittany (see map pages 150-151) was a bonus.

Being a pre-war civil airport, once its concrete runways had been repaired and extended it was used as a resupply and evacuation airfield after the night fighters were moved to bases further east. The Americans held A-33 until June 1945.

Today Vannes, also known as Meucon Airport, has a main runway resurfaced with asphalt of 5,020 feet on a bearing of 04/22 and a grass strip of 3,363 feet on 08/26. The old secondary runway (13/31) is now just used for parking.

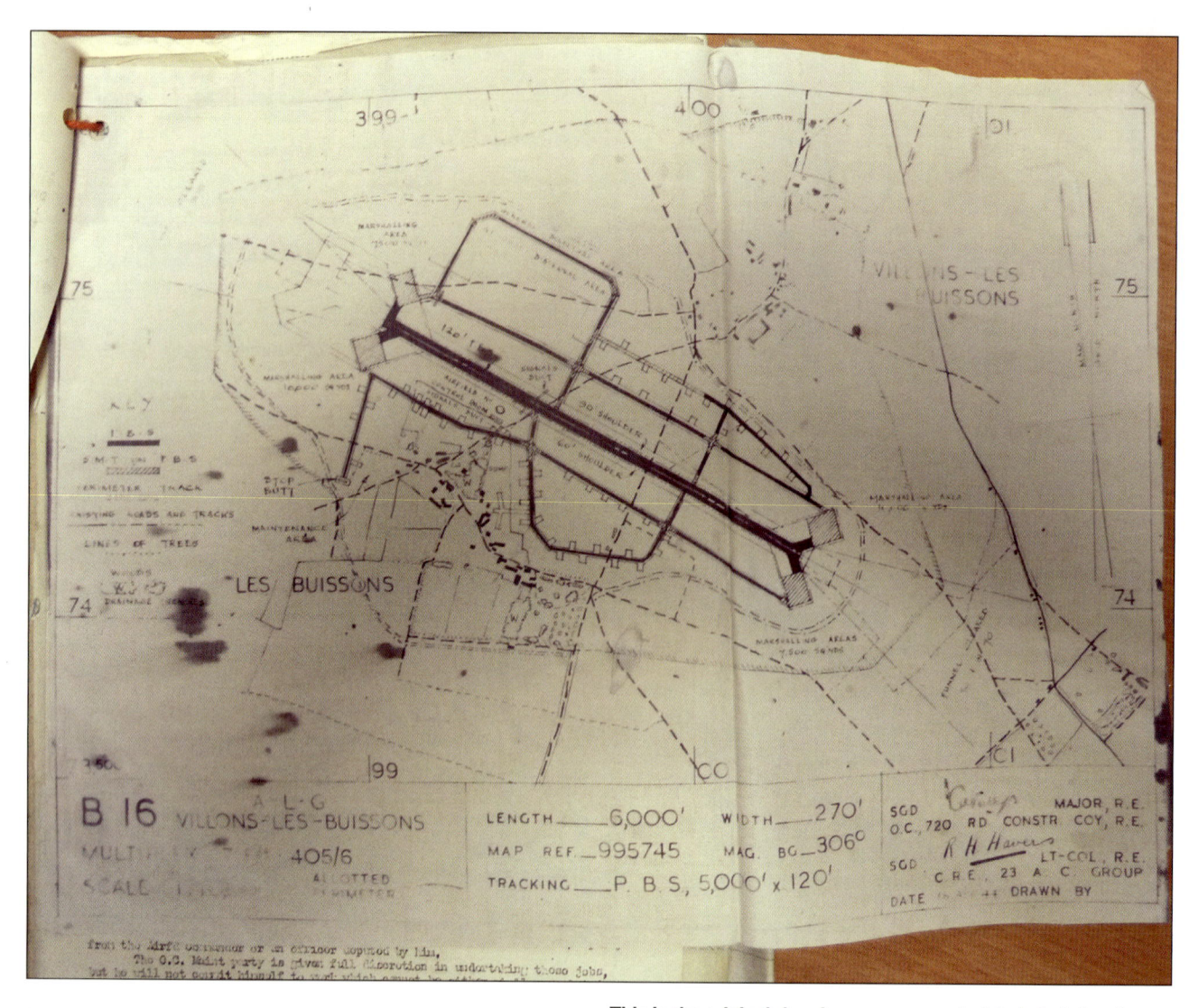

B-16 VILLONS-LES-BUISSONS

This is the original drawing now somewhat faded, dating from a 1944 file, and *(below)* the formal plan issued to the Second Tactical Air Force by the 21st Army Group on August 12.

OPERATIONAL AUGUST 20

Latitude: 49°14'N
Longitude: 00°24'W
Grid reference: T-995745
Altitude 192ft

After touch-down, the Canadian 9th Infantry Brigade, Canadian 3rd Division, had as its D-Day objective the airfield at Carpiquet just west of Caen, a march of about ten miles. However, it took all morning to get clear of the coastal town of Bernières and by the time they reached the half-way point they found the 8th Brigade were still ahead clearing the village of Bény. Without stopping, the North Nova Scotia Highlanders pushed on with the infantry riding on the tanks of the Canadian 27th Armoured Regiment and by dusk the head of the column had reached Villons-les-Buissons. The village was soon cleared the next day although Carpiquet, the original target, did not fall for a month.

B-16 was to have a strip of 5,000ft by 240ft on an alignment of WNW-ESE and surfaced with PBS and SMT. Surveyed by No. 23 Airfield Construction Group on July 12, it was scheduled to be completed by August 7.

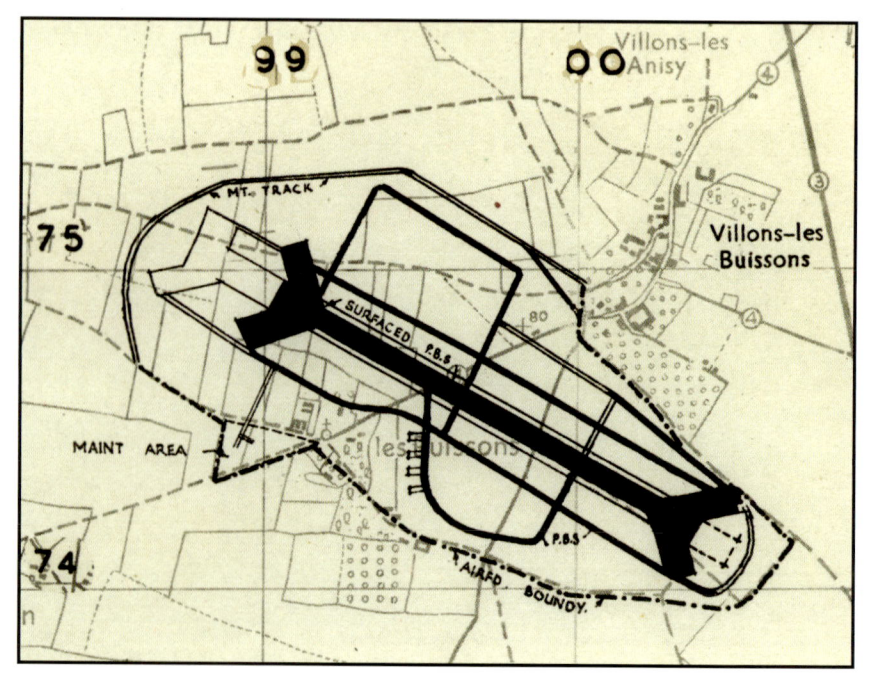

Fortunately with B-16 the technical report has survived and we dipped into the file to be able to include an extract, reproduced on pages 170-171, including a critique on the quality of the Prefabricated Bituminous Surfacing.

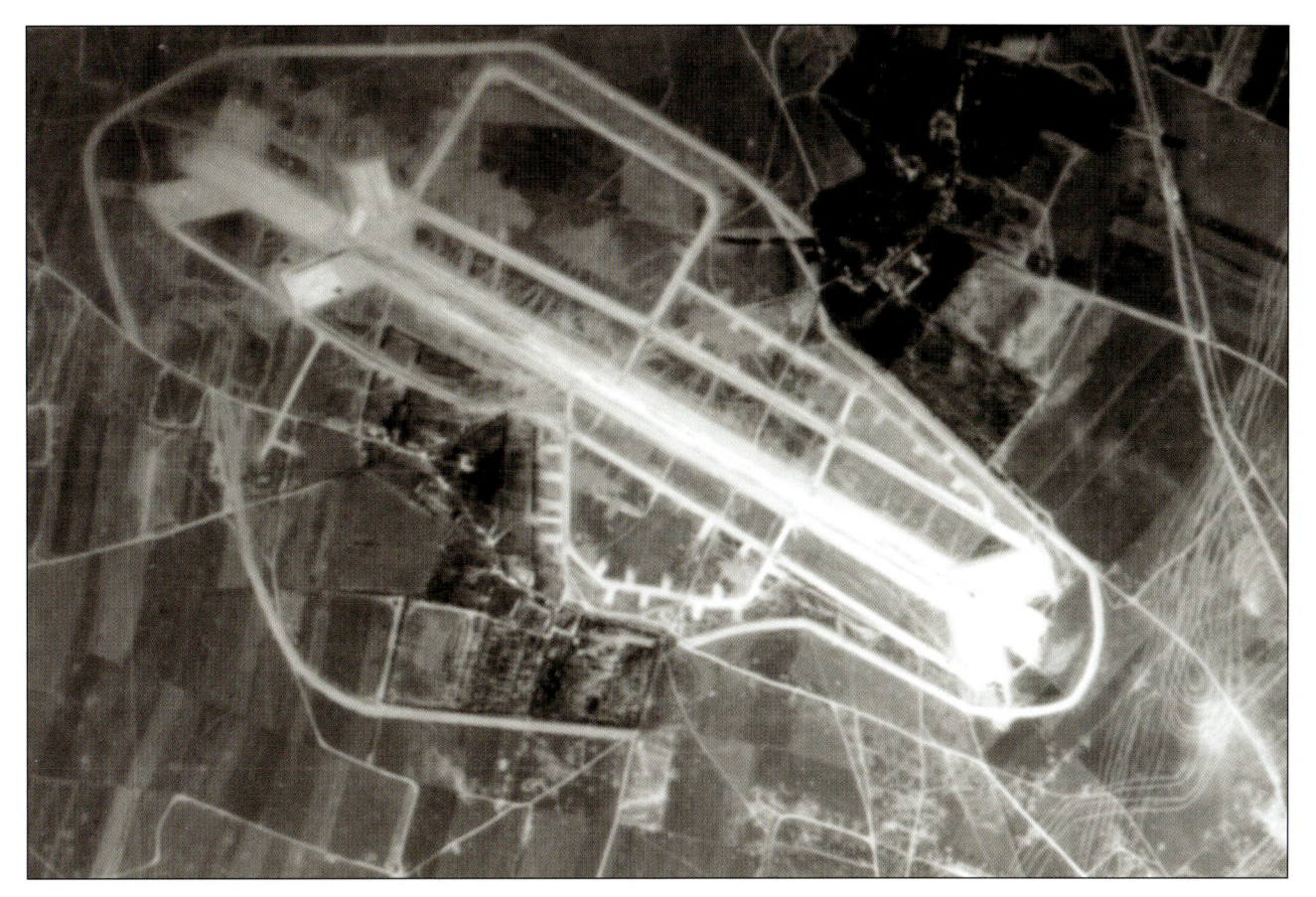

From August 20 it became the home of No. 132 Wing. Two of its squadrons were the Norwegian Nos. 331 and 332 that had moved five times since leaving their main base at North Weald in January. They were joined by Nos. 66 and 127 Squadrons, all flying Spitfires. During September 1-6 they all moved to B-33 at Campneuseville, east of Dieppe. A memorial marker was originally placed on the edge of the runway of the former flying field but has since been moved.

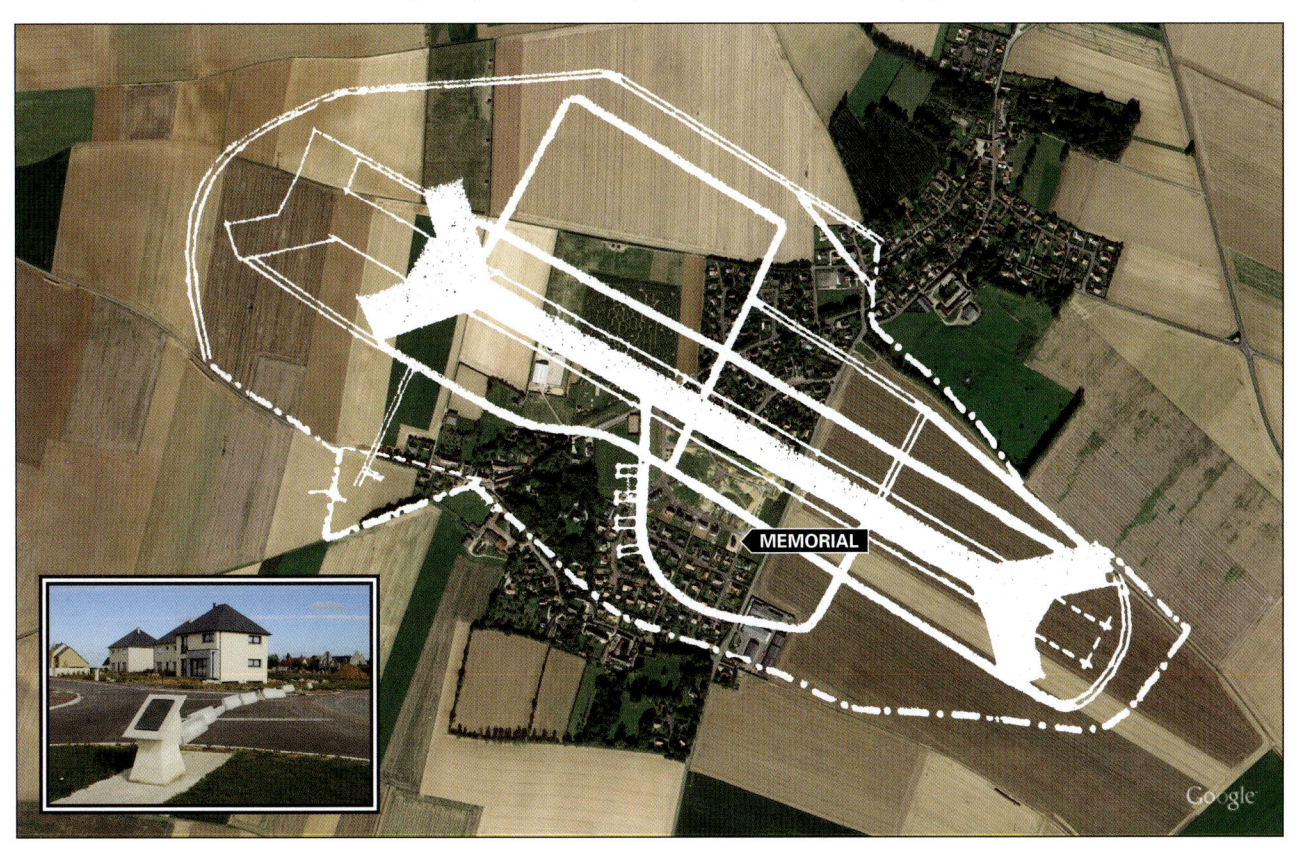

The memorial has been moved from its original location to a new spot at the entrance to the Domaine de Vikland housing development. It now stands on Place Lieutenant Helland, named after the first Norwegian pilot to land in France on June 11 although he was never based at Villons. It was re-dedicated by the Norwegian King, Harald V, on June 5, 2014.

TECHNICAL REPORT OF CONSTRUCTION OF ALG B-16 AT VILLONS-LES-BUISSONS (MAP REF 995745 7F/1 405/406).

Task: To construct an airfield surfaced with PBS to Medium Bomber Specification. Length 6,000 feet. Width 270 feet. (Subsequent modifications noted later.)

Description of Site: Arable land, alluvial silt topsoil and clay and limestone subsoil. 100% cultivated; excellent farmland. Small pockets of soft spongy vegetable matter encountered on the taxi-tracks and marshalling areas.

Time: Work was started on the field on the 14th July and the strip was completed to the requirements then in force for flying on first light 8th August. Additional requirements completed by 15th August. Several days were lost owing to diversions of plant to provide gunpits in the vicinity for the major attack on Caen, and also owing to the closing of roads for operations.

Weather: Except for the period 21st to 25th July inclusive which was showery and gusty, the weather was good particularly in August.

Working Hours: Mechanical Equipment. 0600 hrs to 2200 hrs (2 shifts). Labour. 0800 hrs to 1800 hrs daily except period 1st to 7th August. 0700 hrs to 1800 hrs (1st to 4th) 0700 hrs to 2000 hrs (5th & 6th), 0700 hrs to 2200 hrs (7th). No PBS could be laid on any day before 0830 hrs owing to ground mist, heavy dew and low temperature.

Stores Used: PBS (Rolls) 4,900. Petrol (Galls.) 10,000. Derv. (Galls.) 10,000. Bitumen Emulsion 12,750. Armco Culvert 3,000 ft. run. Sand 200 tons. *Sundry:* Cable ducts, cement for markers, 2" tubular scaffold, Sandbags. Hardcore 5,650 tons (on side drains alone).

Plant and Labour: 720 Rd Constr Coy RE. Working Numbers 140. 201 Coy PC Working Numbers 210. With the addition of 190 from 250 Coy PC on 3rd — 7th Aug (incl.). Scraper Hours 922. Dozer Hours 481. Autopatrol Hours 1,095. Blade Grader 459. 10. RB 501. Machine time was lost owing to mines.

The ground generally had been heavily fought over and there were many unused mortar bombs, Hawkins grenades, etc, lying about. In additon part of the site was over a British minefield which had been reported cleared. In spite of the clearance a D6 was wrecked on a Mark V mine and two tractors damaged with Hawkins with several narrow escapes on mortar bombs. As a result the whole area was swept, holding up work to some extent (total loss approx one day), a bomb disposal section RE being attached for this purpose. The sweeping on the area proved to be difficult and very long job owing to the corps, but visual clearance effected the collection of about one ton of sundry ammunition.

Constructional Data: Crop Cutting 657,800 sq. yds. Excavation 35,800 cu. yds. Drainage Trenches 19,000 ft. run. Incorporating: 3,000 ft. run culvertizing. 5,650 cu yds. hardcore lifted to site (varying in size from rubble stone to dust).

Autopatrol trenching to edges of PBS. 11,000 yds. run. Grading: (reckoned over net area only not including duplication of grading due to bad weather, etc) 429,650 sq.yds. PBS measured net as laid 170,100 sq. yds. Surfacing measured with sand and Bitumen 70,000 sq. yds. Perimeter Road 6,100 lin. yds. SMT 50,000 sq. yds. Control and GOR (each room 30' × 12' intercommunicating and all dug to a depth of 6' 6", covered and splinterproof).

Survey and Plan: The initial survey of the area showed good natural drainage; both cross fall and longitudinal fall existed on the runway. Careful levels were taken on the runway to avoid basins, but the general lines of the ground were followed throughout, and the drainage falls adapted to these lines. The position of taxi-tracks and one marshalling area was amended to avoid soft spots which came to light after grading.

Changes in Specification: The field was orignally designed as a 6,000' strip for the use of night fighters. Medium bomber specifications were decided on. Subsequently the specification was changed to a 5,000' field for fighters, with the extra 1,000' of flightway and the extra taxi-tracks graded out to fair weather specifications only. The field as finally completed has the runway and taxi-tracks covered in PBS to fighter specifications.

Technical Observations:
1. *Drainage:* Consideration was given to the large run-off of water from the runway and it was decided to make a complete and elaborate system to deal with the quantity involved. Such a system cannot be instituted in hasty work, but lack of it will invariably give a soft mushy edge where the PBS goes into the ground and there will be runnels across the strip and untracked fair weather strip which requires attention after even light rain. Loose joint piping is required for this type of job. As those were not forthcoming we had to make do with unsuitable hardcore from damaged houses. The work of the drain will be handicapped by this. Crushed stone for the top was not available until the last two days of working time, and when it came much of it was unsuitable for the work because it appeared to have been crushed from too smaller stones which made consolidation very difficult. For this reason it was necessary to fix the crushed stone nearest the PBS by a sand grout with Bitumen emulsion for about 12" to 18" width throughout the length of the drains.

The drain was dug, for speed, with a D8 towing a Killifor plough which gives a very narrow suction at the bottom. Such a section is not ideal, unless piping is available because there is danger of the water level rising too near the top and possibly seeping through the joints of the PBS and wetting the gound under the runway.

The earth is thrown to both sides and entails the collection of a windrow by a scraper, with resultant damage to the grade unless the grading is worked towards the centre of the runway. A better section could be got with an RB10 excavator, though it would be much slower. This should be done after grading the whole surface, spoil being carted and dumped as part of the operation.

2. *Laying of PBS:* PBS was laid in accordance with the standard drill, but the following should be noted:—
(a) It is advisable to raise the Stamplicker teams to 10 men and one NCO. Owing to the importance of complete coverage by stickum, the NCO should be free to observe the sheet as it comes off the machine. The extra man can cover the odd jobs which invariably crop up.
(b) As the sheet was threaded the men dipped the end in the stickum, this ensures good coverage on the lateral joints.
(c) The best method found to avoid wrinkles in the sheets at the beginning of each length was with link bars and pickets. The sheet is doubled over the link bar and the picket knocked in. The short end which is then holed is cut off and buried after completion of laying. The burying can then be done by machine.
(d) The last roller on the machine was shifted to the lower of the two alternative positions. This makes it easier to thread.
(e) 50% Derv and 50% Petrol was found satisfactory throughout.
(f) Much better results were obtained when the weather was hot. The laying in the heat of the afternoon always gave results free from wrinkles.
(g) Any edges which are not properly stuck should be sealed. With stickum good results are always obtained, but pure diesel should not be used for this nor should bitumen emulsion be rubbed UNDER the sheets. Both diesel and emulsion cause the bitumen on the PBS to remain soft unless it is exposed to the air.

(h) A small part of the PBS in short lengths was laid by hand, the stickum being applied by paint spray. This machine gives too fine a spray and the application is very slow.
(i) Some PBS rolls were defective. A separate report is at Appendix "D".

3. Application of Bitumen and Sand: Materials supplied for this purpose were 55% Bitumen Emulsion and a good coarse-grained sand. Bitumen Emulsion is not suitable for either spraying on PBS or for sealing the joints. It remains too soft and clogs sprays and cans. A cutback bitumen would be more suitable. Suggested reasons for this are given in Appendix "E". Part of the strip was coated with 60 gall sprayer on Coy G.1098. This is a hand pump, but was too slow in use that a paint spray compressor was connected and spraying continued at a pressure of 50lbs per sq. in. The machine still had to be filled by hand however. It takes 1½ days work to spray 300 yards by 40 yards. An Etynro Road Spray was made available on the last day. This holds 1,250 galls and sprays at 10 miles per hour, 5 yards wide. A coverage of 11 yards per gall was found satisfactory. Despite frequent stops for cleaning of jets with petrol, the Etynro sprayed 1,400 yards by 40 yards (the whole of the strip less 300 yards done by hand) in 8 hours. With proper filling facilities it could do it in 4 hours.

Several methods were tried out for covering the strip with sand. A trial was made with the blades raised ½" from the ground; this was fairly successful. An agricultural Spreader was found and used, but gave such a fine coveage that six journeys were required. Owing to pressure of time the majority of the strip was covered by hand shovelling.

A light smooth face and wobble-wheel roller was then applied, and after 24 hours, the sand was brushed off with circular road brooms. Sufficient sand was applied just to prevent the bitumen bleeding through. The result was a reasonable surface and of a fair even nature.

4. SMT: A Havoc landed on the strip without damaging the surface, but a Thunderbolt landing for refuelling on a hot afternoon turned on a locked wheel and tore the upper surface of the PBS.

The Marshalling areas and all taxi-track cross-overs are covered with SMT.

SMT is laid over the safety strip and fairweather strip where the PBS run-offs have to connect to the runway.

We laid the SMT at right-angles to the line of the runway. I now think it would have been better to lay it on the line of the runway i.e. at right-angles to the line of the run-off.

We laid some bad rolls of PBS which were very thinly coated with bitumen, under this SMT to act merely as a dust layer.

The strips have already torn badly and it remains to be seen whether we have done more harm in giving opportunity for soft patches to form, than good in laying the dust.

A very heavy thunderstorm did not cause soft patches there.

Conclusion: For future fields in PBS the following is recommended.
(i) Before starting, the ultimate specification of the field must be known so that drains can be made to fit in with the ultimate development.
(ii) If the field is required quickly the side drains should be left out altogether and the resulting softening of the ground at the edge of the PBS after rain and damage to the fair-weather portions must be accepted.
(iii) If the field is to be extended later the side drains should be omitted until the extension is to be carried out, unless considerable bad weather is expected before development can proceed.
(iv) If the field is to last the winter, drains must be built. They should be built at the edge of the PBS and not at the edge of the shoulders. If an extension is necessary one drain will have to be scrapped. It can be rolled and tarred and blended to ground level and covered with PBS or merely rolled and blended and covered with PBS. I see no reason to expect either a rough surface or subsidence in a drain which has been so treated.
(v) A certain and adequate supply of stores must be available before starting if a good finish is to be expected.
(vi) Cutback bitumen and not emulsion is required for sanding and sealing joints.

APPENDIX. "D"

1. The delivery of PBS to the job was a total of 4,900 Rolls. These were made by several different manufacturers.

2. On the whole 80 per cent of the PBS was reasonably good although lengths of the sheets varied from 80 yds to 130 yds despite recommendations that they should be a standard length of 80 yds.

3. The manufacturer's names were not all decipherable: those that had the full names were:

   (a) Messrs Ruberoid, Ltd. (b) Messrs Anderson & Son, Ltd. (c) Messrs W.S & S, Ltd. (d) No name, but a metal tag as follows: H.B.5369 P.B. Surface. D.T.5. 109864 L. 80 yds. 145 of 168 W.T.31010 Gold 2nd Con. S.S.I. SG. 28E/317. This type of label was attached to the worst quality of PBS.

4. This bad quality PBS suffered from serious defects making it unsuitable for use on airfields.

   (a) It was very thin — almost uncoated in places.
   (b) It was coated by the manufacturers without the hessian being under tension: the result is that the finished PBS is wrinkled before it is laid and therefore the final laid job is very bad.

Messrs Ruberoid and Andersons products are satisfactory. The other manufactures products vary much more. Messrs Ruberoid comply with the standard 80 yards length, which none of the other firms do.

APPENDIX. "E"

The Bitumen Emulsion was not suitable either for spraying on the PBS or for sealing the joints for the following reasons.

(a) It is, like all emulsions of this nature, a bitumen of low viscosity in suspension and not actually in a liquid state. Emulsions are much more sensitive to local conditions than a cutback bitumen would be.

(b) The bitumen, when broken away from the emulsion agent, is very soft and remains so. This softness is not due to volatiles which evaporate as in a cutback. It is a fault in the emulsion itself and usually means that the bitumen in suspension is simply of high penetration, i.e. about 220 plus. The only cure is in the manufacture (further distillation). Bitumen emulsion for use on PBS should have a penetration of not more than 180. Lengthy exposure will harden the coat somewhat and it will no doubt prove satisfactory in cold weather. In view of the foregoing it is suggested that cutback bitumen would be more suitable. (Cutback No. 1 War Specification). Even better would be a hot bitumen applied with the Etnyro Sprayer. A cutback would be easier to apply; emulsion coats itself on any type of sprayer and great difficulty and frequent washing with petrol was necessary.

A-29 ST JAMES

OPERATIONAL AUGUST 20

Latitude: 48°30'N
Longitude: 01°19'W
Grid reference: Y-294972
Altitude: 415ft

Located just under ten miles southeast of A-28 at Pontorson, the site for the strip at St James was overrun by Combat Command A of the US 4th Armored Division on August 1 on their drive to capture Rennes, although it was the 13th Infantry Regiment of the 8th Division which actually secured the area on the 3rd.

The 825th Engineer Aviation Battalion began work on constructing a 5,000ft runway with PBS hessian matting on August 8 which was more or less complete six days later. The three squadrons — the 410th, 411th and 412th — of the 373rd Fighter Group quit Tour-en-Bessin where they had been based since July 19 and touched down at St James on August 20. They remained in residence until moving to Reims (A-62) later in September.

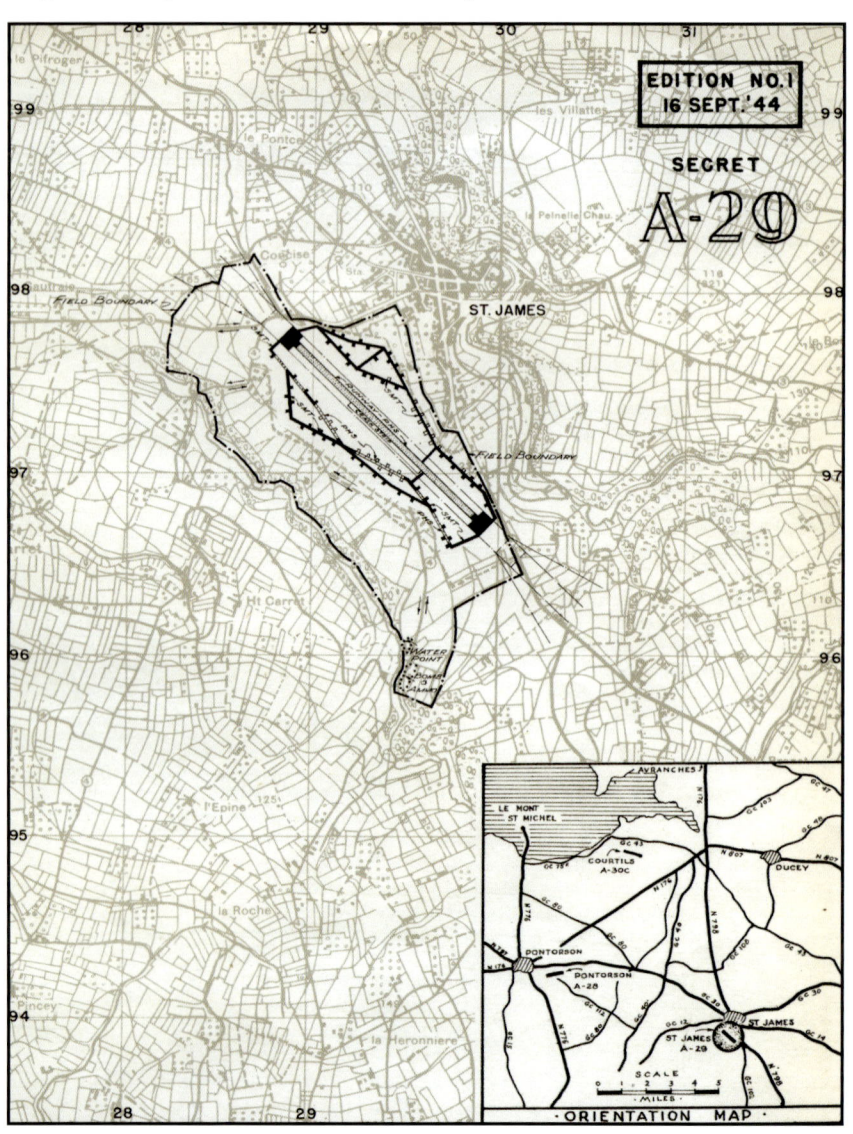

On the day that A-29 became operational, over to the east Allied forces advancing from the north and south met at Chambois (see map pages 162-163), so sealing the pocket at Falaise. Altogether the Allies captured 40,000 to 50,000 men in the pocket while several thousand others lost their lives while trying to escape, much due to the relentless attacks from the air. During the four-day period following August 20, poor visibility and heavy rain prevented SHAEF air forces from operating enabling the German withdrawal towards the Seine to continue unabated. Meanwhile French Resistance forces decided to take a hand in the liberation of Paris. Général de Gaulle had only just arrived in France and on the 21st he went to see Eisenhower with an ultimatum: if he did not send troops into the capital immediately, the French were prepared to do so unilaterally. Eisenhower gave the order the following day, the advance to be led by the armour of the French 2ème Division Blindée.

The PBS runway at St James, aligned 134 degrees, was laid down by the 825th Engineers in six days, somewhat of a record with this surfacing material. It served the 373rd Fighter Group until its squadrons moved nearer the front, the 410th on September 21, 412th on September 23 and the 411th on September 29.

Virtually no landmarks remain to identify the line of the airstrip at St James today which lay just west of the town.

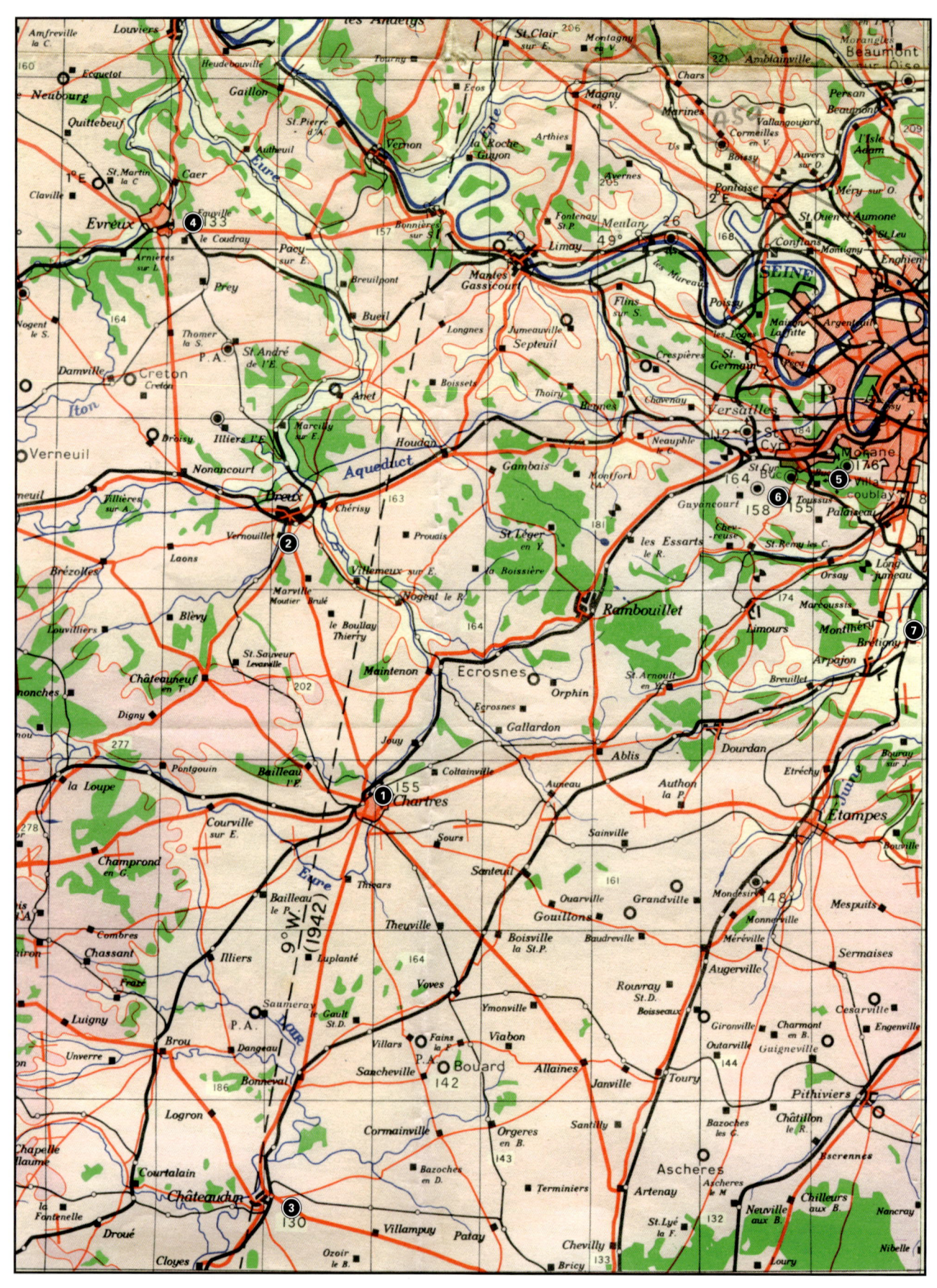

It was planned next to develop virgin sites in the Chartres plain, but the armies moved so swiftly that Chartres, too, was soon left far behind and instead the many aerodromes around Paris were becoming available in the latter part of August while the Germans were still withdrawing. Once Paris had fallen, several permanent French airfields like [1] Chartres, [2] Dreux, [3] Châteaudun, [4] Évreux, [5] Villacoublay, [6] Toussus-le-Noble and [7] Brétigny were taken over by American forces and by the end of August airfields in the Orléans-Paris areas had been made ready for supply and evacuation work. On these airfields the planes bringing food from England to the Parisian populace landed during the last days of August and the first days of September.

A-40D CHARTRES

OPERATIONAL AUGUST 23

Latitude: 48°27'N
Longitude: 01°30'E
Grid reference: R-405033
Altitude: 492ft

The history of Chartres aerodrome, some 50 miles south-west of Paris, begins during the First World War when it was established as a military flying training school. After the war the 22ème Régiment Aérien de Bombardement — a night bombing squadron — was based there from 1923, and the 6ème Escadre de Chasse fighter squadron from 1936.

Following the Armistice, the Luftwaffe used it as a main base for Luftflotte 3 in operations against Britain. Units based there between July 1940 and June 1943 included KG55, KG100, KG53 and KG66. From July 1943 to June 1944 the FW190s of KG55 were in residence and the Ju88s of NKG13 at the time of the invasion.

Consequently, the airfield was the target for repeated attacks by the Eighth Air Force in 1943 and 1944, with additional raids by the Ninth in the run-up to D-Day.

Many of the former Armée de l'Air bases had been used by the Luftwaffe but as they were grass airfields, which became unsafe or unusable in wet weather, during the winter of 1940-41 much was done to improve them, sometimes using French civilian labour to lay concrete runways, taxiways and dispersals. This picture shows such work in progress while mechanics are servicing the engines of the Heinkel. The aircraft are believed to belong to KG55, the Griffon Geschwader based at Villacoublay, Chartres and Dreux.

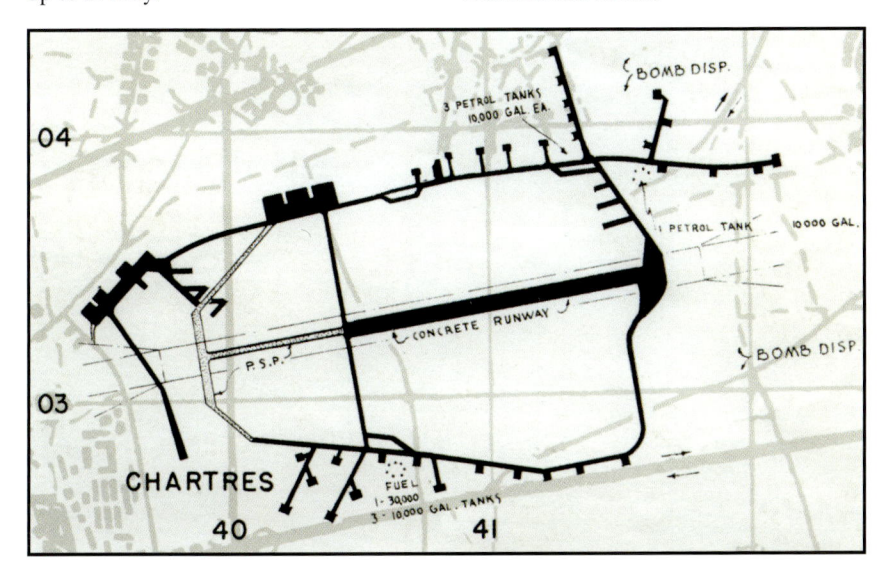

On August 18, the 11th Infantry of the US 5th Division, in conjunction with the 7th Armored Division, captured the airfield which had already been allotted the code A-40. The 832nd and 833rd Engineer Aviation Battalions moved in to rehabilitate the single concrete runway that was extended with pierced steel planking to 5,500ft. Formally declared operational on the 26th, the 395th and 396th Squadrons of the 368th Fighter Group brought in their Thunderbolts the following day, although the third squadron — the 397th — had already flown in to Chartres five days earlier from their strip at Cardonville, A-3 being one of the earliest airstrips that had been established in the beachhead.

On September 11 the 368th moved forward 125 miles to A-69 at Laon to be replaced at Chartres by the 323rd Bomb Group. Its four squadrons (453rd, 454th, 455th and 456th) had been at A-20 at Lessay since August 26, switching bases to Chartres on September 21. They moved to Laon on October 13.

Returning to French control in June 1945, it required almost total reconstruction to repair the damage caused by Allied bombing, being reopened as the major French Air Force Base Aérienne 122 Chartres-Champhol (BA 122). The military base closed in 1977, being replaced by a much smaller civilian facility on the southern side of the wartime airfield.

Chartres was provided with taxiways 35ft wide with dispersals for 75 aircraft, complete airfield lighting for night landings, with VHF homing on 7550 kcs. There were 60,000 gallons of aviation fuel on hand with refuelling carried out by truck.

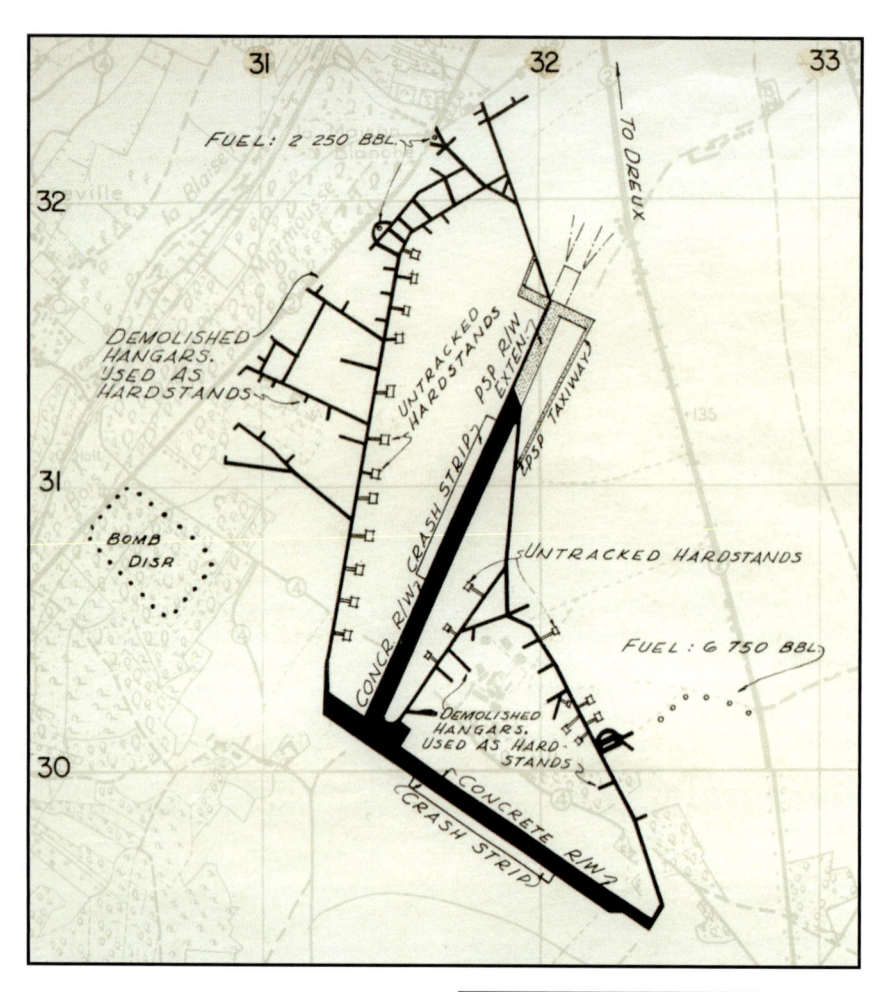

A-41 DREUX

OPERATIONAL AUGUST 24

Latitude: 48°42'N
Longitude: 01°21'E
Grid reference: R-318313
Altitude: 453ft

Dreux lies 40 miles west of Paris, its aerodrome lying two miles south of the town. Originally when built in the 1920s it was a simple grass field but later two concrete runways were added. The Luftwaffe made good use of it as a base for Luftflotte 3, initially for bombing missions against England by KG55. In April and May 1944 the Me410s of KG51 were at Dreux and it became a fighter base for FW190s of JG3 and SKG10, and the Bf109s of JG3 in attempts to counter the invasion.

Already listed as airfield A-41, on August 16 it fell to the US 5th Armored Division. On the 21st its rehabilitation was begun by the 840th Engineer Aviation Battalion which had declared Dreux operational by August 26. The two runways were NE-SW at 5,500ft, including a PSP extension, with the secondary 4,400ft from NW-SE.

Today Dreux (see map page 174) is but a shadow of its former self, almost indistinguishable from the wartime layout when it was A-41. Virtually all the concrete from the two runways has been removed leaving a 2,362-foot grass runway on 04/22.

A-41 was destined to become a major American base for fighters, bombers and troop-carrying aircraft. First to arrive was the 366th Fighter Group, its three squadrons — 389th, 390th and 391st — bringing their P-47s in from St Pierre-du-Mont on the 24th-25th. When they departed for Laon on September 12 they were replaced by the B-26 Marauders of the 397th Bomb Group from Gorges (A-26) on September 15-16. The four squadrons (596th, 597th, 598th and 599th) were moved to A-72 at Péronne in October.

Arriving on November 3-4 was the 441st Troop Carrier Group, comprising the 99th, 100th, 301st and 302nd Squadrons, all of which stayed there for the remainder of the war.

The US tenure of Dreux ended with the departure of the 441st Group in February 1946 but, with the onset of the Cold War, the United States Air Force wanted to establish airbases and station combat wings in France. The airfield at Dreux was one site proposed but the French government turned the request down stating that increased air traffic there would impinge on the expansion of the Paris airport at Orly. Instead an alternative USAF airbase was built two miles to the south-west called Dreux-Louvilliers.

As a result, Dreux was closed and the wartime structures demolished, the runway concrete being lifted in the process. Today, renamed Vernouillet Airport, a grass strip remains for light general aviation.

During its heyday — August 1944 to February 1946 — Dreux carried out a mixture of roles, first as a base for the fighters of the 366th Fighter Group which flew in from A-1 as the early Normandy strips were now too far away from the action.

In September, B-26 Marauders arrived at Dreux. We have included this shot taken from the late Roger Freeman's collection although it shows the 394th Bomb Group pictured at their base A-74 at Cambrai/Niergnies. They were first at Tour-en-Bessin (A-13), then moved to A-50 at Orléans-Bricy in September, before moving to A-74 in October.

Another of Roger's shots shows the third aircraft type to occupy Dreux — the C-47 Skytrain, the 441st Troop Carrier Group (50th Troop Carrier Wing) being the longest residents. This picture illustrates 42-100766 *Lilly Bell II* of the 89th Troop Carrier Squadron, 438th Troop Carrier Group, which was stationed at A-79 at Prosnes in February 1945.

177

A-20 LESSAY

OPERATIONAL AUGUST 26

Latitude: 49°12'N
Longitude: 01°30'W
Grid reference: T-201741
Altitude: 86ft

A grass aerodrome had been opened at Lessay on the west coast of the Cotentin in 1923, its future in the history books of aviation being assured when on June 4, 1927 Charles Lindbergh landed there in *The Spirit of St Louis* prior to boarding a liner at Cherbourg to return to the United States. He had won the $25,000 prize set by Raymond Orteig in May 1919 for the first person to fly non-stop from New York to Paris, which he achieved in 33½ hours.

The airfield had been earmarked for a medium bomber base and was captured by the 315th Infantry Regiment of the US 90th Division on July 26. The 830th Engineer Aviation Battalion began work on August 1 and within two weeks two intersecting runways, surfaced with PSP, had been laid down with the taxiways constructed from a mixture of SMT and PSP.

The 323rd Bomb Group flew in from Beaulieu in Hampshire and landed its three squadrons with their B-26 Marauders on August 26. However their stay was short-lived as the 453rd, 454th, 455th, and 456th squadrons relocated to Chartres (A-40) on September 21.

Today, renamed Charles Lindbergh Airfield, it has reverted to grass.

Lessay aerodrome near the western coastline of the Cherbourg peninsula (see map page 133) had been captured on July 26 but it required considerable work to be carried out before it was serviceable. French civilians were employed to fill bomb-craters under the guidance of the 830th Engineers, this being their first assignment in France.

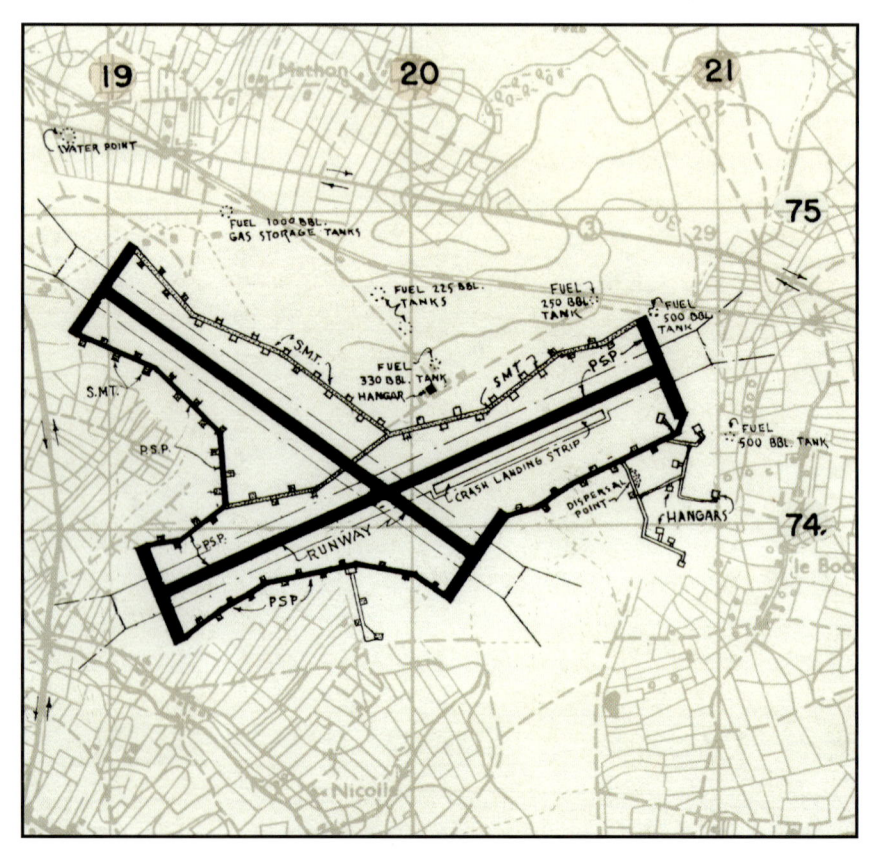

Also, by the time the Marauders of the 323rd Bomb Group arrived on August 26, the front line had moved right out of Normandy. The three squadrons of the group stayed barely a month at A-20 before re-locating to A-40 at Chartres.

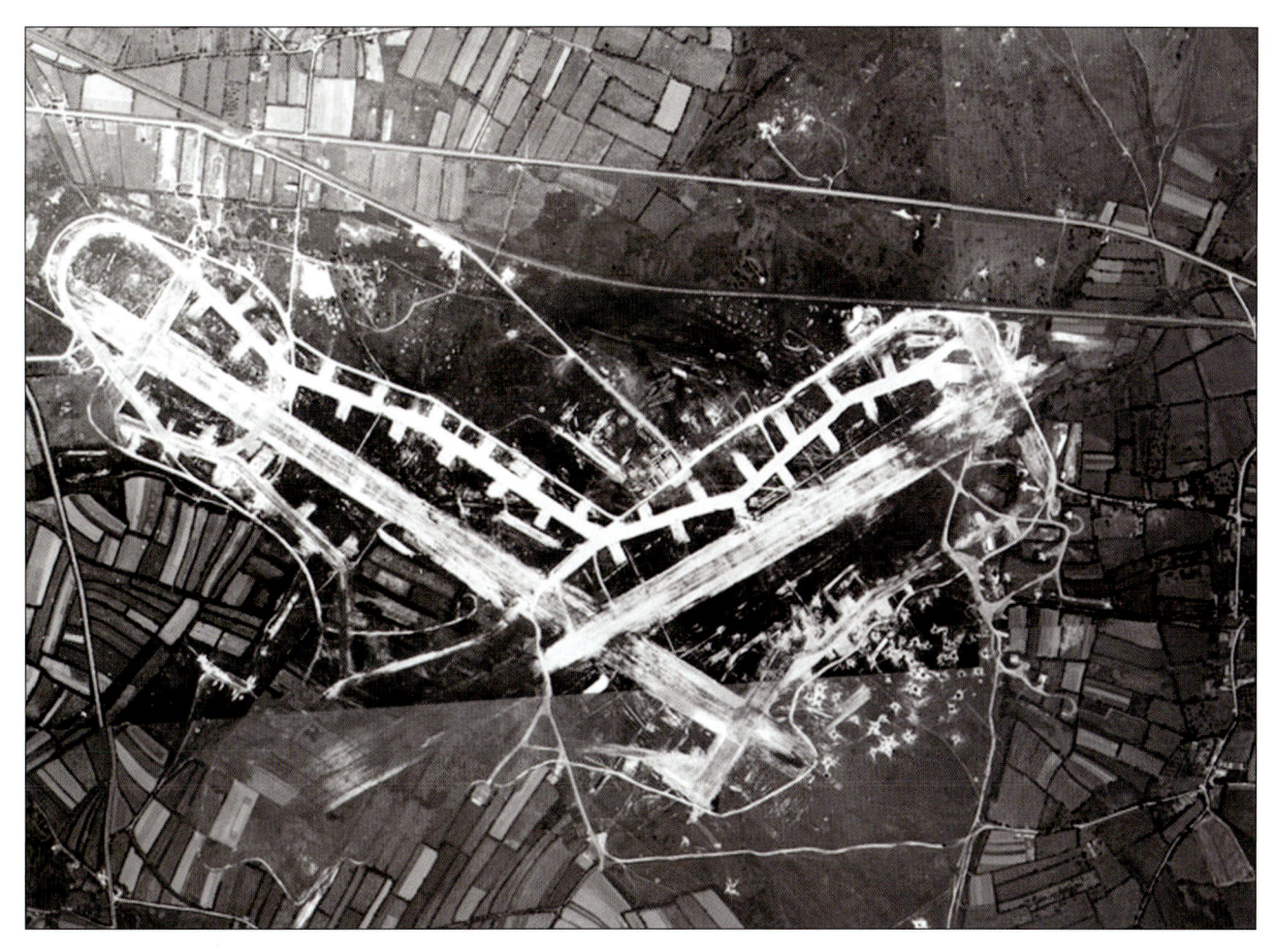

The aerodrome, which dated back to 1923, was abandoned by the Ninth Air Force on September 28, this photo showing its extent in 1947.

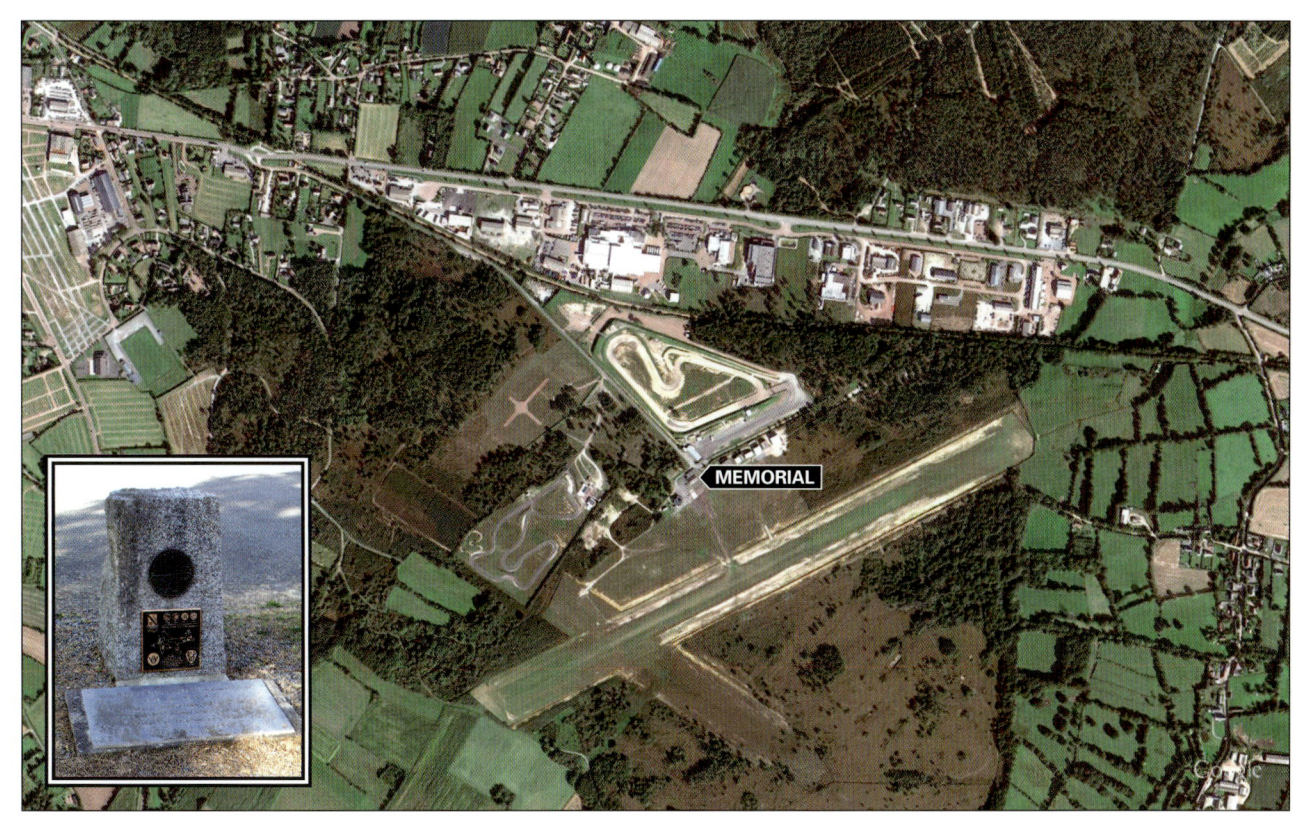

Although the wartime runways were closed in favour of a grass strip, the preservation of Lessay was assured due to its connection with Charles Lindbergh, this being his final stop in France in 1927 before departing for the USA. It was named after him in 1980. The plaque at the foot of the memorial states that A-20 was built by the 850th and 877th Aviation Engineer Battalions but most sources agree that it was laid down by the 830th Battalion.

179

On August 19, the US 79th Infantry Division reached the Seine at Mantes-Gassicourt and had crossed the river early the following morning. This same day Montgomery directed the 21st Army Group to complete mopping up the Falaise pocket while American forces of the 12th Army Group were to drive north to the lower Seine to block the German withdrawal. The 43rd (Wessex) Division reached the river on August 25 and forced a crossing at Vernon that evening. Behind the leading troops, a whole range of aerodromes now became available, most of which did not require building from scratch. B-24 at St André-de-l'Eure provided the second hard runway for the RAF. On August 25, No. 13 Airfield Construction Group completely revised its plans to despatch recce parties to the area of St André but Second TAF reported that it would not require additional airstrips in this area as German forces were in full flight. By the end of the month they were in such dire straits that the withdrawal had to be carried out by night and day, regardless of fighter-bomber attacks, and Allied aircraft roaming the battlefield found themselves presented with a wealth of targets. However, what they effectively achieved has often been exaggerated. Survey teams of No. 2 Operational Research Section of the RAF's Bombing Analysis Unit investigated the area from the Falaise pocket to the Seine to tally up the abandoned and destroyed vehicles and equipment. For descriptive purposes, they divided the sector into three zones. Moving from west to east, the 'Pocket' comprised the area bounded by a line passing through Falaise and Argentan; the 'Shambles', a triangular area encompassing Falaise, Argentan and Vimoutiers, and the 'Chase' between the 'Shambles' and the Seine. The investigation carried out by the Research Section showed that while German losses during their retreat from Normandy in August 1944 amounted to a total of about 15,000 vehicles, of these only 26 per cent were attributable to direct air attacks.

B-24 ST ANDRE-DE-L'EURE

OPERATIONAL AUGUST 28

Latitude: 48°53'N
Longitude: 01°16'E
Grid reference: R-260530
Altitude: 489ft

This French aerodrome, ten miles south-west of Évreux, was a popular regional airport during the 1930s having just a simple circular grass area providing take-offs in any direction. It was improved and extended by the Luftwaffe which laid two concrete runways, one NE-SW the other NW-SE, and was later used as a base for the Ju88s of KG30 and He111s of KG55 during the bombing campaign against Britain between July 1941 and April 1942.

St André had suffered much bombing by both the Eighth and Ninth Air Forces and after its capture by the 120th Infantry of the US 30th Division on August 21, the 877th Engineer Aviation Battalion began work to patch the

St André under attack by the 322nd Bomb Group. One B-26 *Lil' Pork Chop* banks away as a stick of bombs burst along the dispersal area while a fuel dump burns on the eastern side of NW-SE runway.

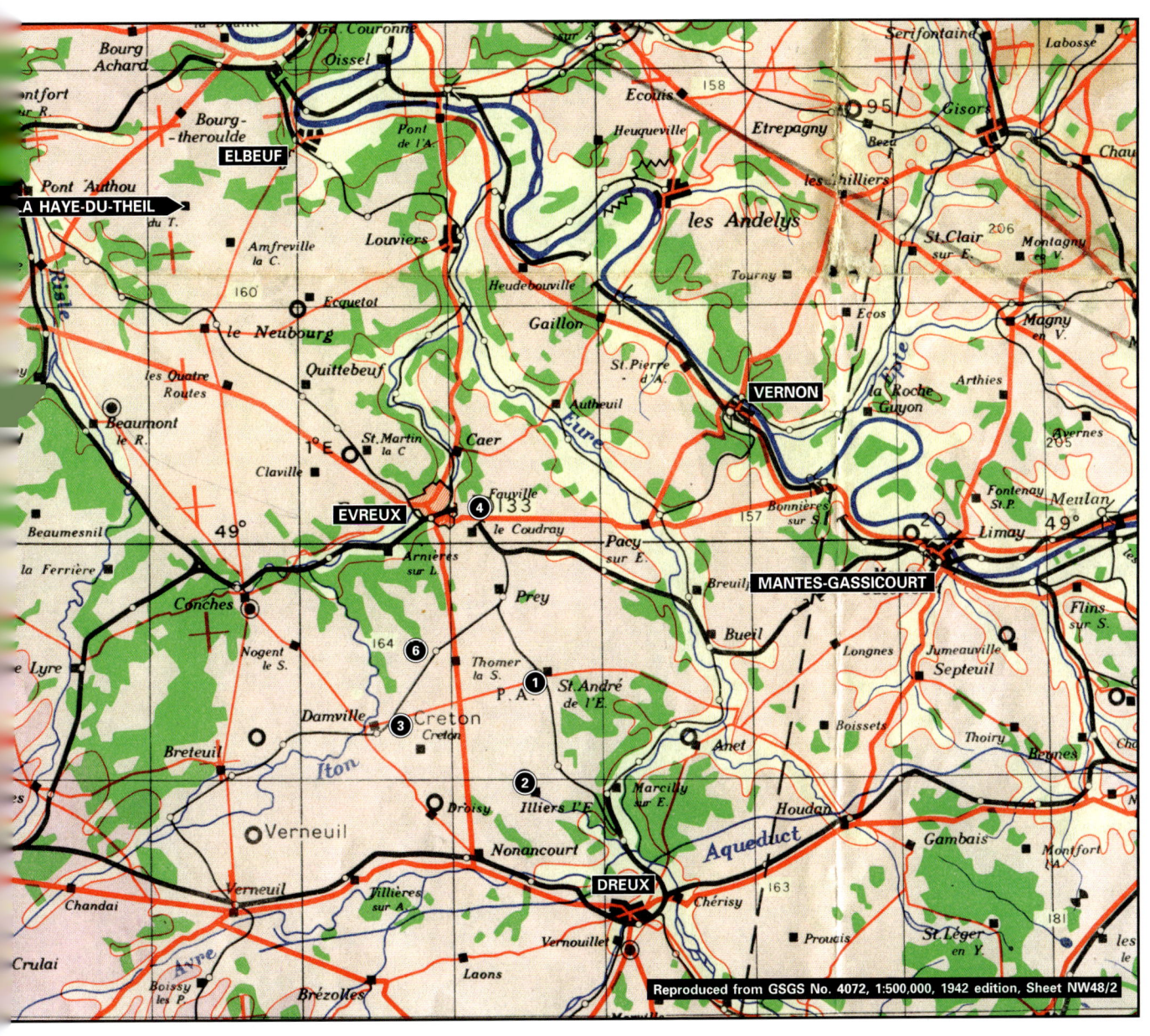

[1] B-24 St André-de-l'Eure, [2] B-26 Illiers-l'Évêque and [3] B-30 Créton, all three airfields becoming operational on August 28. [4] B-28 Évreux was operational the following day. [5] B-27 Boisney and [6] B-34 Avrilly were both operational on September 1, [7] B-29 Valailles on September 2, with [8] B-23 La Rue Huguenot following on September 3.

This attack took place at La Haye-du-Theil just south-west of Elbeuf and German war photographer Kriegsberichter Genzler was on hand to take an extensive sequence of photographs. Jean Paul Pallud, who researched this incident for his book *Rückmarsch!*, believed that this incident took place on either August 21 or 22. He pinpointed the location by referring to a photo showing a German soldier pointing at a spot on his map. It turned out to be on the D80, south of the village.

181

damaged runways. However, as it was more suited to British operations, its maintenance was taken over by the RAF giving the Second TAF its second hard runway airfield after Carpiquet. No. 16 ACG were detailed on August 25 to make the necessary repairs.

By the end of August the Normandy airstrips were now being abandoned as they were too far from the front and the first to arrive at B-24 was No. 121 Wing exiting from B-5 Camilly. The Typhoons of its three squadrons — Nos. 174, 175 and 245 — arriving on August 28, together with No. 184 Squadron of No. 129 Wing. They moved on to B-40 at Tillé, 40 miles north of Paris, on September 2.

On August 31, No. 143 Wing abandoned B-9 at Lantheuil. The three Canadian Typhoon squadrons (Nos. 438,

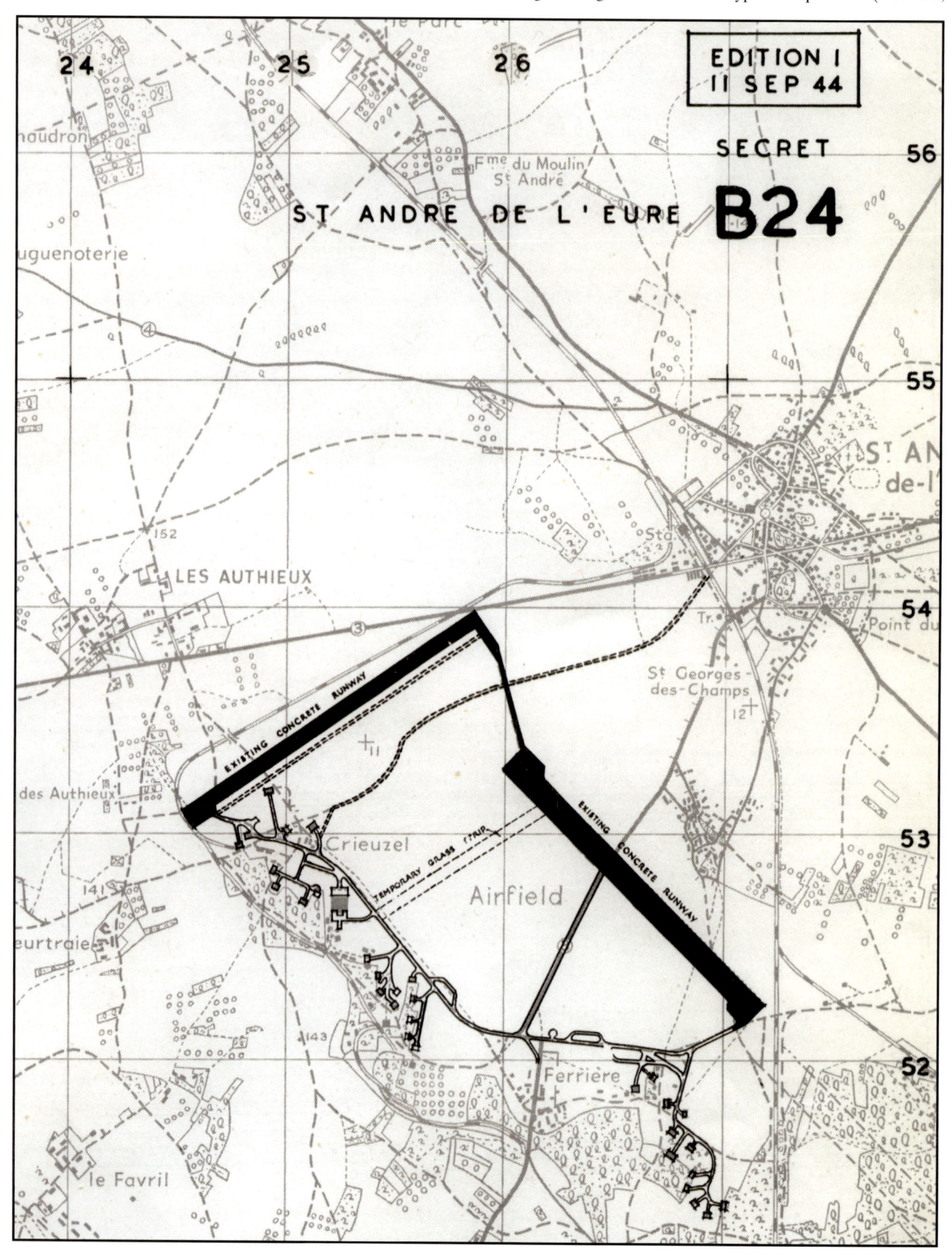

One of the busiest invasion airfields, 15 RAF squadrons passed through St André en route for bases further up the coast.

439 and 440) had been transferred to the airfield at Amiens (B-48), staging through St André which they left on September 3.

The RCAF Spitfire squadrons of No. 126 Wing (Nos. 401, 411 and 412) also spent a night at B-24 before two of them flew on to B-26 at Illiers-l'Évêque while No. 401 went to B-44 Poix near Amiens. No. 442 (RCAF) Squadron arrived the same day from B-18 at Cristot, also moving on to Illiers.

From B-12 at Ellon came Nos. 19, 65 and 122 Squadrons of No. 122 Wing, remaining from September 1-3 before they took their Mustangs on to B-40 at Beauvais, north of Paris. Finally, the Mosquitos of No. 409 Squadron left Carpiquet on September 10, staying at B-24 until the 27th before transferring to B-48 at Amiens.

After the war St André was completely redeveloped into a provincial airport, the two wartime runways being abandoned.

Today the wartime runways remain although now no longer used having been replaced by two grass runways.

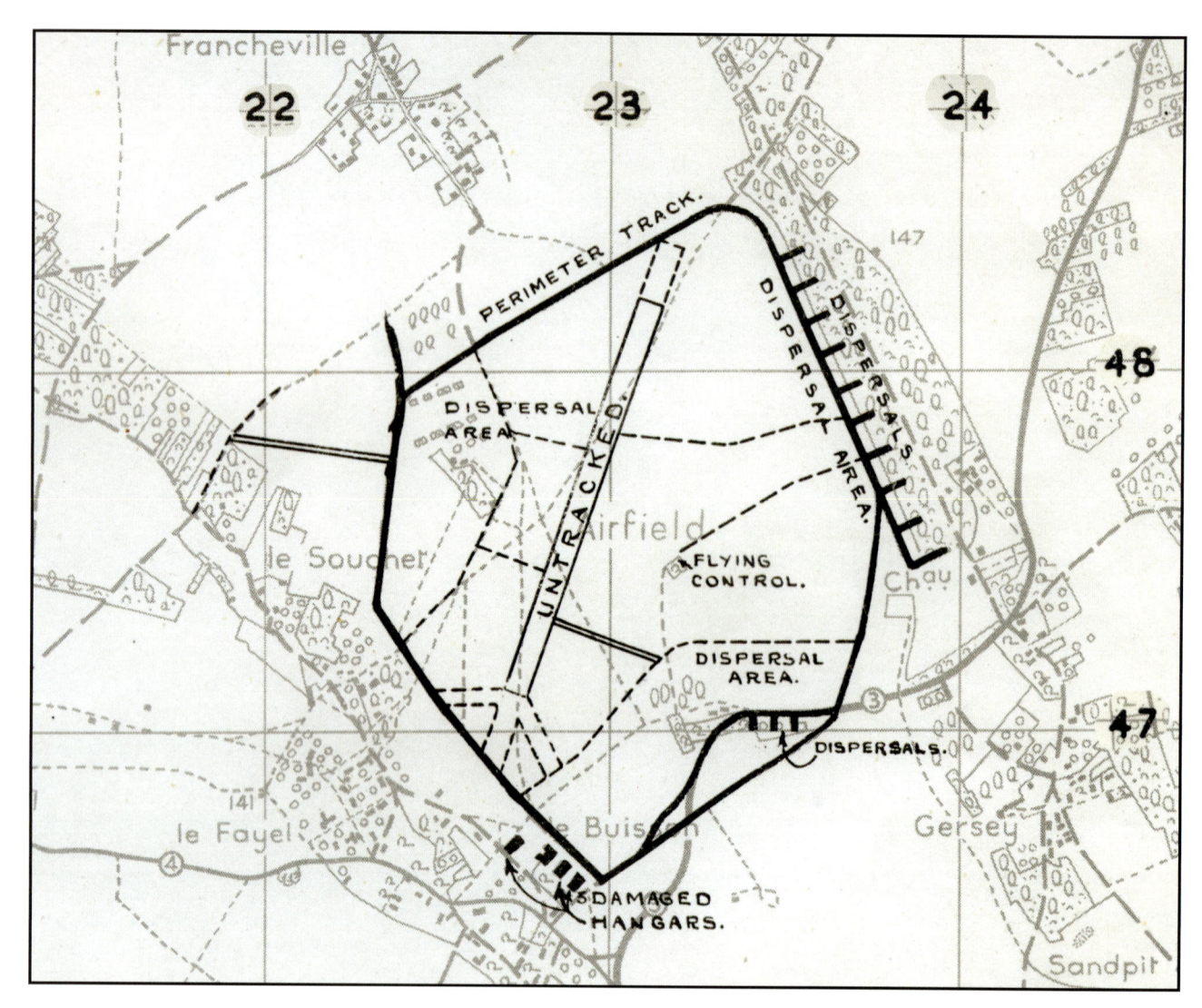

B-26 ILLIERS-L'EVEQUE

Another 'staging' airstrip with only the bare bones of the perimeter track left to identify B-26 at Illiers-l'Eveque today (see map pages 180-181).

OPERATIONAL AUGUST 28

Latitude: 48°50'N
Longitude: 00°13'E
Grid reference: R-230475
Altitude: 475ft

Used briefly by French Air Force fighters in 1940, B-26, five miles south of B-24, was captured by the 120th Infantry of the US 30th Division on August 20 but was turned over to the RCAF so that their Spitfire squadrons would have a forward base from which they could better support the advance of the First Canadian Army. It was already an airfield and an untracked grass strip, 3,600ft long, was cleared and marked out on its longest axis by No. 16 Airfield Construction Group by August 26.

The Canadian ALG at Bazenville (B-2) was abandoned at the end of August, squadrons of Nos. 126, 127 and 144 Wings arriving at B-26 from August 28 to September 2. Nos. 411, 412, 414 and 442 moved on to B-44 at Poix near Amiens, while Nos. 403, 416, 421 and 443 leapfrogged over 230 miles to the combined US-British airfield at Le Culot/Beauvechain (B-68/A-89) in Belgium.

184

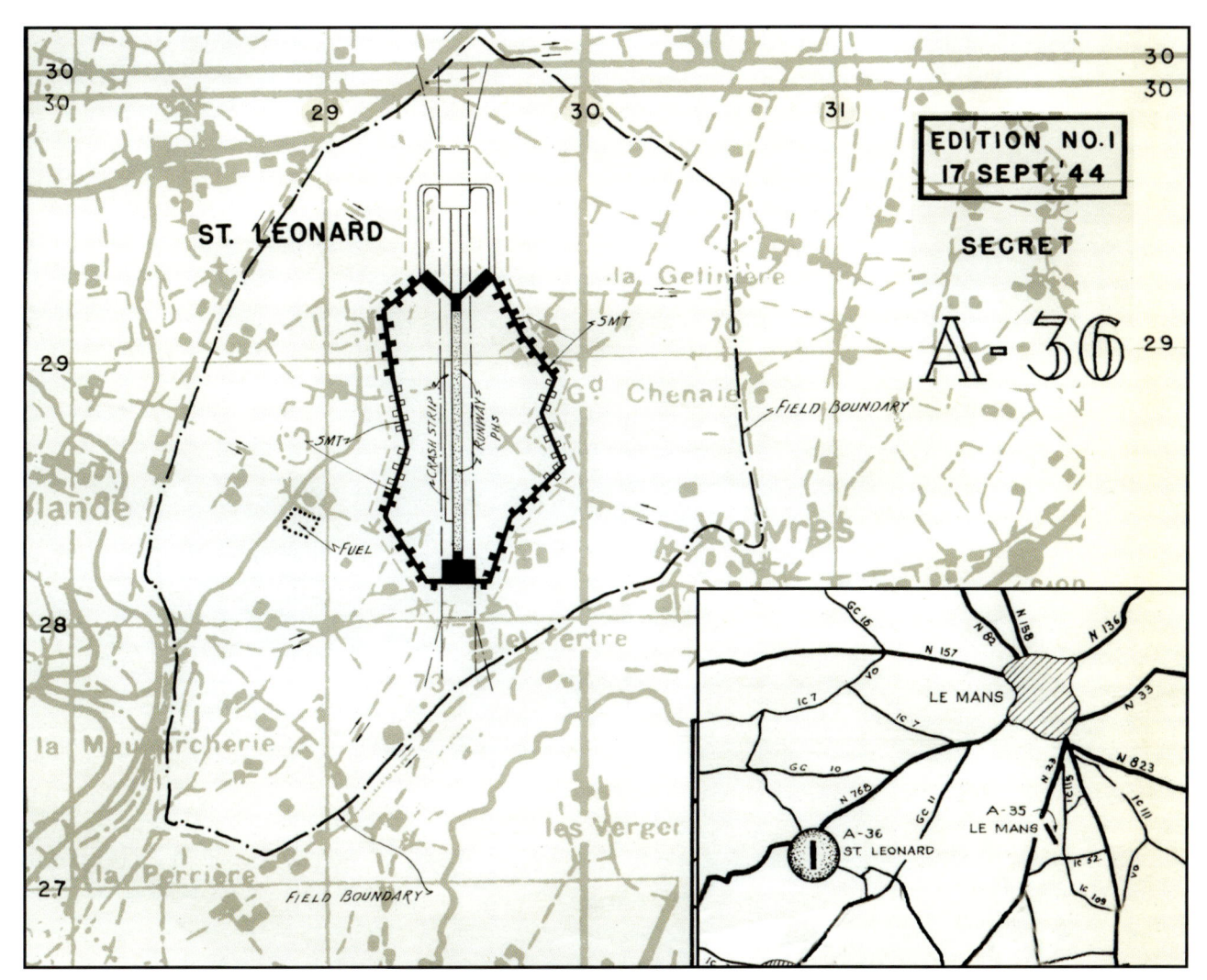

A-36 ST LEONARD

OPERATIONAL AUGUST 28

Latitude: 47°56'N
Longitude: 00°03'E
Grid reference: K-295289
Altitude: 229ft

Lying nine miles south-west of Le Mans, St Léonard, where the 846th Engineer Aviation Battalion were scheduled to lay down a 5,000ft strip, was secured on August 8 by the 315th Infantry Regiment of the US 80th Division and CCB of the 5th Armored Division.

The N-S airstrip — 3,600ft of PBS and 1,400ft earth — had been completed by September 4 but the 514th Squadron of the 406th Fighter Group based at A-14 at Cretteville stole a march by arriving early on August 28. The other two squadrons, the 512th and 513th, followed on September 4, but all had departed for Mourmelon-le-Grand (A-80) by September 24.

At St Léonard absolutely nothing remains of A-36, used briefly by the 406th Fighter Group on its march across France. Next stop 250 miles away at A-80 Mourmelon-le-Grand, south-east of Reims. The group ended the war in Nordholz (R-56) in Germany.

THE CROSSING OF THE SEINE AND ADVANCE TO THE SOMME
21st August to 1st September 1944

Once the Seine had been crossed, the pace of the 21st Army Group advance quickened. Moving up coast, the First Canadian Army was given the chance of recapturing St Valéry and Dieppe — both towns having seen Canadian defeats in earlier years. At the same time, the Second British Army was looking forward to breaking out from the Normandy hedgerow country into the open plains from the Seine to the River Somme. On August 30, the armour advanced 20 miles to Beauvais, driving on through the night another 30 miles to Amiens. At four in the morning of the 31st, the leading tanks of the 29th Armoured Brigade of the 7th Armoured Division, with infantry in close support, were just three miles short of the city and two hours later had reached the city centre.

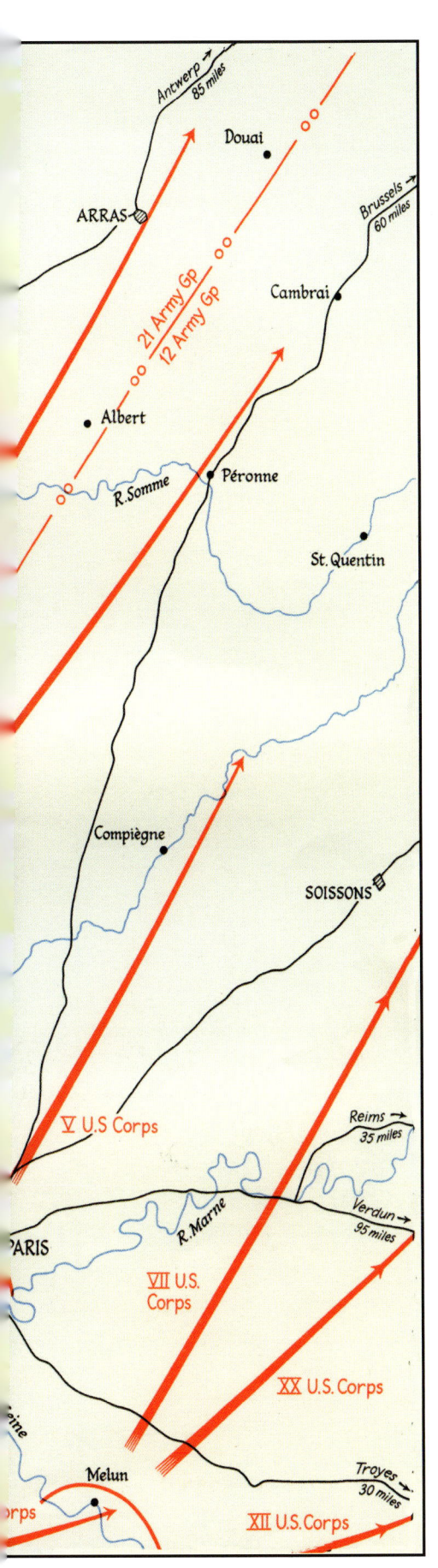

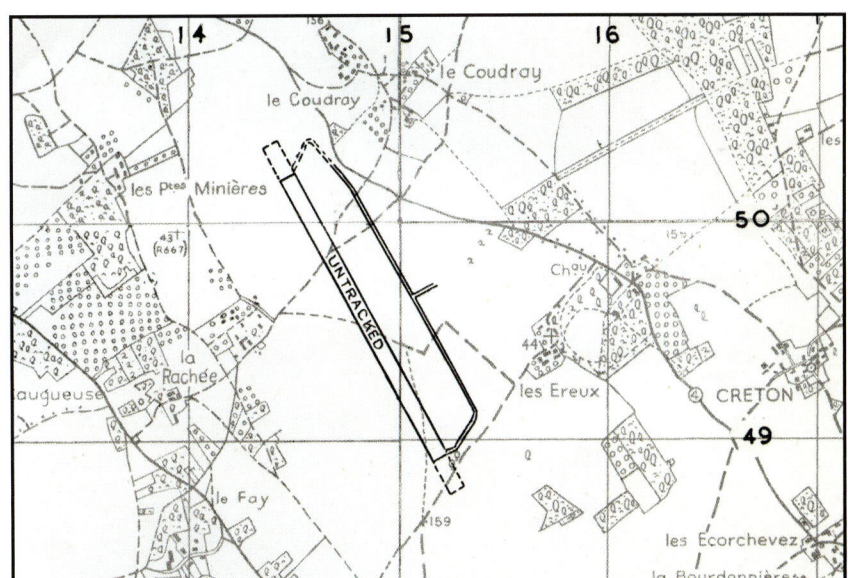

B-30 CRETON

OPERATIONAL AUGUST 28

Latitude: 48°51'N
Longitude: 01°06E
Grid reference: R-149495
Altitude: -526ft

Créton fell to the 119th Infantry of the US 30th Division on August 21. A 5,000ft untracked strip was prepared and on the 28th-31st the Typhoons of No. 124 Wing staged through, bound for the airfield at Amiens that bore the code B-48. Nos. 137, 181, 182 and 247 Squadrons had all been based in Normandy on B-6 at Coulombs but all departed from B-30 on September 3.

No. 124 Wing brought their Typhoons from Coulombs *(above)* **to Créton at the end of August, but all four squadrons quickly moved on to the pre-war aerodrome at Amiens/Glisy, now code-named B-48 — see page 214.**

The simple untracked strip at Créton, 12 miles south of Evreux, was abandoned on September 10.

187

A-39 CHÂTEAUDUN

OPERATIONAL AUGUST 28

Latitude: 48°03'N
Longitude: 01°22'E
Grid reference: vW-269598
Altitude: 426ft

The airfield at Châteaudun, some 70 miles south-west of Paris, was established in 1934 for the Armée de l'Air, basically for supply, storage and maintenance of French Air Force machines.

It became a major Luftwaffe bomber base after the fall of France, being used right up to August 1944. Ju88s of LG1 were there from June 1940-January 1941, and KG76 from February to April 1941. In December 1943 and January 1944 the He177s of KG40 were in residence followed by those of KG100.

This Heinkel He177 was found by US troops in the hangar at Châteaudun. It had belonged to Kampgeschwader 100.

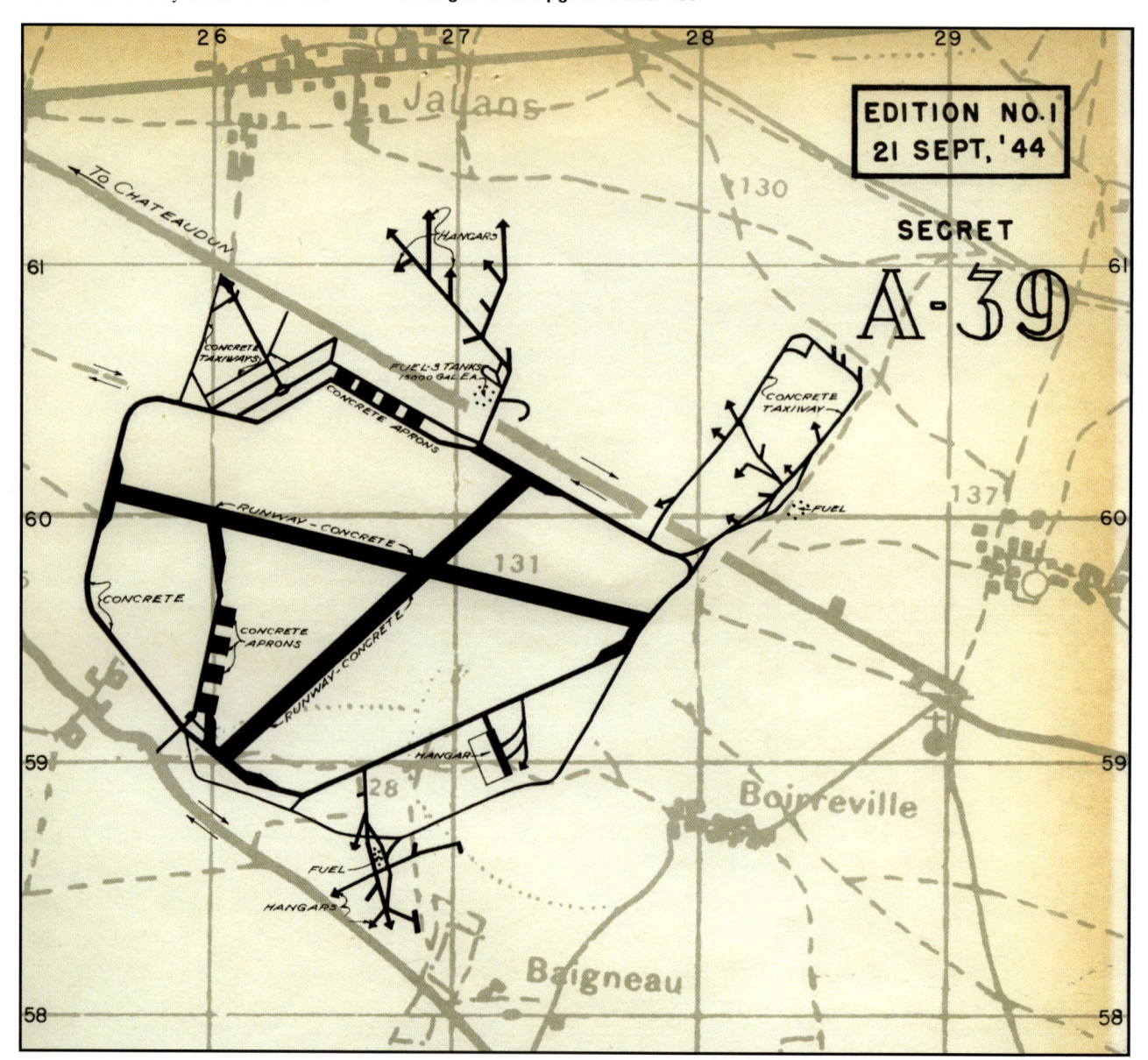

Châteaudun (see map page 174) received constant attention from both the Eighth and Ninth Air Forces from February to August in 1944. It was a premier Luftwaffe base and since July had hosted the Me262 jet fighters of Kampfgeschwader 51 which were a threat to American heavy bomber attacks.

With its two concrete runways repaired it was to become a major American air base for both night fighters and daylight medium bombers until the front moved towards Germany whose frontier was crossed in September. Then, from November to July 1945, it was the home of the 439th Troop Carrier Group.

188

The 320th Infantry of the US 35th Division took the airfield on August 17 and by the 26th the combined efforts of the 832nd and 833rd Engineer Aviation Battalions had made it usable for units of the Ninth Air Force. Its two concrete runways measured 7,500ft ESE-WNW and 5,700ft NE-SW.

The 10th Photo-Recon Group (31st and 34th Photo, 155th Night Photo and 12th and 15th Tactical Recon Squadrons) operated from here from August 11 to September 8, when it moved to A-64 St Dizier.

The 422nd Night Fighter Squadron was based at A-39 with P-61 Black Widows from August 28 to September 16 when in moved to Florennes (A-78).

Two days later the 387th Bomb Group arrived with their B-26 Marauders. The four squadrons — 556th, 557th, 558th and 559th — continued on operations from A-39 until they transferred on November 4 to A-71 at Clastres near St Quentin in northern France.

Châteaudun then became the home of the 439th Troop Carrier Group (23rd, 312th, 313th and 314th Squadrons). They had been based at A-45 at Lonray but they remained at A-39 from November 5 to July 1945.

In August that year it reverted to the French Air Force but was closed in July 2014.

C-47s and WACO gliders pictured at Châteadun in preparation for Operation 'Varsity' in which the American 17th Airborne Division, leaving from airfields in the Paris area, rendezvoused over Belgium with the British 6th Airborne Division flying from bases in England, to land troops to support the crossing of the Rhine in March 1945.

A-39 was returned to the French Air Force on August 8, 1945, and in recent years was used as a base for the preservation of modern jet aircraft by the Groupement d'Entretien Réparation et Stockage des Aéronefs.

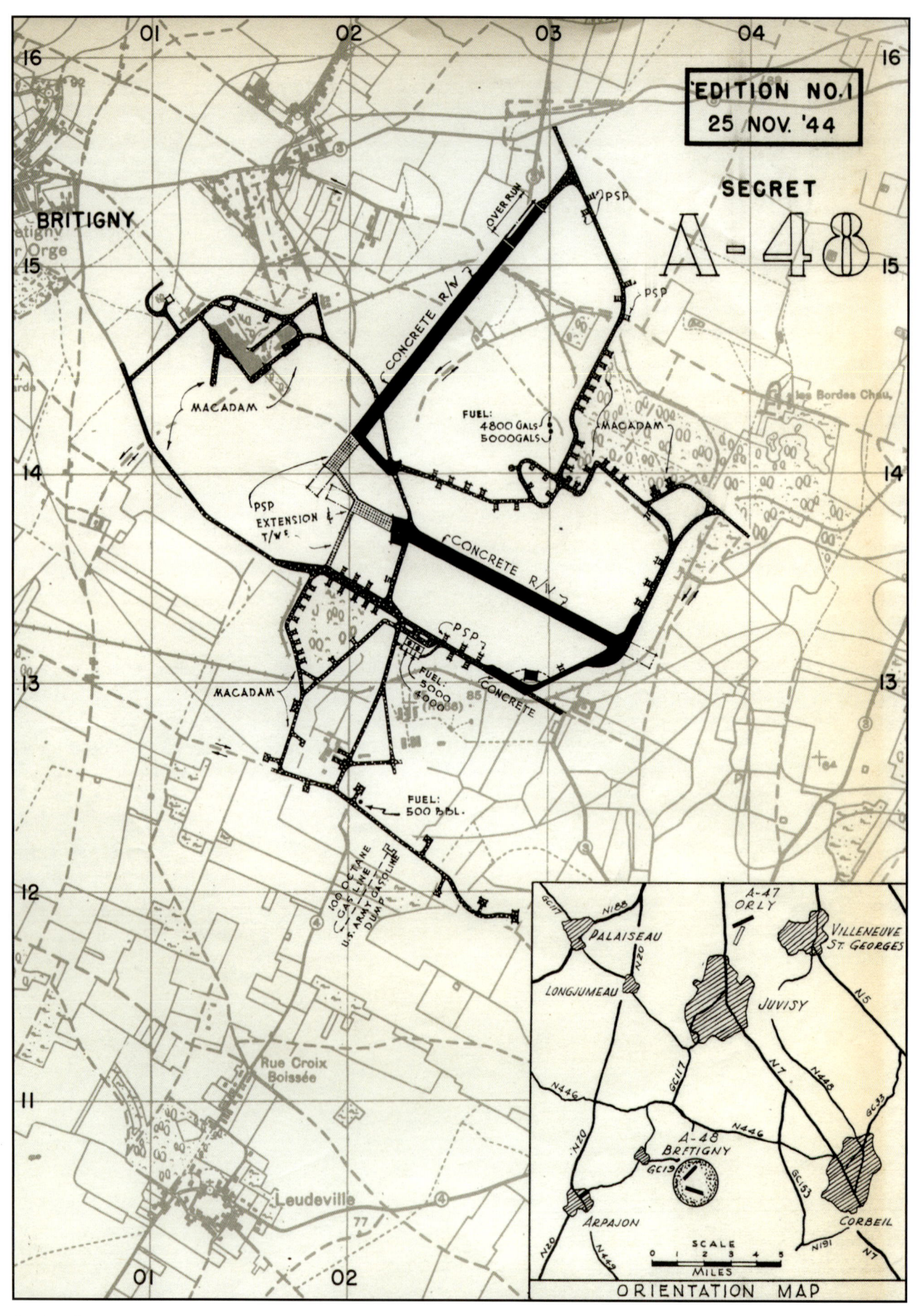

Another former French aerodrome taken over in the Paris area was Brétigny (see map page 174) which gave the Ninth Air Force the opportunity to bring the 409th Bomb Group over to France. A-48 also took part in Operation 'Varsity' with the 75th, 76th, 77th and 78th Troop Carrier Squadrons of the 435th Troop Carrier Group from Little Walden in Essex.

A-48 BRETIGNY

OPERATIONAL AUGUST 28

Latitude: 48°36'N
Longitude: 02°19'E
Grid reference: vS-024139
Altitude: 260ft

The French Air Force base at Brétigny-sur-Orge lies 17 miles south of Paris and just ten miles away from Orly Airport. With two concrete runways, Luftflotte 3 used it as a main base for Ju88s beginning with KG51 (November 1940-March 1941); KG54 (April-May 1941); KG30 (June 1941-January 1942) and KG6 from August 1942 to September 1944.

The US 4th Division's 22nd Infantry Regiment took Brétigny on August 24, the day that French troops first entered the capital.

Three days later the men of the 825th Aviation Engineers set to work to repair the damaged runways and add PSP extensions at their western ends. The NE-SW main then measured 5,100ft while the WNW-ESE secondary was 4,200ft.

The day before the engineers declared A-48 operational, the 507th Squadron arrived to pave the way for the 404th Fighter Group that was leaving A-5 at Chippelle. Its other two squadrons, the 506th and 508th, flew in on August 29 and September 2 respectivly. The 404th remained until mid-September when they moved to A-68 at Juvincourt, north-west of Reims.

On September 3, the three squadrons from another Thunderbolt unit, the 365th Fighter Group, joined them from Lignerolles (A-12) before the 386th, 387th and 388th Squadrons also moved on to Junvincourt.

They were replaced by 409th Bomb Group which flew in direct from their UK base at Little Walden on September 18. Its four squadrons, the 640th, 641st, 642nd and 643rd, equipped with the A-20 Havoc, remained at Brétigny until February 1945.

The 435th Troop Carrier Group replaced them, being based at A-48 from February 21 to June 1945.

The airfield was returned to the French Air Force on August 8, 1945, later being totally rebuilt as BA 217 with a new runway.

Now the French Air Force Base Aérienne 217, the new main runway measuring 3000 metres (9,843ft) was constructed on a bearing of 05/23 alongside the original wartime NE-SW runway of 5,100ft which was then reduced in width to be used as a taxiway. The old E-W runway has been extended from 4,200ft to 7,218ft.

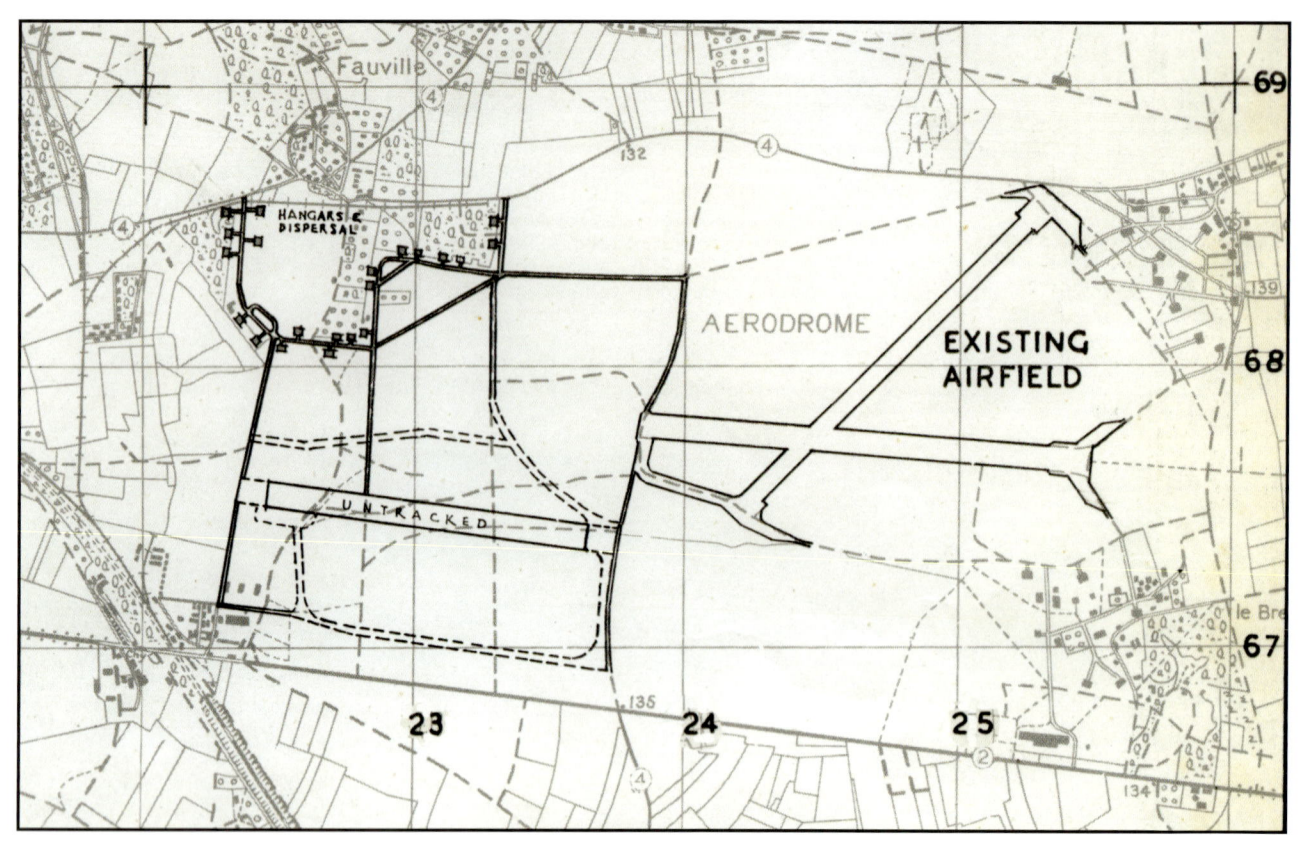

B-28 EVREUX

OPERATIONAL AUGUST 29

Latitude: 49°01'N
Longitude: 01°13'E
Grid reference: R-232678
Altitude: 464ft

An aerodrome had existed at Évreux since the 1920s and two concrete runways had been added in the 1930s. It was used by the French Air Force at the beginning of the war, then being taken over by the Luftwaffe in 1940. They improved the base but it was then severely knocked about in the extensive bombing campaign which was the prelude to Operation 'Overlord'.

The airfield was captured by the US 30th Infantry Division during their drive north towards the River Seine on August 20-22 but it was so badly damaged that it was decided that it would be easier for No. 5357 Wing to lay down a new 3,600ft strip in the south-western corner. However it proved to be little used. Two Spitfire squadrons — Nos. 401 and 412 — having evacuated from

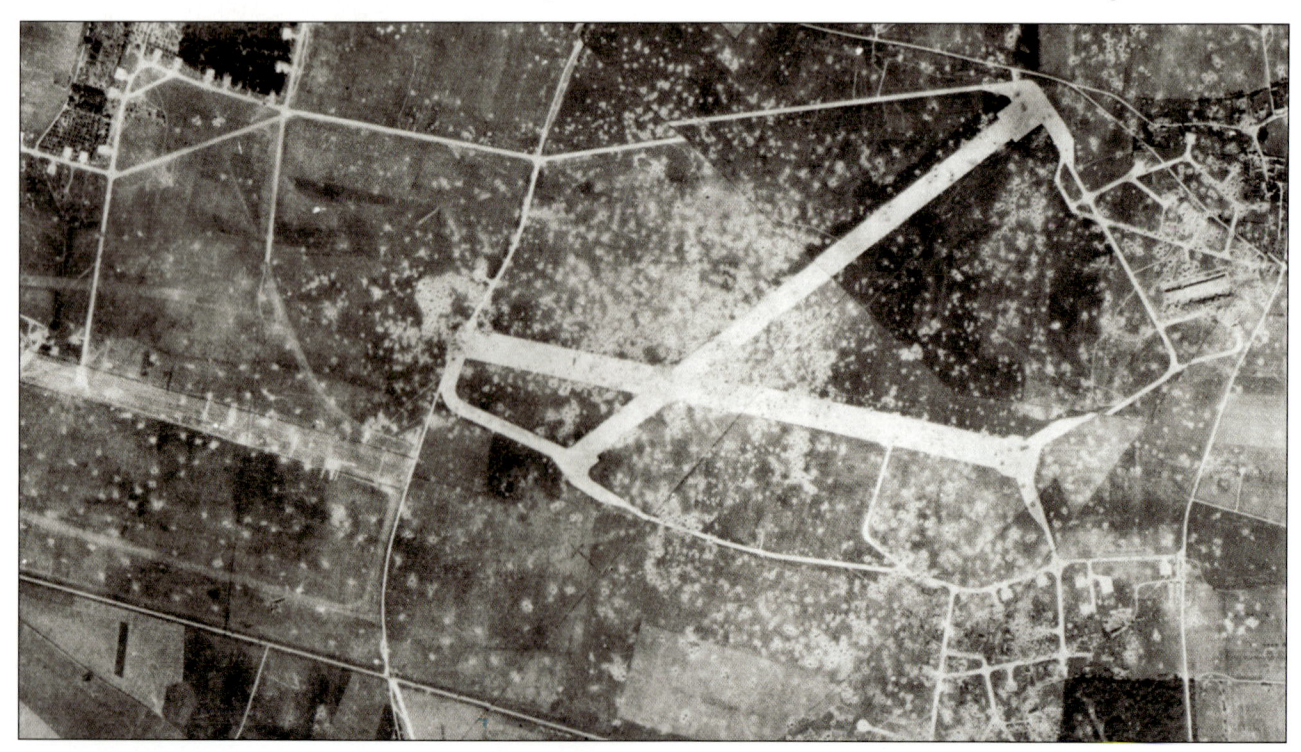

Pictured on September 11, the miriad of bomb craters scattered across Evreux (see map page 174) graphically illustrates the problem facing the RAF's No. 5357 Airfield Construction Wing in quickly making it serviceable, particularly as squadrons were moving beyond the Seine. A new strip was marked out to the west but, in the end, B-28 never supported any units.

B-18 Cristot, dropped in at the end of the month, but within a day both had moved on to St André (B-24).

After the war, Évreux was largely left as it was, the only resident being a small aero club, but in 1950 the United States opened negotiations with France as the Americans wanted to establish bases in Europe to counter the perceived threat from the Soviet Union. It was envisaged to use the airfield as a troop-carrier base once the old runways had been replaced and new dispersals constructed. The 465th Troop Carrier Wing took up residence in May 1955, being replaced in 1958 by the 317th TCW. However, on March 7, 1966, Président Charles de Gaulle announced that he was withdrawing France from NATO, giving the US the deadline of April 1, 1967 to remove all its military forces from the country.

Today Évreux is a French Air Force base, its claim to fame being that the Presidential Airbus A330-200 is based there.

The only recorded use was by Nos. 401 and 412 Squadrons which passed through B-28 on their way to B-24 at St André-de-l'Eure. The Second Tactical Air Force notes for the use of Évreux indicate that it had been abandoned and was for emergency use only. There were dispersals sufficient for four squadrons on the grass. Nevertheless the RAF held on to Évreux until May 1945. In the late 1940s it was earmarked as a suitable location for a NATO base operated by the USAF and work to completely rebuild the airfield began in July 1952, the unique design providing circular hardstands which could later be revetted with earth banks for blast protection. Each provided 15-18 dispersals surrounding a large central hangar, the aircraft being spaced 150 feet apart. The 465th Troop Carrier Wing arrived in May 1955. Two years later this unit was inactivated together with the one based at Dreux. Ten years later Président Charles de Gaulle informed the United States that all its military forces had to be removed from France, and by January 1967 they had been relocated to RAF Mildenhall in Suffolk.

A-35 LE MANS

OPERATIONAL AUGUST 29

Lattitude: 47°56'N
Longitude: 00°11'E
Grid reference: K-407295
Altitude: 161ft

With the nearby Renault factory a target for Allied air attacks, the Luftwaffe established a grass airfield at Le Mans half a mile west of the racecourse to counter the raids. At the time of the invasion it was occupied by JG1 with Focke-Wulf 190As and JG53 with the Bf109G.

Combat Command B of the US 5th Armored Division and the 315th Infantry of the 79th Division reached Le Mans on August 8 and the 816th Engineers lost no time in clearing mines and wrecked Luftwaffe aircraft from the airfield ready for a 5,000ft PBS runway. This was operational by August 12 but the first aircraft from the 36th Fighter Group did not fly in until the end of the month. The 53rd Fighter Squadron arrived first with P-47 Thunderbolts on August 29, followed by the 22nd Squadron on September 5 and the 23rd the following day. Later in September the 440th Troop Carrier Group (95th, 96th, 97th and 98th Squadrons) took their place.

The pre-war airfield two miles south of Le Mans (see map pages 162-163) had been used briefly by the Royal Air Force in June 1940 during the evacuation from France.

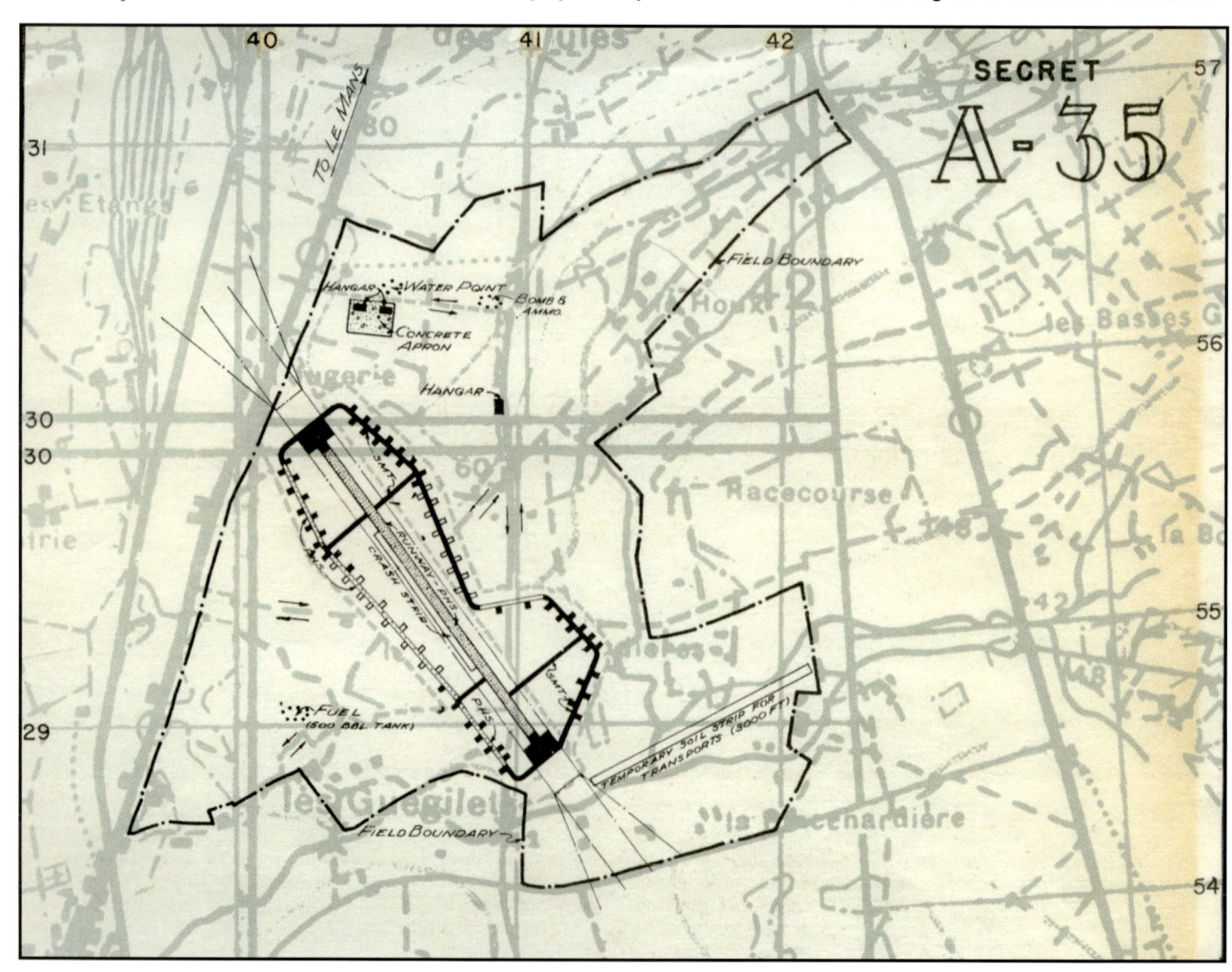

Four years later IX Engineer Command had drawn up plans for a crash strip to be added alongside a runway surfaced with PBS.

On the whole it was found that repairing captured enemy airfields, even though they had cratered concrete runways, was more satisfactory than trying hastily to construct new airfields by laying surfacing materials on unused ground. By the end of August over 60 airfields were in use. Three more airfield construction wings from the RAF arrived in the British sector but it was decided not to bring in a fourth. Some of the wings were temporarily employed on road construction work in addition to the maintenance and construction of airfields. In the American sector the demand for advanced supply and evacuation landing strips was intensified toward the end of August as the First and Third Armies cleared Paris and plunged toward the German frontier. Units of the 2nd Engineer Aviation Brigade, operating in the Third Army area, reached Reims on September 3 and St Dizier on September 7. So rapidly did the Third Army advance that the engineers passed up good fields around Romilly in order to keep close to the advancing ground forces. By September 19, when the Third Army had reached the limits of its eastward advance for the time being, an earth strip at Toul (A-90) was in operation and additional sites were being sought in the neighbourhood of Toul, Verdun and Nancy. The 1st Brigade, meanwhile, was following the advancing First Army to the German frontier at Aachen, rehabilitating airfields primarily for the use of fighter-bombers and medium bombers. By September 9 the 1st Brigade had reached the Florennes/Juzaine airfield in Belgium (A-78), from where it pushed on to Luxembourg on September 13 and to Liège/Bierset (A-93) on September 19. *Left:* On September 5, the 36th Fighter Group relocated from A-16 at Brucheville to Le Mans but by the end of the month, when the 440th Troop Carrier Group were posted in from Reims, the surface of the airfield left a lot to be desired *(right)*. This is the flight line for the 96th Troop Carrier Squadron.

Part of the Le Mans racetrack lies to the east of the airfield on which the runway has now been completely realigned.

A-42D VILLACOUBLAY

OPERATIONAL AUGUST 29

Latitude: 48°46'N
Longitude: 02°12'E
Grid reference: vR-942333
Altitude: 584ft

During the drive of the 2ème Division Blindée on August 24 to liberate Paris, they overran two important airfields on the south-western outskirts of the capital: Villacoublay and Toussus-le-Noble.

Villacoublay was a pre-war French Armée de l'Air base which had been promptly utilised by the Luftwaffe for both fighters and bombers. KG55 and KG77 operated He111s from there during the Blitz on Britain, and Bf109s from June 1941 to August 1943 to intercept Allied air attacks. They were replaced by the FW190s of JG54.

Villacoublay only possessed one concrete runway on a NW-SE alignment which the 818th Engineer Aviation Battalion extended with SMT to 4,200ft.

On August 29 the 48th Fighter Group were transferred in from Deux-Jumeaux (A-4) in Normandy, its three squadrons, the 492nd, 493rd and 494th, operating from Villacoublay until they moved to Cambrai/Niergnies (A-74), 125 miles to the north, on September 15-16.

Thereafter — as the 'D' in the code denotes — A-42D became a transport hub for supply and maintenance by the 370th Air Service Group and the 314th Troop Carrier Group.

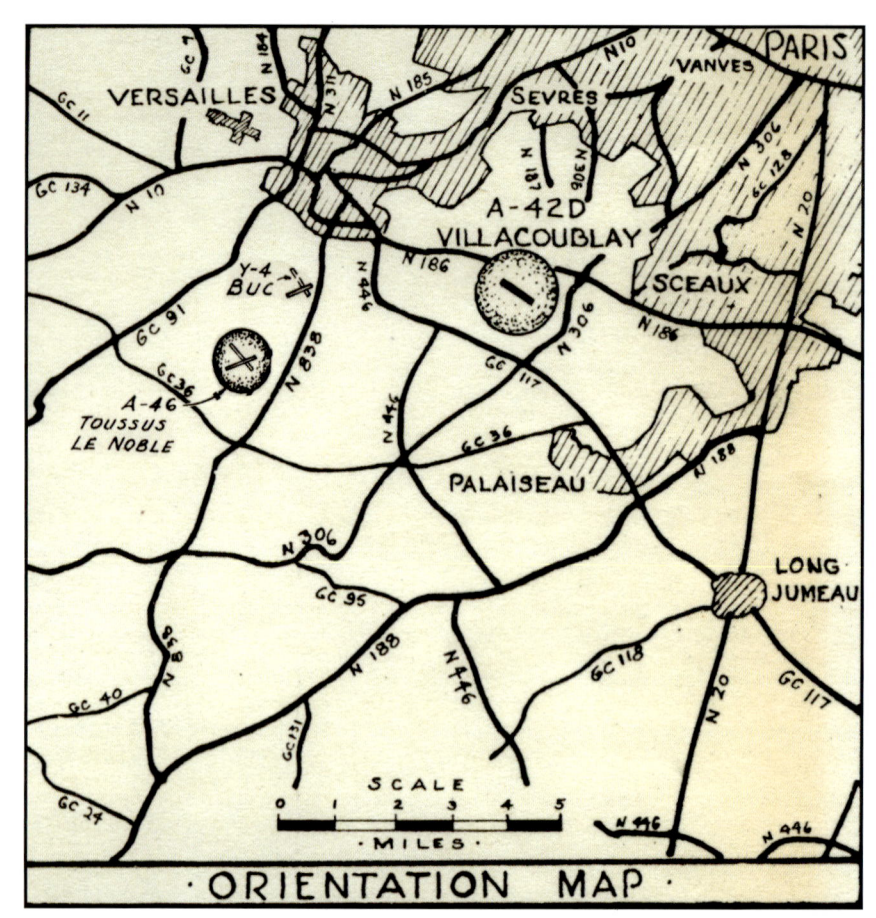

On the southern outskirts of Paris lay several aerodromes, the clutch of Villacoublay, Toussus-le-Noble and Buc being reached by the French 2nd Armoured Division during their drive to liberate the capital on August 24 (see also map page 174). The airfields being captured now were mostly all former French Air Force bases, latterly used by the Luftwaffe.

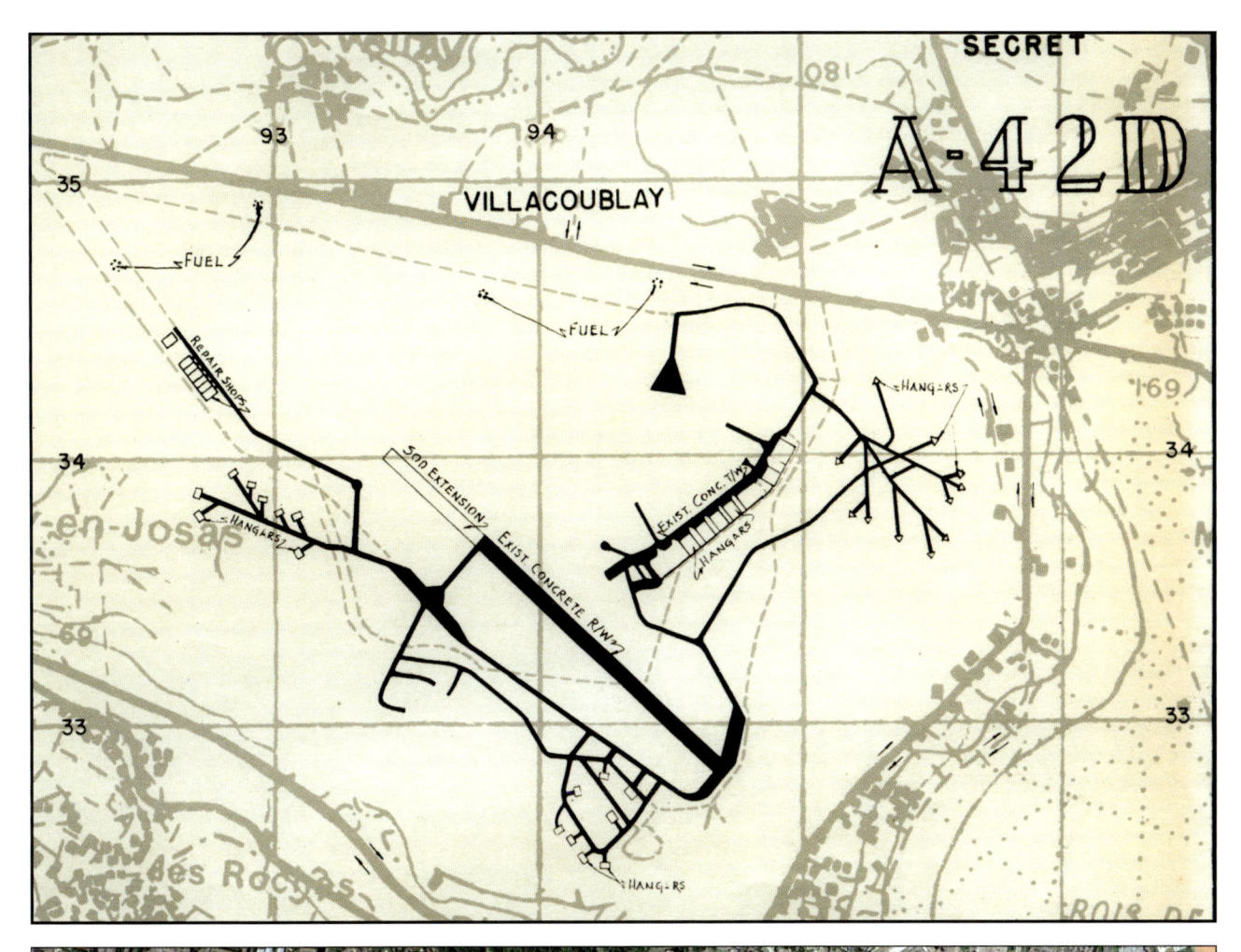

The aerodrome was relinquished by the USAAF in August 1946 whereupon it was reconstructed for the French Air Force with a new E-W runway of 6,000ft, becoming Vélizy-Villacoublay Base Aérienne 107.

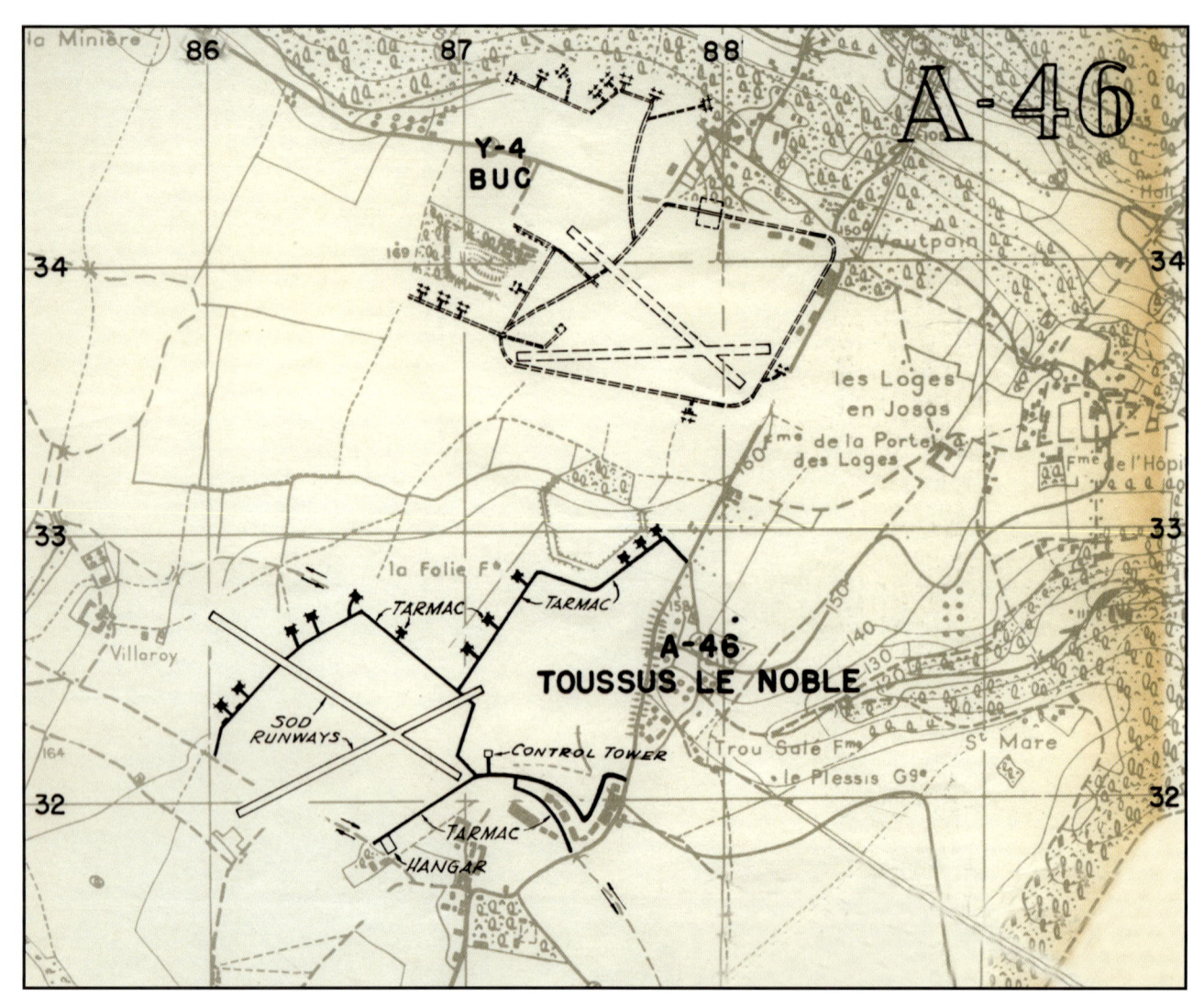

A-46 TOUSSUS-LE-NOBLE

Another French airfield totally reconstructed after the war was Toussus-le-Noble. Buc (Y-4), just to the north, was an historic aerodrome dating back to 1909 and Louis Blériot's flying school.

OPERATIONAL AUGUST 29

Latitude: 48°45'N
Longitude: 02°06'E
Grid reference: vR-867322
Altitude: 500ft

Toussus-le-Noble lay just five miles from Villacoublay with another airfield — Buc which was coded Y-4 — a mile to the north. They both lay on the route of the French 2nd Armoured Division as it advanced to Paris, their capture on August 24 being credited to Combat Command L.

The 818th Engineer Aviation Battalion, already working at Villacoublay, began work on August 28 to prepare a 3,600ft flying strip and surfacing the turf with SMT.

It was assigned to the 67th Tactical Reconnaissance Group and of its seven squadrons, the three currently based at Le Molay (A-9) moved to A-46 — the 107th and 109th TRS on the 29th and the 30th Photographic Reconnaissance Squadron on the 31st. The 109th was moved to Buc on the 31st, while the other two squadrons were transferred to Belgium as soon as A-87 at Charleroi became available in mid-September.

Just as the speed of the advance across France outstripped the airfields, so Eisenhower's Forward Headquarters was left far behind at the base of the Cherbourg peninsula, so on September 20 it was relocated to Versailles, just outside Paris. At the same time Admiral Bertram Ramsay, the Allied Naval Commander, moved to St Germain in the Paris area, using Toussus-le-Noble (see map page 174) as a convenient base. On January 2, 1945, the Admiral had to fly to Brussels to consult with Montgomery about the islands holding out in the Scheldt estuary, his departure being routinely filmed for Paramount News.

The USAAF held on to the airfield until August 1945, using it as a base for liaison aircraft assigned to Allied headquarters in Paris, and it was there that a serious crash resulted in the death of Admiral Bertram Ramsey, the Allied Naval Commander. On January 2 he was about to take off in a Hudson to fly to Brussels to meet with General Montgomery regarding the German defences still active in the Scheldt which were preventing the use of Antwerp, when the aircraft crashed on take-off, killing all on board. (See *After the Battle* No. 87.)

This crudely annotated photo was presented to the Board of Enquiry which believed the crash of his aircraft had been caused by a combination of a failure to de-ice the airframe properly in the sub-zero temperature, and the pilot not applying full power causing the Hudson to crash just beyond the western end of the NE-SW runway.

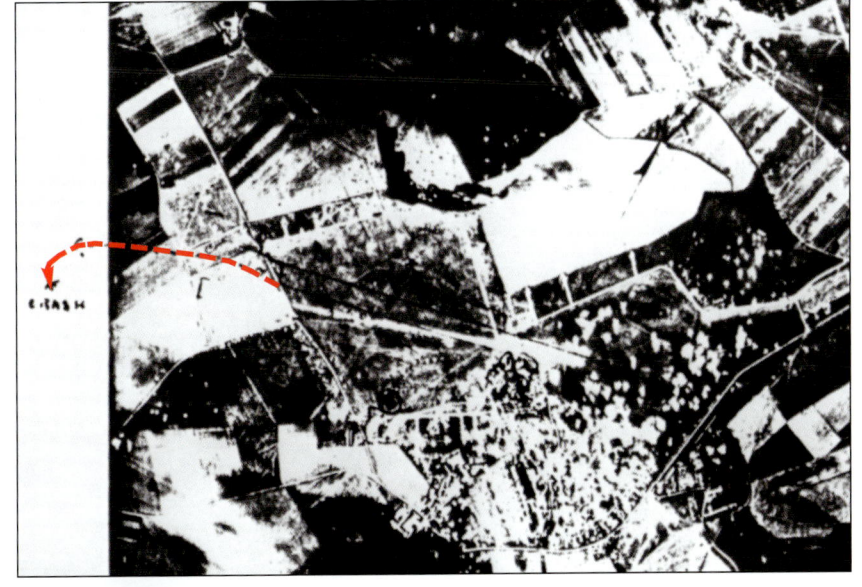

Unfortunately the Admiral, the passengers, and crew were all beyond help.

199

It is important to remember that although the development of the invasion airfields followed the advance across France, the Atlantic ports were still in German hands. The 'Overlord' plan had designated Brittany as the stage for the Third Army's initial operations. The peninsula was important to the Allies because of its ports: Saint-Malo, less than 40 miles west of Avranches; Brest, on the western extremity of the peninsula; Lorient and Saint-Nazaire, along the southern seashore; Nantes, 30 miles east of the estuary of the Loire river; and the many small harbours and beaches useful for discharging cargo. General Eisenhower stated that 'the ideal situation would be to obtain the entire coastal area from Le Havre to Nantes. With such a broad avenue of entry we could bring to the Continent every single soldier the United States could procure for us.' Apart from swinging round to the east, the second part of Patton's orders were therefore to launch armoured columns into Brittany. Rennes was captured on August 4 (see page 150) and Vannes the following day (page 166), but St Malo did not fall until August 17.

A-26 GORGES

OPERATIONAL AUGUST 30

Latitude: 49°14'N
Longitude: 01°24'W
Grid reference: T-275784
Altitude: 60ft

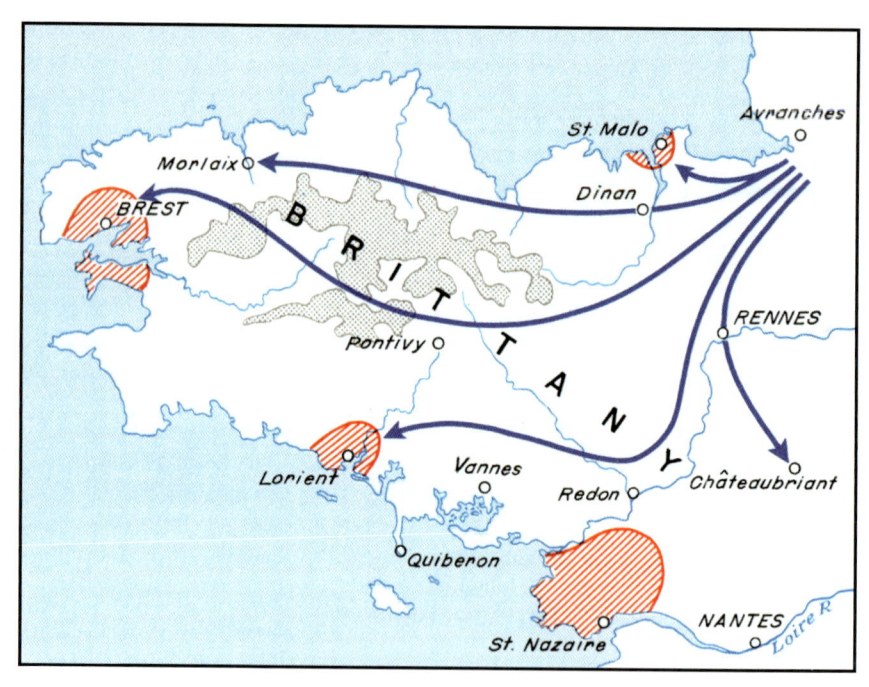

Located five miles north of Périers, Gorges was captured by the 358th Infantry of the US 90th Division on July 12. The 826th Engineer Aviation Battalion laid down a single 120ft-wide runway, 6,000ft long, on a NE-SW axis, surfaced with PSP, as this was to be used as a base for medium bombers. Seventy-five dispersals were provided, with 48,000 gallons of aviation fuel on site in trucks.

The 596th Squadron from the 397th Bomb Group at Hurn, Hampshire, touched down on August 30, the other three squadrons, the 597th, 598th and 599th, arriving the next day.

The group remained at A-26 until September 15-16 when they transferred to A-41 at Dreux, 130 miles to the east.

On August 30-31, the 397th Bomb Group were brought over from their British base at Hurn, near Bournemouth, to add weight to the bombing campaign to secure Brest. They were based at Gorges in the south of the Cherbourg peninsula, where a 6,000ft runway, surfaced with pierced steel planking had been prepared for them (see map page 133).

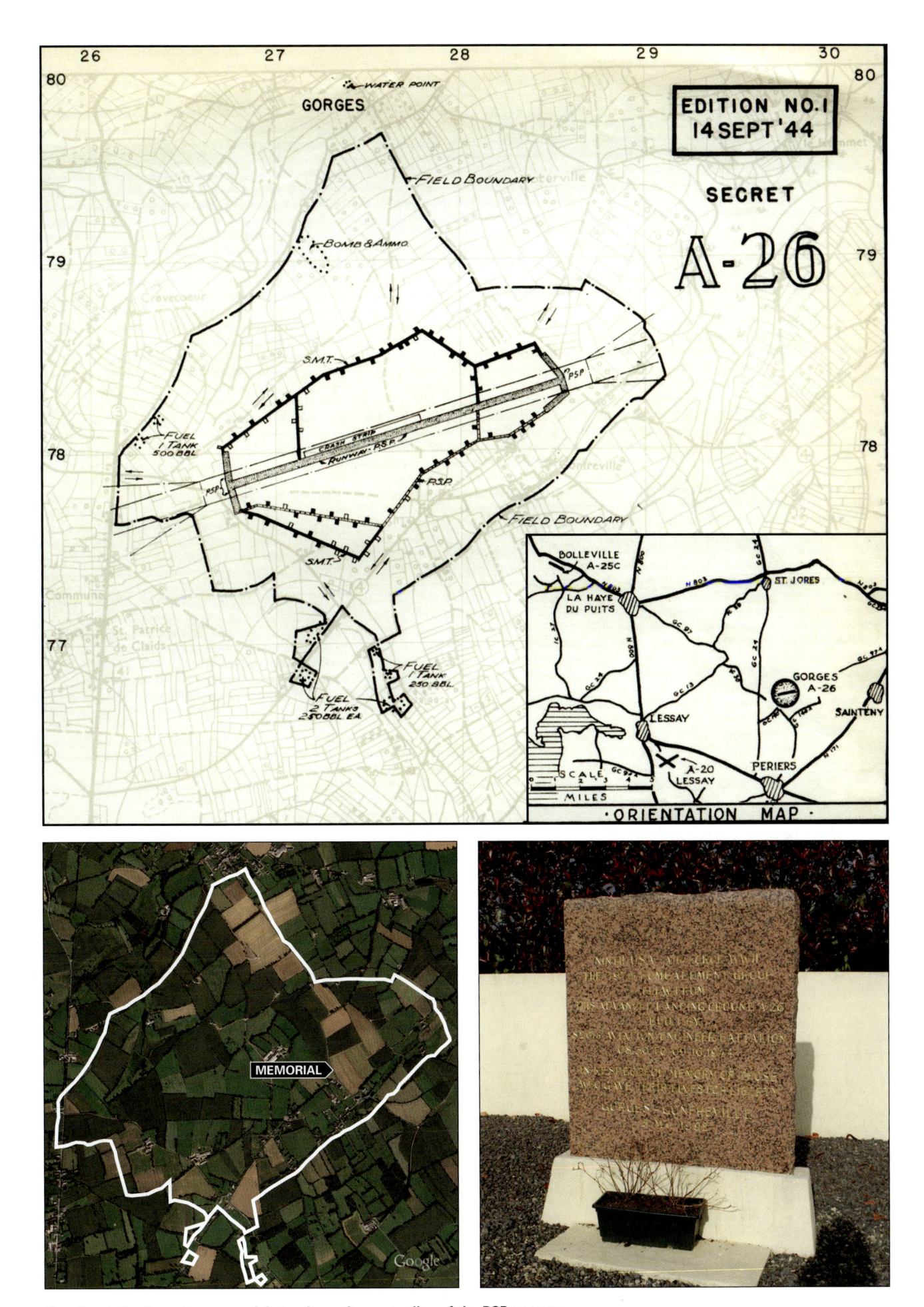

On a lonely back road, a memorial stands on the centre line of the PSP runway.

A-18 ST JEAN-DE-DAYE

OPERATIONAL AUGUST 31

Latitude: 49°13'N
Longitude: 01°09'W
Grid reference T-455744
Altitude: 148ft

On the morning of July 10, the German front line ran just in front of Saint Jean-de-Daye, some eight miles south of Carentan, and although the 47th Infantry Regiment of the US 9th Division took the area that day, the Panzer-Lehr-Division counter-attacked on the 11th and the location was not secure until the following day.

The site chosen for A-18 lay parallel to the GC8 (now the D8) at Saint Jean-de-Daye and the 843rd Engineer Aviation Battalion began work on July 31. A 5,000ft strip was laid down, 3,600ft being surfaced with PBS hessian and 1,400ft of graded earth at the eastern end. A crash strip was also marked out for aircraft in difficulties to avoid them damaging the PBS.

It was completed by August 31 but it was now too late for fighters to be positioned so far behind the lines, and the ALG had no resident units although liaison aircraft are reported to have used it. It was also the last PBS-surfaced airfield to be built by the Americans in the beach-head area and was abandoned on September 9.

The Allied advance had exceeded all the forecasts of the 'Overlord' planners (see pages 6-7) and on September 12 American forces crossed the German frontier. The following day the Seventh Army, which had landed in the south of France, joined up with the armies in the north.

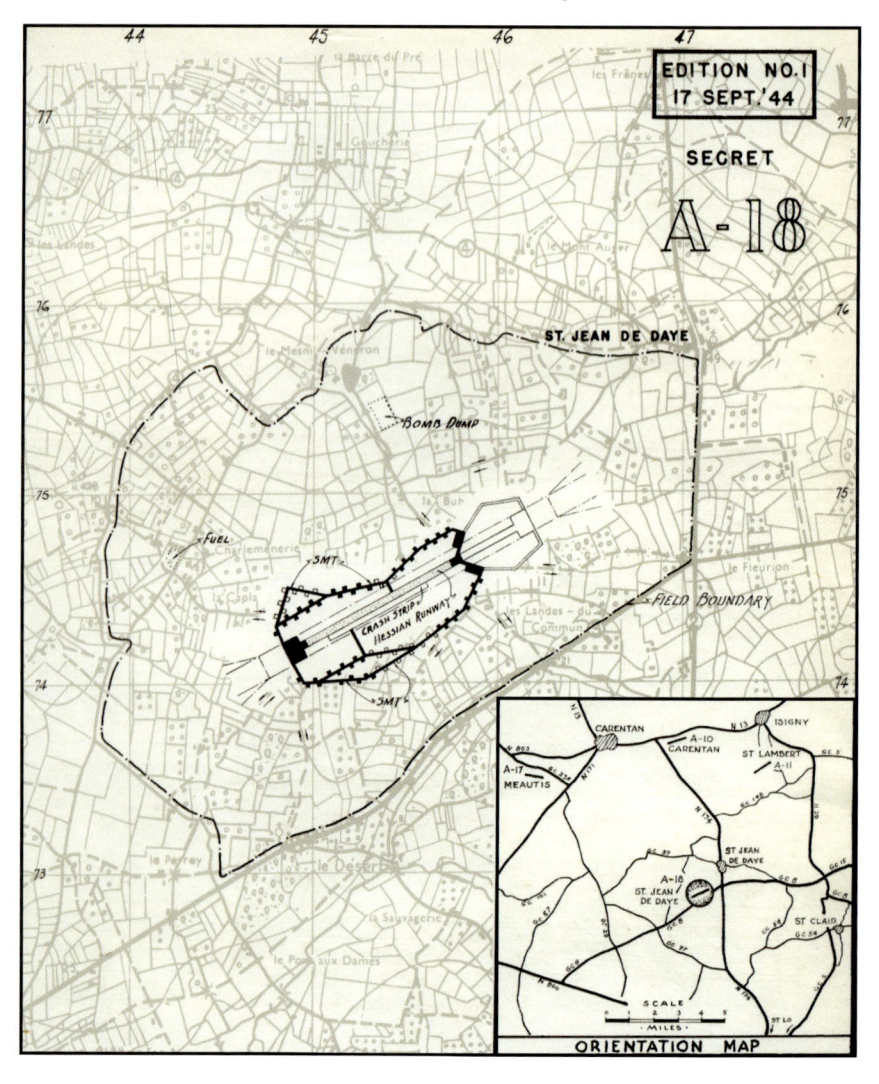

The 843rd Engineers put a lot of effort into completing a 5,000ft PBS strip south of Carentan but by the time it was operable, the front line was 300 miles away.

B-27 BOISNEY

OPERATIONAL SEPTEMBER 1

Latitude: 49°09'N
Longitude: 00°39'E
Grid reference: Q-835865
Altitude: 518ft

Boisney, six miles north-east of Bernay, lay in the sector of the Canadian II Corps and its 3rd Division secured the site for the airfield on August 25.

The single untracked runway, prepared by No. 24 Airfield Construction Group, was only used for a week at the beginning of September after B-4 at Bény-sur-Mer was abandoned. On September 1, three squadrons of No. 39 (Recce) Wing arrived from there: No. 2 with their Mustangs; No. 4 with Spitfires, and No. 268 with Typhoons, but they all moved to B-31 at Fresnoy near Dieppe on the 6th.

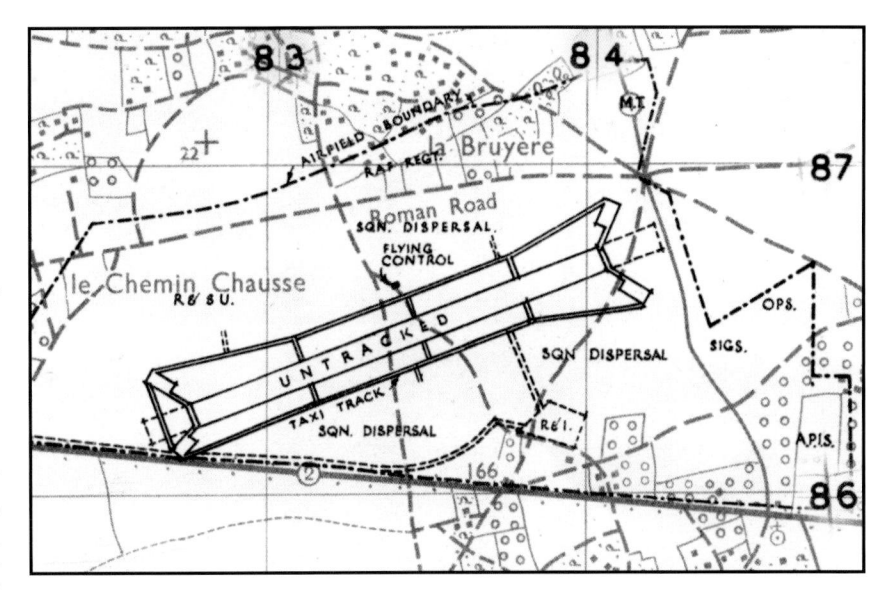

Another short-lived airstrip was B-27 at Boisney (see map pages 180-181), merely used as a staging post to places further north.

However B-27 does have one lasting legacy in that this section of the E46 Autoroute de Normandy uses the line of the runway!

B-33 CAMPNEUSEVILLE

One of the squadrons which used Campneuseville (see map pages 186-187) was No. 66, seen here during its four-day stay at the beginning of September before moving on to Belgium.

OPERATIONAL SEPTEMBER 1

Latitude: 49°51'N
Longitude: 01°39'E
Grid reference: M-631569
Altitude: 678ft

Campneuseville, south-west of Amiens, was overrun by the British 4th Armoured Brigade on September 1 and an east-west strip of rolled earth was quickly prepared for B-33 as the Spitfires from the Norwegian No. 331 Squadron touched down the same day from B-16 at Villons-les-Buissons. Its sister squadron, No. 332, joined it on the 6th by which time the other Villons' Spitfire squadrons — No. 66 and 127 — had arrived. All departed for B-57 at Lille-Nord which had been captured by the 53rd Recce Regiment of the 53rd (Welsh) Division on September 5. On the 11th B-33 was abandoned.

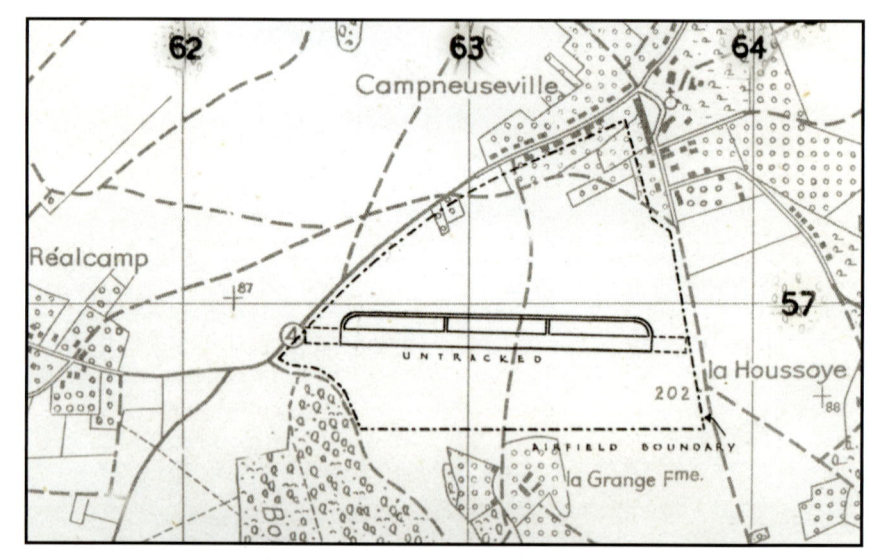

It should be mentioned at this point that on September 1 General Montgomery ceased to act as the Allied ground forces commander, Eisenhower having taken over that role for himself. He now commanded a continuous front stretching from the North Sea to the Swiss frontier with three army groups about to enter Germany: the 21st Army Group in the north, the 12th Army Group in the centre, and the 6th Army Group in the south.

B-34 AVRILLY

OPERATIONAL SEPTEMBER 1

Latitude: 48°55'N
Longitude: 01°09'E
Grid reference: R-180565
Altitude: 483ft

Two miles north of Créton lay the small village of Avrilly which was captured on August 22 by the 119th Infantry of the US 30th Division. The airstrip, which measured 5,000ft, was prepared by No. 23 Airfield Construction Group by rolling the stubble, and on September 1 the Spitfires of No. 400 Squadron and the Mustangs of No. 430 arrived from B-21 (St Honorine). The following day the Mustangs of No. 168 joined them. All stayed until the 21st when they departed for B-66 at Blankenberg, east of Brussels.

Now back on the western side of the River Seine, a strip was laid down at Avrilly, just five miles north of Créton (see map pages 186-187). The Americans overran the area on August 22 and an untracked strip had been marked out by September 1, parallel with the Rouen-Caen railway line.

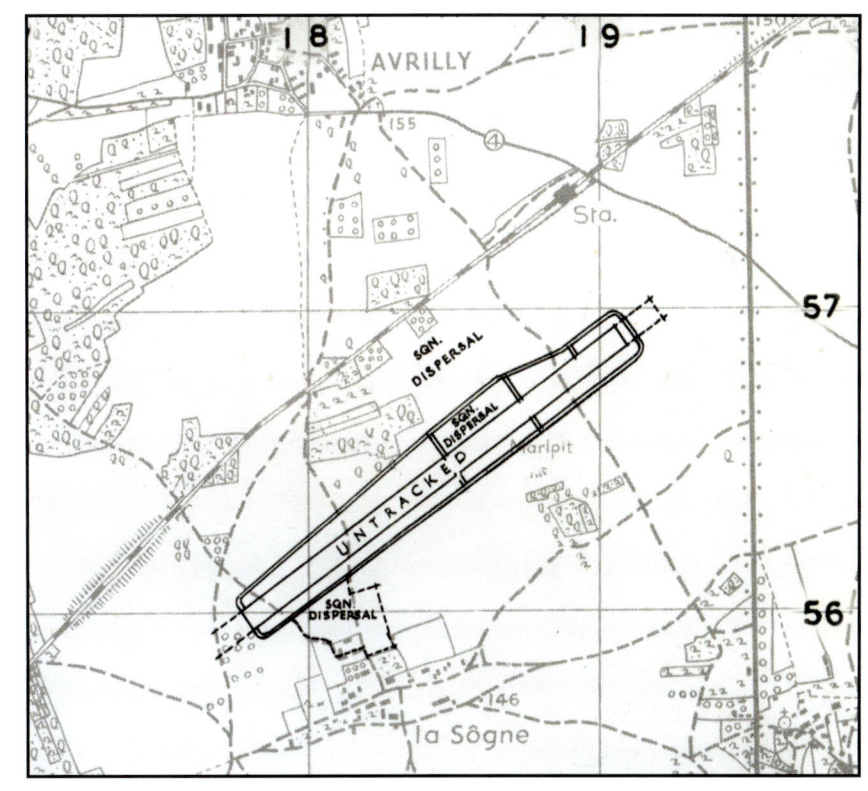

The aerial photograph was taken on September 12 but two weeks later it was just another abandoned airstrip.

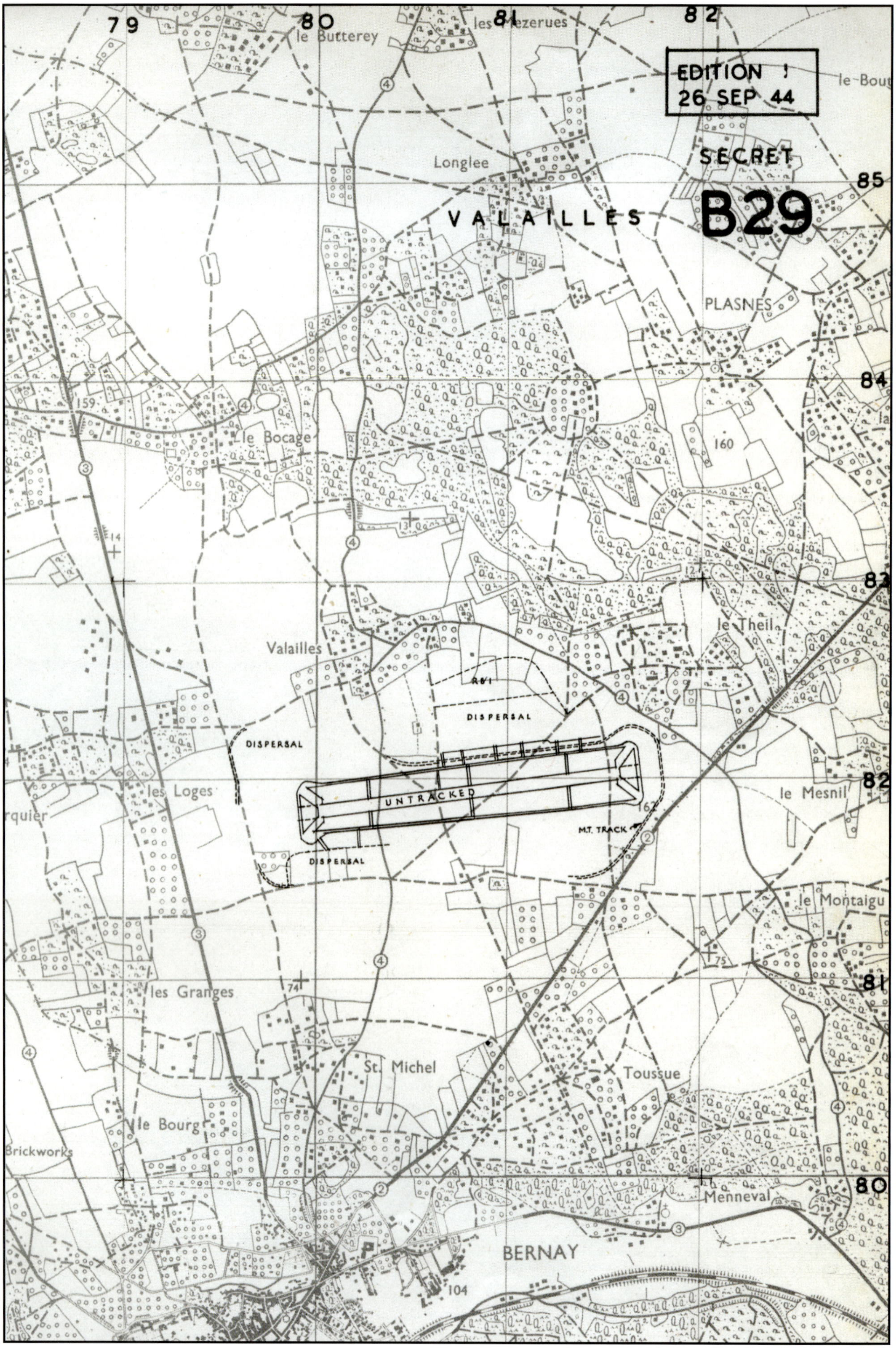
79
80
81
82
le Butterey
les Mezerues
EDITION !
26 SEP 44
SECRET
B29
Longlee
VALAILLES
PLASNES
85
84
83
82
81
80
le Bocage
160
le Theil
Valailles
R&I
DISPERSAL
DISPERSAL
UNTRACKED
M.T. TRACK
DISPERSAL
les Loges
le Mesnil
le Montaigu
les Granges
St. Michel
Toussue
le Bourg
Brickworks
Menneval
BERNAY
104

Just north of Bernay (see map pages 180-181), and ten miles south-east of La Rue Huguenot, B-29 became operational too late to be of any significance. Laying far behind the front line, it saw only brief use at the beginning of September. This faded plan in a long-forgotten archive file remains to show that it once existed, even though no trace of it remains to be seen today.

B-29 VALAILLES

OPERATIONAL SEPTEMBER 2

Latitude: 49°07'N
Longitude: 00°36'E
Grid reference: Q-808819
Altitude: 522ft

Also referred to as Bernay in some records, B-29 was situated just to the north of the town. It fell to Keane Force of the Canadian 4th Armoured Division on August 24.

With the speed of the advance across France, airstrips now had a finite life so nothing elaborate was constructed. A simple E-W untracked runway of 5,000ft was marked out and the three Free French squadrons of No. 145 Wing — Nos. 329, 340 and 341 — which had left their ALG at Sommervieu (B-8), landed their Spitfires at B-29 on September 2. No. 74 Squadron came with them but all departed for B-37 at Corroy, north of Dieppe, on September 10 when B-29 was abandoned by the RAF.

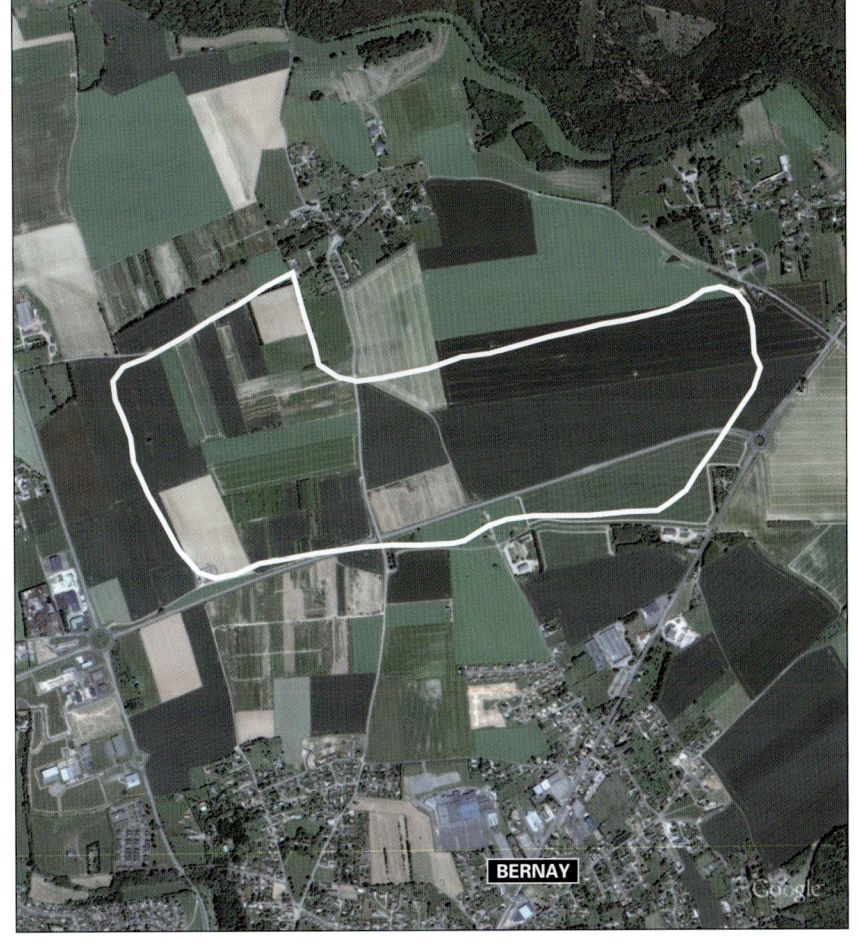

Taken at Beauvais in June 1943, on the right is Hauptmann Gerhard Lucke, the Staffelkapitän of 2./Kampfgeschwader 6. The aerodrome, 50 miles north-west of Paris (see map pages 186-187), was one of approximately 100 airfields that lay within 350 miles of Normandy. Some of these bases were well built up as a result of several years of use by, in turn, French commercial airlines, the Royal Air Force and the Luftwaffe. By the spring of 1944 most of the bases were empty except for odd reconnaissance units. The Allied master plan to achieve air supremacy depended on three main programmes: continued policing to keep the Luftwaffe at its reduced state; heavy bomber missions deep into Germany, just before and soon after the invasion to discourage the Germans from removing their fighters to France, and wholesale attacks on airfields in France during the three weeks before D-Day. But even then the attacks would have to be spread out in such a way as to conceal any connection with Normandy.

B-40/A-61 BEAUVAIS/TILLE

Coded by the Second Tactical Air Force as B-40, when it became a Ninth Air Force base the Americans applied A-61 to the aerodrome, which lay two miles north-east of the town of Beauvais.

OPERATIONAL SEPTEMBER 2

Latitude: 49°27'N
Longitude: 02°06'E
Grid reference: vM-936107
Altitude: 361ft

By the beginning of May, Leigh-Mallory had his airfield programme prepared and in the hands of the various air force commanders. Of the airfields and usable landing grounds in an arc 130 miles around Caen (designated Area I), eight were assigned to RAF Bomber Command, 12 to the Allied Expeditionary Air Force, and 20 to the Eighth Air Force. Area II extended from the 130-mile line to an arc 350 miles around Caen, reaching into Germany and the Netherlands, where 59 airfields were to be bombed by heavy bombers of the Eighth and Fifteenth Air Forces. Each air commander was to decide for himself when and how to hit the airfields based on the general plans and current reports on target conditions. Fortunately, the airfields were grouped around Paris in such a fashion that the invasion plans were unlikely to be given away in the bombing pattern if all were attacked. Beauvais had received the attention of the Eighth on seven occasions back in September 1943, but the campaign against enemy-held airfields began in earnest by the Ninth Air Force on May 11. Two days later 42 A-20s bombed the airfield while 200 P-47s attacked a range of bases, including Beauvais, on the 19th. On May 22 two B-26 groups again attacked the airfield. The wartime caption to this striking photo runs as follows: 'Luftwaffe Nemisis. Here you see a "Silver Streak" Martin B-26 Marauder medium bomber of the 9th AF leaving the Nazi airfield at Beauvais Tillé in France after a recent attack. A large dispersal area took a heavy pounding during the daylight operation, and hits were scored on an important hangar, crews reported. Thirty-three separate attacks were carried out by both Marauders and Havocs of the 9th AF on Luftwaffe airfields in May 44.'

Dating from the 1930s, the Luftwaffe made extensive use of the aerodrome, initially as a bomber base stationing a number of units there from Luftflotte 3. First to arrive in June 1940 were the Do17s of KG76, followed by the Ju87s of StG1 in July. In September, the He111s of KG26 came in for six months followed by the Ju88s of KG77 in March 1941. KG4 with He111s were based at Beauvais in June-July, while KG54 with Ju88s were there from July

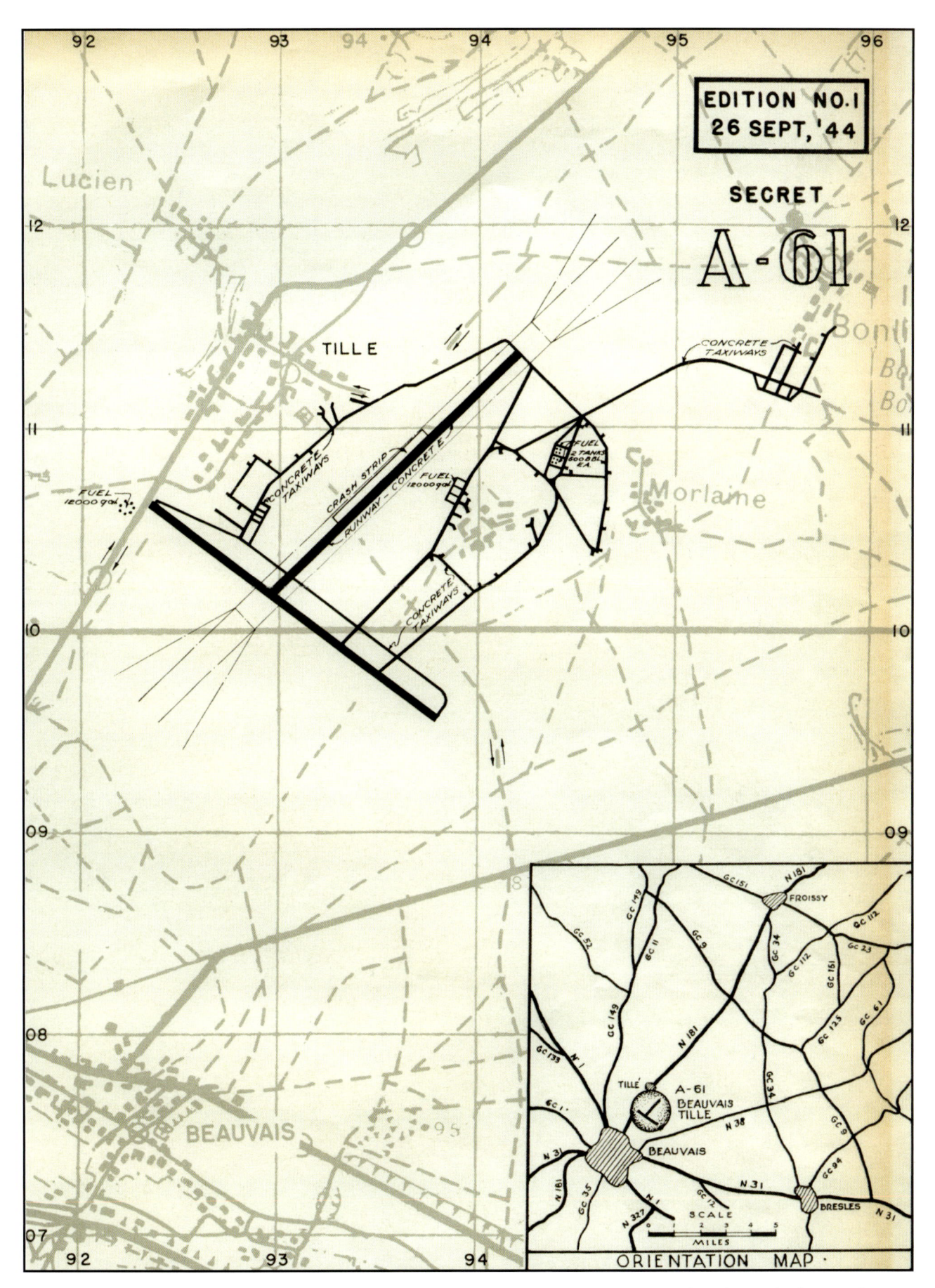

By D-Day, airfields in Area I had received 6,717 tons of bombs, 3,197 of which were delivered by the Ninth Air Force, 2,638 by the Eighth, and the remaining 882 tons by the RAF although the results were disappointing as only four of the 32 targets in Area I were classified as 'Category A', this description denoting that destruction was so complete that no further attacks were considered necessary. However, the Eighth Air Force missions were so effective that few repetitions were required, although Ninth Air Force and RAF fighter-bombers still worked over all of the important airfields for good measure.

The RAF's Film Production Unit visited B-40 at Beauvais to cover the work to repair it for operations, and were on hand to record the arrival of the Typhoons of No. 121 Wing from B-24 St André-de-l'Eure on September 2. However, the three squadrons — Nos. 174, 175 and 245 — stayed only briefly before departing up country to Vitry-en-Artois (B-50) on September 4.

to August in 1942. They were replaced by KG6 from December to February 1943. Finally, FW190s of JG26 were stationed at the airfield from August-October 1943, and Bf109s from JG1 briefly in June 1944.

In September 1943, the US Eighth Air Force had selected the airfield as a target for a series of seven raids, returning in 1944 for post-D-Day attacks on June 11 and 16.

It was the British 8th Armoured Brigade that liberated the area on August 30, the RAF staging through Typhoons of Nos. 175, 184 and 245 Squadrons on September 2 on their way from B-24 at St André-de-l'Eure to Vitry-en-Artois (B-50).

The RAF code for Beauvais was B-40 but it became A-61 when the US 843rd and 852nd Engineer Aviation Battalions moved in on the 6th. They had made it operational by the 10th having repaired the 5,500ft concrete runway but it was not until the 23-29th that the 322nd Bomb Group transferred to the Continent from their base in the UK. The 449th, 450th, 451st and 452nd Squadrons had been waiting at Andrews Field — the Essex base having been so renamed from Great Saling following the death of General Frank M. Andrews in May 1943 (see *After the Battle* No. 123).

Beauvais/Tillé remained in US hands until August 1945. The French offered the airfield to NATO in 1950 to be developed as a Cold War emergency base with an 8,000ft runway but the proposal was scrapped due to lack of finance in 1953. Instead it was rebuilt as a civil airport in 1956, but was redeveloped again in 2005 with an 8,000ft runway to be able to handle medium-size passenger jets.

The main resident at Beauvais was the 322nd Bomb Group, its Marauders flying in direct from their Essex base of Andrews Field.

Bombing up *Patricia Ann* (43-34132) sometime during the winter. The 322nd Bomb Group remained at A-61 until the spring of 1945.

In post-war years, Beauvais has been used mainly by charter airlines to save on landing fees for flights to Paris, becoming known as Paris/Beauvais airport, even though it lies some 50 miles north of the capital.

Two and a half miles south-west of Beauvais lies the village of Allonne, its dubious reputation being that it was there that the world's then-largest flying machine — the *R101* airship — crashed on October 5, 1930 on its maiden flight.

211

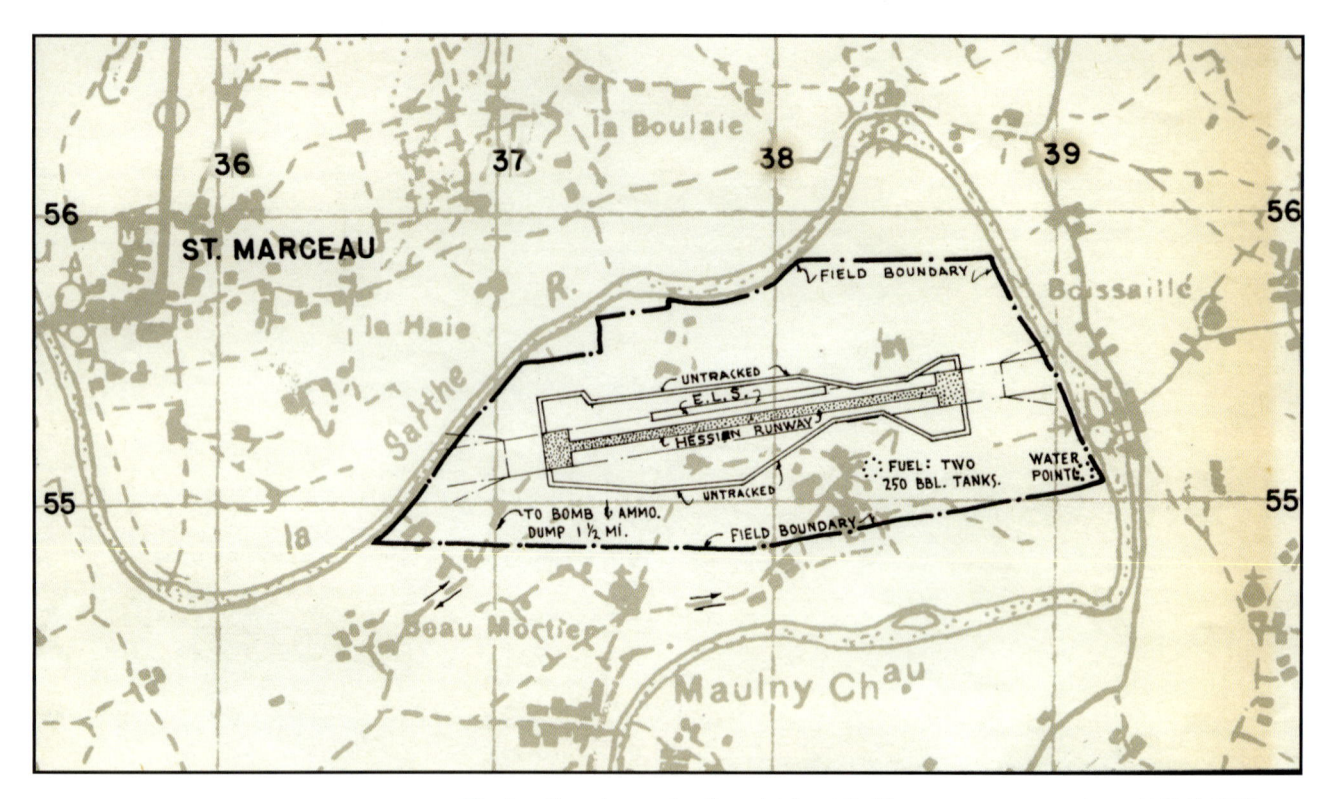

A-43 ST MARCEAU

OPERATIONAL SEPTEMBER 2

Latitude: 48°10'N
Longitude: 00°09'E
Grid reference: Z-380553
Altitude: 187ft

The location chosen for the airstrip at St Marceau was unusual as a 5,000ft PBS runway was shoehorned into a bend in the River Sarthe north of Le Mans (see map pages 162-163). It possessed dispersals for 75 aircraft and 35,000 gallons of aviation fuel. Complete airfield lighting was available. The first squadrons to take up residence were those from the 474th Fighter Group previously based at A-11 St Lambert, although the official records books seem to prefer to refer to that airstrip as Neuilly. The Ninth Air Force retained it until the 441st Troop Carrier Group moved out at the beginning of November and it was formally abandoned on the 20th of the month. It is another wartime airfield now bisected by an autoroute: the A28-E402 Le Mans to Rouen.

Situated nine miles north of Le Mans, St Marceau fell to the 2ème Division Blindée on August 10.

The 819th Engineer Aviation Battalion arrived on August 20 to lay down a 5,000ft hessian runway, the first units arriving on September 2 being the three squadrons (428th, 429th and 430th) of the 474th Fighter Group from A-11 at St Lambert. Then, at the beginning of October, the 441st Troop Carrier Group (99th, 100th, 301st and 302nd Squadrons) transferred in from Villeneuve (A-63) until they moved on to A-41 at Dreux.

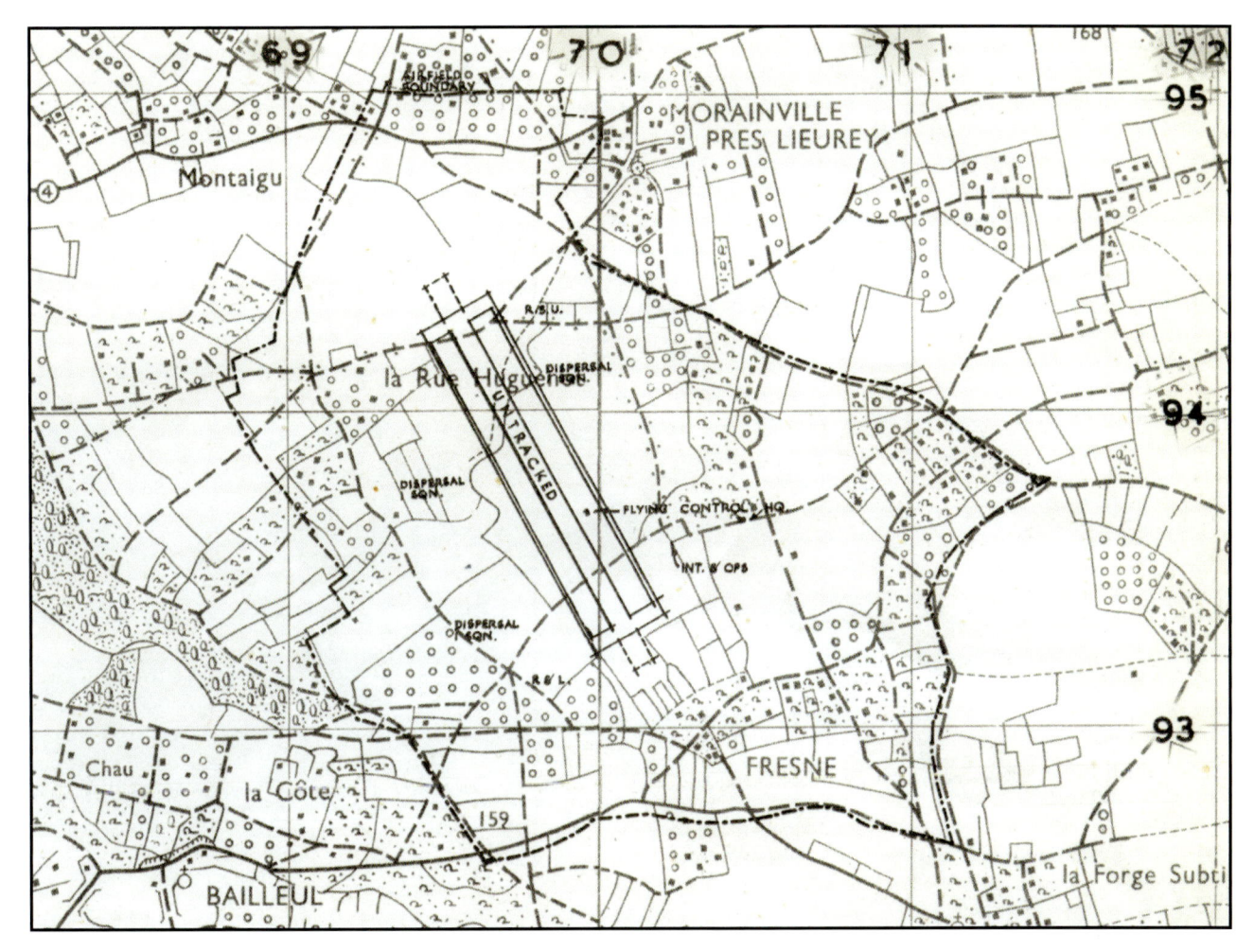

B-23 LA RUE HUGUENOT

Back on the Normandy battlefield, a staging post had been quickly set up north of Lisieux (see map pages 180-181) for squadron transfers to bases further north.

OPERATIONAL SEPTEMBER 3

Latitude: 49°12'N
Longitude: 00°26'E
Grid reference: Q-698938
Altitude: 533ft

B-23 was located 12 miles north-east of Lisieux and is referred to in some records as Morainville after the town which lies close by.

The site for the ALG had been taken by the 11th Hussars of the British 7th Armoured Division on August 24 and a basic untracked runway of 3,600ft over rolled stubble was quickly available for intermediate staging as some squadrons were now moving on as far as Lille on the Franco-Belgian border, and even into Belgium.

On September 3 Typhoons arrived from No. 123 Wing (Nos. 198 and 609 Squadrons) and No. 136 Wing (No. 164 and 183 Squadrons) that had been based at Martragny, leaving three days later for B-35 at Godelmesnil north-east of Dieppe. Three days later, the Typhoons of No. 146 Wing abandoned B-3 Ste Croix and B-8 Sommervieu, Nos. 193, 257 and 266 Squadrons dropping into Morainville on their way to their next posting at Lille/Vendeville (B-51) via Manston in Kent.

B-23 was abandoned by the RAF on September 10.

The runway of compacted wheat stubble was really busy for six days at the beginning of September but then became surplus to RAF requirements and was abandoned.

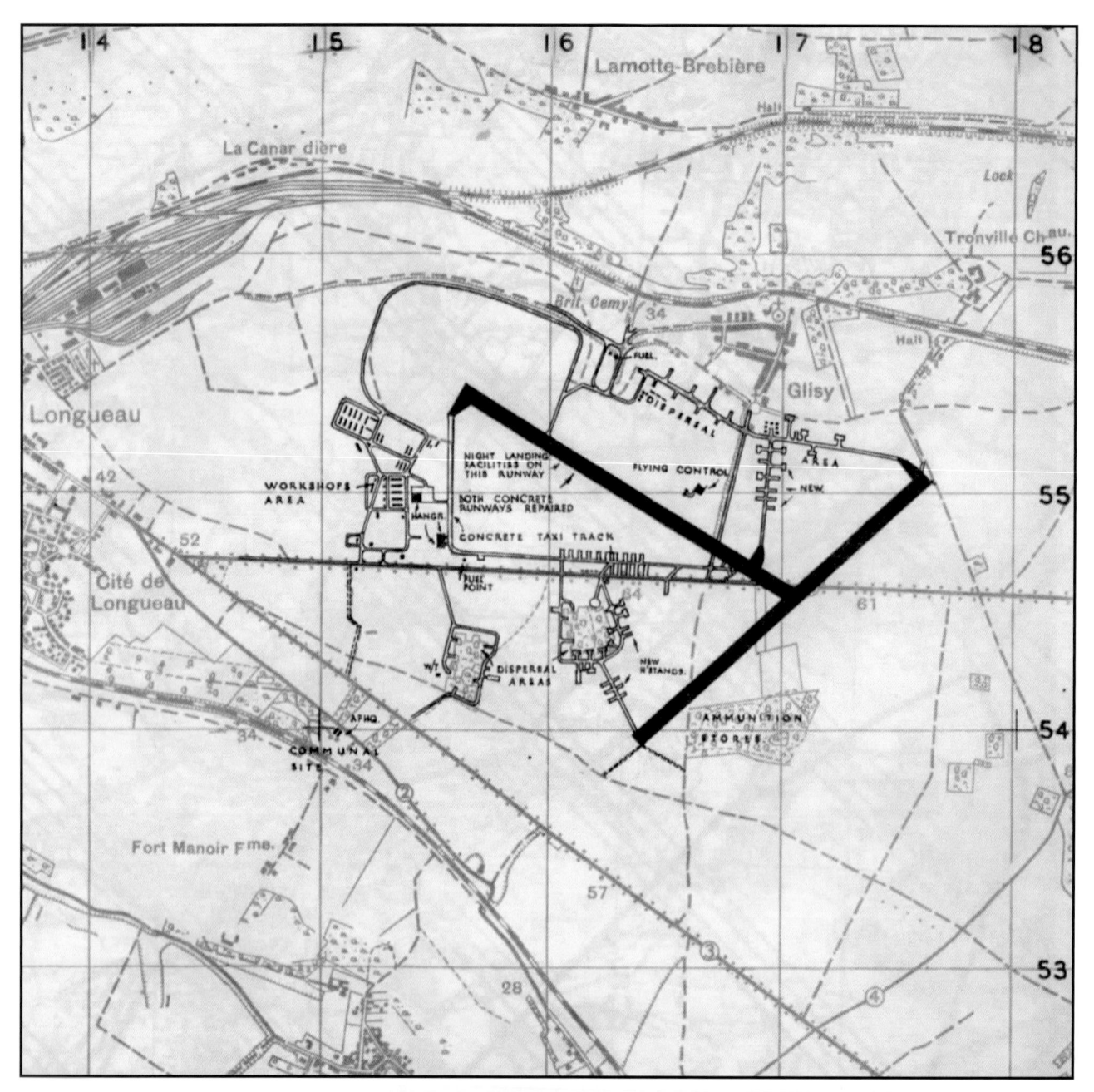

B-48 AMIENS/GLISY

OPERATIONAL SEPTEMBER 3

Lattitude: 49°52'N
Longitude: 02°23'E
Grid reference: N-162551
Altutude: 197ft

The aerodrome at Amiens lay four miles east of the town and had been established for the French Armée de l'Air in 1937. In 1940 it was briefly used by the Air Component of the British Expeditionary Force until it fell into German hands that June. It then became an important Luftwaffe base for operations against Britain with several units from Kampfgeschwader 1 being based there. There were two concrete runways, NW-SE of 5,640 feet and NE-SW at 5,340 feet, and 38 large covered aircraft shelters along with nine dispersals.

Amiens airfield (see map pages 186-187) was subjected to repeated bombing throughout the war, this particular attack occurring in July 1940. Bombs can be seen falling in the top left-hand corner. The airbase was softened up by the Ninth Air Force on February 6 and March 2, 1944 with another low-level attack taking place on August 7.

By the time the aerodrome had been captured, the surface was pitted with dozens of partially repaired craters.

Several bombing attacks were carried out on the airfield by the Eighth Air Force, the largest by 105 B-17s taking place on August 25, 1943. Amiens was hit again by Ninth Marauders in March 1944 when the airfield and runways were heavily cratered, resulting in the ESE-WNW runway being abandoned. P-47s carried out a low-level strafing attack on August 7.

The swift advance by the British Second Army's XXX Corps led to Amiens being captured on August 31. The runway was quickly made serviceable and for a month the airfield was used as a staging post for squadrons moving north. First to arrive on September 3 were the squadrons of No. 124 Wing — Nos. 137, 181, 182 and 247 — but all departed three days later to B-58 at Melsbroek, just outside Brussels, the Belgian capital having been entered on September 3. Other squadrons passing through were No. 16 (September 9-27), No. 69 (September 11-26), No. 140 (September 9-26), Nos. 438, 439 and 440 of the RCAF's No. 143 Wing (September 3-6/7), also Nos. 219, 276, 409, 410, and 488.

Then in 1945 the USAAF used B-48 as a C-47 troop carrier base. The 315th Troop Carrier Group were in residence in April and May, and the 1st Troop Carrier Pathfinder Squadron (Provisional) from March 5 to June 20, 1945.

Today it facilitates general and private aviation.

As airfield B-48, Amiens/Glisy possessed two concrete runways but now there is only a single runway, designated 12-30, of 1300 metres, bordered by a grass strip of 900 metres. The feint trace of the second wartime runway is still just visible.

215

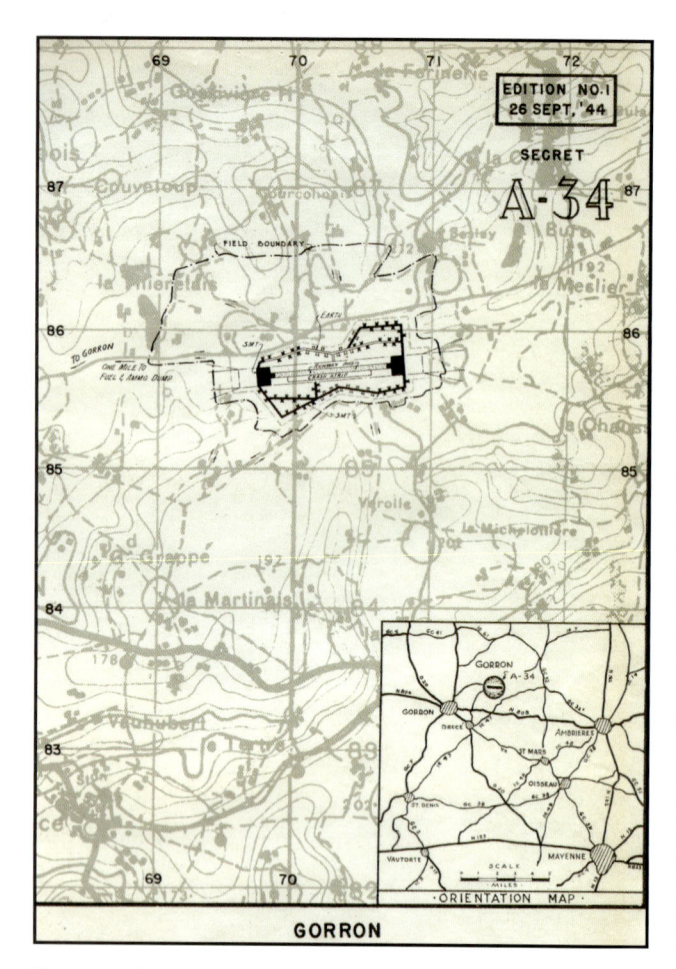

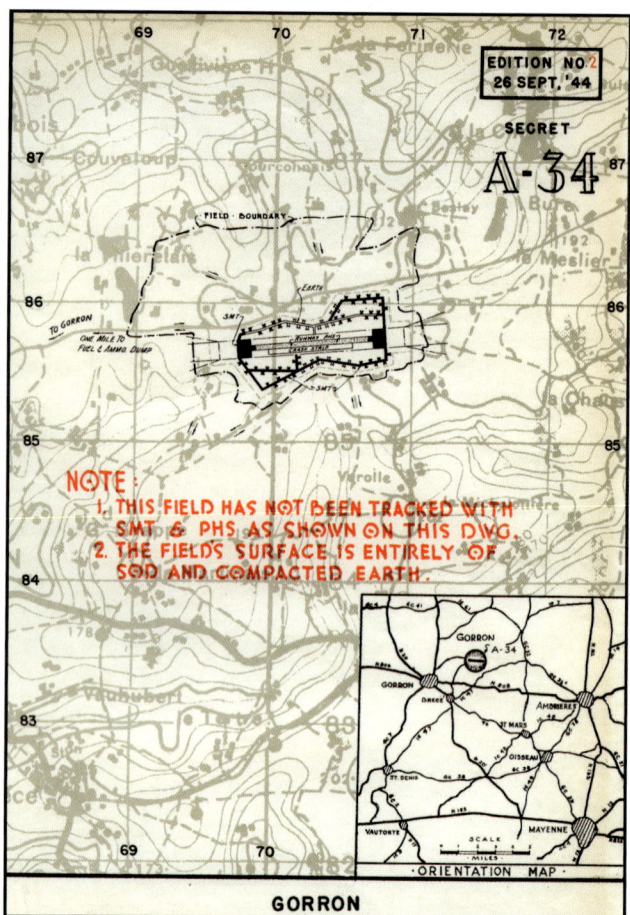

The pace of the American advance and the capture of ex-Luftwaffe bases eliminated the need for more ALGs to be constructed, so airstrips like that at Gorron were never completed as planned.

Mayenne lies mid-way between Rennes and Le Mans (see map pages 162-163) where aerodromes with hard runways were already in use. A revised plan for A-34 with overprint was then issued.

A-34 GORRON

OPERATIONAL SEPTEMBER 3

Latitude: 48°25'N
Longitude: 00°46'W
Grid reference: Y-703857
Altitude: 668ft

IX Engineer Command had prepared a drawing for a hessian-surfaced strip to be constructed at Gorron, ten miles north-west of Mayenne, but in the event the 846th Engineer Aviation Battalion improvised with a 3,600ft runway of compacted earth.

The area had been secured by Combat Command A of the US 3rd Armored Division on August 6, the engineers beginning work on the 14th. It was specified for use as an Emergency Landing and Refuelling strip although by the time it was declared operational on August 27, there was little need for such, and there is no recorded use. It was abandoned on November 4.

By now there had been a change of commander for the Ninth Air Force as Lieutenant General Brereton had been appointed commander of the new First Allied Airborne Army on August 8. Command was turned over to the Deputy Air Commander-in-Chief, AEAF, Major General Hoyt S. Vandenberg, on August 8.

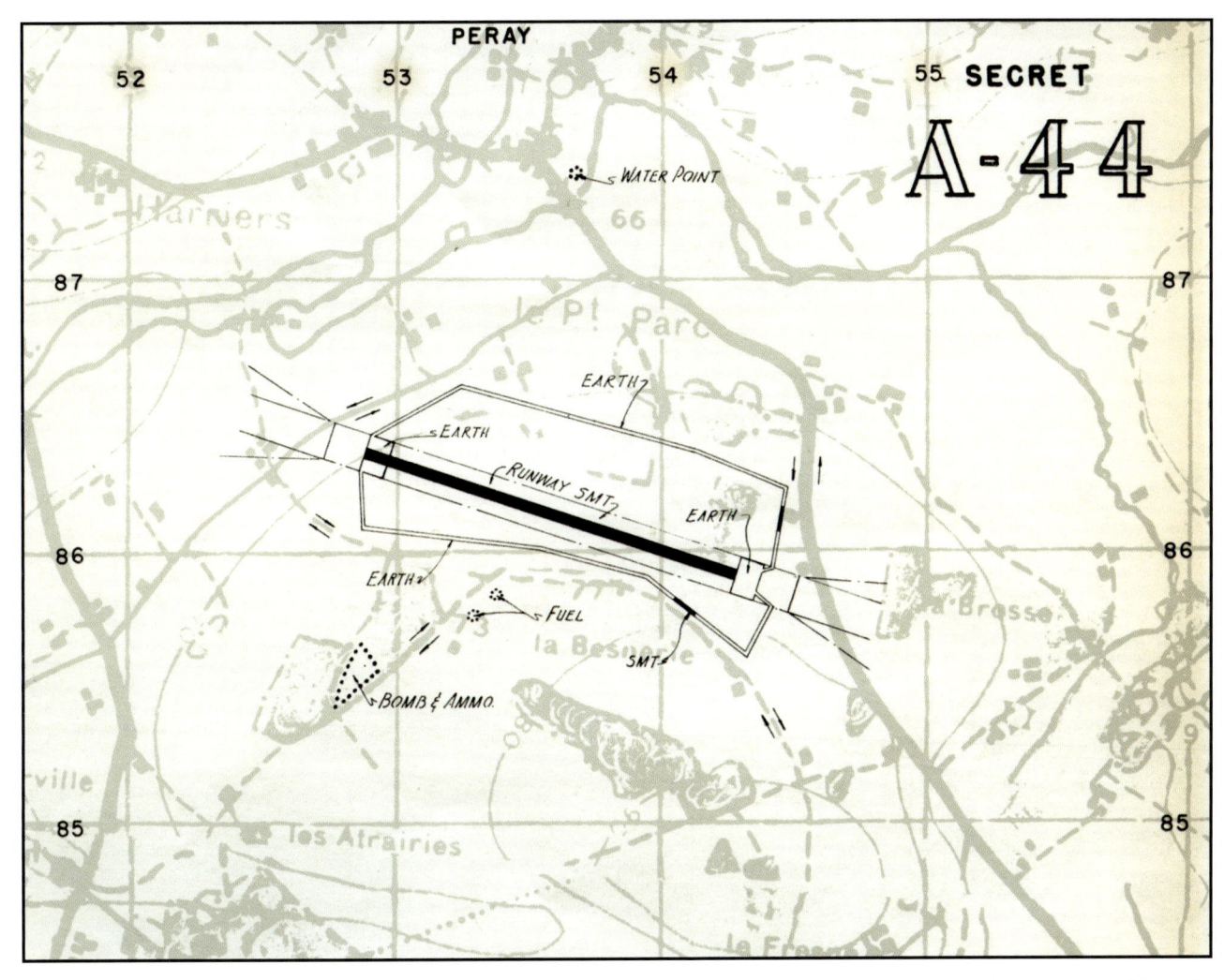

The last airfield to become operational within Leigh-Mallory's D+90 plan was A-44 at Peray, a small village some 12 miles south of Alençon (see map pages 162-163). A single SMT-surfaced runway had been completed by September 2, the P-38s of the 367th Fighter Group transferring from A-2 at Criqueville, the 393rd Fighter Squadron heralding the arrival on September 4. After they moved on to A-71 Clastres, the strip was empty until the C-47s of the 442nd Troop Carrier Group had it as their base from October 4 to November 11.

A-44 PERAY

OPERATIONAL SEPTEMBER 4

Latitude: 48°14'N
Longitude: 00°21'E
Grid reference: V-536861
Altitude: 229ft

Located 18 miles north-east of Le Mans (A-35), the location was captured on August 11 by CCR of the US 5th Armored Division in conjunction with the 314th Infantry Regiment of the 78th Division.

Between August 20 and September 2, a SMT runway, 5,000ft long, was laid down by the 819th Engineer Aviation Battalion. The first unit to arrive was the 393rd Squadron from A-2 at Cricqueville on the 4th, the other two squadrons of the 367th Fighter Group — the 394th and 392nd — transferring in on the 5th and 7th respectivly. They all moved out a week later.

Then in October the 442nd Troop Carrier Group relocated from Italy, remaining at A-44 for a month. Peray was abandoned on November 20.

No outward trace can be seen today, a new woodland having been planted on the line of the runway.

Type of Field	American Sector Operational	American Sector Under construction	U.S. Total	British Sector Operational	British Sector Under construction
Fighter ALG	24	8	32	23	5
Medium Bomber	5	1	6	1	—
Transport	9	1	10	2	—
Tactical Aerodrome	1	—	1	—	—
Liaison Strip	1	—	1	—	—
	40	10	50	26	5

This table, reproduced from Leigh-Mallory's despatch published in January 1947, shows the position at D+90, the end of the planned period, showing that a total of 81 airfields had been built to date. Between D-Day and VE-Day British and American engineers constructed or rehabilitated a total of over 400 continental airfields.

Leigh-Mallory closed his report stating that 'the IX Engineer Command proved very effective and I feel that the Royal Air Force could well consider the adoption of a comparable organisation to ensure immediate operational facilities in overseas theatres. In particular, I feel that more heavy earth-moving equipment should be provided for British units and that the organisation should be reviewed to allow smaller and more flexible companies than the present Wings. These companies should be under the direct control of the air commander in the theatre and not under a ground commander.

'The fact that airfield construction was still a little behind schedule at the end of the planned period [D+90], was due mainly to tactical reasons in the assault phase and to the consequent lack of adequate and suitable ground area, and to some delay in shipping sufficient material. The men of the American Aviation Engineer Battalions of the IX Engineer Command and of the British Airfield Construction units worked exceptionally well, as was proved by the setting-up of the first three Emergency Landing Strips at Pouppeville, St Laurent-sur-Mer and Asnelles by D+1. These men worked right in the battle area, through shelling and bombing, and as well as constructing the airfields often had to lay down their tools to deal with stray snipers in the area around the airfield strip.'

General Eisenhower shakes hands with Air Chief Marshal Leigh-Mallory, the new Allied Air Commander-in-Chief for the Southeast Asia Command, whom he had just decorated with the US Legion of Merit. On Leigh-Mallory's right is Air Chief Marshal Sir Arthur Harris, head of RAF Bomber Command, and at his left is Lieutenant General Carl A. Spaatz, commander of the US Strategic Air Forces, both of whom were also decorated. The awards ceremony was held at Eisenhower's headquarters in the Trianon Palace Hotel at Versailles on November 4; ten days later Leigh-Mallory lay dead on a French mountain top having crashed while on his way to the Far East (see *After the Battle* No. 39).

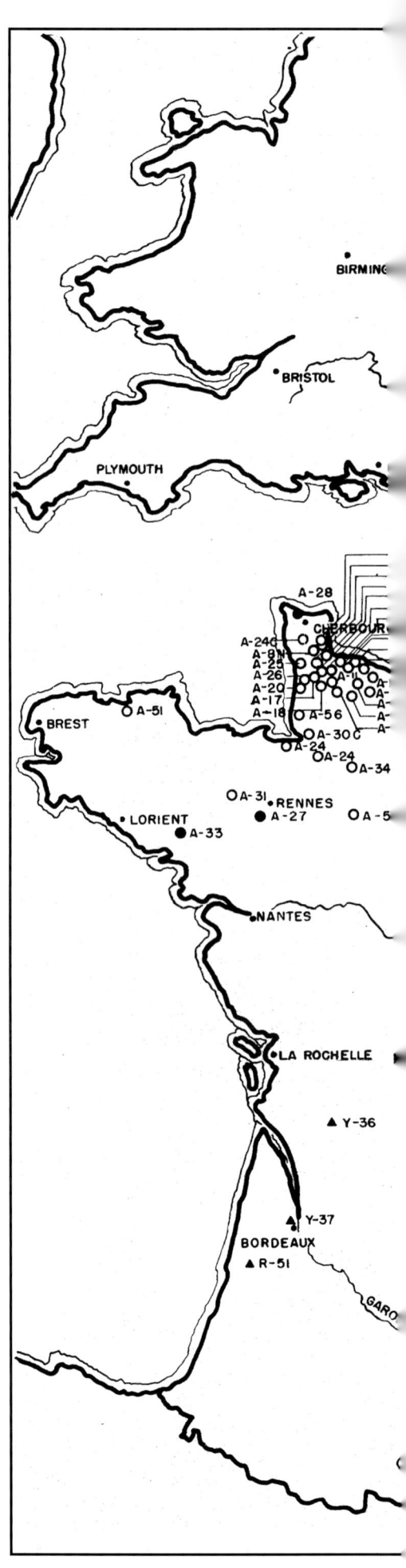

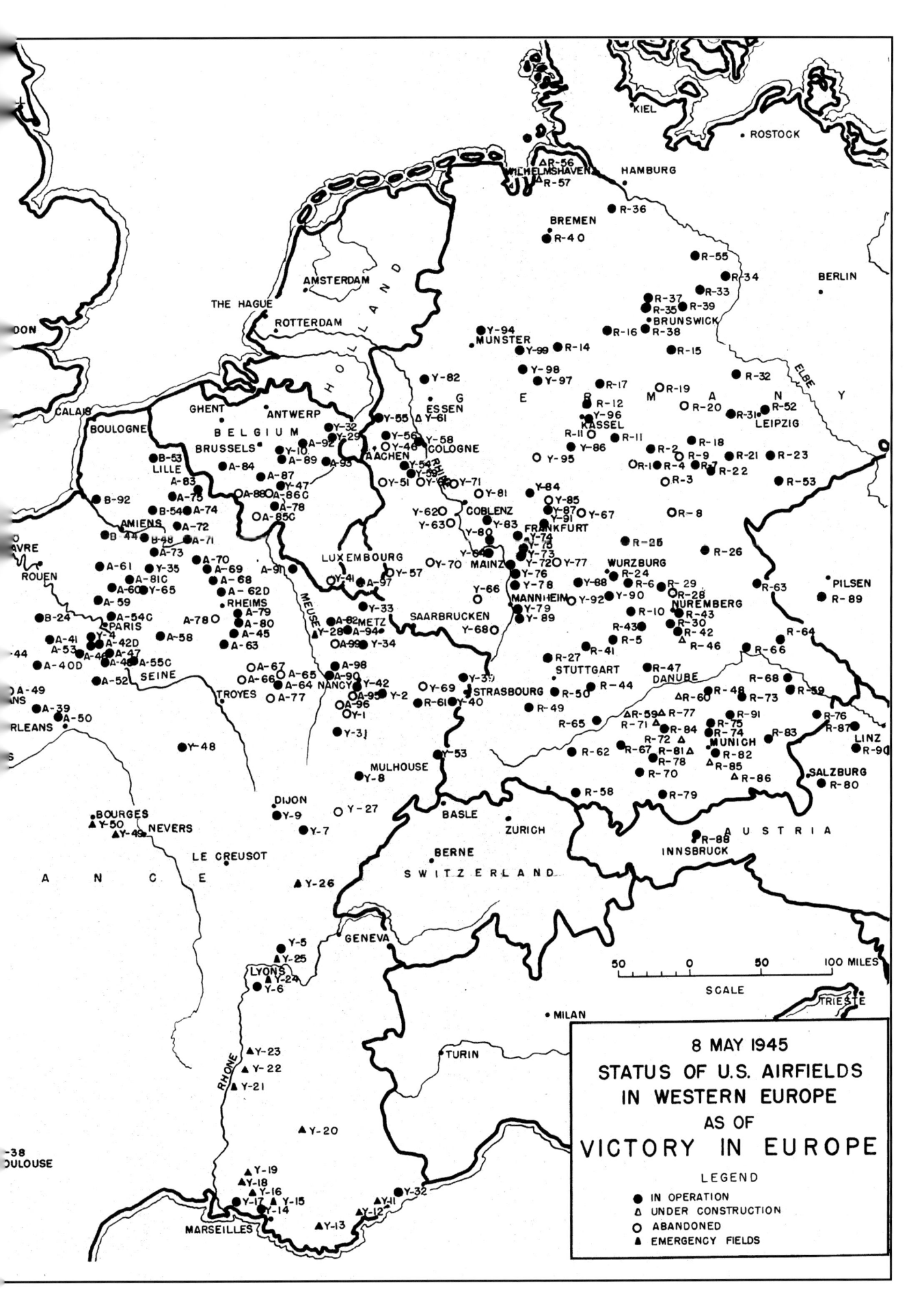

**8 MAY 1945
STATUS OF U.S. AIRFIELDS
IN WESTERN EUROPE
AS OF
VICTORY IN EUROPE**

LEGEND
● IN OPERATION
△ UNDER CONSTRUCTION
○ ABANDONED
▲ EMERGENCY FIELDS

INDEX

COMPILED BY PETER GUNN

Note: Page numbers in *italics* refer to illustrations. There may also be textual references on these pages.

A-1 *see* St Pierre-du-Mont
A-2 *see* Cricqueville
A-3 *see* Cardonville
A-4 *see* Deux-Jumeaux
A-5 *see* Chippelle
A-6 *see* Beuzeville
A-7 *see* Azeville
A-8 *see* Picauville
A-9 *see* Le Molay
A-10 *see* Carentan
A-11 *see* St Lambert (Neuilly)
A-12 *see* Lignerolles
A-13 *see* Tour-en-Bessin
A-14 *see* Cretteville
A-15 *see* Maupertus
A-16 *see* Brucheville
A-17 *see* Méautis
A-18 *see* St Jean-de-Daye
A-19 *see* La Vieille
A-20 *see* Lessay
A-21C *see* St Laurent-sur-Mer
A-22C *see* Colleville
A-23C *see* Querqueville
A-24C *see* Biniville
A-25C *see* Bolleville
A-26 *see* Gorges
A-27 *see* Rennes
A-28 *see* Pontorson
A-29 *see* St James
A-30C *see* Courtils
A-31 *see* Gaël
A-33 *see* Vannes
A-34 *see* Gorron
A-35 *see* Le Mans
A-36 *see* St Léonard
A-38 *see* Montreuil
A-39 *see* Châteaudun
A-40D *see* Chartres
A-41 *see* Dreux
A-42D *see* Villacoublay
A-43 *see* St Marceau
A-44 *see* Peray
A-45 *see* Lonray
A-46 *see* Toussus-le-Noble
A-47 *see* Orly
A-48 *see* Brétigny
A-50 *see* Orléans-Bricy
A-55 *see* Melun
A-61 *see* Beauvais/Tillé (B-40/A-61)
A-62 *see* Reims
A-63 *see* Villeneuve
A-64 *see* St Dizier
A-66 *see* Orconte
A-67 *see* Vitry-le-François
A-68 *see* Juvincourt
A-69 *see* Laon
A-71 *see* Clastres
A-72 *see* Péronne
A-73 *see* Roye/Amy
A-74 *see* Cambrai/Niergnies
A-78 *see* Florennes/Juzaine
A-79 *see* Prosnes
A-80 *see* Mourmelon-le-Grand
A-87 *see* Charleroi
A-89 *see* Le Culot/Beauvechain (B-68/A-89)
A-90 *see* Toul
A-93 *see* Liège/Bierset
Aachen 15, *195*
Aircraft
    A-20 Havoc 22
    A-26 Invader 22
    Airbus A330-200 (French Presidential Airbus) *193*
    Auster (AOB) 23, 58, *59*
    B-26 Marauder 22
        43-34132 *Patricia Ann* (US 322nd BG) *211*
        Lil' Pork Chop (US 322nd BG) *180*
    Boston 23
    C-46 Commando 23
    C-47 Skytrain 22–23
        41-18513 *147*
        42-100766 *Lilly Bell II* (US 89th TCS) *177*
    F-5 Lightning 22
    F-6 Mustang 22
    Fieseler Storch 43, *84*
    Mitchell 23

Mosquito 23
Mustang (RAF version) 23
    FZ190 (19 Sqn) *130*
P-38 Lightning 12, 22, *46*
P-47 Thunderbolt 12, 22
    Lethal Liz II (US 81st FS) *75*
P-51 Mustang 12, 22
    44-13309 *Fools Paradise IV* (US 363rd FG) *111*
P-61 Black Widow 22, *104*
R101 airship disaster *211*
Seafire (FAA) 23
The Spirit of St Louis (Lindbergh) *178*
Spitfire 23
    Mk IX MJ627 (403 Sqn) *40*
    Mk IX MK277 (442 Sqn) *40*
    Mk IX MK464 (442 Sqn) *60*
Stearman *77*
Tempest 23
    MN1526 (198 Sqn) *6*
Typhoon 23, *34*, *72*
    JP656 (184 Sqn) *81*
    JR427 (182 Sqn) *69*
    MN125 (198 Sqn) *81*
    MN464 (439 Sqn) *81*
    MN667 (184 Sqn) *81*
    MN809 (247 Sqn) *81*
    MN928 (247 Sqn) *69*
    MP137 (245 Sqn) *81*
    Roll of Honour 80–81
Wellington 23
Airfields
    Advanced Landing Grounds (ALGs) 6, 9, 10
    All-Weather 10
    construction requirements 106–107
    Emergency Landing Strips (ELS) 6, 9, 10
    Pierced Steel Plank (PSP) 12, 15, 16, *18–19*
    Prefabricated Bituminous Surfaces (PBS) 10, 12, 15, *20–21*, *102*, *147*, *168*, *170–171*
    Refuelling and Re-arming Strips (R&RS) 6, 9, 10
    Sommerfeld tracking 57, *157*
    Square Mesh Track (SMT) 10, 12, *13*, 15, *16–17*, 21, *34*, *72*, *147–148*, *155*
    standards established 12
    Supply & Evacuation (S&E) 15
Aldington *150*
Alençon 161, *217*
Allied Airborne Army, First 216
Allied Expeditionary Air Force (AEAF)
    logistics *78*
    planning 8, *208*
Allied Expeditionary HQ (SHAEF) *172*
    airfield planning 32
    invasion planning 8
Allonne, *R101* airship disaster *211*
Amblie (B-14) 32, *144–145*
Amiens *186–187*
Amiens/Glisy (B-48) *183*, *187*, *214–215*
Amy *see* Roye/Amy (A-73)
Anderson, F/Lt William *81*
Andrews, Gen. Frank M. 210
Andrews Field (formerly Great Saling) *210*
Antwerp *199*
Appleton, G/Capt. Charles *69*
Argentan 161, *180*
Arromanches 82, *125*
    Mulberry harbour 10, *43*, *61*
Asboe, F/O Arnold *13*
Asch *see* Zwartberg/Asch (Y-29)
Aschenbrenner, Hptm. Kurd *166*
Ascot *see* Sunninghill Park
Ashford, S/Ldr Herbert (padre) *93*
Ashworth, F/O Corran (RNZAF) *131*
Ashworth, Vince *131*
Asnelles-sur-Mer (B-1) 28–29, 32, *106*
Au Gay (HQ US First Army) *52*

Aubertin, Capt. Pierre *83*
Authie (B-22) *137*
Avranches *200*
Avrilly (B-34) *159*, *181*, *205*
Azeville
    Château de Fontenay *94*, *112*
    German coastal batteries 26, *94*
Azeville (A-7) *74*, *94–97*, *106*

B-1 *see* Asnelles-sur-Mer
B-2 *see* Bazenville
B-3 *see* Ste Croix-sur-Mer
B-4 *see* Bény-sur-Mer
B-5 *see* Le Fresne-Camilly
B-6 *see* Coulombs
B-7 *see* Martragny
B-8 *see* Sommervieu
B-9 *see* Lantheuil
B-10 *see* Plumetot
B-11 *see* Longues-sur-Mer
B-12 *see* Ellon
B-14 *see* Amblie
B-15 *see* Ryes
B-16 *see* Villons-les-Buissons
B-17 *see* Carpiquet
B-18 *see* Cristot
B-19 *see* Lingèvres
B-21 *see* Ste Honorine-de-Ducy
B-22 *see* Authie
B-23 *see* La Rue Huguenot
B-24 *see* St André-de-l'Eure
B-26 *see* Illiers-l'Évêque
B-27 *see* Boisney
B-28 *see* Évreux
B-29 *see* Valailles (Bernay)
B-30 *see* Créton
B-31 *see* Fresnoy
B-33 *see* Campneuseville
B-34 *see* Avrilly
B-35 *see* Godelmesnil
B-37 *see* Corroy
B-40/A-61 *see* Beauvais/Tillé
B-44 *see* Poix
B-48 *see* Amiens/Glisy
B-50 *see* Vitry-en-Artois
B-51 *see* Lille/Vendeville
B-56 *see* Brussels-Evere
B-57 *see* Lille-Nord
B-58 *see* Melsbroek
B-66 *see* Blankenberg
B-68/A-89 *see* Le Culot/Beauvechain
Balleroy *120*
Banville 58, *144*
Barneville-sur-Mer *146*
Bayeux 11, *78*, *79*, 82, *128*, *134*
    see also Tournières ('Shellburst' Advanced CP)
Bazenville (B-2) 25, 32, 33, 35, *40–43*, *67*, *106*, *145*, *184*
Beaches, D-Day assault
    Gold *35*, 51, 66, *78*, 82
    Jig Green *28*
    Juno 51
        Mike Sector 32, *43*, 58, 70, 90, *115*, *144*
        Nan Sector 58
    Omaha 10, *39*, *51–53*, 75, *111*, *126*
        Charlie Beach 44
        Easy Green *30*
        Easy Red *30*
    Sword *51*, *136*
    Utah 26, 27, *39*, *43*, 48, 51, 52, *75*, *111*, *123*
Beaulieu *178*
Beauvais *186*
    R101 airship disaster (Allonne) *211*
Beauvais/Tillé (B-40/A-61) *154*, *182*, *183*, *208–211*
    later Paris/Beauvais Airport *211*
Beauvechain *see* Le Culot/Beauvechain
Beck, SS-Hstuf. Wilhelm *69*
Benn, P/O C. E. *69*
Bennet, P/O Sam *99*
Bentley Priory, Stanmore, RAF Fighter Command HQ 8
Bény (village) *168*
Bény-sur-Mer (B-4) 25, 33, 35, *58–61*, *67*, *85*, *86*, *87*, *88*, *106*, *149*, *203*
Bernay *see* Valailles
Bernières *168*
Beuzeville (A-6) 16, *46*, *54–57*, *95*, *97*, *106*
Bierset *see* Liège/Bierset (A-93)

Biéville-Quétiéville *81*
Biggin Hill 40
BIGOT cross-Channel operation *128*
Biniville (A-24C) *126*, *132*
Bisterne ALG, New Forest *57*
Blackett, LAC *155*
Blankenberg (B-66) *205*
Blary, fuel pipeline *11*
Blay, 21st Army Gp Tac HQ *115*, *117*, *118*, *158*
Blaziek, 1st Lt Jacob C. *48*
Blériot, Louis *198*
Bletchley Park 69
Boisney (B-27) *61*, *181*, *203*
Bolleville (A-25C) *126*, *146–147*
Book: *Le Grand Cirque* (*The Big Show*) (Closterman) 42, *85*
Bournemouth *136*
Bracknall *see* Ramslade House, Bracknall
Bradley, Gen. Omar N.
    commands US ground forces *132*, *161*
    establishes foothold in Normandy 53
    HQ St Sauveur *142*
Brannagan, S/Ldr Tommy *82*
Breadnor, AM Lloyd *60*
Bregman, P/O Sid *40*
Bréhin, Jacques *80*, *81*
Brereton, Lt Gen. Lewis H.
    CG First Allied Airborne Army 216
    CG US Ninth Air Force 8, *9*
Brest 200
Brétigny (A-48) *118*, *121*, *174*, *190–191*
    later French Air Force Base (BA 217) *191*
Bricy *see* Orléans-Bricy
British Army
    British Expeditionary Force (1940) *214*
    21st Army Group
        advance to Somme *186–187*
        airfield construction 16, *30*, *68*, *102*, *154*, *168*
        Churchill visits *142*
        communications with US 53
        Eisenhower commands *204*
        and Falaise pocket *180*
        operational planning 6–7, 14
        Tac HQ Blay *115*, *117*, *118*, *158*
        Tac HQ Creully 90, *115*
    Armies, Second *121*, *124*, *134*, *157*, *159*, *186*, *215*
    Corps
        I Corps 70
        XXX Corps 98, 149, 215
    Divisions
        3rd Infantry 29
        6th Airborne 100, *189*
        7th Armoured *128*, *159*, *187*, *213*
        43rd (Wessex) *180*
        49th (West Riding) 149
        50th (Northumbrian) 66, *78*, 82, 99
        53rd (Welsh) 204
        59th (Staffordshire) 148
    Brigades
        4th Armoured 204
        8th Armoured 210
        22nd Armoured 128
        29th Armoured 187
        56th 78
        69th 66
        151st 99
        231st 82
    Regiments
        11th Hussars 213
        53rd Recce Regt 204
        Durham Light Infantry, 9th Bn 99
        Hampshire Regt, 1st Bn 29, 82
        King's Own Yorkshire Light Infantry, 1st/4th Bn 149
        Nottinghamshire Yeomanry 29
    Pioneer Corps
        No. 135 Coy 98
        No. 164 Coy 91
        No. 201 Coy 170
        No. 214 Coy 58, 87
        No. 217 Coy 58, 87
        No. 222 Coy 91
        No. 231 Coy 29, 79
        No. 250 Coy 170

220

British Army — continued
  Royal Engineers (RE)
    Airfield Construction Groups
      10
      No. 13 *34*, 66, 67, *79*,
        90–91, 148, 149, *158, 180*
      No. 16 *28*, *33*, 40, 67, 78,
        79, *128*, *159*, 182, 184
      No. 23 *67*, 70, *71*, 83, *144*,
        168, 205
      No. 24 *32*, *67*, *82*, *98*, 99,
        101, *124*, 125, *138*, 139, *203*
      No. 25 *58*, *67*, 86, *87*, 89
    Army Troops Coy, No. 575 *158*
    Road Construction
      Companies
      No. 64 *58*, *87*
      No. 75 *98*
      No. 88 *70*
      No. 609 *79*
      No. 614 *66*, *148*
      No. 653 *91*
      No. 681 *58*, *59*, *87*
      No. 689 *29*
      No. 720 *70*, *82*, *170*
    Assault Squadron, 82nd *29*
    No. 1 Dog Platoon *138*
  Royal Electrical and
    Mechanical Engineers (REME)
    11
  Medical *11*
    No. 77 General Hospital *145*
    No. 81 General Hospital *145*
British Lodgement Area: Rear
  Maintenance Area (RMA) *10–12*
  Advanced Ordnance Depot
    (AOD) *11*
  Ammunition (AMN) *11*
  Army Post Office (APO) *11*
  Base Ammunition Depot
    (BAD) *11*
  Civil Affairs (CA) *11*
  Field Ammunition Repair
    Factory (FARF) *11*
  Forces Institute (NAAFI) *11*
  Medical (MED) *11*
  Ordnance (ORD) *11*
  Petrol Oil and Lubricants
    (POL) *11*
  Prisoners of War (PW) *11*
  Reinforcements (RFTS) *11*
  Royal Electrical and Mechanical
    Engineers (REME) *11*
  Salvage (SAL) *11*
  Supplies (SUPS) *11*
Brittany 120, *142*, *150–151*, 200
Broadhurst, AVM Harry
  escorts Churchill on tour *24–25*, *43*
  lands in Normandy 35
  visits airfields *84*
Bruceville (A-16) *122–123*, 195
Brussels 199
Brussels-Evere (B-56) *43*
Buc (Y-4) *196*, 198
Buchheim, Rittmeister *69*
Burgsthaler, Maj. i.G. Hugo *69*
Butler, Maj. Gen. William O.,
  Deputy C-in-C AEAF *8*
Butler Manufacturing Company,
  Kansas City 116

Caen 80, 159, *208*
  Airport (ex-Carpiquet) *139*
  battle area *43*
  bombing of 89, *91*
  operational planning for 9, 10,
    138
Cambrai/Niergnies (A-74) *177*, 196
Camilly *see* Le Fresne-Camilly
Campneuseville (B-33) *169*, *204*
Canadian units
  First Army *142*, 157, 184, *186*
  II Corps 203
  Divisions
    3rd Infantry *136*, 149, 203
    4th Armoured 207
  Brigades
    7th Infantry *144*
    8th Infantry *136*, 168
    9th Infantry 168
  Regiments
    6th Armoured *32*
    27th Armoured 168
    North Nova Scotia
      Highlanders 168
    Royal Winnipeg Rifles *32*, *144*

Cap de la Hague 140
Cardonville (A-3) *7*, *36–39*, 46, 62,
  97, *102*, *106*, 126, *161*, 175
Carentan, Normandy Tank
  Museum 75, *77*
Carentan (A-10) *46*, *74–77*, 97,
  106, *118*, *164*, *202*
Carpiquet (B-17) *66*, 104,
  136–140, 149, 168, 182, 183
Caumont 159
Cemetery: Bayeux *128*
Chalgrove 150
Chambois 172
Charleroi (A-87) 198
Charles Lindbergh Airfield *see*
  Lessay
Charney, F/Lt Ken *85*
Chartres 161
Chartres (A-40D) *38*, *174*, 175,
  178
  later French Air Force Base
    Chartres-Champhol (BA 122) 175
Châteaudun (A-39) 112, 151, *174*,
  188–189
  later French Air Force base *189*
Cherbourg *43*, *104*, *167*
  port *26*, *61*, *110*, 111, *141*
Cherbourg peninsula 75, 94, *118*,
  133, 134
  Allied plans *26*, *200*
  US advance *61*, *146*
  US bogged down at 13
Cherbourg-Théville (later Cher-
  bourg Airport) 111, *113*
  see also Maupertus (A-15)
Chesters, S/Ldr Frank *100*
Cheux 81
Chicago: O'Hare Airport *141*
Chilbolton *36*
Chippelle (A-5) *114*, *118–119*, 120,
  191
Churchill, Winston
  tours airfields *24–25*, *43*, *73*
  visits Normandy front *142*
Clark, F/O N. S. *73*
Clark, Greg (war correspondent)
  100
Clark, Lt-Col George 86, *87*
Clarke, F/O Ross *40*
Clastres (A-71) *189*, *217*
Closterman, Sous-Lt Pierre (602
  Sqn) *8*, *42*, 83, *85*
Colleville (A-22C) *126–127*
Colombelles 86
Coningham, AM Sir Arthur (AOC
  2nd TAF) *8*, *9*, *158*
Corroy (B-37) *207*
Cotentin peninsula *see* Cherbourg
  peninsula
Coulombs (B-6) *11*, *60*, *66–69*, 90,
  91, *106*, *136*, *139*, *148*, *187*
Courseulles-sur-Mer *58*, *70*, *154*
Courtils (A-30C) *126*, *151*, *156*, 157
Crépon *40*, *79*
Créton (B-30) *66*, *181*, *187*, 205
Cretteville, Château de Franque-
  tot *109*
Cretteville (A-14) *46*, *74*, *102*,
  106–109, *134*, *157*, 185
Creully, Château de Creullet (21st
  Army Gp Tac HQ) *90*, *91*
Cricqueville (A-2) *16*, *48–49*, 52,
  55, 75, *97*, *106*, 120, *152*, *217*
Crisbecq, German battery 94, *95*
Cristot (B-18) *131*, *148–149*, 183,
  193
Croissanville *81*

Davis-Monthan Field, Arizona
  141
Davoud, G/Capt. Paul, DSO, DFC
  92, *93*
Dawans, Genmaj. Sigismund-Hell-
  muth Ritter und Edler von *69*
De Gaulle, Gén. Charles *172*, *193*
Dean, Basil *100*
Deux-Jumeaux (A-4) *61*, *62–65*,
  97, *102*, *106*, 126, *196*
Dieppe *186*
Douville 64
Douvres-la-Délivrande *70*
  Hindenburg radar station *86*
Dreux 161
Dreux (A-41) *174*, 175, *176–177*,
  200, *212*
  later Vernouillet Airport 176

Dreux-Louvilliers (USAF AFB)
  176, *193*

Eastchurch 80
Ehrgott, Col Herbert W. *39*
Eisenhower, Gen. Dwight D.
  Adv. CP 'Shellburst' *114*, *115*,
    116, *158*
  air operations report *6*
  appointed Supreme Commander
    8
  becomes ground forces com-
    mander *204*
  CP 'Sharpener' *115*, *116*, *118*
  Forward HQ to Versailles *199*,
    218
  German defences bombed 13
  liberation of Paris 172
  Normandy advance plan *200*
  regroups forces *132*, *142*
Elbeuf *181*
Ellis, S/Ldr Dick *100*
Ellon (B-12) *80*, *128–131*, 183
Elphinstone, Maj. Harold (RE) *29*
ELS-1 *see* Pouppeville
ENSA (Entertainments National
  Service Association) *100*
Évreux (B-28) 149, *174*, *181*,
  192–193
Ezanno, Gén. Yves *73*, *80*

Falaise *60*, *142*, *161*, 172, *180*
Flers *69*
Florennes/Juzaine (A-78) *161*,
  189, *195*
Ford *70*, 83, *104*
Forêt de Cerisy *120*
  Montgomery's Tac HQ *118*
Formby, George *100*
Ford, F/Lt Charley *85*
Freeman, Roger (historian) *46*, *177*
Freeman Field, Indiana, USA *141*
French units
  2ème Div. Blindée (2nd
    Armoured Div.) 172, *196*, 198,
    212
  Armée de l'Air
    6ème Escadre de Chasse
      (fighter sqn) 175
    22ème Régt (night bombing
      sqn) 175
Fresnoy (B-31) *88*, *203*
Fugh, Oblt *69*

Gaël (A-31) *151–153*
Genzler, Kriegsberichter *181*
George VI, King *115*
German Army
  Panzergruppe West *69*
  Divisions
    2. Panzer 89
    12. SS-Panzer 'Hitlerjugend'
      136
    Panzer-Lehr *202*
  see also Luftwaffe
Ghesla, Uffz Willi 150
Glisy *see* Amiens/Glisy
Godelmesnil (B-35) 213
Gordon, F/Lt N. *91*
Gorges (A-26) *176*, *200–201*
Gorron (A-34) *216*
Grandcamp-les-Bains *53*
Graye-sur-Mer *58*, *144*
Great Saling *see* Andrews Field
Green, W/Cdr Charles *43*
Grigson, Maj. Reginald (RE) *16*

Hall, Rear Adm. John L. *51*
Hancock, Lt-Col Leslie, RE *128*
Hardy, George *80*
Harris, ACM Sir Arthur *218*
Havers, Lt-Col Richard, RE *70*,
  72
Headcorn *120*
High Halden *48*, *157*
Hill, AM Roderic M., as AOC
  ADGB *8*
Hillingdon House *see* Uxbridge,
  RAF
Hoge, Gen. William M. *53*
Holland, F/Lt Frank *81*
Holmsley South 71, *135*
Hôtels-Sainte-Bazille *81*
Hughes, Cpl J. *130*
Hunsdon *139*
Hurn *66*, *200*

Ibsley *57*
  Station 347 *62–63*
Illiers-l'Évêque (B-26) 40, 159,
  181, 183, *184*
Ingham, Beryl *100*
IRA (Irish Republican Army) *51*
Isigny *36*, *53*, *75*

Johnson, Johnnie *60*
Josupeit, SS-Rottenf. Werner *89*
Judd, W/Cdr Michael *43*
Juvincourt (A-68) *191*
Juzaine *see* Florennes/Juzaine
  (A-78)

Kansas City, Butler Manufacturing
  Company *116*
Kingsnorth *123*
Kühl, Rittmeister Herbert *69*
Kuhn, Sgt Jack *52*

La Caine château *69*
La Cambe *49*
La Haye-du-Puits *146*
La Rue Huguenot (B-23)
  (Morainville) 80, *101*, *181*, *207*, 213
La Vieille (A-19) *38*, *160–161*
La-Haye-du-Theil *181*
Lallemant, F/Lt Ray *78*
Lane, George *80*
Lantheuil (B-9) *90–93*, *106*, *148*,
  182
Laon (A-69) 175, *176*
Le Culot/Beauvechain
  (B-68/A-89) *184*
Le Fresne-Camilly (B-5) *33*, *35*,
  43, *67*, *70–73*, 80, *88*, *106*, *182*
Le Hamel *66*
Le Havre *110*, *200*
Le Mans 9, *106*, *143*, *165*, *167*, *212*
Le Mans (A-35) *96*, 123, *194–195*,
  216, 217
Le Molay (A-9) *13*, *114–117*, *158*,
  198
Le Roux, S/Ldr 'Chris' *83*, *85*
Le Tronquay, 2nd TAF HQ *158*
Leary, Capt. Richard E. *36*
Lee, Cpl N. *130*
Leigh-Mallory, ACM Sir Trafford
  Allied Air C-in-C *8*
  death *6*, *218*
  invasion planning 9, *208*, *217*
  operational report *6*, *10*, *218*
Les Moulins 30, 31
Lessay (A-20) *133*, 151, 175,
  178–179
  later Charles Lindbergh Airfield
    178, *179*
Liège/Bierset (A-93) *195*
Lignerolles (A-12) *96*, *120–121*,
  150, *159*, 191
Lille-Nord (B-57) 204
Lille/Vendeville (B-51) 213
Lindbergh, Charles 178, *179*
Lingèvres (B-19) *12*, *16–17*, *67*, 83,
  129, *131*, *154–155*
Lisieux 213
Little Walden *190*, 191
Livarot 83, *85*
Loire, River *161*, *200*
Lommel, Sgt Leonard *52*
London, Air Traffic Control
  Centre, Uxbridge *51*
Longues-sur-Mer (B-11) *33*, *35*,
  82–85, *106*, *154*
Lonray (A-45) *161*, *189*
Lorient *200*
Lucke, Hptm. Gerhard *208*
Luftwaffe
  Luftflotte 3 175, *176*, 191, *208*
  JG1 *194*, 210
  JG2 *166*
    10./JG2 *136*
  JG3 *176*
  JG11 150
  JG26 210
    10./JG26 *136*
  I./JG27 111, 140
  III./JG27 111, 140
  Stab JG27 *140*
  JG51 *166*
  JG53 *166*, *194*
    1./JG53 150
  JG54 *196*
  III./JG54 140
  III./JG77 111

Luftwaffe — *continued*
  KG1 214
  KG4 208
  KG6 191, 210
  2./KG6 *208*
  KG26 150, 208
  KG27 150
  KG30 180, 191
  KG40 188
  KG51 176, *188*, 191
  KG53 175
  KG54 191, 208
  KG55 *175*, 176, 180, 196
  KG66 175
  KG76 *188*, 208
  KG77 150, 196, 208
  KG100 175, *188*
  KG806 136
  Kgr100 *166*
  LG1 188
  NKG13 175
  SKG10 150, 176
  13./SKG10 *136*
  StG1 208
  I./ZG2 136
Luttwitz, Genlt Heinrich von 89
Luxembourg 157, *195*

McBee, Capt. Lawrence (27th PRS) 27
McCall, Maj. Evan 111
McDowell, Lt-Col William, RE *128*
MacNeely, Lt Col Carlton O. (US 8th Inf.) 26
Maitland-Thompson, S/Ldr Bastian 104
Manston 213
Mantes-Gassicourt 180
Marseilles 110
Martragny (B-7) 78–80, 88, *106*, 128, *130*, 213
Maupertus (A-15) 43, 104, 110–113, *133*, 140, *142*, 151
Méautis (A-17) 75, *122*, *164–165*
Melsbroek (B-58) 215
Melun (A-55) 18
Memorials
  Azeville (A-7) 97
  Bazenville (B-2) *41*, 42
  Bény-sur-Mer (B-4) 61
  Beuzeville (A-6) 57
  Blay, Montgomery's Tac HQ *117*
  Brucheville (A-16) *123*
  Cardonville (A-3) *38, 39*
  Cherbourg-Théville (later Maupertus/Cherbourg Airport) 113
  Chippelle (A-5) 118, *119*
  Coulombs (B-6) *67, 68*
  Cretteville (A-14) *109*
  Cricqueville (A-2) *49*
  Deux-Jumeaux (A-4) *62, 65*
  Ellon (B-12) 128, *131*
  Gaël (A-31) 152, *153*
  Gorges (A-26) *206*
  Lantheuil (B-9) *93*
  Le Fresne-Camilly (B-5) *71, 73*
  Le Molay (A-9) 116, *117*
  Lignerolles (A-12) (the Hodam) *121*
  Longues-sur-Mer (B-11) 83, *85*
  Martragny (B-7) *79, 80*
  Méautis (A-17) *164, 165*
  Picauville (A-8) *105*
  Runnymede Memorial to the Missing *131*
  St Lambert (A-11) *143*
  St Laurent-sur-Mer (A-21C) *30, 31*
  St Pierre-du-Mont (A-1) *45, 46*
  Ste Croix-sur-Mer (B-3) 35
  Tour-en-Bessin (A-13) *135*
  Villons-les-Buissons (B-16) *169*
Merderet, River 102
Metz 15, 157
Meucon Airport *see* Vannes
Meyers, Col Gilbert 36
Middle Wallop 114
Mildenhall *193*
Miron, F/Lt Arthur *81*
Moncrieff, G/Capt. Ernest *100*
Montebourg *118*

Montgomery, Gen. B. L.
  and Adm. Ramsay 199
  Allied communications on beaches 53
  Churchill visits *43*, 142
  and Falaise pocket 180
  and George Formby *100*
  King George VI visits *115*
  replaced as ground forces commander 204
  TAC HQ at Blay *115*, 117, *118*, *158*
  TAC HQ at Creully *90*, 115
Montreuil (A-38) 120
Monts-en-Bessin *81*
Moore, Maj. Gen. Cecil R. (US Chief Engineer) 12
Morainville *see* La Rue Huguenot
Mortain 89, *142*
Mourmelon-le-Grand (A-80) 185
Mulberry harbours *43, 53*, 61, *110*, 111
  Arromanches *10*, 61
  Omaha beach *10*, 111
Museums
  Carentan, Normandy Tank Museum *75, 77*
  Tangmere Aviation Museum *85*

Nancy 15, *195*
Nantes 200
NATO (North Atlantic Treaty Organisation) 113, *193*, 210
Néhou 132, *133*
Nelson-Smith, Lt-Col David 29
Nerrant, Olivier *75*
Nerrant, Patrick *75*
Nerrant, Stéphane *75*
Neuilly-la-Forêt *143*
  see also St Lambert
Newark Army Airfield, USA 141
Niergnies *see* Cambrai/Niergnies
Nordholz (R-56) 185
North Weald 169
North-Lewis, S/Ldr (later Air Cdre) Christopher 'Kit' *67*
Northolt 51, *142*
Noyers-Bocage 80

O'Hare Airport, Chicago 141
Oissel 131
Olympic village, Uxbridge (post-war) 51
Operation
  'Cobra' *13*, 159
  'Goodwood' 89
  'Lusty' 141
  'Totalize' 142
  'Varsity' 189, *190*
  'Windsor' 136, *138*
Orconte (A-66) 152
Orléans *161, 174*
Orléans-Bricy (A-50) 135, *177*
Orly (A-47) *164*, *165*, 176, 191
Orteig, Raymond 178
'Overlord' *see* Beaches, D-Day assault

Page, W/Cdr Geoffrey *83*
Paimpont forest *153*
Paris
  airfield locations 15, *174*, *208*
  liberation 172, *195*, *196*
  St Germain 199
  see also Beauvais; Orly
Park Ridge, Illinois (later Chicago's O'Hare Airport) 141
Pas de Calais 150
Patton, Gen. George S.
  advance in Brittany 142, *200*
  commands US Third Army 132, *161*
Peray (A-44) 49, *217*
Périers *13*, 118, 200
Péronne (A-72) 176
Picauville (A-8) 74, 75, *102–105*, *106*, *139*
Ploesti oil refineries raid 9
Plumetot (B-10) 6, 58, 80, *86–89*, 102, *106*, *140*
Pointe-du-Hoc 44, 46, *47*, *52*, *53*
Poix (B-44) 183, 184
Polley, LAC L. *130*
Pontorson (A-28) 14, 106, *151*, 157, *172*
Popp, Sgt Michael (Eisenhower's tailor) *13*

Port-en-Bessin, as petroleum port *10*
Portal, MRAF Sir Charles *84*
Portsmouth 58
Pouppeville 26
Pouppeville (ELS-1) *27*, *106*
Price, F/O F. H. *130*
Prizer, Edward *85*
Prosnes (A-79) 150, *177*

Querqueville (A-23C) *126*, *133*, *140–141*
  later École des Fourriers (French Navy) *141*

R-56 *see* Nordholz
Ramsay, Adm. Bertram 199
Ramslade House, Bracknall, 2nd TAF HQ 8
Redhill 60
Reims 195
Reims (A-62) 15, 172, *195*
Remlinger, Sous-Lt Jacques *83, 85*
Renault, Robert 128, *131*
Renault factory (Le Mans) 194
Rennes (A-27) 114, 120, 132, *150–151*, *216*
  later St Jacques Airport *151*
Rennes (city) 120, *172*, *200*
Resistance, French 172
Rhine, River, Allied crossing 189
Romilly 195
Rommel, FM Erwin 83, *85*
Roper, F/Lt Peter *81*
Rowland, F/Sgt John *81*
Royal Air Force
  Second Tactical Air Force 8, 9, 19, *42*, *50*, 69, 104, 139, *158*, *161*, *168*, *180*, *182*, *193*, *208*
  Operation 'Goodwood' 89
  Order of Battle 7
  Bomber Command 208
  Fighter Command HQ (Bentley Priory) 8
  Groups
    No. 2 23, *69*
    No. 11 8, *50*
    No. 46 Transport 145
    No. 83 23, *35*, *42*, *43*, *60*, 145
    No. 84 23
    No. 85 23
  Wings
    Airfield Construction *10*, 67
    No. 5352 *138*, 139
    No. 5357 *17*, 149, *154*, *192*
    No. 34 (PR) 23
    No. 35 (Recce) 23
    No. 39 (Recce) 23, *100*, 101, 159, 203
    No. 121 23, *43*, *71*, *72*, *182*, *210*
    No. 122 23, 128, *183*
    No. 123 23, *80*, 213
    No. 124 23, *66*, *67*, *69*, *81*, *187*, *215*
    No. 125 *17*, 23, *83*, *154*
    No. 126 (RCAF) 23, *58*, *59*, *60*, 149, *183*, 184
    No. 127 (RCAF) 23, *40*, *42*, 184
    No. 129 23, *72*, 182
    No. 131 23, 88
    No. 132 23, *154*, 169
    No. 133 23
    No. 134 23, 88
    No. 135 23
    No. 136 23, *80*, *81*, 128, 213
    No. 137 23, *66*
    No. 138 23
    No. 139 23
    No. 140 23
    No. 141 23
    No. 142 23
    No. 143 23, *43*, *90*, *92*, *182*, 215
    No. 144 23, *32*, *35*, 184
    No. 145 23, 101, 207
    No. 146 23, *33*, *43*, *81*, 101 *125*, 213
    No. 147 23
    No. 148 23
    No. 150 23
  Squadrons
    No. 2 (RAF) 23, *58*, *61*, 88, 203
    No. 3 (RAF) 23
    No. 4 (RAF) 23, *58*, *61*, 88, 203
    No. 16 (RAF) 23, 215
    No. 19 (RAF) 23, 128, *130*, 183
    No. 21 (RAF) 23, *152*
    No. 26 (Air Spotting Pool) 23

Royal Air Force, Squadrons — *cont.*
  No. 29 (RAF) 23
  No. 33 (RAF) 88, 139
  No. 56 (RAF) 23
  No. 63 (Air Spotting Pool) 23
  No. 65 (RAF) 23, 128, *130*, *131*, 183
  No. 66 (RAF) 23, 169, *204*
  No. 69 (RAF) 23, 215
  No. 74 (RAF) 101, 207
  No. 88 (RAF) 23
  No. 91 (RAF) 23
  No. 98 (RAF) 23
  No. 107 (RAF) 23
  No. 122 (RAF) 23, *78*, 128, *130*, 183
  No. 124 (RAF) 23
  No. 127 (RAF) *13*, 169, 204
  No. 129 (RAF) 23
  No. 130 (RAF) *35*
  No. 132 (RAF) 23, 83
  No. 137 (RAF) *81*, *187*, 215
  No. 140 (RAF) 23, 215
  No. 164 (RAF) 23, *80*, *81*, 101, 213
  No. 168 (RAF) 23, *99*, 101, 159, *205*
  No. 174 (RAF) 23, *40*, *43*, *71*, *81*, *182*, *210*
  No. 175 (RAF) 23, *33*, *35*, *43*, *71–73*, *81*, *182*, *210*
  No. 180 (RAF) 23
  No. 181 (RAF) 23, *66*, *67*, *81*, *136*, *187*, 215
  No. 182 (RAF) 23, *66*, *69*, *81*, *187*, 215
  No. 183 (RAF) 23, *80*, *81*, 213
  No. 184 (RAF) 23, *71*, *72*, *81*, 88, *182*, 210
  No. 193 (RAF) 23, *33*, *35*, *81*, *125*, 213
  No. 197 (RAF) 23, *33*, *35*, *81*, 125
  No. 198 (RAF) *6*, 23, *71*, *73*, *78*, *80*, *81*, *86–87*, 88, 213
  No. 219 (RAF) 215
  No. 222 (RAF) 23, 139
  No. 226 (RAF) 23
  No. 245 (RAF) 23, *35*, *43*, *71*, *81*, *182*, *210*
  No. 247 (RAF) 23, *66*, *69*, *81*, *187*, 215
  No. 257 (RAF) 23, *33*, *35*, *81*, *125*, 213
  No. 263 (RAF) *33*, *35*, *81*
  No. 264 (RAF) 23, *66*, *67*, *104*, *139*
  No. 266 (RAF) 23, *33*, *35*, *81*, *99*, 101, *125*, 213
  No. 268 (RAF) 23, *58*, *61*, 88, 203
  No. 276 (RAF) 215
  No. 302 (Polish) 23, *88*
  No. 303 (RAF) *35*
  No. 305 (Polish) 23
  No. 306 (Polish) 23
  No. 308 (Polish) 23, *70*, 88
  No. 310 (Czech) 23, 88
  No. 312 (Czech) 23, 88
  No. 313 (Czech) 23, 88
  No. 315 (Polish) 23
  No. 317 (Polish) 23, *88*
  No. 320 (Dutch) 23
  No. 322 (Dutch) 23
  No. 329 (French) 23, 101, 207
  No. 331 (Norwegian) 23, 169, 204
  No. 332 (Norwegian) 23, 169, 204
  No. 340 (French) 23, 101, 207
  No. 341 (French) 23, 101, 207
  No. 342 (French) 23
  No. 349 (Belgian) 23, 139
  No. 400 (RCAF) 23, *100*, 101, 159, *205*
  No. 401 (RCAF) (ex- No. 1 Canadian Sqn) 23, 58, *59*, 149, 183, *192*, *193*
  No. 403 (RCAF) 23, *40*, 184
  No. 409 (RCAF) 23, *139*, 183, 215
  No. 410 (RCAF) 23, 215
  No. 411 (RCAF) 23, *58*, *59*, 60, 149, 183, 184
  No. 412 (RCAF) 23, *58*, *59*, *85*, 149, 183, 184, 192, *193*
  No. 414 (RCAF) 23, 101, 159, 184

Royal Air Force, Squadrons — cont.
  No. 416 (RCAF) 23, 40, 184
  No. 421 (RCAF) 23, 40, 184
  No. 430 (RCAF) 23, *100*, 101, 159, 205
  No. 438 (RCAF) 23, 81, 90, 92, *182*, 215
  No. 439 (RCAF) 23, *81*, 90, *182*, 215
  No. 440 (RCAF) 23, 81, 90, *91*, *182*, 215
  No. 441 (RCAF) 23, 32–33, *35*, *82*, 83, *84*, 154
  No. 442 (RCAF) 23, 32–33, *35*, 58, *60*, 149, 183, 184
  No. 443 (RCAF) 23, 32–33, *35*, 40, *42*, 184
  No. 453 (RAAF) 23, *83*, 154
  No. 464 (RAAF) 23
  No. 485 (RNZAF) 23, 139
  No. 486 (RNZAF) 23
  No. 487 (RNZAF) 23
  No. 488 (RNZAF) 23, 215
  No. 602 (RAF) 8, 23, *42*, *83*, *85*, 154
  No. 604 (RAF) 23, *104*, 139
  No. 609 (RAF) 23, 71, *78*, 80, 81, 88, 213
  No. 613 (RAF) 23
  No. 652 (AOP) 23, 58, *59*, 88
  No. 653 (AOP) 23
  No. 658 (AOP) 23, 128
  No. 659 (AOP) 90
  No. 660 (AOP) 23
  No. 661 (AOP) 23, 145
  No. 662 (AOP) 23
  No. 5022 (Airfield Construction) 149
Flights
  No. 1320 (Ah Spotting Pool) 23
  No. 1401 (Met) 23
RAF Regiment, Queen's Colour Sqn 51
Bombing Analysis Unit 69, *180*
Film Production Unit *210*
Royal Navy (FAA)
  No. 808 (FAA) 23
  No. 885 (FAA) 23
  No. 886 (FAA) 23
  No. 897 (FAA) 23
Roye/Amy (A-73) *161*
Rudder, Lt Col James E. 52
Runnymede Memorial to the Missing *131*
Russel, Hugh 60
Russel, W/Cdr 'Dal' ('Deadeye Dick') 60
Ryes (B-15) *32*, *124–125*

St André-de-l'Eure (A-24) 71, *72*, 90, 128, 149, *180–183*, *193*, *210*
St Dizier *195*
St Dizier (A-64) 102
St Germain, Paris *199*
St Jacques Airport (ex-Rennes A-27) *151*
St James (A-29) *134*, *172–173*
St Jean-de-Daye (A-18) *202*
St Lambert (A-11) (Also Neuilly) *143*, *212*
St Laurent-sur-Mer (A-21C) *30–31*, *46*, *106*, *126*
St Léonard (A-36) *106*, *185*
St Lô 12, *13*, 114, 161
St Malo *200*
St Marceau (A-43) *143*, *212*
St Marcouf, German coastal batteries *26*
St Martin-de-Varreville *26*, 27
St Nazaire *200*
St Pierre-du-Mont (A-1) *30*, 31, *44–47*, 48, *97*, *102*, *106*, 114, *176*, *177*
St Sauveur-le-Vicomte *132*
  see also Biniville
St Sauveur-Lendelin *143*
  Château des Mares *142*
St Valéry *186*
Ste Colombe *132*
Ste Croix-Grand-Tonne *66*, *67*
Ste Croix-sur-Mer (B-3) *32–35*, *43*, *60*, *67*, *98*, *101*, *106*, *125*, 213
Ste Honorine-de-Ducy (B-21) 101, *159*, 205
Ste Marguerite-de-Viette *81*
Ste Mère-Église *46*, 54
  see also Beuzeville

Sarthe, River *212*
Scheldt estuary *199*
Schilling, Col Karl B. *165*
Seine, River
  Allied advance to *161*, *162–163*, *172*, *180*, *192*
  crossing of *186–187*
Severson, Lt Col *104*
'Shellburst' Advanced CP *see* Tournières
Sheppard, S/Ldr Jack 59
Ships
  British
    Ajax 82
    Ambitious 100
    Argonaut 82
    Enterprise 43
    Hilary 51
    Largs 51
  United States
    Ancon 51–52
    Bayfield 51
    Bulolo 51, 82
Smith, F/O Bill (245 Sqn) *35*
Smith, Sgt Clide W. *118*
Smyser, Col Rudolph E. *165*
Smythe, Col George *132*
Somme, River *186–187*
Sommervieu (B-8) 80, *98*, *99–101*, *106*, *159*, 207, 213
Spaatz, Lt Gen. Carl A. *218*
Stanmore *see* Bentley Priory
Stars and Stripes
  (US Army newspaper) 36
Stecker, Col Ray 96
Stoney Cross *112*
Strickland, Brig. Gen. Aubrey C., Deputy Senior Air Staff Officer 8
Sunninghill Park, Ascot, USAAF Ninth Air Force HQ 8
Sweeting, Denis 80

Tangmere *13*, *59*, 88
  Aviation Museum *85*
Tedder, ACM Sir Arthur
  appointed deputy Supreme Commander 8
  invasion planning 9
  need for Tac HQ on Continent *13*, *115*, 116
Thomas, F/O Frank *81*
Thompson, P/O John *99*
Thursby, F/Sgt Reg *81*
Tillé (B-40/A-61) *see* Beauvais/Tillé
Tilly-sur-Seulles 128, 149
The Times 98
Tipton, Col James B. 96
Toul (A-90) *195*
Tour-en-Bessin (A-13) *106*, *134–135*, *151*, *172*, *177*
Tournières, Eisenhower's Adv. CP 'Shellburst' *13*, *115*, 116, *118*, *158*
Toussus-le-Noble (A-46) 114, 151, *174*, *196*, *198–199*
Trenchard, MRAF Lord *84*

Ultra decoding 69
United States Air Force (USAF)
  317th Troop Carrier Wing *193*
  465th Troop Carrier Wing *193*
United States Army
  Army Groups
    6th Army Group 12, *204*
    12th Army Group 12, *132*, *142*, *161*, *180*, *204*
  Armies
    First *13*, *106*, *121*, *134*, *142*, *146*, 157, 159, *165*, *195*
    HQs *52*, *53*
    Third *132*, *142*, 157, *161*, *165*, *195*, *200*
    Seventh 157, *202*
  AAA Group, 18th *64*
  Corps
    V Corps *53*, 75, 159
    VII Corps *26*, 75
    VIII Corps *146*
    XV Corps *161*
  Divisions
    1st Infantry 120, *135*, 159
    2nd Infantry *53*, 114, 118, 161
    3rd Armored 216
    4th Armored 120, 166, 172
    4th Infantry *26*, 27, 54, 94, 111
    5th Armored *161*, *176*, *185*, *194*, 217

United States Army, Divisions — cont.
  5th Infantry 175
  6th Armored 152, 156, 157
  7th Armored 175
  8th Infantry *146*, 172
  9th Infantry *132*, 140, *202*
  17th Airborne *189*
  29th Infantry 30, 36, 44, 48, 118
  30th Infantry *180*, 184, *187*, 92, 205
  35th Infantry *189*
  78th Infantry 217
  79th Infantry *146*, 147, *161*, *180*, 194
  80th Infantry *185*
  82nd Airborne *26*, 54, 106
  90th Infantry 102, 178
  101st Airborne *26*, 27
Regiments
  8th Infantry *26*, 27
  11th Infantry 175
  12th Infantry 54
  13th Infantry 120, 150, 172
  22nd Infantry 94, 111, *191*
  23rd Infantry 161
  26th Infantry 120, *135*, 159
  38th Infantry 114
  39th Infantry 95
  47th Infantry 132, 140, *202*
  115th Infantry *62*, 118
  116th Infantry 30, 44, 48
  119th Infantry *187*, 205
  120th Infantry *180*, 184
  175th Infantry 36, *53*
  314th Infantry 147, 217
  315th Infantry 178, *185*, 194
  320th Infantry *189*
  357th Infantry 102
  358th Infantry *102*, 200
  501st Parachute Infantry *26*, 27
  502nd Parachute Infantry *26*
  505th Parachute Infantry 54
  508th Parachute Infantry 106
Battalions
  2nd Ranger 44, 46
  5th Ranger 30
  35th Signal Construction *53*
  552nd AAA AW 57
  660th Engineer Topographical *32*, *44*
  747th Tank 36
United States Army Air Force (USAAF)
  Eighth Air Force 150, *208*, *209*, *210*, 215
  Ninth Air Force 8, 9, 49, 50, 52, *89*, *113*, *123*, *142*, *208*, *209*, *214*, 215, *216*
  airfield building 12, *39*, 48, *104*, *150*
  deployments *97*, *134*, *179*, *190*, *212*
  HQ St Sauveur-Lendelin *143*
  Order of Battle *22–23*
  Fifteenth Air Force *208*
  IX Air Force Service Command *150*, *167*
  IX Bomber Command 22
  IX Engineer Command 12, *14*, 15, *102*, *150*, *194*, *216*
Brigades
  Engineer Aviation 12
    1st *165*, *195*
    2nd *165*, *195*
Regiments
  1st Airfield Maintenance (Provisional) *150*
  923rd Engineer Aviation 12
Battalions
  Airborne Aviation Engineering 10
  Engineer Aviation *10*, 12
  816th *37*, 38, *62*, *126*, 194
  818th 161, 196, 198
  819th 27, 55, *56*, *94*, 95, 106, 157, *212*, 217
  820th 48, *118*, *120*, 150
  825th *172*, 191
  826th 75, *102*, *140*, 200
  830th *18*, 132, *178*, *179*
  832nd *143*, 175, *189*
  833rd *18*, 134, *135*, *147*, 175, *189*
  834th *30–31*, *30*, 44, 114, *115*, *156*
  840th *164*, 176

USAAF, Battalions — continued
  843rd *122*, 123, *202*, *210*
  846th 134, *135*, *185*, *216*
  850th *14*, *111*, 112, *140*, 141, 152, 166, *179*
  852nd *210*
  877th *111*, 112, *179*, 180
  878th *18*
  942nd Engineer Aviation Topographical *47*, *65*, *76*, *95*
IX Fighter Command *22*
IX Tactical Air Command 22, *53*, *142*, *151*, *161*
IX Troop Carrier Command *22–23*
XIX Tactical Air Command 22, *142*
Wings
  50th Troop Carrier *22–23*, *177*
  52nd Troop Carrier 23
  53rd Troop Carrier 23
  70th Fighter 22, *52*
  71st Fighter *22*
  84th Fighter *22*
  97th Bomb *22*
  98th Bomb 22, 135, *150*
  99th Bomb *22*
  100th Fighter *22*
  302nd Transport 141, 147
  303rd Fighter *22*
Groups
  7th Photo Reconn. *27*
  10th Photo Reconn. *22*, *150–151*, 189
  31st Transport 147
  36th Fighter 22, *123*, 194, *195*
  48th Fighter 22, *62–63*, 97, 196
  50th Fighter 22, *75*, *97*, *164*
  61st Troop Carrier 23
  67th Tactical Reconn. *22*, 114, 198
  313th Troop Carrier 23
  314th Troop Carrier 23, 196
  315th Troop Carrier 23, 215
  316th Troop Carrier 23
  322nd Bomb 22, *180*, *210*, 211
  323rd Bomb 22, *150*, 175, 178
  344th Bomb 22
  349th Troop Carrier 23
  354th Fighter 22, *49*, *97*, 152, *153*
  358th Fighter *14*, 22, *48*, 106, *157*
  362nd Fighter 22, 120, 150–151
  363rd Fighter (later Tactical Reconn. Gp) 22, *96*, *97*, *111*, 112
  365th Fighter 22, *96*, *97*, 121, 191
  366th Fighter 22, *46*, 97, 176, *177*
  367th Fighter 22, *46*, *49*, 55, *75*, 106, *217*
  368th Fighter *7*, 22, *36*, *38*, 97, 175
  370th Air Service 196
  370th Fighter 22, *38*, *46*, *161*
  371st Fighter 22, 55, *56–57*, 97
  373rd Fighter 22, *134*, *135*, *172*
  386th Bomb *22*
  387th Bomb 22, *112*, *150*, 189
  391st Bomb *22*
  394th Bomb 22, 135, *150*, *177*
  397th Bomb 22, 176, *200*
  404th Fighter 22, *118*, *191*
  405th Fighter *22*, 102
  406th Fighter 22, *106*, *109*, *134*, *135*, *185*
  409th Bomb 22, *190*, *191*
  410th Bomb *22*
  416th Bomb *18*, 22
  434th Troop Carrier 23
  435th Troop Carrier 23, *190*, *191*
  436th Troop Carrier *18*, 23
  437th Troop Carrier 23
  438th Troop Carrier 23, *177*
  439th Troop Carrier 22, *188*, *189*
  440th Troop Carrier 22, *194*, *195*
  441st Troop Carrier 23, 176, *177*, *212*
  442nd Troop Carrier 23, *217*
  474th Fighter 22, *143*, *212*
  IX TCC Pathfinder (P) 22

United States Army Air Force — cont.
  Squadrons
    1st Pathfinder (P) 22, 215
    2nd Pathfinder (P) 22
    3rd Pathfinder (P) 22
    4th Pathfinder (P) 22
    9th Weather Reconn. (P) 22
    10th Fighter 22, 75, 164, *165*
    12th Tactical Reconn. 22, 114, 150, 189
    14th Troop Carrier 23
    15th Tactical Reconn. 22, 150, 189
    15th Troop Carrier 23
    22nd Fighter 22, 123, 194
    23rd Fighter 22, 123, 194
    23rd Troop Carrier 23
    27th Photo Reconn. *27*
    29th Troop Carrier 23
    30th Photo Reconn. 22, 198
    31st Photo Reconn. 22, 150, 189
    32nd Troop Carrier 23
    33rd Photo Reconn. 22
    34th Photo Reconn. 22, 150, 189
    34th Troop Carrier 23
    36th Troop Carrier 23
    37th Troop Carrier 23
    43rd Troop Carrier 23
    44th Troop Carrier 23
    45th Troop Carrier 23
    47th Troop Carrier 23
    48th Troop Carrier 23
    49th Troop Carrier 23
    50th Troop Carrier 23
    53rd Fighter 22, 123, 194
    53rd Troop Carrier 23
    59th Troop Carrier 23
    61st Troop Carrier 23
    62nd Troop Carrier 23
    71st Troop Carrier 23
    72nd Troop Carrier 23
    73rd Troop Carrier 23
    74th Troop Carrier 23
    75th Troop Carrier 23, *190*
    76th Troop Carrier 23, *190*
    77th Troop Carrier 23, *190*
    78th Troop Carrier 23, *190*
    79th Troop Carrier 23
    80th Troop Carrier 23
    81st Fighter 22, 75, *164*, *165*
    81st Troop Carrier 23
    82nd Troop Carrier 23
    83rd Troop Carrier 23
    84th Troop Carrier 23
    85th Troop Carrier 23
    86th Troop Carrier 23
    87th Troop Carrier 23
    88th Troop Carrier 23
    89th Troop Carrier 23, *177*
    90th Troop Carrier 23
    91st Troop Carrier 22
    92nd Troop Carrier 22
    93rd Troop Carrier 22
    94th Troop Carrier 22
    95th Troop Carrier 22

USAAF, Squadrons — continued
    96th Troop Carrier 22, *195*
    97th Troop Carrier 22
    98th Troop Carrier 22
    99th Troop Carrier 23, 176, 212
    100th Troop Carrier 23, 176, 212
    107th Tactical Reconn. 22, 114, 198
    109th Tactical Reconn. 22, 114, 198
    125th Liaison 132, 151
    153rd Liaison 22
    155th Night Photographic 22, 150, 189
    301st Troop Carrier 23, 176, 212
    302nd Troop Carrier 23, 176, 212
    303rd Troop Carrier 23
    304th Troop Carrier 23
    305th Troop Carrier 23
    306th Troop Carrier 23
    309th Troop Carrier 23
    310th Troop Carrier 23
    312th Troop Carrier 23
    313th Fighter 22, 75, 164, *165*
    313th Troop Carrier 23
    314th Troop Carrier 23
    353rd Fighter 22, 49, 152
    355th Fighter 22, 49, 152
    356th Fighter 22, 49, 152
    365th Fighter *14*, 22, 106, *157*
    366th Fighter *14*, 22, 106
    367th Fighter *14*, 22, *48*, 106
    377th Fighter 22, 120, 150
    378th Fighter 22, 120, 150
    379th Fighter 22, 120, 150
    380th Fighter 22, 96, *97*, 112
    381st Fighter 22, 96, 112
    382nd Fighter 22, 96, *111*, 112
    386th Fighter 22, 96, 121, 191
    387th Fighter 22, 96, 121, 191
    388th Fighter 22, 96, 121, 191
    389th Fighter 22, 46, 176
    390th Fighter 22, 46, 176
    391st Fighter 22, 46, 176
    392nd Fighter 22, *46*, 49, 75, 217
    393rd Fighter 22, *46*, 49, 106, *217*
    394th Fighter 22, *46*, 49, 55, 217
    395th Fighter 22, 38, 175
    396th Fighter 22, 38, 175
    397th Fighter 22, *36*, 38, 175
    401st Fighter 22, 38, *46*, 161
    402nd Fighter 22, 38, *46*, 161
    404th Fighter 22, 55
    405th Fighter 22, 55
    406th Fighter 22, 55
    410th Fighter 22, 134, *172*
    411th Fighter 22, 134, *172*
    412th Fighter 22, 134, *172*
    422nd Night Fighter 22, *104*, *112*, 189
    425th Night Fighter 22, *104*, *166*
    428th Fighter 22, 143, 212
    429th Fighter 22, 143, 212

USAAF, Squadrons — continued
    430th Fighter 22, 143, 212
    449th Bomb 22, 210
    450th Bomb 22, 210
    451st Bomb 22, 210
    452nd Bomb 22, 210
    453rd Bomb 22, 175, 178
    454th Bomb 22, 175, 178
    455th Bomb 22, 175, 178
    456th Bomb 22, 175, 178
    485th Fighter 22, 38, *46*, 161, *161*
    492nd Fighter 22, 62, 196
    493rd Fighter 22, 62, 196
    494th Bomb 22, 62, 196
    494th Fighter 22
    495th Bomb 22
    496th Bomb 22
    497th Bomb 22
    506th Fighter 22, 118, 191
    507th Fighter 22, 118, 191
    508th Fighter 22, 118, 191
    509th Fighter 22, 102
    510th Fighter 22, 102
    511th Fighter 22, 102
    512th Fighter 22, 106, 134, 185
    513th Fighter 22, 106, 134, 185
    514th Fighter 22, 106, 134, 185
    552nd Bomb 22
    553rd Bomb 22
    554th Bomb 22
    555th Bomb 22
    556th Bomb 22, 112, 189
    557th Bomb 22, 112, 189
    558th Bomb 22, 112, 189
    559th Bomb 22, 112, 189
    572nd Bomb 22
    573rd Bomb 22
    574th Bomb 22
    575th Bomb 22
    584th Bomb 22, 135
    585th Bomb 22, 135
    586th Bomb 22, 135
    587th Bomb 22, 135
    596th Bomb 22, 176, 200
    597th Bomb 22, 176, 200
    598th Bomb 22, 176, 200
    599th Bomb 22, 176, 200
    640th Bomb 22, 191
    641st Bomb 22, 191
    642nd Bomb 22, 191
    643rd Bomb 22, 191
    644th Bomb 22
    645th Bomb 22
    646th Bomb 22
    647th Bomb 22
    668th Bomb 22
    669th Bomb 22
    670th Bomb 22
    671st Bomb 22
United States Navy Squadron, VCS-7 23

Units *see* British; Canadian; French; German; Luftwaffe; Royal Air Force; United States
Uxbridge, RAF, Hillingdon House: Allied Air Forces HQ (formerly RAF 11 Gp HQ) 8, *50–51*, *53*

V1 flying bombs 89
Valailles (Bernay) (B-29) 101, *181*, 206–207
Vandenberg, Maj. Gen. Hoyt S. *216*
Vannes (A-33) *104*, *151*, 166–167, 200
  now Meucon Airport 166, *167*
VE-Day 15
Vélizy-Villacoublay *see* Villacoublay (A-42D)
Vendeville *see* Lille/Vendeville
Venlo 15
Verdun *195*
Vernon *180*
Vernouillet Airport *see* Dreux
Versailles, Trianon Palace: Eisenhower's Forward HQ *199*, *218*
Ver-sur-Mer 33
Vienne-en-Bessin *81*
Vierville-sur-Mer *61*
Villacoublay (A-42D) 62, *63*, *174*, 175, *196–197*, 198
  later French Air Force Vélizy-Villacoublay Base Aérienne 107 *197*
Villeneuve (A-63) 212
Villers-Bocage *69*, *80*, *159*
Villons-les-Buissons (B-16) *33*, *58*, *58*, *67*, *87*, 168–169, 170–171, 204
Vimoutiers *80*, *85*, *180*
Vire *69*
Vitry-en-Artois (B-50) 210
Vitry-le-François (A-67) *14*, 15, 152, *157*

Waldow, Maj. i.G. Friedrich-Wilhelm von *69*
Ward, Sgt W. G. *130*
Warfield, Lt Col Benjamin M. *57*
Warmwell *143*
West, WO Chester *99*
Wethersfield *18*
Wharry, F/O George *99*
White, Lt-Col Peter, RE *98*, *101*
Wigglesworth, AVM Philip, Senior Air Staff Officer AEAF 8
Wilbur Wright Field, USA *141*

X-Verfahren radio navigation *166*

Y-4 *see* Buc
Y-29 *see* Zwartberg/Asch
Yank (US Services magazine) *127*

Ziegler, Uffz Josef *69*
Zwartberg/Asch (Y-29) *161*

The memorial at Martagny (B-7) is dedicated to all those serving at the RAF airfields in Normandy.

224

A-6 BEUZEVILLE